THE NEW LAW OF INSOLVENCY

Related titles by Law Society Publishing

Enterprise Act 2002

The New Law of Mergers, Monopolies and Cartels
Tim Frazer, Susan Hinchcliffe and Kyla George
1–85328–896–9

Titles from Law Society Publishing can be ordered from all good legal bookshops or direct from our distributors, Marston Book Services (telephone 01235 465656 or e-mail **law.society@marston.co.uk**). For further information or a catalogue call our editorial and marketing office on 020 7320 5878.

THE NEW LAW OF INSOLVENCY

Insolvency Act 1986 to Enterprise Act 2002

Vernon Dennis and Alexander Fox
of Manches Solicitors London

The Law Society

ISBN 1–85328–812–8

Published in 2003 by the Law Society
113 Chancery Lane, London WC2A 1PL

Typeset by J&L Composition, Filey, North Yorkshire
Printed by TJ International Ltd, Padstow, Cornwall

This book is dedicated to

Sarah-Jane and Philippa
With thanks for all of their love and support

CONTENTS

Preface   x
Acknowledgements   xii
About the authors   xiii
Abbreviations   xv
Table of cases   xvi
Table of statutes   xix
Table of statutory instruments   xxvii
Table of European legislation   xxix

PART I   THE REFORM PROCESS IN CONTEXT   1

1   An historical perspective   3

1.1   Credit, risk and insolvency   3
1.2   Corporate insolvency   3
1.3   The changing perception of insolvency practitioners   7
1.4   The reform of corporate insolvency law   9
1.5   Bankruptcy   14

2   An international perspective   21

2.1   Global trends   21
2.2   The United States   22
2.3   Europe   26
2.4   The Commonwealth   28
2.5   Asia   30

PART II   CHANGES IN INSOLVENCY CUSTOM AND
           PRACTICE SINCE 1986   33

3   Insolvency Act 2000   35

3.1   A glimpse of what is to come?   35
3.2   Company Voluntary Arrangements for small companies   36

3.3   General reforms to the CVA regime   50
3.4   General reforms to the IVA regime   53
3.5   The nominee's role   55
3.6   Company Directors Disqualification Act 1986 proceedings   56
3.7   Landlord's rights of action and administration   58
3.8   Miscellaneous reforms made by the Insolvency Act 2000   59
3.9   When did it come into force?   60

4   Major legislation affecting insolvency law and practice   61

4.1   Human Rights Act 1998   61
4.2   Welfare Reform and Pensions Acts 1999   71
4.3   The family home   81
4.4   Employment law reform   92
4.5   Cross-border insolvency   97
4.6   International corporate reconstruction   106

PART III   ENTERPRISE ACT 2002 – CORPORATE
           INSOLVENCY REFORM   113

5   The abolition of administrative receivership?   115

5.1   Receivership   115
5.2   Debentures entered into prior to the Enterprise Act 2002   120
5.3   The future of secured lending post-Enterprise Act 2002   121

6   The abolition of Crown preference   129

6.1   Preferential debts and the Enterprise Act 2002   129
6.2   Officeholder's proceedings   133
6.3   The ring-fenced sum   135

7   The new administration procedure   138

7.1   Introduction to the Enterprise Act 2002 reforms   138
7.2   The purpose of administration   139
7.3   Appointment of an administrator by the court   144
7.4   Appointment by floating chargeholder   149
7.5   Appointment by company or its directors   154
7.6   The effect of administration   158
7.7   The process of administration   163
7.8   The functions of an administrator   170
7.9   Challenge regarding an administrator's conduct   174
7.10 Ending the administration   176
7.11 Replacing an administrator   184

PART IV   ENTERPRISE ACT 2002 – PERSONAL INSOLVENCY REFORM 187

8   The new bankruptcy regime 189

8.1   The duration of the Bankruptcy Order   189
8.2   The transitional provisions   193
8.3   Bankruptcy Restrictions Orders ('BROs')   196
8.4   Bankruptcy Restrictions Undertaking ('BRU')   199
8.5   The effect of annulment on a BRO or BRU   200
8.6   Will the new regime work?   201

9   Further reforms to personal insolvency law 204

9.1   Investigatory duties of the Official Receiver   204
9.2   Income Payment Orders/Agreements   207
9.3   Fast-track Individual Voluntary Arrangements   213
9.4   Bankruptcy restrictions   221

PART V   CONCLUSIONS 227

10   Into the future 229

10.1   The future of corporate insolvency   229
10.2   The future of personal insolvency   236
10.3   When do the Enterprise Act 2002 reforms come into force? 240

APPENDICES

Appendix 1   Insolvency Act 2000   241

Appendix 2   Enterprise Act 2002, Part 10   285

Appendix 3   Enterprise Act 2002, Schedules 16–23   301

Bibliography   362
Index   369

PREFACE

We want an enterprising economy to make the UK the best place in the world to do business

The Rt Hon Patricia Hewitt MP
Secretary of State for Trade and Industry

Foreword to the White Paper
'Productivity and Enterprise – Insolvency – A Second Chance'
July 2001

Central to the Government's platform of structural economic reform is the stated intention to foster enterprise and productivity, so releasing the entrepreneurial skills of the British people. The Government believes that a dynamic economy is one in which risk-taking is an essential factor in releasing enterprise and encouraging entrepreneurial flair. However, the Government believes that the fear of failure has been a powerful disincentive to potential entrepreneurs. It therefore proposes that the legal, economical and social framework must be geared towards encouraging responsible risk-taking so as to promote enterprise.

Underpinning these laudable aims is the radical remodelling of competition, consumer and insolvency law which is tackled in the Enterprise Act 2002.

The Enterprise Act 2002 itself is divided into 11 Parts, containing 281 sections and no fewer than 26 highly detailed Schedules. The Act covers diverse areas such as fair trading, competition, mergers, market investigations, consumer affairs and disclosure of information. This book concerns itself only with Part 10 of the Act which deals with insolvency law reform. Part 10 will bring about radical changes to both the corporate and personal insolvency regimes. The Government must take credit for its bold attempt to reform this area of law, in particular its championing of corporate rescue. There is, however, unease in many quarters over how major parts of the reform package will work in practice and, indeed, whether the reforms to the personal insolvency regime are advisable in light of previous experience in other jurisdictions.

This book is primarily intended as a guide to the recent reforms to insolvency law. The reforms clearly have not come out of thin air and consequently, it is also the aim of this book to put the reform process in context both historically and by comparison with other major industrialised nations. Commentary on other important legislative changes since the introduction of the Insolvency Act 1986 (which is referred to throughout this work as the '1986 Act') is also included, thus providing the reader with an overview of the new law of insolvency.

The Enterprise Act 2002 received Royal Assent on 7 November 2002. It is anticipated that the provisions dealing with corporate law reform will be implemented from April 2003 onwards. Those dealing with personal insolvency law reform will be implemented from April 2004. For the most part these reforms will be incorporated into the 1986 Act. However some of the transitional provisions set out within the Enterprise Act 2002 retain old 1986 Act provisions.

At the time of writing, the draft Insolvency Rules to accompany the new statutory provisions are still awaited. Where possible, we have provided comment on the key issues which are still subject to debate and provided an assessment of how the reforms are likely to work in practice, based on statements made by Government Ministers during the passage of the Enterprise Bill through Parliament. However, some important areas were simply not discussed and we must hope that such issues are dealt with in the new Insolvency Rules.

The book is therefore written on the basis of available information as at the end of November 2002.

Vernon S Dennis
London
30 November 2002

ACKNOWLEDGEMENTS

The authors would like to thank their colleagues Esra Kingsbury and Hester Jewitt for their contributions on the Insolvency Act 2000 and employment law reform respectively.

Thanks also go to Ross Risby, Kirstie Gibson, Nicola Kay, Janice Usher and Lynne Metcalfe for their helpful suggestions, research and proofreading. Our task in attempting to provide a summary of legislative changes to insolvency law since 1986 would have been far harder but for the invaluable assistance of our colleagues at Manches.

ABOUT THE AUTHORS

Vernon S Dennis

Vernon studied law at Essex University and was trained at a Tunbridge Wells firm, Cripps Harries Hall. Qualifying in 1993, he joined their commercial litigation department. He went on to obtain a diploma in the subject and joined Manches in March 1999, where he is now a Partner.

He is a member of the firm's Commercial Dispute Resolution Team and has responsibility for insolvency and banking work throughout Manches.

Vernon edits CRIB sheet, the firm's newsletter to corporate recovery insolvency and banking clients. He has also published a large number of articles and spoken at a variety of seminars and conferences on litigation and insolvency issues.

Vernon is married to Sarah Jane and has a young son Thomas.

Alexander P S Fox

Alex studied economics at Leeds University. After qualifying at the West End banking law firm, Glovers, he joined Manches in December 1998 and is now the senior solicitor within Manches' Commercial Dispute Resolution Team.

Alex has advised on a variety of different substantial national and cross-border commercial disputes. His particular experience and interests have led him to focus on resolving both banking and insolvency related issues. He has published a wide number of articles and spoken on insolvency and banking issues. When not disseminating the Enterprise Act 2002, Alex is a keen traveller and in his spare time has worked on building projects in remote parts of South America; closer to home he is an enthusiastic wind-surfer, off-road runner and mountain biker. Alex is married to Philippa, who is a specialist registrar in gastroenterology.

Manches

Manches is an innovative commercial law firm with offices in London and Oxford, providing a full service practice, with particular focus on the industry sectors of corporate and technology, property and construction law.

Manches' commercial dispute resolution experts have a wealth of experience across the broad spectrum of insolvency and pre-insolvency issues such as the creation, review and enforcement of security rights, corporate reconstruction, matters relating to creditors' rights and post-insolvency administration and liquidation issues.

MANCHES
Aldwych House
81 Aldwych
London
WC2B 4RP

ABBREVIATIONS

BRO	bankruptcy restrictions order
BRU	bankruptcy restrictions undertaking
CDDA 1986	Company Directors Disqualification Act 1986
CVA	company voluntary arrangement
DTI	Department of Trade and Industry
European Convention	European Convention on the Protection of Human Rights and Fundamental Freedoms
FLA 1986	Family Law Act 1986
FSA	Financial Services Authority
FSMA	Financial Services and Markets Act 2000
HRA 1998	Human Rights Act 1998
INSOL	International Federation of Insolvency Practitioners
IVA	individual voluntary arrangement
Model Law	UNCITRAL Model Law on Cross-Border Insolvency
OPPS Regs	Occupational and Personal Pension Schemes (Bankruptcy) Regulations 2002
PPP	public private partnership
TLTA 1996	Trusts of Land and Appointment of Trustees Act 1996
TUPE	Transfer of Undertakings (Protection of Employment) Regulations 1981, SI 1981/1794
TUREA	Trade Union Reform and Employment Rights Act 1993
UNICTRAL	United Nations Commission on International Trade

TABLE OF CASES

Abels v. Administrative Board of the Bedrijfsvereniging voor de Metaal-industrie en de
  Electrotechnische Industrie [1987] 2 CLMR 406, ECJ 4.4.12
Agnew and Bearsley v. Inland Revenue Commissioner (Brumark Investments Limited)
  (2001) 3 WLR 454, 1 BCLC 353 . . . . 10.1.5, 10.1.6, 10.1.7, 10.1.8, 10.1.10
Banke Geselleschaft Berlin International SA v. Zihnali [2001] WL 753380 . . . . 4.1.20
Re: Blackspur Group Plc [1998] 1 WLR 422 . . . . 3.6.2
Bower v. Schroder Securities Ltd (3203104/1999) EAT 4.4.6
British Eagle International Airlines Limited v. Compagnie National Air France
  [1975] 2 All ER 390 . . . . 4.2.16
Brown v. Stott [2001] 2 WLR 817 . . . . 4.1.23
Centros Limited v. Erhvervs-og Selskabsstryrelsen [1999] 1 ECR I-1459 . . . . 4.5.13
China and South Seas Bank Limited v. Tan Soon Gin [1990] 1 AC 536 . . . . 5.1.17
Clarence Café v. Comchester Properties [1991] L&TR 303 . . . . 3.7.1
Clarks & Co Limited v. Rockwell International Corp (1977) 441 F.SUPP 792 . . . . 5.1.4
Cuckmere Brick Co Limited v. Mutual Finance Limited [1971] 2 All ER 633 . . . . . . 5.1.16
Daniels v. Walker 17.05.00 TLR, CA 4.1.8
Dear v. Reeves [2001] 3 WLR 467, EWCA Civ277 . . . . 4.3.7
Dennison v. Krasner [2000] 3 All ER 234; 3 WLR 720 . . . . 4.2.11
DPP v. Manners [1978] AC 43 HL 4.1.10
Dudgeon v. UK (1981) 4 EHRR 149 . . . . 4.1.13
Ex Parte Cleo Lightfoot [2000] WLR 319 . . . . 4.1.27
Ex Parte Huggins (1882) 21 Ch.D 835 . . . . 4.2.6, 4.2.7, 4.2.32
Exchange Travel Agency v. Triton Property Trust Plc [1991] BCLC 396 . . . . 3.7.1
Ezekiel v. Orakpo [1977] QB 260 CA 3.7.1
Foreningen af Arbejdsledere i Danmark v. Daddy's Dance Hall A/S [1988]
  ECR 739; IRLR 315 . . . . 4.4.7
Foxley v. UK The Times 4 July 2000 . . . . 4.1.29
Ghaidan v. Mendoza The Times 5 November 2002, CA 4.3.20
GJ v. Luxembourg [2000] BPIR 1021 . . . . 4.1.19
Grant v. South West Trains Limited (Case 249/96) [1998] All ER (EC) 193;
  CR 449 . . . . 4.3.20
H v. Mental Health Review Tribunal N&E London Region, The Times 4 April 2001 . . 4.1.9
Haig v. Aitken [2001] 3 All ER 80 . . . . 4.1.30
Hall v. Simons [2000] 3 All ER 673 . . . . 4.1.28
Handyside v. UK (1979–80) 1 EHRR 737 . . . . 4.1.13
Helen Mountney v. Stephen Treharno [2002] EUCA 174 . . . . 4.3.19
Hopkins v. Worcester and Birmingham Canal (Proprietors) (1868) LR 6 EQ 437 . . . . 5.1.2
Hughes v. Hannover-Rucksversicherungs AG [1997] BCC 921 . . . . 4.5.6
Ireland v. United Kingdom or Lawless v. Ireland (No.3) paragraph 28 (1961) 1
  EHRR 15 . . . . 4.1.6

Jones v. Patel [1999] BPIR 509; [2001] EWCA Civ779. . . . . 4.2.14
Judd v. Brown [1997] BPIR 470. . . . . 4.3.18
Katz v. McNally (1997) BCC 784. . . . . 6.2.4
Kennedy v De Trafford [1897] AC 180 . . . . 3.1.13
King v. Walden [2001] BPIR 1012. . . . . 4.1.19
Kleinwort Benson Limited v. Lincoln C.C. [1998] 3 WLR 1095. . . . . 4.1.16, 4.2.20
Lawrence v. Lesser [2001] Ch.76; [2000] BPIR 410 . . . . 4.2.11, 4.2.12
Malcolm v. Official Receiver [1999] BPIR 97. . . . . 9.2.10
Meade and Baxendale v. British Fuels Limited [1998] 4 All ER 609. . . . . 4.4.7
Medforth v. Blake [1999] 3 All ER 97 . . . . 5.1.18
Mond v. Hammond Suddards (No.2)[2000] Ch 40. . . . . 6.2.4
Mond v. Hyde [1998] 3 All ER 833 . . . . 4.1.28
MTI Trading Systems Limited v. Winter [1998] BCC 591. . . . . 7.7.17
On Demand Information Plc v. Michael Gerson (Finance) Plc [2001]
    1 WLR 155 CA. 7.6.13
Osman v. UK (2000) 29 EHRR 245 . . . . 4.1.28
Powdrill v. Watson; Re: Paramount Airways Limited (No.2) (1994) 2 All ER 513,
    CA. 7.11.9
R v. Carass [2002] BPIR 821 . . . . 4.1.25
R v. Frank Faryab; unreported 22 February 1999, CA 4.1.26
R v. Kearns (2002) EWCA Crim748; The Times 4 April 2002. . . . . 4.1.23
Rayatt [1998] BPIR 495. . . . . 4.2.26
Razzaq v. Pala [1997] 1 WLR 1336 . . . . 3.7.1
Re: ARV Aviation Limited (1998) 4 BCC 708 . . . . 7.8.13
Re: Atlantic Computers [1992] Ch 505 CA 3.7.4, 7.6.15, 7.8.16
Re: Bailey (1977) 2 All ER 26 . . . . 4.3.18
Re: Carecroft Construction Co Ltd [1994] 1 WLR 172 . . . . 3.6.2, 8.4.1
Re: Cedarwood Productions Limited, Re Inter City Print and Finishing Lts,
    the Secretary of State for Trade and Industry v. Rayna and Another, CA
    12.07.01 TLR. 4.1.20
Re: Charnley Davies (No.2) [1990] BCC 605 . . . . 7.9.3
Re: Citro (1990) 3 All ER 952. . . . . 4.3.18
Re: Consumer and Industrial Press Limited (No.2) [1998] 4 BCC 72 . . . . . . 7.7.17, 7.8.13
Re: Coslett Contractors Limited (2001) 1 All ER 292; 3 WLR 1347;
    (2002) 1 BCLC 77 . . . . 10.1.5
Re: Floor Fourteen Limited; Lewis v. Commissioners of Inland Revenue & Others
    [2001] All ER 499. . . . . 6.2.7, 6.2.10
Re: Focus Insurance Co Limited [1996] BCC 659 . . . . 4.5.6
Re: Gorman (A Bankrupt) [1990] WLR 616 . . . . 4.3.7, 4.3.11
Re: Instrumentation Electrical Services Limited (1998) 4 BCC 301. . . . . 7.5.3
Re: J N Taylor Finance Pty Limited [1998] BPIR 347 . . . . 4.5.6
Re: Landau [1998] Ch. 233; 3 All ER 322. . . . . . . 4.2.8, 4.2.10, 4.2.11, 4.2.14, 4.2.15
Re: M C Bacon Limited (No.2) [1990] 3 WLR 646; BCC 430 . . . . 6.2.4
Re: Manchester and Norford RLY Company (1888) 14 ChD 641. . . . . 5.1.5
Re: Mark One (Oxford Street) Plc [1999] 1 WLR 1445; [1998] BCC 984 . . . . 7.10.27
Re: Mirror Group (Holdings) Limited [1993] BCLC 538 . . . . 7.2.20
Re: New Bullas Trading Limited [1994] BCC 36; 1 BCLC 455,
    2 WLR 197 . . . . 10.1.6
Re: Novditrack (UK) Limited [2000] 1 WLR 343. . . . . 7.10.27
Re: Olympia & York Canary Wharf [1993] BCC 154. . . . . 3.7.1
Re: Park Air Services Plc [2000] 2 AC 172. . . . . 3.7.1
Re: Pavlou (A Bankrupt) [1993] 1 WLR 1046; 3 All ER 955 . . . . 4.3.7
Re: Philip Alexander Securities and Futures [1998] BCC 819 . . . . 7.10.27
Re: Pittoriou (A Bankrupt) [1985] 1 WLR 58; 1 All ER 285. . . . . 4.3.7
Re: Powerstore (Trading) Limited [1997] 1 WLR 1280; [1998] 1 BCLC 90 . . . . . . 7.10.27

Re: Sevenoaks Stationers (Retail) [1991] Ch.164 . . . . 8.6.5
Re: Rayatt (A Bankrupt) [1998] 2 FLR 264. . . . . 9.2.10
Re: Trusts of the Scientific Investment Pension Plan [1998] 3 All ER 154 . . . . 4.2.16
Re: UCT (UK) Limited (2001) 2 All ER 186 . . . . 7.10.27
Rowe v. Saunders [2002] EWCA Civ242. . . . . 4.2.12, 4.2.19
Royal Bank of Scotland v. Etridge (No.2) and Others [2001] UKHL 44 . . . . 4.3.7
Saunders v. UK [1998] 1 BCLC 362; [1997] BCC 872; *The Times*
    18 December 1996 . . . . 4.1.25, 4.1.26
Siebe Gorman [1979] 2 Lloyd's Rep 142. . . . . 10.1.7
Southern Equities Corporation Ltd (In Liquidation) (2000) 2 WLR 1141 . . . . 4.5.6
T&D Industries Plc (In Administration) [2000] 1 WLR 646;
    1 BCLC 471 . . . . 7.2.13, 7.7.17, 7.7.21
Taylor v. (1) Serviceteam Ltd (2) London Borough of Waltham Forest IDS
    December 1997 Brief 602. . . . . 4.4.6
Trustee of the Estate of Bowe (A Bankrupt) v. Bowe [1997] BPIR 744 . . . . 4.3.18
Tyrer v. UK (1979–80) 2 EHRR 1. . . . . 4.1.5
Wilson v. St Helens Borough Council [1999] 2 AC 52 . . . . 4.4.7

TABLE OF STATUTES

Bankruptcy Act 1861 . . . . 1.5.4
Bankruptcy Act 1883 . . . . 1.5.4, 1.5.5
Bankruptcy Act 1914. . . 1.5.5, 4.2.9, 9.2.1,
                             10.2.3
Building Societies Act 1986. . 3.3.13, 5.3.25
Companies Act 1862 . . . . 1.2.1
Companies Act 1908 . . . . 1.2.1
Companies Act 1929 . . . . 1.2.1
Companies Act 1948 . . . . 1.2.1
Companies Act 1985 . . . 1.2.1, 2.4.4, 3.2.5
  Part VII, Ch.I
    s.247
        (3) 3.2.5
        (4) 3.2.5
        (5) 3.2.5
        (7) 3.2.5
  Part XII, Ch.I
    s.395 . . . . 7.4.9
Companies Act 1989
    s.173. . . . . 5.3.19
Company Directors Disqualification
  Act 1986 . . . 1.5.19, 3.6.1, 4.1.20, 8.4.1,
                         8.6.5, 10.2.6
    s.1A 3.6.3, 8.6.4, 9.2.6
        (4) 3.6.4
    s.2. . . . . 3.6.5
    s.3. . . . . 3.6.5
    s.4. . . . . 3.6.5
    s.5. . . . . 3.6.5
    s.6. . . . . 3.6.5, 3.6.6
    s.8. . . . . 3.6.5
    s.8A 3.6.6
    s.11
        (1) 9.4.10
Deeds of Arrangement Act 1914
  (c.47). 9.3.12
Employment Rights Act 1986. . . . . . 6.1.13
    s.198
        (4) 6.1.13
English Bankruptcy Act 1542. . . . . . . 1.5.2
Enterprise Act 2002. . . 1.2.11, 1.3.8, 1.4.5,

     1.4.11, 1.4.14, 1.4.15, 1.5.7, 1.5.10,
     1.5.11, 1.5.15, 1.5.18, 1.5.19, 2.2.18,
    3.1.2, 3.4.1, 3.4.2, 3.8.4, 4.1.32, 4.1.33,
    4.3.1, 4.3.10, 4.3.18, 4.3.21, 4.3.23,
    4.3.24, 4.3.25, 4.3.26, 4.3.27, 4.3.28,
    4.3.29, 4.3.30, 5.1.7, 5.2.3, 5.2.5, 5.2.7,
     5.3.1, 5.3.2, 5.3.7, 5.3.22, 5.3.26,
  5.3.31, 6.3.9, 7.2.2, 7.2.5, 7.2.7, 7.2.18,
  7.3.11, 7.3.19, 7.4.3, 8.1.1, 8.1.2, 8.1.3,
  8.1.7, 8.1.8, 8.1.9, 8.1.10, 8.1.11, 8.2.1,
    8.2.7, 8.3.1, 8.6.2, 8.6.4, 8.6.5, 9.1.4,
  9.1.6, 9.1.8, 9.2.2, 9.2.5, 9.2.13, 9.2.15,
    9.3.8, 9.3.14, 9.3.20, 10.1.1, 10.1.2,
  10.1.3, 10.1.4, 10.1.5, 10.1.10, 10.1.12,
  10.1.15, 10.2.1, 10.2.5, 10.2.7, 10.2.8,
            10.2.9, 10.3.1, 10.3.4
Part 10
    s.248. 7.1.4
    s.249. . . . . 5.3.25
    s.250. 5.2.2
    s.252. . . . . 6.3.2, 6.3.8
    s.253. . . . . 6.2.11
    s.254. . . . . 5.3.27
    s.255. . . . . 5.3.28
    s.256 . . . 8.1.5, 8.1.10, 8.1.11, 8.2.2,
      8.2.3, 8.2.7, 8.2.9, 9.2.3, 9.4.10
    s.257 . . . . 4.2.31, 8.3.2, 8.3.7, 8.4.1,
        8.4.2, 9.3.20, 9.4.3, 9.4.8,
                9.4.10, 9.4.13
    s.258. 9.1.1
    s.259. 9.2.3
    s.260. 9.2.3
    s.261. . . . . 4.3.26
    s.262. 9.1.5
    s.264. 9.4.2
    s.266. 9.4.3
    s.267. 9.4.4
    s.268. 8.3.2
    s.269 . . . . 8.1.6, 8.1.11, 8.6.1, 8.6.7,
            9.1.7, 9.3.11, 9.3.22
        (3) 8.2.5

Sched.16 . . . . 7.1.4
Sched.19 . . . . 8.2.1
   para.3 . . . . 8.2.2
   para.4
         (2) 8.2.3
   para.7 . . . . 9.2.13
   Part 6 . . . . 8.2.5
   Part 8 . . . . 8.2.11
Sched.20 . . . . 4.2.31, 9.4.3
Sched.21 . . . . 9.4.1
   para.4 . . . . 9.4.8
   para.5 . . . . 9.4.10
Sched.22 . . . . 9.3.1
Sched.23 . . . . . . 8.1.6, 8.3.2, 9.3.11, 9.3.22
   para.3 . . . . 8.1.11
   para.13 . . . . 9.1.7
   para.16 . . . . 9.3.22
         (3) 8.6.1
Family Law Act 1996 . . . . . . 4.3.10, 4.3.11
   Part IV
     s.33 . . . . 4.3.11
     s.40 . . . . 4.3.13
Financial Services and Markets Act
   2000 . . . . 3.8.6
   Part VIII
     s.124A 7.6.2
   Part XXIV
     s.356 . . . . 3.8.6
     s.367 . . . . 7.6.2, 7.6.20, 7.10.19
Greater London Authority Act
   1999 . . . . 5.3.25
Housing Act 1996
   Part I 5.3.20
Human Rights Act 1998 . . . . 3.3.11, 4.1.1,
              4.1.2, 4.1.3, 4.1.4, 4.1.6,
            4.1.7, 4.1.8, 4.1.10, 4.1.12,
          4.1.13, 4.1.16, 4.1.17, 4.1.18,
          4.1.20, 4.1.22, 4.1.25, 4.1.30,
          4.1.31, 4.1.32, 4.1.33, 4.2.12,
          4.3.3, 4.3.19, 4.3.20, 8.3.3,
              9.2.11, 9.3.4, 9.4.12
   s.1 . . . . 4.1.2
   s.2 . . . . 4.1.2
   s.3 . . . . 4.1.2, 4.1.9
   s.4 . . . . 4.1.2, 4.1.9
   s.5 . . . . 4.1.2
   s.6 . . . . 4.1.2
     (3)
        (b) 4.1.10
   s.7 . . . . 4.1.2
     (1) 4.1.11
     (5)
        (a) 4.1.11
        (b) 4.1.11
   s.8 . . . . 4.1.2, 4.1.17
   s.9 . . . . 4.1.2

s.10 . . . . 4.1.2
s.11 . . . . 4.1.2
s.12 . . . . 4.1.2
s.13 . . . . 4.1.2
s.14 . . . . 4.1.2
s.15 . . . . 4.1.2
s.16 . . . . 4.1.2
s.17 . . . . 4.1.2
s.22
   (4) 4.1.2
Art.6 . . . . 3.6.6
Sched.1
   Part I 4.1.3
Insolvency Act 1986 . . . . 1.2.2, 1.2.5,
       1.2.8, 1.2.9, 1.2.10, 1.3.2, 1.3.3,
       1.3.4, 1.4.1, 1.4.13, 1.5.8, 1.5.9,
     1.5.11, 1.5.16, 1.5.17, 3.7.2, 4.2.5,
       4.2.8, 4.2.9, 6.1.14, 6.2.10, 7.1.1,
      7.7.3, 8.1.4, 8.1.7, 8.1.9, 9.2.2,
     9.2.5, 9.2.15, 9.3.5, 9.3.22, 10.1.1
   Part I 3.2.1
   s.1 . . . . 3.2.4
     (1) 3.2.1
     (2) 3.2.1
     (3) 3.2.1
   s.1A 3.2.4, 3.3.9
     (2) 3.6.3
     (3) 3.6.3
   s.2 . . . . 3.3.2, 3.3.3
   s.3 . . . . 3.3.4
   s.3A 6.2.11
   s.4 . . . . 3.3.4
   s.4A 3.3.4, 3.3.5, 3.3.9, 3.3.12
   s.7A 3.3.9
     (1) 3.3.10
     (2) 3.3.10
     (3) 3.3.11
     (4) 3.3.11
     (5) 3.3.11
     (6) 3.3.11
   s.7B 3.3.12
   Part II 7.1.4
   s.8 . . . . 7.1.4
     (1)
        (a) 7.3.2, 7.3.3
        (b) 7.3.2
   s.8
     (3) 7.2.1
       (i) 7.2.6
   s.10
     (1)
       (b) 3.7.1
       (c) 3.7.1
   s.11
     (3)
       (c) 3.7.1

(d). 3.7.1
s.14
  (1)(A). 7.7.18
s.15. . . . . 7 8 13
s.19. . . . . 7.11.12
  (4) 7.11.9
  (5) 7.11.9
s.23. . . . . 7.7.11
s.27. . . . . 7.9.2, 7.9.3

Part III, Ch.I
s.29. . . . . 5.1.7
  (2) 7.4.5
s.31. . . . . 9.4.7
s.33. . . . . 4.3.10
s.34. . . . . 7.4.10
s.40. . . . . 7.6.9

Part III, Ch.II
s.59. . . . . 7.6.9
s.63. . . . . 9.3.11

Part III, Ch.III
s.72A–72G 5.3.3
s.72A(1) 5.3.3, 5.3.4, 5.3.6
  (4)(a) 5.2.2
    (b). 5.3.6
s.72B–72G 5.3.7, 5.3.22
s.72B. 5.3.8
s.72C 5.3.11
s.72D 5.3.15
s.72E. 5.3.16
s.72F. 5.3.19
s.72G 5.3.20
s.72H 5.3.22

Part IV, Ch.I
s.73. . . . . 3.4.3

Part IV, Ch.V
s.115. . . . . 6.2.5

Part IV, Ch.VI
s.123. . . . . 7.3.3, 7.3.4, 7.3.5
s.124A 7.6.20, 7.10.19
s.125. . . . . 7.3.21
s.127. . . . . 3.2.25
s.135. . . . . 7.4.6
s.156. . . . . 6.2.9

Part IV, Ch.VII
s.165. . . . . 6.2.11
s.167. . . . . 6.2.11

Part IV, Ch.VIII
s.176A 6.3.2, 10.1.1
  (2)
    (a). 7.7.20, 7.10.8
  (3) 6.3.6
s.178. . . . . 7.8.4

Part IV, Ch.X
s.206. . . . . 4.1.25
  (4) 4.1.22

s.213. . . . . 6.2.2, 6.2.11
s.214. . . . . 6.2.2, 6.2.11, 8.3.2
Part IV, Ch. X
s.219. . . . . 3.8.2
Part VI
s.236. . . . . 4.1.22
s.238 . . . . 4.1.20, 6.2.2, 6.2.11,
7.4.9, 7.10.24,
10.1.11
s.238–9. . . . . 7.10.3, 7.10.24
s.238–40. . . . . 7.3.15, 7.6.5
s.239 . . . . 4.1.20, 6.2.2, 6.2.11,
7.4.9, 10.1.11
s.244. . . . . 7.4.9
s.245. . . . . 7.3.15, 7.4.9, 7.6.5
Part VIII 3.4.1
s.253. . . . . 9.3.6, 9.3.10
s.256A 3.4.2
  (3) 3.4.4
  (4) 3.4.7
  (5) 3.4.4
s.257. . . . . 3.4.8, 9.3.3
s.258
  (1) 3.4.9
s.259. . . . . 9.3.4
s.260
  (2)
    (b). 3.4.10
      (i) 3.4.14
    (2A) 3.4.10
  (3) 9.3.12
s.261. . . . . 8.5.3, 9.3.1, 9.3.4, 9.3.20
s.262. . . . . 9.3.4
  (1) 3.4.11
    (b). 8.5.3
  (2) 3.4.11
  (3)
    (a). 3.4.11, 9.3.4
    (b). 3.4.11
s.262A 3.4.12
s.262B. 3.4.13
s.262C 3.4.14
s.263B. 9.3.8, 9.3.9
  (3) 9.3.15
  (4) 9.3.9
s.263C 9.3.11, 9.3.16
s.263D 8.5.3
  (4) 9.3.11
  (7) 9.3.12
s.263F. 9.3.11
  (1) 9.3.14
  (3) 9.3.16
Part IX, Ch.I
s.264
  (1)

Insolvency Act 1986 *cont.*
    (d). 8.1.4, 8.1.11, 8.2.5
  s.279. . . . . 8.1.5, 8.2.2, 9.2.3
    (1)
      (b). 8.2.2
    (3) 8.2.3
    (3)–(5). 8.2.4, 8.2.9, 8.3.3
    (6) 8.1.11
    (7) 8.1.10
  s.280. . . . . 8.2.5, 8.2.7, 9.1.4
    (1) 8.1.11
    (2)
      (b). 8.2.7
      (c). 8.2.7
    (3) 8.2.7
  s.282. . . . . 8.2.10, 9.3.11
    (1)
      (a). 8.5.2
    (2) 8.5.2
    (4) 8.1.10
Part IX, Ch.II
  s.283
    (2) 9.2.1
  s.283A 4.3.25, 4.3.28
    (2) 4.3.27
    (4) 4.3.25, 4.3.26
    (5) 4.3.26
    (6) 4.3.26
    (7) 4.3.26
    (7)–(8). 4.3.28
    (9) 4.3.26
  s.284
    (1) 4.3.8
  s.289. . . . . 9.1.1
    (1) 9.1.2
    (2) 9.1.3
    (3)–(4). 9.1.4
  s.291
    (4) 8.3.2
Part IX, Ch.IV
  s.306 . . . . 1.5.16, 1.5.17, 4.1.30,
    4.2.4, 4.2.14, 4.2.25, 4.3.4, 9.2.1
  s.306A 1.5.16
  s.307. . . . . 9.2.1, 9.2.12
  s.308. . . . . 9.2.1
  s.310 . . . . 4.2.4, 4.2.11, 4.2.18,
               4.2.22, 4.2.26
    (1) 9.2.3, 9.2.4, 9.2.7
      (a). 9.2.7
    (2) 9.2.9
    (6) 9.2.3, 9.2.4
    (6A) 9.2.4
    (7) 9.2.5
    (7)–(9). 9.2.7
    (8) 9.2.14
    (9) 9.2.14

  s.310A 9.2.3, 9.2.7
    (2) 9.2.7
    (3) 9.2.7
    (4)
      (a). 9.2.7
      (b). 9.2.7
    (5) 9.2.7
    (6) 9.2.7
    (7) 9.2.7
      (a). 9.2.7
  s.313. . . . . 4.3.26, 4.3.27
  s.333
    (2) 9.2.12
  s.335A 4.3.16, 4.3.17
    (3) 4.3.18
    (4) 4.3.16
Part IX, Ch.V
  s.336. . . . . 4.3.10
    (1) 4.3.11
    (4) 4.3.14
    (5) 4.3.15
  s.337. . . . . 4.3.10
  s.339. . . . . 4.3.8, 8.3.2, 9.1.5
  s.340. . . . . 4.3.8, 8.3.2, 9.1.5
  s.342A 4.2.28, 8.3.2
  s.342B. 4.2.28
  s.342C 4.2.28
    (1) 4.2.30
Part IX, Ch.VI
  s.350
    (A) 9.4.9
    (3A) 9.4.1
  s.354
    (3). 4.1.22, 4.1.23
  s.355. . . . . 9.1.6
    (3) 9.1.7
  s.360. . . . . 9.4.13
    (5)–(6). 9.4.9
  s.361. . . . . 9.4.12
  s.362. . . . . 9.4.12
Part IX, Ch.VII
  s.366. . . . . 4.1.22
  s.371. . . . . 4.1.29
Part XIII
  s.388. . . . . 3.5.1
  s.389. . . . . 1.3.2
  s.389A 3.5.2
  s.389B. 9.3.1
  s.390. . . . . 1.3.3, 9.4.8
Part XV
  s.412A 3.8.3
  s.415A 8.6.7
  s.417A 3.2.27
Part XVI
  s.423 . . . . 4.3.8, 6.2.2, 6.2.11,
                  7.4.9, 9.1.5

Part XVII
   s.426A 9.4.3
   s.426B 9.4.3
   s.429
      (2)
         (b) 9.4.11
Part XVIII
   s.436 . . . . 4.2.9
Sched.A1 . . . . 3.9.1
   para.2 . . . . 3.2.5
      (2) 3.2.8
   para.3 . . . . 3.2.5
   para.4 . . . . 3.2.8
   para.5 . . . . 3.2.7
   para.6
      (1) 3.2.10
      (3) 3.2.12
   para.7 . . . . 3.2.13
   para.8 . . . . 3.2.14
      (3) 3.2.14, 3.2.43
   para.9 . . . . 3.2.22
      (2) 3.2.22
   para.10 . . . . 3.2.22
   para.11 . . . . 3.2.23
   para.12
      (1) 3.2.24
   para.13
      (1) 3.2.26
      (3) 3.2.26
      (5) 3.2.26
   para.15 . . . . 3.2.22
      (2) 3.2.27, 3.2.29
   para.16 . . . . 3.2.22
   para.17
      (1) 3.2.27
      (2) 3.2.27
      (3) 3.2.27
      (4) 3.2.27
   para.18
      (1) 3.2.28
      (2) 3.2.28
      (3) 3.2.28
   para.19 . . . . 3.2.28
   para.20
      (1) 3.2.29
      (2) 3.2.29
      (3) 3.2.29
      (4) 3.2.29
      (6) 3.2.29
      (7) 3.2.29
      (8) 3.2.29
      (9) 3.2.29
   para.23
      (1) 3.2.33

      (2) 3.2.33
      (3) 3.2.33
   para.24 . . . . 3.2.15
      (1) 3.2.35
      (2) 3.2.37
      (3) 3.2.37
   para.25
      (2) 3.2.21
      (4) 3.2.21
      (5) 3.2.21
      (6) 3.2.21
   para.26
      (1) 3.2.39
      (2) 3.2.39
      (3) 3.2.39
      (4) 3.2.21, 3.2.39
   para.27
      (1) 3.2.40
      (2) 3.2.40
      (3) 3.2.40
      (4) 3.2.41
      (5) 3.2.41
   para.28 . . . . 3.2.42
   para.29
      (2) 3.2.43
   para.31
      (2) 3.2.44
      (4) 3.2.45
      (5) 3.2.45
      (7) 3.2.46
   para.32
      (2) 3.2.15
      (5) 3.2.16
      (6) 3.2.16
   para.33 . . . . 3.2.17
   para.34 . . . . 3.2.17
   para.35 . . . . 3.2.24
      (5) 3.2.16
      (6) 3.2.16
   para.36 . . . . 3.3.9, 3.3.12
      (1) 3.2.47
      (2) 3.2.47
      (3) 3.2.47
      (4) 3.2.47
      (5) 3.2.47
   para.37 . . . . 3.2.48
   para.38
      (1) 3.2.50
      (2) 3.2.50
      (3) 3.2.51
      (4)
        (a) 3.2.51
        (b) 3.2.51
      (5) 3.2.51

Sched.A1 *cont.*
        (6) 3.2.51
        (7) 3.2.51
        (8) 3.2.51
   para.39
        (2) 3.2.52
        (3) 3.2.52
        (4) 3.2.52
        (5) 3.2.53
        (6) 3.2.54
   para.40
        (1) 3.2.18
        (2) 3.2.18
        (3) 3.2.18
        (4) 3.2.19
        (5) 3.2.19
        (6) 3.2.20
   para.41 . . . . 3.2.55
        (4) 3.2.55
        (5) 3.2.56
        (6) 3.2.56
        (7) 3.2.56
   para.42 . . . . 3.2.57
   para.43 . . . . 3.3.14
   para.44 . . . . 3.3.4, 3.3.14
Sched.B1
   para.1–9 . . . . 7.1.4
   para.3 . . . . 7.2.4
        (1) 7.2.2
        (2) 7.2.3
        (3) 7.2.4
        (4) 7.2.18
   para.5 . . . . 7.2.19
   para.6–9 . . . . 7.2.21
   para.10–39 . . . . 7.1.4
   para.11 . . . . 7.3.5
   para.12 . . . . 7.11.1
        (4) 7.3.7
   para.13
        (1) 7.3.11
        (e) 7.3.21
   para.14 . . . . 7.6.2
        (2) 7.4.4
        (3)
        (c) 7.4.4
   para.15
        (1)
        (b) 7.4.6
        (2) 7.4.6
   para.20 . . . . 7.11.1
   para.21 . . . . 7.4.10
   para.22 . . . . 7.5.10
   para.35
        (1) 7.3.1

para.36 . . . . 7.3.11
para.37 . . . . 7.3.22
        (3) 7.4.8
para.38 . . . . 7.2.21, 7.3.22
para.39 . . . . 7.6.5
   (1)
        (a) 7.3.13
para.40–45 . . . . 7.1.4
para.40
        (1) 7.6.1
        (2) 7.6.2
        (3) 7.6.2
para.41
        (1) 7.6.5
        (2) 7.6.7
        (4)
        (a) 7.6.8
para.44
        (4) 7.6.12
para.45
        (1) 7.6.21
        (2) 7.6.22
para.46 . . . . 7.7.1
        (9) 7.7.2
para.46–58 . . . . 7.1.4
para.48
        (4) 7.7.6
para.49 . . . . 7.7.7
        (5) 7.7.11
para.51 . . . . 7.7.28
para.52 . . . . 7.10.8
        (2) 7.7.22
para.53
        (1) 7.7.18
para.59–75 . . . . 7.1.4
para.59
        (1) 7.8.1
        (3) 7.8.3
para.63 . . . . 7.8.6
para.68
   (1)
        (b) 7.8.10
        (3) 7.8.6
para.70 . . . . 7.8.3
para.71
        (6) 7.7.15
para.74 . . . . 7.10.17
        (1) 7.7.10, 7.9.1
para.75 . . . . 7.8.10
        (6) 7.9.7
para.76 . . . . 7.10.1
        (2) 7.10.4
para.76–86 . . . . 7.1.4
para.77
        (3) 7.10.9

para.79
    (2) 7.10.10
para.80
    (2) . . .   7.10.13
    (5) 7.10.14
    (6) 7.10.14
para.81 . . . . 7.10.16
para.83 . . . . 7.10.28
para.84
    (1) 7.10.30
para.86 . . . . 7.10.11
para.87 . . . . 7.11.1
para.87–99 . . . . 7.1.4
para.88 . . . . 7.11.1
para.89 . . . . 7.11.1
para.91 . . . . 7.11.3
para.92 . . . . 7.11.4
para.94 . . . . 7.11.5
para.95 . . . . 7.11.3
para.96 . . . . 7.11.4
para.97 . . . . 7.11.5
para.98 . . . . 7.9.7
    (4) 7.11.8
para.99
    (4) 7.11.7
    (5) 7.11.12
para.100–116 . . . . 7.1.4
para.104 . . . . 7.2.22
para.105 . . . . 7.5.3, 7.7.12
Sched.1 . . . . 7.8.2
para.6
    (1) 3.2.10
    (2) 3.2.12
Sched.1A 7.5.4
Sched.2A 5.3.22
para.1 . . . . 5.3.9
para.2 . . . . 5.3.8
para.3 . . . . 5.3.8
para.7 . . . . 5.3.11
para.9 . . . . 5.3.12
para.10 . . . . 5.3.15
Sched.4
Part I 6.2.11
Sched.4A 4.2.31, 8.1.11, 9.4.3
para.2
    (2) 8.3.2, 8.4.1
    (3) 8.4.1
para.6 . . . . 8.3.7
para.7 . . . . 8.4.2
para.11 . . . . 9.3.20
Sched.5
Part I
para.2A 9.1.5
Sched.6 . . . . 6.1.11, 6.1.14

Sched.9
para.29A 8.6.1
Sched.17 . . . . 6.1.13
Insolvency Act 1994 . . . . . 7.11.9, 7.11.10,
              7.11.11, 7.11.12
Insolvency Act 2000 . . . 1.4.5, 1.4.9, 3.1.2,
         3.1.3, 3.4.1, 3.6.1, 3.6.6,
         3.7.4, 3.9.1, 8.4.1, 9.2.6
s.1 . . . . 3.9.1, 3.2.4
s.2 . . . . 3.3.1, 3.9.1
s.3 . . . . 3.9.1
s.4 . . . . 3.4.9, 3.9.1
    (2) 3.5.1
    (4) 3.5.2
s.6 . . . . 3.6.3, 3.6.6
    (3) 3.6.5
    (4) 3.6.5
s.9 . . . . 3.7.2
s.10 . . . . 3.8.1
s.11 . . . . 3.8.2
s.12 . . . . 3.8.3
s.13 . . . . 3.8.4
s.14 . . . . 3.8.5, 3.9.1
s.15 . . . . 3.8.6, 3.9.1
Sched.2 . . . . 3.3.1, 3.3.9, 3.9.1
para.3 . . . . 3.3.2, 3.3.3
para.5 . . . . 3.3.4, 3.3.5
para.6 . . . . 3.3.6
para.7 . . . . 3.3.6
para.8 . . . . 3.3.8
para.10 . . . . . . 3.3.10, 3.3.11, 3.3.12
para.13 . . . . 3.3.13
para.14 . . . . 3.3.13
Sched.3 . . . . 3.9.1
para.7 . . . . . 3.4.3, 3.4.4, 3.4.5, 3.4.7
para.8 . . . . 3.4.8
para.9 . . . . 3.4.9
para.10 . . . . 3.4.10
para.11 . . . . 3.4.11
para.12 . . . . 3.4.12, 3.4.13
Sched.4 . . . . 3.9.1
Sched.5 . . . . 3.8.6, 3.9.1
Joint Stock Companies Act 1844 . . . . 1.2.1
Justices of the Peace Act 1997
Part VIII
s.65 . . . . 9.4.2
Land Registration Act 1925
s.42
    (1) 4.3.4
Law of Property Act 1925
s.30 . . . . 4.3.16
Limited Liability Act 1855 . . . . 1.2.1
Local Government Act 1972
Part V
s.80

Local Government Act 1972 *cont.*
    (1)
        (b). 9.4.4
    s.81
        (1) 9.4.4
        (2) 9.4.4
Magistrates Court Act 1980
    s.87
        (A) 7.3.7
Pensions Act 1995
    Part I
        s.92
            (2)
                (b). 4.2.17
Sched.3
    para.15 . . . . 9.2.14
Pension Schemes Act 1993
    Part XI
        s.159A 4.2.31
        (1) 4.2.13
Social Security Contributions and Benefits
    Act 1992
    Part II 4.2.24
Trade Union Reform and Employment
    Rights Act 1993. . . . . 4.4.1

Part II
    s.33
        (2) 4.4.4
        (5) 4.4.5
Trusts of Land and Appointment of
    Trustees Act 1996 . . . . 4.3.26
Part I
    s.14. . . . . 4.3.16
Welfare Reform and Pensions Act
    1999. . . . 4.2, 4.2.3, 4.2.8, 4.2.33, 8.6.7
Part II
    s.11. . . . . 4.2.21
        (1) 4.2.22
        (2) 4.2.22
    s.12. . . . . 4.2.21
        (1) 4.2.24
    s.14. . . . . 4.2.13, 4.2.17
        (1) 4.2.31
    s.15 . . . . 4.2.28, 4.2.30,
                              9.2.14
        (2)
            (b). 4.2.28
        (6) 4.2.28

TABLE OF STATUTORY INSTRUMENTS

Collective Redundancies and Transfer of Undertakings (Protection of
    Employment)(Amendment) Regulations 1999, SI 1999/1925. . . . . 4.4.1
Co-operation of Insolvency Courts (Designation of Relevant Countries and Territories)
    Order 1986, SI 1986/2123 . . . . 4.5.4
Employment Rights (Increase of Limits) Order 2002, SI 2002/10
    Sched.1
        para.1. . . . . 4.4.6
Financial Markets and Insolvency Regulations 1996, SI 1996/1469. . . . . 5.3.19
Financial Markets and Insolvency (Settlement of Finality) Regulations 1999, SI
    1999/2979. . . . . 5.3.19
Financial Services and Markets Act 2000 (Regulated Activities) Order 2001,
    SI 2001/544. . . . . 5.3.8
        art.77. . . . . 5.3.8
        arts.83–85. . . . . 5.3.9
Fixed-term Employees (Prevention of Less Favourable Treatment) Regulations 2002,
    SI 2002/2034. . . . . 4.4.6
Insolvency Act 1986 (Amendment)(No.3) Regulations 2002, SI 2002/1990 . . . . 3.2.9
Insolvency (Amendment)(No.2) Rules, SI 2002/2712 . . . . 3.2.9, 6.3.9
Insolvency ((ECSC) Levy Debts) Regulations 1987, SI 1987/2093 . . . . 6.1.14
Insolvency Practitioners (Recognised Professional Bodies) Order 1986,
    SI 1986/1764. . . . . 1.3.3
Insolvency Practitioners Regulation 1990, SI 1990/439 . . . . 1.3.4
Insolvency Rules 1986, SI 1986/1925
        r.2.2. . . . . 7.3.6, 7.3.17, 7.3.18, 7.4.1
        r.2.7. . . . . 7.3.14
        r.4.181(1) 6.1.3
        r.4.218(1)(a). 6.2.6
Occupational and Personal Pension Schemes (Bankruptcy) Regulations 2002,
    SI 2002/427. . . . . 4.2.21
        reg.3 . . . . 4.2.24
        reg.3(c). 4.2.24
            (1)
                (a) 4.2.25
                (b) 4.2.25
        reg.6
            (4). 4.2.25
            (5). 4.2.25
Part-time Workers (Prevention of Less Favourable Treatment) Regulations 2000, SI
    2000/1551. . . . . 4.4.6
Transfer of Undertakings (Protection of Employment) Regulations 1981,
    SI 1981/1794. . . . . 4.4.3, 4.4.11, 4.4.12, 4.4.20

reg.2
   (1) 4.4.4
reg.3
   (1) 4.4.4
reg.5 . . . . 4.4.7
   (2)
      (a) 4.4.6
      (b) 4.4.6
reg.7 . . . . 4.4.5
reg.8(1) 4.4.9
   (2) 4.4.9
reg.10 . . . . 4.4.14
Transfer of Undertakings (Protection of Employment) (Amendment) Regulations
  1987, SI 1987/442 . . . . 4.4.1

TABLE OF EUROPEAN
LEGISLATION

Conventions and Treaties

European Coal and Steel Community (ECSC) Treaty 1951
 art.49. . . . . 6.1.14
 art.50. . . . . 6.1.14
European Convention on Human Rights and Fundamental Freedoms 1950 . . 4.1.5, 4.1.6,
                                                                4.1.16, 4.1.20, 4.1.32
 art.1. . . . . 4.2.12
 art.2. . . . . 4.1.4, 4.1.13
 art.3. . . . . 4.1.4
 art.4. . . . . 4.1.4
 art.6 . . . . 4.1.4, 4.1.11, 4.1.18, 4.1.22, 4.1.23, 4.1.27. 4.1.28, 9.3.4
  Clause 2. . . . . 4.1.22
 art.8 . . . . 4.1.4, 4.1.14, 4.1.28, 4.1.29, 4.3.19, 4.3.20
  Clause 1. . . . . 4.3.19
 art.13. . . . . 4.1.4
 art.14. . . . . 4.1.4, 4.3.20
  First protocol. 4.1.4

Regulations

Regulation 1346/2000 (Insolvency proceedings). 4.1.10, 4.5.8, 4.5.20, 4.5.21, 4.5.25,
                                                4.5.29, 4.5.36, 5.3.28, 7.3.9
 art.2. . . . . 4.5.16
 art.3. . . . . 4.5.13
 art.3.1 . . . . 4.5.14
 art.3.2 . . . . 4.5.16
 art.3.3 . . . . 4.5.16
 art.4. . . . . 4.5.17
 art.5–15. . . . . 4.5.17
 art.18.1 . . . . 4.5.17
 art.18.2 . . . . 4.5.17
 art.25(1) 4.5.22
 art.31. . . . . 4.5.19
 art.33.1 . . . . 4.5.19
 art.37. . . . . 4.5.18
 recital 12. . . . . 4.5.13

Directives

Acquired Rights Directive 77/187/EEC 4.4.1, 4.4.4
Acquired Rights Directive 2001/23/EC 4.4.3
Reorganisation and Winding Up of Insurance Undertakings Directive 2001/17/EC . . 4.5.8
Reorganisation and Winding Up of Credit Institutions Directive 2001/24/EC 4.5.8

PART I   THE REFORM PROCESS IN CONTEXT

1 AN HISTORICAL PERSPECTIVE

1.1 CREDIT, RISK AND INSOLVENCY

1.1.1 The extension of credit is essential to the development of any economic system. It may take the form of the provision of capital by means of a loan, which in turn may be used to fund acquisitions or facilitate commercial development. Alternatively, credit may be extended to grant the immediate use of goods and of services with agreement for deferred payment. In either case, the extension of credit will create a debt, with both creditor and debtor accepting a degree of risk in entering into the transaction.

1.1.2 Risk exists for the lender because, whether through personal failings, market forces, unforeseen contractual or tortious liability or just plain misfortune, some debtors default on their repayment obligations. The risk for the borrower is the potential penalty incurred for failing to repay the creditor on time.

1.1.3 Insolvency is therefore the inevitable by-product of any market economic system as not all borrowers will repay the debts they incur; indeed, the very nature of a free market economy means that not all parties can succeed. The way in which the law deals with the problem of insolvency has developed slowly. Whilst the concept of personal insolvency is as old as the earliest commercial markets (bankruptcy was recognised in Roman law), the development of modern corporate insolvency law is a relatively new phenomena in the UK.

1.2 CORPORATE INSOLVENCY

The development of modern corporate insolvency law

1.2.1 A company is an association of individual members formed together for a common purpose. Until the nineteenth Century, 'companies' were created by Royal Charter (e.g. The East India Company in 1600), or by Special Acts of Parliament. The Joint Stock Companies Act 1844 first introduced the concept that a company could have a separate legal personality from its members. It was not, however, until the Limited Liability Act 1855 that limited liability for members was given statutory recognition. It is, therefore, unsurprising that until the emergence of limited liability there was little need for a separate code dealing with corporate insolvency; bankruptcy law remained sufficient. The Companies Act 1862 introduced the first specific regulation and procedure for the winding up of a company. Provisions in the Companies Acts 1908, 1929, 1948 and 1985 followed.

1.2.2   A lengthy period of economic prosperity also meant that there was little need for a distinct code to deal with corporate insolvency. Until the Insolvency Act 1986 (the '1986 Act'), most issues regarding corporate insolvency were left to be determined by general legal principles, the control and regulation of corporate insolvency thus remaining piecemeal.

1.2.3   However, in the 1970s a number of factors arose which moved the question of corporate insolvency reform to the foreground:

- Increased commercial activity and the growth of worldwide markets led to an escalation in corporate failure rates.
- In post-war Britain, the days of full employment soon faded and unemployment started to rise. The political importance of avoiding corporate failure and saving jobs became more urgent.
- Valuable businesses were lost to the liquidation process. This led to a growing acceptance that it would not only benefit the company, its employees and its creditors, but also the economy as a whole, if a company could potentially be rescued from insolvency.
- It became increasingly recognised that an efficient insolvency system which facilitates corporate rescue where possible is a vital cog in the process required to avoid the spiralling recessionary effect that can be produced by corporate failure, and thus ensure economic stability.

The development of corporate rescue

1.2.4   It is, perhaps, paradoxical considering the Government's reasoning behind the recent fundamental changes to insolvency law, that the emergence of a rescue culture owes much to the skill and inventiveness of banks and their legal draftsmen. Indeed, during the 1960s the only method of preserving the business of an insolvent company was at the instigation of a secured lender. It was generally a company's bank, using powers conferred by a debenture, who could appoint a receiver and manager of the company. The receiver, in exercising powers contained in a floating charge, could usually then carry on the company's business as he saw fit. The receiver would generally try to preserve the business in order to sell it as a going concern, thus realising a greater sum than would be obtained if the business were to be sold on a break-up basis. In light of these developments, it is not surprising that the Cork Committee[1] considered receivership to be the obvious and preferred means of business rescue.

---

1   The Review Committee on Insolvency Law and Practice set up in 1976 to review insolvency law and practice and to consider what reforms were necessary and desirable, chaired by Sir Kenneth Cork.

1.2.5   Until the 1986 Act came into force, the only insolvency procedures available to a company were the three forms of liquidation: members' or creditors' voluntary liquidation, or compulsory liquidation. The Cork Committee saw great value in the furthering of a rescue culture and sought to bolster the receivership process by statutory recognition; i.e. the definition of administrative receivers and the creation of two new forms of rescue procedure: administration and the company voluntary arrangement (CVA).

1.2.6   The administration procedure was primarily intended to enable corporate rescue where a company was not subject to a floating charge, or where the floating chargeholder had no interest or benefit in appointing an administrative receiver.

1.2.7   The CVA procedure was an attempt to formalise the company's ability to make arrangements with its creditors. Importantly, it provided a mechanism for binding minority creditors (holding less than 25 per cent of the total unsecured debt) who wished to object to and hinder an arrangement which was seen as beneficial by the larger majority of creditors (holding at least 75 per cent of the total unsecured debt).

1.2.8   The Cork Committee's report[1] was published in 1982 and although some of the major proposals of the Committee were not enacted, the greater proportion of the report was accepted and the recommendations incorporated into the provisions now in force as the 1986 Act.

1   'Report of the Review Committee on Insolvency Law and Practice', Cmnd 8558.

Table 1.1 Corporate insolvency proceedings in England and Wales 1987 to 2001

	Liquidation		Administrative receiverships	Administration orders	Company voluntary arrangements
	Compulsory	Creditors' voluntary			
1987	4116	7323	1265	131	21
1988	3667	5760	1094	198	47
1989	4020	6436	1706	135	43
1990	5977	9074	4318	211	58
1991	8368	13459	7515	206	137
1992	9734	14691	8324	179	76
1993	8244	12464	5362	112	134
1994	6597	10131	3877	159	264
1995	5519	9107	3226	163	372
1996	5080	8381	2701	210	459
1997	4735	7815	1837	196	629
1998	5216	7987	1731	338	470
1999	5209	9071	1618	440	475
2000	4925	9382	1595	438	557
2001	4675	10297	1914	698	597

Source: DTI Statistical Directorate

1.2.9   The economic recession of the early 1990s sorely tested the statutory regime introduced by the 1986 Act. In particular, the newly introduced forms of corporate rescue, namely administration and voluntary arrangements, came under close scrutiny. As is evident from the available statistical data, the new statutory procedures were little used. Indeed, in the first four years after their introduction, fewer than 200 voluntary arrangements were proposed and accepted. Furthermore, the number of administration appointments, although steadily rising, has remained dwarfed by administrative receivership, particularly during the recession of the early 1990s.

1.2.10   However, the fact that administrative receivership was more widely used than administration is perhaps unsurprising when one considers the positive endorsement the Cork Committee had given to receivership as a method of corporate rescue. Indeed, the 1986 Act saw administration as a means to complement administrative receivership, not to replace it. Furthermore, in times of

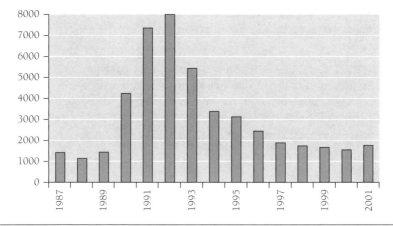

Figure 1.1 Administrative receivership

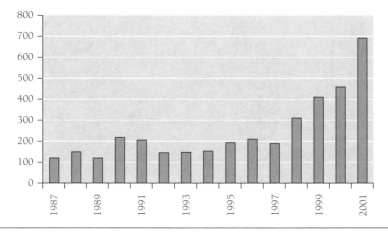

Figure 1.2 Administration appointments

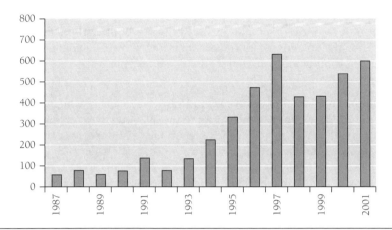

Figure 1.3 Company voluntary arrangements 1987–2001

economic downturn, swift and decisive action is called for, and thus banks relied on tried and tested methods of corporate rescue.

1.2.11 There may also have been an initial reluctance on the part of insolvency practitioners to try out new methods and procedures. It is clear that the use of administrative receivership has dramatically declined since the early 1990s. This may be due to a number of factors (the more benign economic conditions certainly being one of them), but it has been suggested that banks have been under pressure, whether political or otherwise, not to appoint administrative receivers. This in turn was driven by the blame attached to the banks for the unduly hasty appointment of administrative receivers, which in turn depressed the property market still further. During the 1990s, the banks refined their lending practices, set up specialist insolvency units and adopted a more sophisticated approach to corporate recovery. All of these factors have contributed to the decline in appointments of administrative receivers. Allied to this is the growing acceptance that administration and voluntary arrangements provide a viable means to effect corporate rescue, which assists not only the company but also its secured and unsecured creditors. As we shall see, however, even though the use of administrative receivership has declined in recent years it has not been spared the reforms initiated by the Enterprise Act 2002.

1.3   THE CHANGING PERCEPTION OF INSOLVENCY PRACTITIONERS

1.3.1 Just as important as statutory reform in the development of insolvency practice in the UK, has been a perceptible sea-change in the regard in which insolvency practitioners are held by the public at large. In its investigation of insolvency practice and procedure in the UK, the Cork Committee found that a small minority of unscrupulous practitioners had caused disproportionate harm to the reputation of the insolvency profession. The main problems were associated with unqualified practitioners acting in cahoots with debtors, ensuring a poor return for creditors. Examples included the sale of property to associates of the debtor (or the practitioner) for a low value and allowing a company to enter into creditors' voluntary liquidation without creditor approval.

1.3.2   Various recommendations were made by the Cork Committee to improve the regulation and control of insolvency practitioners, many of which found their way into the 1986 Act. For instance, prior to the 1986 Act, any person other than a bankrupt could act as an insolvency practitioner. An important change post-1986 was to make it unlawful for any person to act as an insolvency practitioner in relation to any company or individual unless qualified to do so.[1] Contravention of this section is punishable by a fine and/or imprisonment of up to two years.

1   Insolvency Act 1986, s.389.

1.3.3   The 1986 Act provides that a person is not qualified to act as an insolvency practitioner unless authorised by a recognised professional body[1] or by the Secretary of State. The Insolvency Practitioners (Recognised Professional Bodies) Order 1986[2] provides that the following bodies are 'recognised':

- The Chartered Association of Certified Accountants.
- The Institute of Chartered Accountants of England and Wales.
- The Institute of Chartered Accountants of Scotland.
- The Institute of Chartered Accountants of Ireland.
- Insolvency Practitioners Association.
- The Law Society of Scotland.
- The Law Society of England and Wales.

1   Insolvency Act 1986, s.390.
2   SI 1986/1764.

1.3.4   As part of the transitional provisions for the 1986 Act, established practitioners of substantial experience and good record were allowed authorisation even if they lacked the necessary professional qualification. However, since 1 April 1990[1] it has been necessary for any insolvency practitioner newly seeking authorisation to pass the examination set by the Joint Insolvency Examination Board, or to have obtained a similar overseas qualification.

1   Insolvency Practitioners Regulations 1990, SI 1990/439.

1.3.5   As well as ensuring proper educational qualification, measures have been taken to ensure that professional and ethical standards are maintained. The DTI has issued ethical guidelines stressing the importance of insolvency practitioners being able to act free from any potential or actual conflict of interest. Accordingly, it is regarded as unethical for individuals to take an appointment if a member of that person's firm has been an auditor, director or had any other material professional relationship with the debtor company within the three years preceding insolvency. Professional standards are also maintained by the regular inspection of insolvency practitioners' offices by the Joint Insolvency Monitoring Unit. This Unit is responsible for monitoring the practice and procedures of insolvency practitioners authorised by the Secretary of State, the Institute of Chartered Accountants or the Insolvency Practitioners Association.

1.3.6   The work of the Association of Business Recovery Professionals (R3) has also been of vital importance in raising the profile and reputation of the profession. Although not authorised to grant insolvency licences, R3 is the principal professional body of the insolvency profession and has promoted the training and education of members, ensuring common professional and ethical standards throughout the profession. R3 regularly issues statements of insolvency practice which, although not binding on its members, provide guidance for practice and create greater uniformity in the standard of advice provided to the public.

1.3.7   Insolvency practitioners provide unique skills and imaginative solutions in the area of business recovery and have been vital in saving jobs and businesses, consistently bringing value to the economy as a whole. Since 1986, one of the growth areas in insolvency has been the development of specialists who advise on the successful turnaround of underperforming companies for the benefit of stakeholders, outside the statutory framework. This has transformed the role of the insolvency profession over the course of the last two decades and is explored in detail in section 4.6.

1.3.8   The undoubted improvement in the skill and professionalism of insolvency practitioners has led to a gradual rise in the profile and reputation of the profession (at least within the business community) and the trust and confidence engendered has been instrumental in the development of insolvency practice since 1986. The important role of insolvency law and of insolvency practitioners is recognised by the major role that insolvency plays in the Enterprise Act 2002. The 2002 Act is central to the Labour Government's plans to undertake economic reform in order to foster enterprise and productivity.

1.4   THE REFORM OF CORPORATE INSOLVENCY LAW

Why was reform thought necessary?

1.4.1   As we have discussed, the 1986 Act was certainly put through its paces by the recession of the early 1990s. However, the new procedures, namely administration and CVAs were, in the years immediately following the introduction of the 1986 Act, comparatively little used. Indeed, administrative receivership is still the most common form of corporate rescue procedure. However, if the recession had occurred a few years later, when the 1986 Act had become more refined and battle hardened, might the results have been somewhat different?

1.4.2   Throughout the current reform process, the Government has consistently voiced its opinion that the large number of administrative receivership appointments in the early 1990s was evidence of precipitate behaviour on the part of lenders, which in turn caused companies to fail and the economic recession to worsen.[1] The recession of the early 1990s has been widely viewed as property based, exacerbated by the misuse or overuse of administrative receivership. As margins of security evaporated this in turn increased the likelihood that lenders would appoint an administrative receiver. As so-called 'fire sales' caused property prices to fall, the property market was depressed still further and the recessionary spiral increased.

1   For example, see comments of Douglas Alexander, Minister for E-Commerce & Competitiveness, 15th Sitting, Standing Committee Enterprise Bill, 9 May 2002.

1.4.3   In addition to its economic impact, the following arguments were put forward to support the Government's position that the use of administrative receivership needed radical reform:

- Administrative receivership puts too much power in the hands of one creditor, namely the floating chargeholder. This may lead to unnecessary business failure and undermine corporate rescue, as the floating chargeholder has no need to take into account the interests of any other creditors nor those of the company.
- There is a lack of transparency and accountability, as the floating chargeholder takes decisions which have a significant impact on the returns to other creditors without their consent. Furthermore, there is no equivalent of the duty owed by an administrator to act in the interest of creditors as a whole.
- The absence of an incentive to obtain greater realisations once the secured creditors are assured that their claims will be met from the asset realisations may lead to early sales with low values. It may also prohibit the continued operation of the business as a going concern.
- As insolvency becomes increasingly transnational there is a growing need for international recognition of insolvency procedures. Administrative receivership is not generally recognised outside the UK; it is a contractual remedy for a single creditor, not a collective statutory procedure.
- With the growth of asset based lending, factoring and discounting, there is an increasing diversity of parties holding security. This means that corporate rescue is more difficult to effect, as parties may have conflicting interests and some may be more inclined to appoint earlier to realise their security and not stand in line behind other parties. It is also more difficult to rely on self-regulatory measures introduced by secured creditors, such as the banks' Statement of Principles.

1.4.4   Therefore, the overall impression left by the recession of the early 1990s on members of the current Government was that administrative receivership was often used to pull the plug on a company with no thought given to whether, with breathing space, the company could trade out of its difficulties and survive. With the Government's apparent conversion to the US system which we will discuss later[1], there were also some suggestions that the adoption of a system similar to Chapter 11[2] of the US Federal Bankruptcy Code would be a panacea to all ills. It was against this background that the review process was initiated.

1   See further paras.1.5.12 to 1.5.13.
2   For further comment on the Chapter 11 procedure, see section 2.2.

The review process

1.4.5   The review process commenced in 1997 by the Labour Government contrasts starkly with the review of insolvency law by the Cork Committee between 1976 and 1982. Whereas the Cork Committee looked at all aspects of insolvency reform, both personal and corporate, over a period of six years, the present Government, in its clamour to reform the system, set up a whole raft of different review groups. Three consultation papers were issued over a period of four years and time was still found to introduce the Insolvency Act 2000. The consultation process was criticised for being highly perfunctory in nature and not working well in practice. Nevertheless, the reform process did stimulate feedback which in turn produced an Enterprise Act very different from that first envisaged.

1.4.6   A joint DTI/Treasury Review Group was set up in 1999 with the following terms of reference:

> to review aspects of company insolvency law and practice in the United Kingdom and elsewhere relating to the opportunities for, and the means by which, businesses can resolve short to medium term financial difficulties, so as to preserve maximum economic value; and to make recommendations.

1.4.7   The Review Group's remit was to look at the development of a rescue culture, to reassess the rights and remedies of secured and unsecured creditors in insolvencies (including the Crown as preferential creditor), and to consider the duties of a director of a company experiencing financial difficulties. A consultation paper was released on 20 September 1999 with responses being sought by 12 November 1999. The report of the joint Review Group was eventually published in May 2000.

1.4.8   This was a surprisingly short period of time in which to seek comment on such fundamental reforms. It is also surprising that after the conclusion of the review, the report awaited publication for some six months. In some quarters, the delay was put down to the continuing battle between the DTI and the Treasury over the issue of Crown preference. Indeed, the May 2000 report avoided this issue by stating that this was in reality a political matter. Instead, the report limited its scope of recommendations to how the revenue departments could amend practice and procedures in order to develop a more commercial approach to CVAs.

The Enterprise Act 2002 reforms

1.4.9 The initial proposals mooted in the consultation papers seemed to indicate a fundamental willingness by the Government to undertake root and branch reform of insolvency law. After much criticism, entrenchment followed and only relatively minor tinkering with the 1986 Act system was provided for in the Insolvency Act 2000 (see Chapter 3). Indeed, when the White Paper 'Productivity and Enterprise: Insolvency – A Second Chance' was published in July 2001,[1] the CBI commented that it seemed to have taken little account of the proposals considered in the previous consultation papers. For instance, much of the detail for the eventual non-court route administration had not been proposed earlier (e.g. non-court appointments of administrators by the company and for its directors).

---

1 Cmnd 534.

1.4.10 It is also noteworthy that after the publication of the White Paper and a further short consultation process, the Enterprise Bill was published on 26 March 2002. Given that the Bill introduced very different measures to those foreshadowed in the consultation stages, and constituted genuinely fundamental reform, this was a remarkably swift piece of drafting.

1.4.11 Before looking closely at the reforms initiated by the Enterprise Act 2002, it is perhaps instructive to look at those reforms which were considered and rejected during the reform process, as some appear to have disappeared after pressure from various industry groups and their omission sheds light on the thinking behind the eventual reforms.

1.4.12 To some, the eventual reforms are seen as a clear indication that the Government has bowed to pressure exerted by the banking industry to introduce new procedures to replace administrative receivership; the effect of which has been to provide banks with powers very similar to those that they enjoyed pre-reform. The proposals of the initial consultation papers were significantly more radical and would have severely reduced the role of banks in the process of corporate recovery.

1.4.13 The September 1999 Consultation Paper[1] made clear that the long promised provision of a moratorium prior to the approval of a CVA would be introduced, and provisions regarding the moratorium were introduced in the Insolvency Act 2000. The following suggestions were also put forward in the Consultation Paper as ways of promoting the rescue culture:

■ The reduction of the requisite majority of creditors required to approve a company voluntary arrangement from 75 per cent (in value) to a simple majority (in value).
■ Requiring debenture holders to give advance notice of an intention to appoint an administrative receiver.

- Relaxation of the criteria for companies entering into administration, including removing the requirement that the company must be insolvent.
- Removing the floating chargeholder's veto over administration.
- Ensuring the enforcement of floating charge securities by way of court appointed receivers with wider duties to the court.
- The introduction of a unified insolvency procedure (such as that in Germany) whereby all insolvent companies enter into what would effectively be a form of compulsory administration. During this period, an independent insolvency practitioner would recommend to the court and creditors whether the company should be preserved as a going concern or whether it should be liquidated. The company would be subject to a moratorium until the insolvency practitioner reported to the court and to the creditors his recommendations. The proposal would then be put to the creditors for a vote and court approval sought.
- Disallowing fixed charges over book debts, or allowing a company to collect only a certain percentage of book debts subject to a fixed charge.
- Allowing a company to raise funds by the sale of its assets covered by fixed charge up to a certain percentage level.
- Allowing super-priority financing whereby a creditor giving finance to a company during a period of rescue would be given priority in respect of any realised funds.

1   DTI/Treasury Group Consultation Paper on Company Rescue Mechanisms, published 20 September 1999.

1.4.14   It is surprising how few of these initial proposals found their way into the eventual Enterprise Act 2002. Whilst it was clear that measures would be proposed which would limit the role of secured creditors, the central role of administration was not evident. Furthermore, it was not initially proposed that administration would be available through a non-court appointment route for either the company itself or a floating chargeholder.

1.4.15   Briefly, the Enterprise Act 2002 reforms introduced to corporate insolvency law are:

- The abolition of administrative receivership as a generally available means of corporate rescue (see Chapter 5).
- The abolition of Crown preference (see Chapter 6).
- Provisions to ensure that a certain part of the floating chargeholder's realisation will be made available to the unsecured creditors (see Chapter 6).
- The requirement that creditors' consent be obtained before officeholders take certain proceedings (see Chapter 6).
- The introduction of an entirely new procedure for administration (see Chapter 7).

1.5   BANKRUPTCY

Bankruptcy – criminal conduct and stigma

1.5.1   As trade across the continent increased in the Middle Ages, the customs and practice of traders developed into a distinct body of law known as the 'law merchant'. The law merchant applied to much commercial activity carried out between traders across the continent and was itself derived from Roman law and the subsequently developed mercantile law of Italy. These systems recognised the concepts of merchant bankruptcy, creditors' rights over a bankrupt's property and even composition with creditors. From the fourteenth Century onwards, in England the law merchant was increasingly superseded by the common law, which distinguished between traders and non-traders.

1.5.2   The first English Bankruptcy Act of 1542 was concerned with absconding trade debtors. This Act allowed creditors to seize the debtor's property and allowed for rateable distribution of the proceeds of sale between the creditors. The close correlation between bankruptcy and criminal conduct continued for several centuries. Indeed a bankrupt fraudulent trader could face the death penalty until well into the eighteenth Century.

1.5.3   As regards non-traders, the common law developed severe powers for creditors to enforce payment of the debts through seizure of the debtor's property and/or imprisonment of the debtor. The establishment of privately run debtors' prisons began in the fourteenth Century and continued until the closure of the Queen's Prison, the last debtors' jail, in 1862. Imprisonment was a private arrangement whereby the debtor was forced to rent space within the prison and was responsible for his own food and welfare and would remain in prison until the debt to his creditor was repaid. Without recourse to trade or employment, the debtor was entirely dependent upon his family, alms or the mercy of the creditor. Many debtors lived in squalid, disease ridden 'apartments' until they died. The appalling state of debtors' prisons was an issue tackled by Victorian social reformers, including Charles Dickens. This led to growing public unease with the arbitrary nature of the bankruptcy regime and the fact that the privately run administration of a bankrupt's estate was haphazard and abused. As the industrial revolution took hold, the dire and uncertain consequences of business failure were seen as a major disincentive to enterprise.

1.5.4   The Bankruptcy Act 1861 abolished the distinction between traders and non-traders and in 1869 creditors' powers of imprisonment for debt were all but extinguished. The Bankruptcy Act of 1883 codified the bankruptcy regime and formed the basis of a modern bankruptcy system which survived until the 1986 Act. The 1883 Act firmly established that bankruptcy was a matter of public concern for the entire community. The administration of a bankrupt's estate would therefore be carried out in the best interests of the creditors as a whole and any misconduct by the bankrupt would be dealt with appropriately. Whilst the bankrupt could apply for discharge from bankruptcy at any time, he would have to undergo a public examination after an investigation and a report by an Official

Receiver. In practice, however, the majority of bankrupts did not apply for dis-charge and the stigma of bankruptcy permeated their entire lives.

1.5.5   The 1883 Act and the Bankruptcy Act 1914 did, however, contain pro-visions which allowed a debtor to apply to court for a 'certificate of misfortune'. This was an early attempt to distinguish between culpable and non-culpable bankrupts and allowed for a different procedure to apply where the court found that the bankruptcy of an individual was through 'misfortune'. However, a cer-tificate of misfortune was rarely granted, as misfortune was very narrowly defined. It was not until the Insolvency Act 1976 that limited rights to automatic discharge were introduced.

1.5.6   The need for bankruptcy reform was not immediately apparent in the post-war days of full employment and economic prosperity. The number of bank-ruptcy orders made remained small, running at a few hundred per year, the stigma attached to bankruptcy probably being a factor in keeping this rate so low. However, economic uncertainties from the 1970s onwards, the explosion of home ownership (and therefore mortgage debt) and the wider availability of credit to individuals, all contributed to a rise in the level of personal insolvency. The long term trend over the last 25 years has been of a steadily rising number of bank-ruptcies with an explosive increase in the late 1980s/early 1990s. Interestingly, compared to many other developed countries, the rate of individual consumer bankruptcy remains small, with approximately 65 per cent of bankruptcies being business related.[1] In contrast, in the US the vast majority of individual bank-ruptcies are consumer related (in 1998 1.35 million out of 1.4 million bankruptcy filings were by consumers).

---

1   Consultation Paper 'Bankruptcy: A Fresh Start'.

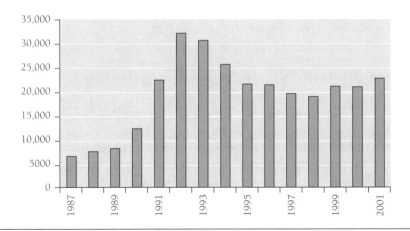

Figure 1.4 Bankruptcy orders 1987–2001
Source: DTI Statistical Directorate

1.5.7   Against the background of rising levels of personal insolvency, in 1982 the Cork Report recommended that the bankruptcy system urgently be reformed. The Cork Committee considered that the function of a bankruptcy regime was to provide a framework for debt recovery and a means by which commercial morality can be policed by investigation, disciplinary measures and restrictions. As a result, it recommended an automatic review of a bankrupt's conduct and affairs after five years which would lead to discharge, unless there was strong opposition by the Official Receiver. The committee also recommended the availability of an early discharge procedure for some bankrupts after 12 months, although the onus would be on the bankrupt to prove that discharge was warranted. These recommendations present an interesting contrast to the reforms introduced by the Enterprise Act 2002 particularly with the differing onus of proof to obtain discharge. The committee also recommended that the Official Receiver undertake an investigation of the bankrupt's affairs which would in turn determine how the bankruptcy and liquidation of the bankrupt's assets should proceed.

1.5.8   In introducing the 1986 Act, the Government did not take up these recommendations. Instead it introduced a system of automatic discharge after three years, with no distinction between culpable and non-culpable bankrupts. The principally cited reason for rejecting the Cork Committee's recommendations was the economic cost of introducing such a system of investigation. Added to this was the desire to avoid increasing bureaucracy at a time when the Civil Service was being pared back.

1.5.9   The 1986 Act also introduced, for the first time, limited protection for a bankrupt's family in respect of the matrimonial home, something echoed again in the more recent reforms.

1.5.10   An historical overview of bankruptcy is illuminating, in that it reveals that many of the considerations behind the reforms embodied in the Enterprise Act 2002 have been debated in the past. The historical trend can also be seen to be one of progressive liberalisation of the bankruptcy laws, despite the reservations of many insolvency professionals.

Bankruptcy since 1986

1.5.11   After the introduction of the 1986 Act, the level of bankruptcy orders made annually exploded. Although not reaching the heights of the early 1990s, the number of orders made each year has remained high, with a growing proportion of consumer related bankruptcies as opposed to those that are business related. Furthermore, although starting out at a very low level, individual voluntary arrangements ('IVAs') have grown steadily in number. Indeed, used properly, IVAs have proved to be an extremely successful tool for debtor rehabilitation and recovery for creditors. As we shall see, however, the success of this procedure may be imperilled by the reforms introduced by the Enterprise Act 2002. At a time when the number of bankruptcies has been rising, why has there been a call for reform of this procedure?

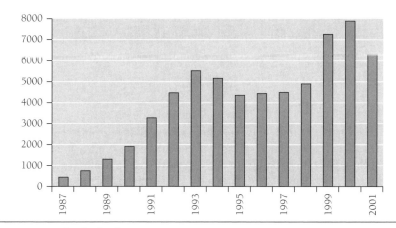

Figure 1.5 Individual voluntary arrangements 1987–2001
Source: DTI Statistical Directorate

1.5.12   In respect of personal bankruptcy, the influence of the US Bankruptcy Code on Government thinking can be clearly seen. In the early days of the incoming Labour Government of 1997, Peter Mandleson, the then Secretary of State for Trade and Industry, travelled to California to undertake a fact finding mission. What he saw in 'Silicon Valley', was a greater percentage of owner managed businesses,[1] greater stakeholding by employees in their employers and a culture of business risk taking, reward and enterprise. He concluded that one of the important factors in fostering this culture was the absence of any fear of failure. In contrast, the stigma attached to bankruptcy in the UK mitigated against risk-taking and therefore enterprise. Peter Mandleson considered that if there was a reform to the bankruptcy procedures, a change in attitude would follow.

1   Global Entrepreneurship Monitor report published in November 2002 showed that 1 in 9 adults own their own business in the US, compared to 1 in 18 in the UK. This level is also well below other European Countries (source: *The Times*, 14 November 2002).

1.5.13   Between 1997 and 2001 there were between 1.3m and 1.4m bankruptcy filings in the US courts annually. The vast majority of these were personal filings and the cost of consumer bankruptcy to each US citizen is said to be $400 per year. Indeed, this problem was being addressed by Congress which was to have introduced legislation making it more difficult for consumers to file for Chapter 7 bankruptcy and forcing them into Chapter 13 compositions, whereby debts are not completely dismissed but instead are reorganised into a repayment plan. Pressure also exists to reduce the disparity between individual State law over debtor protection, central to this debate being the so-called 'homestead exemption'.[1] It appears, however, that after the success of the Republican Party in the November 2002 Congressional elections, the reforms have for the time being been shelved. Whether it is prudent for the UK to follow the US model and risk an explosion in consumer bankruptcy remains to be seen.

1   See section 2.2 for a full description of the US bankruptcy system.

Enterprise Act 2002 reforms

1.5.14   Underpinning the UK Government's view that reform is necessary are the findings of the Official Receiver's office, which has reported that the vast majority of those becoming bankrupt do so despite having dealt responsibly with their creditors and making considerable efforts to avoid bankruptcy.[1]

1   See Consultation Paper 'Bankruptcy: A Fresh Start', Section 7.

1.5.15   In parallel to the review of corporate insolvency procedure, a Consultation Paper entitled 'Bankruptcy: A Fresh Start' was issued by the DTI as part of its review of personal insolvency law. The review set out to consider the social and economic impact of bankruptcy upon the individual and to promote a system which ensured that, over time, financial irresponsibility was identified and the responsible use of credit risk-taking was promoted. Even more clearly than in the area of corporate insolvency, the Government's suggested proposals for personal insolvency reforms appear to emanate from the US experience. The Consultation Paper put forward a number of proposals which, in the main, appear in the Enterprise Act 2002. However, the following proposals were rejected:

- The period before automatic discharge should be six months or sooner (a 12-month period has eventually appeared).
- Legislation which would make it illegal to discriminate against an individual solely on the ground of bankruptcy. This proposal was inspired by US legislation.

1.5.16   One aspect of personal insolvency legislative reform which was certainly not considered at any time during the consultation process was the provision contained in s.261 of the Enterprise Act 2002 (introducing a new s.306A into the 1986 Act), which puts a guillotine period of three years on a trustee in bankruptcy to commence action and dispose of his interest in the matrimonial home. This was in fact a very late amendment proposed by a back bencher and supported by the Government, lyrically referred to as the 'sunset provision'.

1.5.17   It should, however, be noted that the early discharge does not affect the realisation of the bankrupt's estate, as the property of the bankrupt will still vest in the trustee in bankruptcy.[1] However, since the 1986 Act, there have been a number of statutory reforms with the effect that the trustee in bankruptcy's ability to realise the debtor's assets has been restricted (for example, see section 4.2 dealing with the bankrupt's pension and section 4.3 dealing with the family home). The shortening of the bankruptcy period does, however, reduce the creditor's ability to receive benefit from any 'after acquired property' of the debtor. The Government has suggested that few bankrupts acquire property and generally only do so as a matter of chance, for example through inheritance. The effect of this provision was therefore of limited value to creditors and thus the disadvantages to creditors of shortening the period of bankruptcy are small.

1 Insolvency Act 1986, s.306. See para.4.3.24.

1.5.18 The reduction in the period of bankruptcy also has an effect on income payments.[1] The continuation of income payment orders and agreements post-discharge undermines the fundamental principle of the Enterprise Act 2002 reforms; namely, giving a bankrupt a second chance, allowing him to try again and recommence business activity. In order to tackle this dichotomy, the Enterprise Act 2002 has introduced post-bankruptcy individual voluntary arrangements,[2] which have the effect of annulling the bankruptcy.

1 See section 9.2.
2 See section 9.3.

1.5.19 The most radical reform introduced by the Enterprise Act 2002 is the distinction between the culpable and non-culpable bankrupt. Similar to that used in the Company Directors Disqualification Act 1986, a non-exhaustive list of misconduct has been drawn up and the Official Receiver is empowered to apply for a so-called 'bankruptcy restriction order' ('BRO') lasting for a period of between two and 15 years. As we have seen, there have in the past been calls for such a distinction and for different procedures to apply to different types of bankrupts. In the Enterprise Act 2002 reforms, the Government has not provided for different bankruptcy procedures to apply in respect of the liquidation of bankrupt's assets, but rather for different disabilities and restrictions to be imposed upon the bankrupt.

1.5.20 However, whilst it is recognised that an individual's financial failure is often due to circumstances beyond his control, this does not necessarily lead to the conclusion that an individual is non-culpable. By its very nature, taking a risk entails the chance of disaster or loss. A risk-taker should balance the possibility of loss against the prospect of reward and benefit. The individual must take into account circumstances which may be beyond his control. Consequently, although far from being dishonest, an individual's financial failure could be a result of recklessness, naivety or plain stupidity; moreover, the bankrupt individual has taken a risk, as a result of which he has lost not only his own money, but also that of other parties.

1.5.21 These factors seem to have been ignored or overlooked as the Government seeks to encourage an entrepreneurial culture. The fear exists, however, that this encouragement of entrepreneurial risk-taking will instead simply cause an explosion in the rate of consumer bankruptcies. The policing of bankruptcies via the BRO regime seems the best way to prevent this and to ensure that a socially acceptable degree of personal accountability for a bankrupt's actions is maintained. However, this will require significant resources to be allocated to the Insolvency Service, something that may unfortunately be very doubtful. An increase in bankruptcy levels has economic consequences which, as can be seen from the United States' experience, can lead to higher prices, a restriction in the availability of credit and the demand for greater security by lenders. This would be particularly damaging to owner managed businesses: the very sector that the Government seeks to encourage by these reforms. The experience of different insolvency regimes across the world is considered in the next chapter.

2 AN INTERNATIONAL PERSPECTIVE

2.1 GLOBAL TRENDS

2.1.1 A comparative study of foreign insolvency regimes was undertaken as part of the reform process.[1] Although the various review groups made clear that they did not intend to draw any particular conclusions on the efficiency of each system investigated, it is quite clear that the thinking behind the reform process and the eventual Enterprise Act 2002 have been greatly influenced by experiences abroad. This appears particularly true when considering the view of the incoming 1997 Government towards insolvency and its apparent infatuation with the US Bankruptcy Code.

---

1 See in particular *A Review of Company Rescue and Business Reconstruction Mechanisms*, Report by Review Group Department of Trade and Industry and HM Treasury published by The Insolvency Service, May 2000, which looked closely at how business failures are addressed and compared directors' obligations in respect of insolvent companies in the US, Germany, France, Australia, Ireland, Sweden and New Zealand.

2.1.2 The then Secretary of State for Trade and Industry Peter Mandleson, undertook a fact finding trip to the US in early 1997 at the height of the dotcom boom. The lessons he drew from his time in California were that thrusting entrepreneurial businessmen had often 'failed' in the past, but were unhindered from trying again. There was no stigma attaching to a former bankruptcy. Allied to the lack of stigma (it seems an almost established part of US business culture that a successful businessman has not earned his spurs until he has suffered at least one corporate failure) were the apparent attractions of Chapter 11 and the opportunities it provided for business reconstruction.

2.1.3 It is however easy to take too simplistic a view of the Enterprise Act reforms and describe all reforms as a pale imitation of the US System. Douglas Alexander, Minister for E-Commence and Competitiveness, in the committee stage of the Enterprise Bill made clear to opposition committee members that the Bill was not formed just by looking at the US, but that lessons were learnt from reviewing differing approaches to enterprise throughout the world.

We make no apology for seeking to learn from overseas instances of best practice.

2.1.4   It is therefore instructive to view how overseas jurisdictions deal with corporate and personal insolvency. What can be seen is that the need for further insolvency law reform is a pressing issue in the majority of jurisdictions, many procedures share common roots and that, increasingly, insolvency systems are moving closer together, possibly due in part to a wish to develop agreed international principles in respect of insolvency.[1]

1   This development is looked at more closely in section 4.5.

2.1.5   It is perhaps surprising that, when viewed against the background of rising corporate globalisation, insolvency law remains deeply rooted in local legal, economic and social cultures. Differences in various regimes can appear more obvious than similarities and drawing comparisons and learning lessons from foreign jurisdictions appears difficult. Terminology can be confusing; for example in certain jurisdictions, the bankruptcy of an individual and the insolvency of a company are so closely intertwined that the statutory governance is shared and the word 'bankruptcy' is used for both corporate and individual insolvency. However, it is evident that countries across the world have increasingly been regarding insolvency legislation as a means of rescuing valuable businesses, in order to preserve jobs and retain investor value. Furthermore, many of the more draconian restrictions imposed on bankrupts have been removed, as across the world bankruptcy is slowly losing its stigma. It is against this background that the UK reform process has been carried out.

2.2   THE UNITED STATES

2.2.1   In the United States the term 'bankruptcy' applies to all forms of court supervised insolvency proceedings, both corporate and individual. The US legislature has long favoured a policy which encourages the financial rehabilitation of businesses as a going concern. In 1978, Congress enacted a new Bankruptcy Code in which the provisions relating to business reconstruction are primarily to be found in Chapter 11. It is important to look closely at Chapter 11, as this is credited with being the model of business reconstruction which has been followed in the Enterprise Act reforms. It is also a tool used widely in international corporate reconstruction. There are similarities between Chapter 11 and the new administration procedure, but there remain some very significant differences.

Chapter 11 – the US corporate reconstruction model

2.2.2   Chapter 11 is of equal application to both individuals and companies, but individuals generally will have recourse to Chapter 13.[1]

1   Chapter 13 provides a statutory framework by which an individual debtor may put a proposal to his creditors, comparable to the IVA procedure in the UK.

2.2.3   The purpose of the Chapter 11 procedure is to provide a moratorium[1] for the company and to allow the company to put forward a proposal to its creditors in order to preserve the business by restructuring its debt and/or its equity. During the period of moratorium, the debtor formulates a 'plan of reorganisation'. The effect of the moratorium is that the debtor is temporarily relieved of responsibility for paying pre-petition debts and will only need to pay post-petition wages, expenses, taxes and administrative expenses.

---

1   The commencement of the procedure triggers an automatic stay against all actions affecting the debtor and its property. This stay is effective against both secured and unsecured creditors. Any action taken in violation of this stay will be void, and the person contravening the stay will be liable in damages. A stay is binding irrespective of notice to the creditor.

2.2.4   In contrast with most other countries, the existing management of the company will continue to manage and control the business (so-called 'debtor in possession'). The court will only appoint a trustee to take over control of the company in cases where there is shown to be fraud, dishonesty or gross mismanagement of the business. This is the most significant difference between the US and UK system. Administration passes the control and management of the company to an insolvency practitioner. Although certain powers may be delegated back to the existing management the insolvency practitioner remains in control of the company, taking all important business decisions.

2.2.5   It should also be noted that there is no prior requirement that the company or individual should be insolvent before entering Chapter 11. Accordingly, Chapter 11 has been used by companies facing product liability claims as a means to satisfy future claims through a structured settlement. Chapter 11 has no application to banking or insurance institutions.

2.2.6   The procedure is commenced by the debtor company (a voluntary application) or by the creditors (an involuntary application) filing a petition at court. An involuntary application is permitted when three bona fide unsecured creditors whose claims exceed a certain prescribed amount wish to petition. However, this procedure is rarely used, as great care needs to be exercised by such petitioning creditors as irregular petitions can lead to harsh penalties against them.

2.2.7   It is hoped that the period of moratorium will allow negotiation between the company and its creditors, leading to a consensual plan of reconstruction. A trustee appointed by the US Department of Justice Division will also be responsible for the administrative formalities required under Chapter 11. This includes the overseeing of the appointment of the creditors committee and the filing of certain financial information. The creditors committee, in theory, holds a tremendous influence over the company during Chapter 11, as it must be consulted on major decisions.

2.2.8   As actions by secured creditors are also stayed, the US Bankruptcy Code also seeks to protect them against any decline in collateral asset value during the moratorium process. The secured creditor, and indeed any other creditor, has a right to apply for release against the provision of the automatic stay, but a secured creditor has further protection on application to the court. The court can order that:

- the company offer periodic cash payments to the secured creditor as a result of the decreasing value of secured creditor's interests; or
- the company offer an additional and/or replacement lien over property; or
- such other relief as will result in the secured creditor obtaining 'indubitable equivalent' of the value of their secured interest.

Furthermore, if despite such protection, a secured creditor ultimately realises less than the value of the pre-petition security, then the loss in value will be treated as a 'super-priority' claim payable as an expense of the administration.

2.2.9   One of the most significant difficulties in restructuring any business is where the company needs to obtain credit to ensure liquidity. In the US this is dealt with via section 364 of the Bankruptcy Code which deals with the provisions regarding 'debtor in possession financing'. This means that, with court approval, the company can obtain further credit and the court may order the following:

- The creditor will be granted 'super super-priority' over all administrative expenses in respect of the additional credit provided.
- The creditor will be granted a lien on unencumbered property or a junior lien on encumbered property.
- In special circumstances, the creditor can be granted a lien in priority over any existing lien.

The provision of super-priority financing remains missing from UK insolvency law.

2.2.10   Chapter 11 also provides the debtor company with significant flexibility regarding ongoing contracts (i.e. where material performance is required from both parties). The debtor company can assume, assign or reject the contract, depending on its financial needs. If rejected, the other party simply has an unsecured claim for damages. Pending any decision, the debtor's company can continue to enforce the obligations of other parties under the contract. The debtor must however obtain court approval to assign or assume a lease of non-residential real estate.

2.2.11   During the Chapter 11 moratorium, the debtor has a 120-day exclusivity period in which to file a plan of reorganisation. This period is capable of extension by court order. It is only after that exclusivity period has expired that any creditors can put forward an alternative plan. The reorganisation plan will deal with changes to the financial and business structure and may deal with how the debt and/or equity of the company is to be restructured. The debtor also has the ability to deal with and realise any secured property, with the secured creditors' rights attaching to the proceeds.

2.2.12   The rules for approval of the plan for reorganisation are complex, with creditors with similar interests being grouped into various classes, e.g. employees, unsecured and secured creditors. Within each class the creditors will be treated equally and each will receive a disclosure statement giving them enough information to make an informed decision upon the reorganisation plan. Approval of the plan for reorganisation is required by the majority of those voting in each class and two-thirds of the value of the debt in each class.

2.2.13 In the absence of approval from all classes, the court can impose by 'cram down' the reorganisation plan if it considers that the treatment to creditors is fair and equitable and it does not unfairly discriminate against any creditors, and if at least one class of creditors has accepted the plan. The fact that the court can impose a restructuring plan if it considers it to be in the best interest of creditors is a significant feature of the US system and differs from the UK, where creditor approval is required.

2.2.14 Superficially, US Chapter 11 proceedings and UK administration appear to have much in common. Both are court imposed and both provide a moratorium in which time the company is given an opportunity to put proposals to its creditors. Both are procedures with the intention of rescuing and restructuring the business or obtaining a better realisation for creditors than would be effected on winding up.

2.2.15 However, as we have seen, the differences are significant, for instance in the US:

- There is no requirement that the company be insolvent.
- The existing management remains in control of the company.
- The company may be able to obtain credit during the moratorium, giving super-priority to new lenders.

2.2.16 In the last decade, many global corporate rescues have seen the combination of US Chapter 11 and UK administration procedures. This utilises the benefits of the Chapter 11 procedure, such as its flexibility and ability to deal with the corporate group as a whole rather than as individual insolvency corporate entities. It also provides a better stay against worldwide creditors action. Indeed, co-operation between courts on a case-by-case basis has led to formal cross-border protocols to ensure successful co-ordination.

Bankruptcy in the US

2.2.17 Chapter 7 of the US Bankruptcy Code deals with the liquidation of the assets of both individuals and companies. In the case of Chapter 7, a trustee is appointed to collect in and realise the debtor's assets to distribute net proceeds to creditors. There is no fixed period for bankruptcy under Chapter 7, although the process is usually finished within three to four months. The new system of bankruptcy for non-culpable individuals in the UK will have marked similarities.

2.2.18 The application of Chapter 7 differs in various States, as State laws significantly differ on restrictions during bankruptcy and what falls within or outside the bankrupt's estate; the so-called 'homestead exemption' is one such example. This may prevent a trustee from realising the individual bankrupt's interest in a residential property. In Texas, for instance, the homestead exemption is up to a ceiling of $1m; however in Florida there is no limit. The homestead exemption was considered by the UK reform consultation process and an exception of £20,000 considered. This did not find its way into the Enterprise Act 2002, although significant reform has been introduced in respect of this important issue (see section 4.3).

2.2.19   While the UK liberalises its bankruptcy laws, in the US there have been significant calls for stricter measures.[1] Since the reform of bankruptcy law in the US in the late 1970s, individual bankruptcies have steeply risen from around 300,000 in 1980 to over 1,500,000 in 2001. The overwhelming majority (some 98 per cent) are consumer bankruptcies. Non-payment of consumer debt is said to be costing each American $400 per year.

1   Reform of the US Bankruptcy Code has been subject to debate in Congress for the last four years. In November 2002 after the Republican Party's success in the Congressional elections, proposed stricter reforms have been shelved.

2.2.20   There are fears that the UK could follow the US experience. Traditionally, bankruptcy in the UK has been as a result of business failure. The rise in consumer bankruptcy has, however, been gathering pace and now exceeds business bankruptcy; in 2001 the split was approximately 43 per cent to 57 per cent. The further reduction of the stigma attached to bankruptcy and the introduction of provisions allowing early release are intended to encourage enterprise by responsible risk taking. However, if lessons are to be drawn from the US experience, a probable rise in consumer bankruptcy may unfortunately have the opposite effect.

2.3   EUROPE

Corporate rescue

2.3.1   Despite increasing European integration, there are marked differences in insolvency procedure across the Continent.

Germany

2.3.2   In Germany, until recently their insolvency code stemmed back to 1877 and it became evident during the 1970s that a coherent rescue culture was lacking. A new German insolvency code was therefore introduced on 1 January 1999. Prior to this, an informal culture had grown up whereby debtors continued to trade during the insolvency process, with the approval of secured creditors, to allow the business to be sold as a going concern. The new insolvency code has put this practice on a statutory footing.

2.3.3   The most significant feature of the German system (and one which was considered during the UK reform process) is the concept of a single gateway to insolvency procedures. This grew from the recognition that a debtor company (particularly one in perilous financial difficulty) might not be aware of the most appropriate course available. Accordingly, the German system provides a single gateway for all insolvency procedures, whereby a court determines what is the most appropriate route, whether it be liquidation or an insolvency plan.

2.3.4   An insolvency plan, similar to the US Chapter 11, which will restructure business or provide for orderly wind down, is put to creditors. The plan must be accompanied by a realistic forecast and sufficient information must be provided to creditors for them to make an informed decision. The creditors are divided into groups of similar interests and within each group, the creditors are treated equally. If a certain creditor in any particular group is to be preferred from other creditors in the same group, all creditors in that group must approve. If the court is satisfied that the formalities of the plan have been met, then the plan will be presented to the classes of creditors for approval. The plan must be approved by a majority of group members and this majority must represent the majority of the claims.

2.3.5   Unlike Chapter 11, however, there is no provision for reorganisation at shareholder level and consequently, the very useful tool of a debt for equity swap is unavailable. When the planned obligations have been fulfilled, the debtor will be discharged from the remaining debt.

2.3.6   The German system of reorganisation has been criticised for being too complex, requiring too many exhibits, calculations and approvals. The lack of super-priority funding means that during the period of reorganisation the company must obtain funding by trading profitably or by obtaining unsecured lending.

France

2.3.7   In France, a corporate rescue procedure is effected by 'Redressement Judicitaire'. The French procedure is highly court based, with the court appointing an insolvency practitioner to oversee the company. Ultimately any reorganisation or restructuring arrangement will be put to the court for approval, not to the creditors.

Ireland

2.3.8   Ireland has both liquidation and receivership provisions very similar to those of the UK and an 'examination procedure' similar to administration. This is a court driven process with strict time limits and is intended to be undertaken within 100 days. The use of this procedure is minimal with only two companies in 2000 and five companies in 2001 actually undergoing an examination procedure. Receivership is also strictly controlled within Ireland, and if a receiver is appointed over the company, the company can apply to the court for protection within three days. If protection is granted, the receiver could be sidelined for the period of the examination.

Bankruptcy

Germany

2.3.9   It is probably worth noting that personal bankruptcy in Germany, as in many other jurisdictions in Europe, differs significantly from the procedure in the UK. Whilst obtaining a discharge from bankruptcy is harder (and consequently the duration of bankruptcy is longer), it is more difficult to enter bankruptcy in the first place. Indeed, in Germany, if the assets in the estate are insufficient to cover the costs of appointing a trustee, then the bankruptcy petition may be rejected. There is no equivalent in Germany of the Official Receiver's office.

2.3.10   The German system is very much geared towards first allowing the parties to come to a negotiated arrangement. It is a condition that before bankruptcy procedures can be initiated, attempts to settle must have failed. If the debtor is able to put a plan for settlement of his debts to the creditors, the bankruptcy will be withdrawn. If no agreement can be reached, bankruptcy will follow. Until 1999, there was no provision for discharge of bankrupts unless their creditors had been paid in full. After much debate, a provision for automatic discharge after seven years has been introduced and even at this point, release only follows if certain conditions have been met.

Ireland

2.3.11   In Ireland, the discharge from bankruptcy takes 12 years; however, personal insolvency is currently extremely uncommon.

Italy

2.3.12   Surprisingly, at present Italy has no formal bankruptcy regime for consumers. The discharge period for a business bankrupt is five years and only then upon the bankrupt's actual application. There are very strict restrictions on a bankrupt's rights, including the requirement to surrender his passport and a restriction on carrying on certain occupations.

2.4   THE COMMONWEALTH

Corporate rescue

2.4.1   The Commonwealth jurisdictions, particularly Australia and New Zealand, share great similarities with UK insolvency law. Indeed, the insolvency law in each country derives its root from UK statute and common law. All these countries continue to use receivership and, unlike most of the rest of the world, have recognised the concept of a floating charge.[1] Accordingly, in each country banks may take a leading role in deciding whether reconstruction or liquidation is a viable option for the company, although in each country recent reforms have encouraged the greater use of collective procedures.

1 The Personal Property Securities Act 1999 came into force in New Zealand in 2000 introducing a new system of registration of secured interests and new rules regarding priority in respect of personal property (i.e. almost all property other than land). These changes had the effect of abolishing the concept of the floating charge in New Zealand.

2.4.2 In Australia, corporate restructuring is effected by a 'voluntary administration' procedure. Although there is a need to follow strict procedural guidelines, no court approval or formal appointment is required. The voluntary administration procedures provide a moratorium against secured and unsecured claims, whilst an administrator takes control of the management of the company. Within five days of appointment, the administrator must call a meeting of creditors, at which stage a creditors' committee is appointed. A second meeting is called 21 days after appointment, when a report is made by the administrator on his investigations and recommendations made as to whether the company should be liquidated or whether it should enter into a deed of arrangement. During the period of voluntary administration, super-priority financing can be obtained with the consent of secured creditors. Depending on the terms of the deed, some or all of the company's debts pre-deed may be cancelled. The deed binds the company, its officers, members and creditors who voted in favour of it. If the terms of the deed are breached, the deed may be terminated by court order or by creditor resolutions.

2.4.3 The reforms to the UK administration procedure owe much to the Australian system. A system of non-court appointed administration offers speed and savings in cost. However, as we shall see in Chapter 7, in the UK significant powers have been left in the hands of secured creditors.

2.4.4 As an alternative to voluntary administration, Australia also has a scheme of arrangement procedure, akin to the UK procedure available in the Companies Act 1985. The scheme of arrangement provides for debt/equity reconstruction and a court orders the meeting of creditors. The scheme must be approved by the majority of creditors voting and that number must represent 75 per cent of the debts of those creditors. If the scheme is approved by the creditor, the company returns to court for final approval and the scheme becomes effective on being lodged at the Australian Securities Investment Commission.

2.4.5 In New Zealand, a system of compromise agreement is available to effect corporate restructuring. This is an arrangement between creditors and companies, although it is very much a matter for agreement and is not regulated. A compromise of creditors will require leave of the court and classes of creditors with similar interests are required to form to consider the proposal. The consent of the majority of the class who represent 75 per cent in value of claims is necessary. There is no necessity to appoint a formal administrator, but the court can provide such appointment if thought necessary. New Zealand also provides for statutory management of companies if there is evidence of fraud or reckless mismanagement. The use of this procedure is, however, rare.

Bankruptcy

2.4.6   In Australia, the bankruptcy provisions are similar to those of the UK, although there are interesting exceptions in the definition of a bankrupt's assets, namely a car up to a maximum value, life insurance and compensation. Bankruptcy discharge is six months in the limited case of consumer debts; otherwise it is three years unless objections are lodged, in which case discharge can be postponed for five to eight years. At present, Australia is undertaking a reform process which may see the reduction of the bankruptcy period in all cases from three to two years and the removal of the six-month period.

2.4.7   In Canada, a period of bankruptcy lasts for nine months, which is by far the shortest of any bankruptcy period in the Commonwealth prior to the Enterprise Act reforms in the UK.

2.4.8   The Commonwealth countries also often have debtor education programmes, which was an idea discussed in the UK reform process. This sensible idea would need to be backed by necessary funding and expansion to the Insolvency Service, which unfortunately appears unlikely.

2.5   ASIA

2.5.1   Insolvency regimes in Asia came under close scrutiny during the recession in the Far East in the mid to late 1990s. It became apparent that many jurisdictions simply had no insolvency regimes as such and accordingly, often with much assistance from UK insolvency practitioners, informal work outs and reconstructions were facilitated.

2.5.2   Cross-border co-operation was often necessary and agreements between various groups of creditors were vital to facilitate recoveries and rescue. However, such agreements, drawing heavily on the 'London Approach', were often a result of economic necessity, as banks sought to avert an economic collapse. The use of such procedures was also of use only at the 'top end' of Asian economic structures, where international interests also existed. The need to facilitate international business reconstruction still arises in Asia, and indeed across the globe, and is dealt with in more detail in section 4.5. Little assistance can be drawn from domestic insolvency laws in these situations, as the laws often have no application cross-border. Moves to rectify this are being initiated, not least with the development of the UNCITRAL model law. As a result, in Asia domestic corporate rescue regimes needed to be updated and developed. The reforms initiated in Asia are therefore interesting, as in many cases the systems were introducing business rescue procedures for the first time.

2.5.3   Cultural differences are also very profound in Asia. Cultural and social philosophy in Asia, as opposed to institutional legislative control, regulates much commercial activity. There is a strong culture of repayment and compromise. A tremendous stigma remains attached to bankruptcy and liquidation is an unpopular concept, with a strong preference for saving face and saving businesses.

2.5.4   Japan, China, South Korea, Taiwan and Indonesia all have insolvency regimes based upon European civil law codes, with Japan, South Korea and Taiwan borrowing heavily from German law.

2.5.5   Malaysia, Singapore, Hong Kong and India all have systems rooted in UK common law and have borrowed heavily from UK legislation. It is important to note that much of the legislation which has been adopted has since been substantially reformed in the UK or is no longer in force.

2.5.6   With the rise of corporate globalisation, it might be assumed that the dominance of Western cultural values and laws would seek to displace local laws. This has not necessarily been the case, although there has been a tendency to follow the US practice.

Corporate rescue

2.5.7   Malaysia and Singapore both have corporate restructure mechanisms that are similar to the UK scheme of arrangement, with the attendant problems of complexity, cost and delay.

2.5.8   Singapore also has a procedure whereby the company or its creditors can petition the court for the appointment of a 'judicial manager'. The judicial manager will take control of the company and put proposals to creditors. During the period of proposals, there is a moratorium from creditor actions.

2.5.9   For cultural and historical reasons, insolvency law is little used in China and Taiwan. Indeed, bankruptcy was not officially recognised in China until 1988 as the country moved from a command economy to a socialist market economy. Insolvency law in China is, accordingly, still in its infancy. Insolvency law in Taiwan has a longer history, with schemes of arrangement and reorganisation procedures being the principal methods of corporate reconstruction. The reorganisation procedure can be initiated by the board of the insolvent company, 10 per cent of its shareholders or 10 per cent of its creditors. It is however criticised for its delays, the fact that creditors have little say in the process and for allowing companies to avoid liquidation when they should have been wound up. As in the US, the existing management of the company remains in control of the business.

2.5.10   In Thailand, an insolvent company can apply to the court to appoint a plan administrator. The planner will put forward a reorganisation plan to creditors, during which period there is a moratorium on creditors' actions. The plan is a cross between administration and a scheme of arrangement, with the planner taking responsibility for managing the company within a five year period.

Bankruptcy

2.5.11   Despite the economic recession in South East Asia, personal bankruptcy still remains rare. The regimes tend to be stricter, with few examples of automatic discharge. In both Taiwan and Singapore, an application to the court is required. Bankruptcy restrictions are also harsher, with the surrender of personal liberties such as the right to leave the country without permission being common.

2.5.12   The experience in Asia is interesting, as in some jurisdictions they have had to deal with an economic crisis in the absence of any established corporate rescue mechanisms. This is being addressed throughout Asia and reforms are being initiated in virtually every jurisdiction. The lessons to be learnt from these newly emerging systems may, in the future, prove to be very instructive.

PART II CHANGES IN INSOLVENCY CUSTOM AND PRACTICE SINCE 1986

3 INSOLVENCY ACT 2000

3.1 A GLIMPSE OF WHAT IS TO COME?

3.1.1 In Chapter 1 we looked at how the reform of insolvency law and practice gained momentum after the election of the Labour Government in 1997. Since then the Government has set about fostering an enterprise culture, with business rescue forming a fundamental part of that process. To that end, the Government set up a number of review bodies seeking recommendations on insolvency law and practice (see para.1.4.5).

3.1.2 The review groups' published proposals were radical and far reaching. Interestingly, however, the appetite for reform was not borne out by the Insolvency Act 2000 (the '2000 Act') which contained far less dramatic proposals. The 2000 Act is something of a ragbag, catch-all piece of legislation dealing with such diverse areas as company voluntary arrangements, director disqualification and landlords' rights. As such, it deals with some of the problems of the 1986 Act that have been identified in practice, rather than seeking to radically reform either the corporate or personal insolvency regimes. It was, however, made clear that the introduction of the 2000 Act would run alongside the continued work of the 1999 DTI/Treasury Review Group, the report of which is the genesis of the Enterprise Act 2002. The 2000 Act was, therefore, a foretaste of the Government's appetite for insolvency law reform. It is to be regretted that there has been very slow progress in implementing the provisions of the 2000 Act (see section 3.9), something which it is hoped will be avoided when the Enterprise Act 2002 is being implemented.

3.1.3 Despite some shortcomings, the 2000 Act introduces some highly useful practical reforms to the 1986 Act and the Company Directors Disqualification Act 1986 which are worthy of more detailed consideration.

3.2   COMPANY VOLUNTARY ARRANGEMENTS FOR SMALL COMPANIES

Former position

3.2.1   Part 1 of the 1986 Act provides companies in financial difficulty with the opportunity of avoiding insolvent liquidation by entering into a company voluntary arrangement ('CVA'). The directors may make a proposal to the company and its creditors for a composition in satisfaction of its debts or a scheme of arrangement of its affairs.[1] However, the directors cannot propose a CVA where the company is under an administration order or being wound up.[2] In those particular circumstances, only the administrator or liquidator can propose a voluntary arrangement.[3] In practice, the CVA will in most cases be drawn up by the nominee at the request of the company's directors.[4]

---

1   Insolvency Act 1986, s.1 (1).
2   Insolvency Act 1986, s.1 (1).
3   Insolvency Act 1986, s.1 (3).
4   Insolvency Act 1986, s.1 (2). Formerly, the nominee must have been a person qualified to act as an insolvency practitioner. The 2000 Act changes this by widening the meaning of nominee: see section 3.5 below.

3.2.2   The primary purpose of the 2000 Act reforms was to give small and start up companies which have fallen on hard times the opportunity to enter into a rescue procedure rather than a terminal one. Smaller companies are at greater risk of insolvency in the first years of inception.[1] Further, older well established companies are more likely to tackle insolvency by using rehabilitative procedures: companies over 10 years old account for 48 per cent of all receiverships and 40 per cent of administrations since, with higher turnovers and greater assets, they tend to be more suited to using those procedures.[2] Start up companies and smaller companies tend towards liquidation. The former CVA system was notable for its underuse: a recent industry survey revealed that CVAs made up only 6 per cent of all insolvency proceedings.[3]

---

1   R3 9th Annual Survey of Business Recovery in the UK.
2   R3 9th Annual Survey of Business Recovery in the UK.
3   R3 9th Annual Survey of Business Recovery in the UK.

3.2.3   The 2000 Act seeks to redress this by tackling the main areas of concern:

- The lack of a moratorium procedure to prevent creditor action while rescue proposals are formulated (to benefit from a moratorium a company had to apply for an administration order which could be costly).
- The inability of the company to bind creditors who do not receive notice of the creditors' meeting to consider the voluntary arrangement.

The CVA moratorium

3.2.4   The 2000 Act provides that directors of eligible companies intending to propose a CVA are now able to obtain a moratorium to provisionally suspend the rights of the company's creditors.[1] The moratorium will prevent creditors from taking enforcement proceedings against the company which could jeopardise the implementation of a CVA, the existence of the company and the other creditors' hopes of recovery. Indeed, by allowing directors to obtain a CVA moratorium, the Government hopes to encourage more director-led CVAs as historically CVAs have usually been initiated by a liquidator.[2] By allowing smaller companies the opportunity to stave off creditors while a CVA is formulated, the company is afforded a real opportunity of pulling away from the brink of insolvency.

1   Insolvency Act 2000, s.1 and Sched.1 insert s.1A and Sched.A1 into the Insolvency Act 1986.
2   Page 9, R3 9th Annual Survey of Business Recovery in the UK.

3.2.5   The moratorium is only available to those companies which meet the eligibility conditions and are not excluded.[1] A company is *eligible* if the following qualifying conditions are met:

■   The company must satisfy two or more of the small companies requirements[2] in the relevant period.[3]
■   The company's financial year must be determined in accordance with the Companies Act 1985.

1   Insolvency Act 1986, Sched.A1, para.2.
2   See Companies Act 1985, ss.247 (3), (4), (5) and (7). (See para.3.2.6).
3   The relevant period is either in the year ending with the date of filing or in the financial year of the company which ended last before that date: Insolvency Act 1986, Sched.A1, para.3.

3.2.6   Essentially, this means that the CVA moratorium will only be available for small companies which satisfy two or more of the following criteria:

■   Turnover no greater than £2.8m.
■   Assets on the balance sheet no greater than £1.4m.
■   No more than 50 employees.

3.2.7   It is worth noting that the Secretary of State for Trade and Industry is able to change the eligibility criteria by introducing secondary legislation.[1] In this way the Government can test the success of the CVA moratorium before making it available to all companies.

1   Insolvency Act 1986, Sched.A1, para.5.

3.2.8   Eligible companies are *excluded* if, on the date of filing, an act or feature of insolvency is in place; for example, where an administrative receiver or provisional liquidator has been appointed.[1] In addition, certain types of companies are also excluded from benefiting from the CVA moratorium. For full details, see para.2 (2), Sched.A1 to the 1986 Act.

1   For a full list of the exclusions, see Insolvency Act 1986, Sched.A1, para.4.

3.2.9   When first drafted, the 2000 Act's definition of an eligible company could encompass various *special purpose vehicles* used within specialist areas of banking and corporate finance. This problem led to a great deal of lobbying by the City and the implementation of these provisions within the 2000 Act had to await detailed new regulations.[1] This has resulted in the following companies not being eligible for the CVA moratorium:

- Insurance companies.
- An authorised deposit taker.
- A party to a market contract or a system-charge.
- A participant or any of whose property is subject to a collateral security charge.
- A holding company which does not qualify as a small or medium sized group.
- A party to a capital market arrangement under which a party has incurred or is expected to incur a debt of at least £10m.
- A project company of a project which is a public-private partnership project which includes step-in rights.
- A company which has incurred a liability under an agreement of £10m or more.

1   Including the Insolvency Act 1986 (Amendment) (No.3) Regulations 2002, SI 2002/1990; Insolvency (Amendment) (No.2) Rules 2002, SI 2002/2712.

3.2.10   The directors of a company must submit their CVA proposal document to the nominee together with a statement of the company's affairs containing such particulars of its creditors, debts, other liabilities, assets and any other information as may be prescribed. In addition, the directors must provide the nominee with any further information necessary to comply with the nominee's obligations to the directors.[1]

1   Insolvency Act 1986, Sched.A1, para.6 (1).

3.2.11   The nominee must submit a statement to the directors in the prescribed form indicating whether or not in his opinion:

- The proposed voluntary arrangement has a reasonable prospect of being approved and implemented.
- The company is likely to have sufficient funds available to it during the proposed moratorium period to enable it to carry on its business.
- Meetings of the company and its creditors should be summoned to consider the proposed voluntary arrangement.

3.2.12 In forming his opinion, the nominee is entitled to rely on the information submitted to him unless he has reason to doubt its accuracy.[1] The nominee must express the statement to be of his own opinion. This places a duty on the nominee to examine the company and proposed CVA with great care since, ultimately, he will incur personal liability where this duty is breached.

1 Insolvency Act 1986, Sched.1, para.6 (3).

3.2.13 The directors of the company must file the following documents with the court:

- The terms of the proposed CVA.
- A statement of the company's affairs, containing particulars of its creditors, debts and other liabilities and assets and any other information as may be prescribed.
- A statement that the company is eligible for a moratorium.[1]
- A statement from the nominee that he has given his consent to act.[2]
- A statement from the nominee that, in his opinion:[3]

  – the proposed CVA has a reasonable prospect of being approved and implemented;
  – the company is likely to have sufficient funds available to it during the proposed moratorium to enable it to carry on its business; and
  – meetings of the company and its creditors should be summoned to consider the proposed voluntary arrangement.[4]

The Secretary of State may, by subordinate legislation, change the documents to be filed at court.

1 These documents must be in the prescribed form.
2 These documents must be in the prescribed form.
3 These documents must be in the prescribed form.
4 Insolvency Act 1986, Sched.A1, para.7.

The moratorium period

3.2.14 The moratorium automatically comes into force when the documents are filed at court.[1] The moratorium lasts for a maximum period of 28 days unless it is extended by the shareholders and creditors for a maximum of two months from the date of the meeting, which must be convened within that first 28-day period.[2] The moratorium will come to end on the day on which the shareholders and creditors meetings are convened to approve the proposals for the CVA (whether it is approved or rejected) or where a meeting is not called or held within 28 days.

1 Insolvency Act 1986, Sched.A1, para.8.
2 Insolvency Act 1986, Sched.A1, para.8 (3).

3.2.15 Before a decision is made to extend or further extend the moratorium, the nominee must inform the meeting of what he has done to comply with his duty to monitor the company's activities during the moratorium[1] and how he intends to continue to comply with this duty if the moratorium is extended. He must also inform the meeting of the costs of his actions for the company to date and the expected costs of his actions for the company if the moratorium is extended.[2]

1   The nominee's duty to monitor the company's activities during the moratorium are discussed at paras.3.2.35 and 3.2.36 below. See also Insolvency Act 1986, Sched.A1, para.24.
2   Insolvency Act 1986, Sched.A1, para.32 (2).

3.2.16 Where the nominee informs a meeting of the expected costs for his actions, the meeting will resolve whether or not to approve that expected cost. If the expected cost is not approved by a decision of the company and creditors then the moratorium comes to an end. It is also open for the moratorium to be ended before it comes to the end of the extended period.[1]

1   Insolvency Act 1986, Sched.A1, para.35 (5) and (6).

3.2.17 One of the conditions which may be imposed when a moratorium is extended or further extended is that the nominee be replaced by another person qualified or authorised to act as nominee. The replacement must submit a statement to the court consenting to act and all duties imposed on the original nominee are conferred onto the replacement nominee.[1] Any decision to extend or further extend the moratorium should be registered at Companies House and the court should be notified. If the moratorium has been extended pursuant to an order of the court then only Companies House should be notified. If the nominee fails to comply with these provisions without reasonable excuse, he is liable to be fined.[2]

1   Insolvency Act 1986, Sched.A1, para.33.
2   Insolvency Act 1986, Sched.A1, para.34.

3.2.18 If a creditor or member of the company is dissatisfied with any acts or omissions of the directors of the company during the moratorium he may apply to court (during or after the moratorium) for an order on one of the following grounds:

- The company's affairs, business or property are being or have been managed by the directors in a manner which is unfairly prejudicial to the interests of its creditors or the members in general or at least to some of the creditors or members including the petitioner.
- Any act or proposed act or omission of the directors is or would be prejudicial.[1]

1   Insolvency Act 1986, Sched.A1, para.40 (1)–(3).

3.2.19   The court may make such order as it thinks fit for giving relief in respect of the matters complained of, adjourn the hearing conditionally or unconditionally, or make any other order as it thinks fit.[1] However the 2000 Act also specifies that such an order may:

- Regulate the management by the directors of the company's affairs, business and property during the term of the moratorium.
- Require the directors to refrain from doing or continuing an act complained of by the petitioner or to do an act which the petitioner has complained they have omitted to do.
- Require the summoning of a meeting of creditors or members for the purpose of considering such matters as the court may direct.
- Bring the moratorium to an end and make such consequential provisions as the court thinks fit.[2]

1   Insolvency Act 1986, Sched.A1, para.40 (4).
2   Insolvency Act 1986, Sched.A1, para.40 (5).

3.2.20   In making such an order the court must have regard for the need to safeguard the interests of the persons who have dealt with the company in good faith and for value.[1]

1   Insolvency Act 1986, Sched.A1, para.40 (6).

3.2.21   The moratorium will come to an end if the nominee withdraws his consent to act.[1] He is obliged to do so if:

- He considers that the proposed CVA (or proposed modifications) no longer has a reasonable prospect of being approved or implemented.
- He considers that the company will not be able to fund the continuance of the business during the remainder of the moratorium.[2]
- He becomes aware that on the date of filing for the moratorium the company was not 'eligible'.
- The directors fail to comply with their duties.

If the nominee withdraws his consent to act he must notify the court, Companies House and any creditor (of whose claim he is aware) of his withdrawal and the reasons. If the nominee fails to do this, without reasonable excuse, he is liable to a fine.[3] The moratorium will also come to an end if a creditor, director or member of the company or any other member affected by the moratorium obtains a court order to that effect.[4]

1   Insolvency Act 1986, Sched.A1, para.25 (4).
2   Insolvency Act 1986, Sched.A1, para.25 (2) and (4).
3   Insolvency Act 1986, Sched.A1, para.25 (5) and (6).
4   Insolvency Act 1986, Sched.A1, para.26 (4).

Notification procedures

3.2.22   When the moratorium comes into force:

- The directors are under an obligation to notify the nominee of the commencement of the moratorium.[1] If they fail to do so without reasonable excuse each director is liable to imprisonment and/or a fine.[2]
- Upon receiving notification, the nominee must advertise the moratorium to creditors (in the *London Gazette* and such newspapers as thought appropriate) and notify Companies House, the company, any creditor who has presented a winding-up petition before the beginning of the moratorium and any sheriff charged with execution or legal process against the company or any person who has distrained against the company. If the nominee fails to carry out these obligations without reasonable excuse he will become liable to a fine.[3]
- Every order form and business letter issued by or on behalf of the company must bear the nominee's name and a statement that the moratorium is in force. If the company fails to comply with this obligation, the company and any officer who authorises or permits the default may be fined if no reasonable excuse can be shown.[4] If the company does not comply with this rule, it does not make the transaction void or unenforceable against the company.[5]

1 Insolvency Act 1986, Sched.A1, para.9.
2 Insolvency Act 1986, Sched.A1, para.9 (2).
3 Insolvency Act 1986, Sched.A1, para.10.
4 Insolvency Act 1986, Sched.A1, para.16.
5 Insolvency Act 1986, Sched.A1, para.15.

3.2.23   When the moratorium comes to an end:

- The nominee must notify the company, court, Companies House and any known creditor.

- The nominee must also advertise the fact (in the *London Gazette* and any other appropriate newspaper).[1]

1 Insolvency Act 1986, Sched.A1, para.11.

The effect of the moratorium

3.2.24   The moratorium will affect creditors in much the same way as a moratorium obtained under an administration order. Paragraph 12 (1) of Sched.A1 to the 1986 Act lists the steps or acts that a creditor is not allowed to take against the company. These prohibitions include the following:

- No winding-up petition may be presented.
- No meeting of the company may be called without the consent of the nominee or the court's permission.
- No resolution to wind up the company may be passed.
- No administration petition may be presented.

- No administrative receiver may be appointed.
- No landlord can exercise rights of forfeiture.
- No creditor can take steps to enforce security.
- No proceedings or legal process can be commenced or continued without leave of the court.

3.2.25   Where a winding-up petition has been presented before the beginning of the CVA moratorium the petition will be stayed during the moratorium. The winding up-petition will then be dismissed if the proposal is accepted. Section 127 of the 1986 Act will not apply during the moratorium nor in the 28 days following submission to the court of the chairman's report, nor when an appeal challenging the decision of the meeting is pending.

3.2.26   The holder of an uncrystallised floating charge is prevented from taking any steps to crystallise it whilst the moratorium is in place. The holder may give notice as soon as it is practicable to do so once the moratorium has ended.[1] If the crystallisation of the floating charge is triggered by an event which would enable the holder to give notice to the company, the event does not take effect until the moratorium is over and notice is given.[2] Furthermore, the holder may not apply to the court for permission to obtain the crystallisation of the floating charge or the imposition of any restriction imposed by the instrument creating the charge.[3]

1   Insolvency Act 1986, Sched.A1, para.13 (1).
2   Insolvency Act 1986, Sched.A1, para.13 (3).
3   Insolvency Act 1986, Sched.A1, para.13 (5).

3.2.27   The company may not obtain credit of £250[1] or more from a person who has not been informed that a moratorium is in force. Credit includes goods which are bailed under a hire purchase agreement or agreed to be sold under a conditional sale agreement. In addition, credit also includes those transactions where the company has been paid in advance for the supply of goods or services.[2] This provision is potentially restrictive, making it difficult for the company to continue its business albeit only for the duration of the moratorium. If the company contravenes this provision it will be liable to a fine and if an officer knowingly and wilfully authorised or permitted the contravention he is liable to imprisonment and/or a fine.[3] However, any contravention does not void the credit agreement or transaction and it remains enforceable against the company.[4]

1   This sum may be increased or reduced by order under s.417A of the Insolvency Act 1986: Insolvency Act 1986, Sched.A1, para.17 (4).
2   Insolvency Act 1986, Sched.A1, para.17 (1) and (2).
3   Insolvency Act 1986, Sched.A1, para.17 (3).
4   Insolvency Act 1986, Sched.A1, para.15 (2).

3.2.28   During the moratorium, the company may only dispose of uncharged property if there are reasonable grounds for believing that the disposal will benefit the company and the disposal is approved by the committee or nominee.[1] This provision does not apply to a disposal made in the ordinary course of the business.[2] Any contravention of these provisions may result in the company being fined and any officer who authorised or permitted the disposal may be imprisoned and/or fined.[3] Similar provisions exist for payments made by the company in respect of debts or other liabilities that existed before the beginning of the moratorium.[4]

1 Insolvency Act 1986, Sched.A1, para.18 (1).
2 Insolvency Act 1986, Sched.A1, para.18 (2).
3 Insolvency Act 1986, Sched.A1, para.18 (3).
4 Insolvency Act 1986, Sched.A1, para.19.

3.2.29   If the company wants to dispose of charged property,[1] the company must obtain the consent of the charge holder or the court's permission[2] upon which it may dispose of it as if it were not charged.[3] If the court grants permission, the order must be filed with Companies House within 14 days of the date of the order. If the directors fail to do so without reasonable excuse they may be fined.[4] Special provisions relate to holders of a floating charge. If property subject to a floating charge is disposed of, the holder of the floating charge has the same priority in respect of any property directly or indirectly representing the property disposed of as he would have had.[5] Any contravention of these provisions may result in the company being fined and any officer who authorised or permitted the disposal being imprisoned and/or fined.[6]

1 Property subject to a security or goods under a hire-purchase agreement: Insolvency Act 1986, Sched.A1, para.20 (1).
2 The charge holder's consent or the court's permission is conditional upon the charge being discharged with the proceeds of sale. If the property is subject to more than one charge, then the charges must be discharged in accordance with their priority: Insolvency Act 1986, Sched.A1, para.20 (6) and (7).
3 Insolvency Act 1986, Sched.A1, para.20 (2) and (3).
4 Insolvency Act 1986, Sched.A1, para.20 (8) and (9).
5 Insolvency Act 1986, Sched.A1, para.20 (4).
6 Insolvency Act 1986, Sched.A1, para.15 (2).

3.2.30   The company may grant security during the moratorium but it may only be enforced if at the time it was granted there were reasonable grounds for believing that this would benefit the company.

3.2.31   Public utility companies cannot refuse to supply services unless outstanding debts are paid but they can require the nominee to personally guarantee payment for supplies during the moratorium period. It will be interesting to see how practice develops as in these circumstances an insolvency practitioner will clearly not want to incur such liability without having sufficient funds in place.

3.2.32   During the moratorium, the company may not:

■   Enter into a market contract, a money market contract or a related contract.
■   Give a transfer order.
■   Grant a market charge, a money market charge or a system-charge.
■   Provide collateral security.

3.2.33   Any officer who without reasonable excuse authorises or permits the company to enter into any one of those transactions is liable to imprisonment and/or a fine.[1] If the company were to enter into such a transaction, the fact that it is in contravention of this provision does not make it void or unenforceable against the company.[2]

1   Insolvency Act 1986, Sched.A1, para.23 (1) and (2).
2   Insolvency Act 1986, Sched.A1, para.23 (3).

3.2.34   A moratorium committee may be established by resolution of either the creditors' or members' meetings if it has been resolved that the moratorium should be extended. In addition, an estimate of the likely expenses to be incurred by the committee must be approved before the committee can take effect. The committee's expenses will be reimbursed by the nominee if they have not exceeded the amount estimated. The committee will exercise the functions conferred on it by the meeting and ceases to exist when the moratorium comes to an end.[1]

1   Insolvency Act 1986, Sched.A1, para.35.

The nominee's role

3.2.35   During the moratorium, the nominee is under an obligation to monitor the company's affairs so that he can form an opinion as to whether:

■   The proposed voluntary arrangement (as may have been amended) has a reasonable prospect of being approved and implemented.
■   The company is likely to have sufficient funds to enable it to carry on its business.[1]

1   Insolvency Act 1986, Sched.A1, para.24 (1).

3.2.36   As discussed previously the nominee is under an obligation to withdraw his consent to act if:

■   he forms the opinion that the proposed arrangement no longer has a reasonable prospect of being approved and implemented;
■   the company will not have sufficient funds to carry on its business;
■   he becomes aware that the company is not 'eligible' for a moratorium (see above);
■   the directors fail to provide him with any information that he requests to enable him to carry out his functions.

3.2.37   The directors are under an obligation to give the nominee any information that he considers necessary to enable him to carry out his obligations. The nominee is entitled to rely on such information unless he has reason to doubt its accuracy.[1]

1   Insolvency Act 1986, Sched.A1, para.24 (2) and (3).

3.2.38   The nominee's actions may be challenged by any creditor, director or member of the company or any other person affected by the moratorium if they are dissatisfied by any act, omission or decision that the nominee has taken during the moratorium.

3.2.39   The challenge must be made by way of an application to the court and may be made during the moratorium or after it has ended.[1] Upon hearing such an application, the court may confirm, reverse or modify any act or decision of the nominee or give him directions or make such an order as it thinks fit. The order may bring the moratorium to an end and make such consequential provisions as the court considers appropriate.[2]

1   Insolvency Act 1986, Sched.A1, para.26 (1) and (2).
2   Insolvency Act 1986, Sched.A1, para.26 (3) and (4).

3.2.40   In circumstances where a creditor considers that an act, omission or decision of the nominee has resulted in the company suffering a loss, but the company does not intend to pursue a claim it may have against the nominee, the creditor may apply to the court during the moratorium or after it has ended.[1] The court may order the company to pursue any claim against the nominee or authorise any creditor to pursue such a claim in the name of the company or make such other order as it thinks fit. The court will not make an order if it is satisfied that the nominee acted reasonably in all the circumstances.[2]

1   Insolvency Act 1986, Sched.A1, para.27 (1) and (2).
2   Insolvency Act 1986, Sched.A1, para.27 (3).

3.2.41   The court may: impose conditions on any authority given to pursue the claim; direct the company to assist in the pursuit of the claim; make directions with respect to the distribution of anything received as a result of the pursuit of a claim or bringing the moratorium to an end; or make such consequential provisions as the court thinks necessary. Upon considering a creditor's application, the court must have regard to the interests of the members and creditors of the company in general.[1]

1   Insolvency Act 1986, Sched.A1, para.27 (4) and (5).

3.2.42   If the nominee fails to comply with any duty imposed on him under the 2000 Act or if he dies, the directors may apply to the court to have him replaced by another person qualified to act as an insolvency practitioner or authorised to act as a nominee. In addition, if it becomes impractical or inappropriate for the nominee to continue to act, the directors or the nominee may make an application for him to be replaced. A replacement nominee can only be appointed if he submits a statement indicating his consent to act to the court.[1]

1   Insolvency Act 1986, Sched.A1, para.28.

Meetings to consider the CVA proposals

3.2.43   During the moratorium, the nominee must summon meetings of both the company and its creditors (the nominee must summon every creditor of the company of whose claim he is aware to the creditor meeting[1]) on such a time, date and at such a place as he thinks fit. The two meetings may be held on separate days although they must be within seven days of each other. The meetings must be held before the end of the 28-day period beginning on the day on which the moratorium commenced. A meeting summoned to consider the proposal may resolve to extend the moratorium by a maximum of two months from the date of meeting. If a meeting is not held before the end of the 28-day period, the moratorium ends at the end of the day on which those meetings were to be held.[2]

1   Insolvency Act 1986, Sched.A1, para.29 (2).
2   If those meetings were summoned to be held on different days, the later of those days applies: see Insolvency Act 1986, Sched.A1, para.8 (3).

3.2.44   The purpose of the meetings is to decide whether to approve the proposed voluntary arrangement with or without modification. Modifications may include conferring the functions proposed to be conferred on the nominee on another person qualified or authorised to act as nominee.[1] The modification must not include a change which effectively makes the proposals contravene Part 1 of the 1986 Act.

1   Insolvency Act 1986, Sched.A1, para.31 (2).

3.2.45   Any meeting summoned must not approve any proposal or modification which affects the rights of a secured creditor of the company to enforce a security except with the agreement of the creditor concerned.[1] Further provisions apply to any proposal affecting preferential debts and creditors.[2]

1   Insolvency Act 1986, Sched.A1, para.31 (4).
2   Insolvency Act 1986, Sched.A1, para.31 (5).

3.2.46   If the directors wish to modify the proposed CVA, they may give notice of the modifications to the nominee seven days before the meetings are due to take place.[1]

1   Insolvency Act 1986, Sched.A1, para.31 (7).

3.2.47   Decisions made to approve the voluntary arrangement, to extend or further extend the moratorium, to end the moratorium, to establish a committee or approve the costs of the nominee's intended actions[1] will have effect if the decision has been taken by both the creditors' and the company's meetings or by the creditors' meeting only.[2] If there is a difference of decision between the creditors' and the company's meeting then the decision of creditors' meeting shall prevail subject to the right of a company member to apply to the court. The court may order the decision of the company meeting to take effect instead of the decision of the creditors meeting or make any such order as it thinks fit.[3] However, the application must be made before the expiry of the 28-day period beginning with the day on which the decision was taken by the creditors' meeting. If the company meeting takes place after the creditors' meeting then the 28-day period runs from the date of the company meeting.[4]

1   Insolvency Act 1986, Sched.A1, para.36 (1).
2   Insolvency Act 1986, Sched.A1, para.36 (2).
3   Insolvency Act 1986, Sched.A1, para.36 (3) and (5).
4   Insolvency Act 1986, Sched.A1, para.36 (4).

Effect of approval of the voluntary arrangement

3.2.48   When the voluntary arrangement has been approved and the decision to approve it is effective, the CVA takes effect as if made by the company at the creditors' meeting and binds every person as a party to the voluntary arrangement who in accordance with the rules:

- was entitled to vote at that meeting whether or not he was present or represented at it; or
- would have been so entitled if he had had notice of it.[1]

1   Insolvency Act 1986, Sched.A1, para.37.

3.2.49   It is this latter provision which is the most radical proposal of the 2000 Act and ensures that creditors who could not be ascertained or identified at the time when the proposal was formulated are also bound by the CVA and cannot prejudice the position of other creditors by taking action in respect of their debt. If such creditors come to light they will be entitled to claim the amount they would have been entitled to receive under the CVA. Whether such additional claims will have an adverse effect on the continuation of the CVA and the prospects of success will be a matter for the supervisor to determine. In such circumstances a modification of the CVA may be necessary.

Challenges to decisions

3.2.50   In general, decisions may be challenged by those people who are entitled to vote at either the creditors' or company's meetings, or would have been so entitled had they had notice. The nominee may also challenge decisions. The challenge is made by applying to court on one or both of the grounds that:

- The voluntary arrangement approved at one or both of the meetings unfairly prejudices the interests of a creditor, member or contributory of the company.
- There has been some material irregularity at or in relation to either of those meetings.[1]

1   Insolvency Act 1986, Sched.A1, para.38 (1) and (2).

3.2.51   The application must be made within the specified time period.[1] The court may, upon determining that the applicant has made out one or both of the two prescribed grounds, give an order revoking or suspending the relevant decision[2] and/or order directions summoning a further meeting.[3] The court has the power to make consequential or supplemental orders or directions where necessary.[4]

1   See Insolvency Act 1986, Sched.A1, para.38 (3) for full details.
2   Insolvency Act 1986, Sched.A1, para.38 (4)(*a*).
3   Insolvency Act 1986, Sched.A1, para.38 (4)(*b*).
4   Insolvency Act 1986, Sched.A1, para.38 (5) to (8).

Implementation of the voluntary arrangement

3.2.52   Once the CVA has been approved and has taken effect, the nominee, whether he be the original or replacement one, becomes known as the supervisor of the voluntary arrangement.[1] If thereafter any of the company's creditors or any other person is dissatisfied by any act, omission, or decision of the supervisor they may apply to the court. On an application to court, the court may confirm, reverse or modify any act or decision of the supervisor, give directions or make such order as it thinks fit.[2]

1   Insolvency Act 1986, Sched.A1, para.39 (2).
2   Insolvency Act 1986, Sched.A1, para.39 (3) and (4).

3.2.53   The supervisor may apply to the court for directions in relation to any particular matter arising under the voluntary arrangement and he may apply to the court for the winding up of the company or for an administration order to be made in relation to it.[1]

1   Insolvency Act 1986, Sched.A1, para.39 (5).

3.2.54   The court has powers to appoint a person qualified or authorised to act as a supervisor in relation to the CVA either to increase the number of supervisors, or to make a substitution of an existing supervisor or to fill a vacancy. This power is exercisable when it is expedient to appoint such a person and it would not have been, amongst other things, practicable to do so without the court's assistance.[1]

1   Insolvency Act 1986, Sched.A1, para.39 (6).

Offences

3.2.55   If at any time during the moratorium, and up until 12 months after the moratorium started, an officer of the company commits (or is privy to the committing of certain) offences he is liable to imprisonment and/or a fine.[1] The offences are:

■   Concealing company property (or part of it) worth £500 or more.
■   Concealing any debt due to or from the company.

- Fraudulently removing any part of the company's property (or part of it) worth £500 or more.
- Concealing, destroying, mutilating, or falsifying any book or paper affecting or relating to the company's property or affairs.
- Fraudulently parting with, altering or making any omission in any document relating to the company's affairs or property.
- Pawning, pledging or disposing of any company property which has been obtained on credit and has not been paid for (except during the course of the company's ordinary business).[2]

---

1   Insolvency Act 1986, Sched.A1, para.41.
2   Insolvency Act 1986, Sched.A1, para.41 (4).

3.2.56   These provisions apply to shadow directors and to any person who accepts the pawning or pledging of company property in the knowledge that it is an offence.[1] A statutory defence is available to those charged with an offence.[2]

---

1   Insolvency Act 1986, Sched.A1, para.41 (5) and (7).
2   For further details see Insolvency Act 1986, Sched.A1, para.41 (6).

3.2.57   It is also an offence for an officer (including a shadow director) to make any false representation or fraudulently do or omit to do something in order to obtain the moratorium (or an extension to an existing one) even if no moratorium or extension is obtained.[1]

---

1   Insolvency Act 1986, Sched.A1, para.42.

3.3   GENERAL REFORMS TO THE CVA REGIME

3.3.1   Section 2 of the 2000 Act amends the 1986 Act by inserting the provisions contained in Sched.2. The most notable amendments are set out below.

The nominee's duty

3.3.2   A nominee (when he is not the liquidator or the administrator and in addition to other obligations), must state in his report to the court filed under s.2 of the 1986 Act that in his opinion the proposed CVA has a reasonable prospect of being approved and implemented.[1] This has the effect of widening the nominee's duty.

---

1   Insolvency Act 2000, Sched.2, para.3.

The replacement of the nominee

3.3.3   The nominee may be replaced if he fails to submit the s.2 report or if he dies. The person proposing the replacement should make an application to court, whereupon the appropriate direction will be made. In addition, if it becomes apparent that it would be impracticable or inappropriate for the nominee to continue to act, either the nominee or the person intending to the make the proposal may apply to court for his replacement.[1]

---

1   Insolvency Act 2000, Sched.2, para.3.

The approval of a CVA

3.3.4   Paragraph 5 of Sched.2 to the 2000 Act introduces s.4A to the 1986 Act. This provision applies to a decision made under s.4 of the 1986 Act to approve the CVA with or without alterations. The decision to approve the CVA will have effect if it has been made by both meetings summoned under s.3 of the 1986 Act or if it has been made by the creditors' meeting summoned under that section. However, if the decision taken by the creditors' meeting differs from that taken by the company meeting, the decision of the creditors' meeting will prevail, subject to the right of a member of the company to apply to the court. Such an application must be made within 28 days from when the decision was made by the creditors' meeting or, where the company's decision was later, from that day. The court, in response to such an application, may order the decision of the company meeting to have effect over the creditors' meeting decision or any other order it thinks fit.[1]

---

1   Insolvency Act 1986, s.4A as amended by Insolvency Act 2000, Sched.2, para.5.

3.3.5   If the company happens to be regulated[1] then the Financial Services Authority is entitled to make representations at the application.[2]

---

1   For the meaning of 'regulated' see Insolvency Act 1986, Sched.A1, para.44, as amended by the Insolvency Act 2000. See para.4.6.20 for further details.
2   Insolvency Act 1986, s.4A as amended by Insolvency Act 2000, Sched.2, para.5.

Binding 'unknown' creditors

3.3.6   Paragraphs 6 and 7 of Sched.2 to the 2000 Act amend ss.5 and 6 of the 1986 Act. An approved CVA will bind all creditors of the company whether or not they voted at the creditors' meeting or had notice of the proposal. (For discussion on this topic, see para.3.2.48 above.) However, if the CVA ends prematurely or ceases to have effect, the company will be liable to those creditors who did not have notice for the amount still outstanding.[1] In addition, if a creditor has not been given notice of the CVA he may make an application to the court to challenge the approved CVA on the ground that it prejudices his interests. This application may be made after the CVA has ceased to have effect unless it ended prematurely. The application must be made within 28 days of the creditor finding out that the creditors' meeting had taken place.[2]

---

1   Insolvency Act 2000, Sched.2, para.6.
2   Insolvency Act 2000, Sched.2, para.7.

3.3.7   Despite binding 'unknown' creditors to the CVA, this right of challenge will provide an incentive for the company to not only disclose all its known creditors but also to carry out investigations to determine whether there are any 'unknown' or 'forgotten' creditors so that the CVA encompasses their claims. There would be no point in going down the CVA route if, at the end of it, there remains a possibility that an unknown or forgotten creditor could appear, claim prejudice and petition for the winding up of the company.

False representations and prosecution of company officers

3.3.8   If a director (including a shadow director) or other officer of the company makes a false representation or fraudulently does something or omits to do something for the purpose of obtaining the members' or creditors' approval for the proposed CVA, he will have committed an offence and is liable for a fine and/or imprisonment. This provision applies even where the CVA has not been approved.[1]

---

1   Insolvency Act 2000, Sched.2, para.8.

3.3.9   Schedule 2 to the 2000 Act inserts s.7A into the 1986 Act. This provision applies where a company has obtained a moratorium under s.1A or a CVA has been approved under s.4A or para.36 of Sched.A1. In other words, it is not just limited to 'small' companies eligible for a CVA moratorium.

3.3.10   Where an officer of the company has committed a criminal offence in connection with a moratorium of the CVA, the nominee or supervisor is under a duty to report it to the Secretary of State and co-operate with his inquiries.[1]

---

1   Insolvency Act 1986, s.7A (1) and (2) as inserted by Insolvency Act 2000, Sched.2, para.10.

3.3.11   Any evidence obtained by the Secretary of State in the course of his investigations may be used against that person within the confines of the investigation.[1] However, such evidence may not be adduced in subsequent criminal proceedings against that person unless it has been properly adduced within the criminal proceedings itself. [2] These provisions have been included to ensure that the 1986 Act (as amended) complies with the Human Rights Act 1998.

---

1   Insolvency Act 1986, s.7A (3), (4) and (5) as inserted by Insolvency Act 2000, Sched.2, para.10.
2   Insolvency Act 1986, s.7A (6) as inserted by Insolvency Act 2000, Sched.2, para.10.

Premature ending of CVAs

3.3.12   An approved CVA which has taken effect either under s.4A of or para.36 of Sched.A1 to the 1986 Act comes to an end prematurely if it has not been fully implemented in relation to all the persons bound by it.[1]

---

1   Insolvency Act 1986, s.7B as amended by Insolvency Act 2000, Sched.2, para.10.

Miscellaneous provisions

3.3.13 The 2000 Act makes various consequential amendments to the 1986 Act. In addition, it contains amendments of the Building Societies Act 1986.[1]

---

1   See Insolvency Act 2000, Sched.2, paras.13 and 14.

3.3.14 The 2000 Act also affects floating charge documents[1] and outlines the functions of the Financial Services Authority where the company is regulated.[2]

---

1   See Insolvency Act 1986, Sched.A1, para.43 (as amended).
2   See Insolvency Act 1986, Sched.A1, para.44 (as amended).

3.4   GENERAL REFORMS TO THE IVA REGIME

3.4.1 The 2000 Act amends individual voluntary arrangements ('IVAs') under Part 8 of the 1986 Act by introducing a procedure for the approval of IVAs to be started without an initial moratorium for the insolvent debtor. Other amendments are also made to the IVA provisions. See further Chapter 9 and the additional amendments made to the IVA procedure by the Enterprise Act 2002.

Individual voluntary arrangements procedure where no interim order made

3.4.2 The 2000 Act inserts a new s.256A into the 1986 Act. The point of this procedure is to allow those debtors who wish to benefit from an IVA but who do not require an interim order or are not granted an interim order, the opportunity of binding their creditors by the IVA. In such a case, the debtor must first submit to the nominee a document setting out his proposals and a statement of affairs. If the debtor is an undischarged bankrupt, notice must be provided to the Official Receiver/trustee in bankruptcy.

3.4.3 This procedure does not apply if a bankruptcy petition presented by the debtor is pending and the court has, under s.73 of the 1986 Act, appointed an insolvency practitioner to enquire into the debtor's affairs and reports.[1]

---

1   Insolvency Act 2000, Sched.3, para.7.

3.4.4 The nominee must within 14 days[1] (or longer if the court allows[2]) submit a report to the court confirming in his opinion:

- That the proposed IVA has a reasonable prospect of being approved and implemented.
- That a meeting of the creditors should be summoned to consider the debtor's proposal.

- If such a meeting should be summoned, the date, time and place when it should be held.[3]

1   Insolvency Act 1986, s.256A (3) as amended by Insolvency Act 2000, Sched.3, para.7.
2   Insolvency Act 1986, s.256A (5) as amended by Insolvency Act 2000, Sched.3, para.7.
3   Insolvency Act 1986, s.256A (3) as amended by Insolvency Act 2000, Sched.3, para.7.

3.4.5   It should be noted that the nominee is not entitled to rely on the information given to him by the debtor. This is different to the nominee's position when acting for a company in a CVA. Investigations must therefore be completed and the accuracy of the debtor's statement of affairs etc. reasonably assessed.

3.4.6   Where there is no interim order and the debtor is not an undischarged bankrupt, the relevant date for determining preferential claims is the date on which the voluntary arrangement takes effect.

3.4.7   The debtor may apply to the court to have the nominee replaced if he has failed to submit his report to the court or if he has died. The debtor or the nominee may also apply to the court in circumstances where either of them consider that it would be impracticable or inappropriate for the nominee to continue to act.[1] Upon such an application the court may direct that the nominee should be replaced.

1   Insolvency Act 1986, s.256A (4) as amended by Insolvency Act 2000, Sched.3, para.7.

General amendments to IVA procedure

3.4.8   The existing provisions for the summoning of a creditors' meeting under s.257 of the 1986 Act are amended so as to apply to a procedure where an interim order is not used.[1]

1   Insolvency Act 1986, s.257 as amended by Insolvency Act 2000, Sched.3, para.8.

3.4.9   The purpose of a creditors' meeting, as stated in s.258(1) of the 1986 Act, is to approve the IVA. As explained below, this section is amended by the 2000 Act to include the wider definition of a nominee as introduced by s.4 of that Act.[1]

1   See Insolvency Act 2000, Sched.3, para.9.

3.4.10   If the creditors approve the debtor's IVA as endorsed by the nominee, the approved IVA binds every person who was entitled to vote at the meeting (whether or not he was present or represented), or would have been so entitled if he had had notice of it.[1] The debtor will become liable to any bound creditor who did not have notice of the meeting if, when the IVA ceases to have effect (and the IVA did not end prematurely[2]), any amount payable remains outstanding.[3]

1   Insolvency Act 1986, s.260 (2)(*b*) as amended by Insolvency Act 2000, Sched.3, para.10.
2   See para.3.4.14 below for the meaning of ending prematurely.
3   Insolvency Act 1986, s.260 (2A) as amended by Insolvency Act 2000, Sched.3, para.10.

3.4.11   Where an IVA has been approved, any creditor so bound may apply to the court on the grounds[1] that the arrangement unfairly prejudices the creditor's interests and/or that there has been some material irregularity.[2] The application must be made by a creditor who had notice of the meeting, within 28 days from the day on which the creditors' report was filed at court under s.59 of the 1986 Act.[3] If the creditor did not have notice, then he must apply within 28 days from the day on which he first became aware that a meeting had taken place.[4]

1   See s.262 (1) of the 1986 Act.
2   Insolvency Act 1986, s.262 (2) as amended by Insolvency Act 2000, Sched.3, para.11.
3   Insolvency Act 1986, s.262 (3)(*a*) as amended by Insolvency Act 2000, Sched.3, para.11.
4   Insolvency Act 1986, s.262 (3)(*b*) as amended by Insolvency Act 2000, Sched.3, para.11.

3.4.12   If the debtor makes a false representation, or fraudulently does or omits to do anything for the purpose of obtaining the creditors' approval for the IVA he will have committed an offence. This applies even if the IVA is not approved. If he is found guilty he will be liable to a fine and/or imprisonment.[1]

1   Insolvency Act 1986, s.262A as inserted by Insolvency Act 2000, Sched.3, para.12.

3.4.13   The nominee or supervisor of the approved IVA is under an obligation to report a debtor to the Secretary of State if it appears that the debtor is guilty of any offence in connection with the IVA. In addition, he must supply the Secretary of State with such information and provide access to facilities for inspection of documents. The nominee or supervisor is also under a duty to give assistance if the debtor is prosecuted. If the nominee or supervisor fails to do so they may be directed to comply by the court.[1]

1   Insolvency Act 1986, s.262B as inserted by Insolvency Act 2000, Sched.3, para.12.

3.4.14   An IVA ends prematurely if when it ceases to have effect it has not been fully implemented in respect of all persons bound by the IVA by virtue of s.260 (2)(*b*)(i) of the 1986 Act. See s.262C of the 1986 Act as inserted by the 2000 Act (para.12, Sched.3) for further details.

3.5   THE NOMINEE'S ROLE

3.5.1   The definition of 'acting as an insolvency practitioner' as set out in s.388 of the 1986 Act has been amended to include any person acting as an nominee in relation to a company voluntary arrangement.[1] This has the effect that a nominee will require a specific bond for each appointment, although, if appointed as the supervisor, the bond will remain in force and there will be no need to take out a new bond.

1   Insolvency Act 2000, s.4 (2).

3.5.2   One widely criticised aspect of 2000 Act was the introduction of a new s.389A into the 1986 Act. This provision enables a person to act as a nominee or supervisor if authorised to do so by a body recognised by the Secretary of State for that purpose and there is in force security for the proper performance of his functions.[1] There was concern that this would lead to persons other than licensed insolvency practitioners becoming involved in this area, although at the time of writing no other body has been recognised by the Secretary of State.

1   Insolvency Act 2000, s.4 (4).

3.6   COMPANY DIRECTORS DISQUALIFICATION ACT 1986 PROCEEDINGS

3.6.1   The Insolvency Act 2000 amends the Company Directors Disqualification Act 1986 ('CDDA 1986') by allowing directors whom the Secretary of State considers are unfit to hold office as a director, to consent to a 'paper disqualification' without the need for the court's involvement. Despite the increase in the number of disqualification orders made under the CDDA 1986[1] the 2000 Act reforms were considered necessary in order to save on the time and cost involved when the application was in reality uncontested.

1   In 1992/93 only 339 orders were made compared with 1,540 orders in 1999/2000.

3.6.2   Indeed, prior to this amendment the majority of proceedings were dealt with under the *Carecraft* procedure based on the 1994 case *Re Carecraft Construction Company Limited*[1] since this method was cheaper and quicker than full disqualification proceedings. Under the *Carecraft* procedure, directors and the DTI disqualification unit would reach a settlement based on an agreed statement of matters of unfit conduct which was then presented to the court for approval. The major drawback with *Carecraft* agreements was that they still required approval by the court, which necessitated further costs to be borne by the director. In addition, the court determined the period of disqualification based on the facts. The court confirmed its involvement by explicitly ruling in *Blackspur Group Plc*[2] that the Secretary of State's decision to continue disqualification proceedings against a director despite an offer of undertaking was not open to review.

1   [1994] 1 WLR 172.
2   [1998] 1 WLR 422.

3.6.3   The 2000 Act has effectively given statutory approval to the *Carecraft* procedure. Under s.6 of the 2000 Act, a new s.1A is inserted into the CDDA 1986 which provides that the Secretary of State may accept a disqualification undertaking by a person to the effect that he will not act as a director of a company nor take part in its formation or management without the permission of the court and that he will not act as an insolvency practitioner. The maximum period which may be specified in a disqualification undertaking is 15 years and the minimum period is two years.[1] The Act also provides that if a person is already subject to a disqualification undertaking and enters into a new disqualification undertaking, the period for disqualification will run concurrently.[2]

1   Insolvency Act 1986, s.1A (2).
2   Insolvency Act 1986, s.1A (3).

3.6.4   The Secretary of State when determining whether or not to accept a disqualification undertaking, may take account of matters other than criminal convictions notwithstanding that that person may be criminally liable in respect of those matters.[1] Undertakings can be accepted either before proceedings for disqualification commence or during such proceedings.

1   Company Directors Disqualification Act 1986, s.1A (4).

3.6.5   Undertakings can only be accepted where a disqualification is sought for unfitness as set out under ss.6 and 8 of the CDDA 1986. Therefore disqualification for general misconduct in terms of ss.2 to 5 cannot be avoided by an undertaking. In order to accept an undertaking, the Secretary of State must be satisfied that a course of conduct has taken place that makes the director unfit and that it appears expedient in the public interest that a disqualification order be made.[1]

1   Insolvency Act 2000, s.6 (3) and (4).

3.6.6   Under s.8A of the CDDA 1986[1] a person subject to a disqualification undertaking may apply to the court to reduce the period for which the undertaking is to be enforced or ask for it to come to an end. The Secretary of State may also address the court so that he is aware of any matters relevant to the disqualification undertaking. This provision prevents the undertaking from falling foul of the Human Rights Act 1998 (for example, Article 6 – see Chapter 4 for more detailed analysis on this point). Without it, the DTI would be open to criticism that it had acted as the 'judge, jury and executioner' in the disqualification.

1   As amended by Insolvency Act 2000, s.6.

3.6.7   The director's undertaking is registered at Companies House. A breach of the undertaking is a criminal offence and means the director becomes liable for the debts of the company in which he is involved whilst in breach of the order or undertaking.

3.6.8   Effectively, the 2000 Act removes certain disqualifications from the courts. By doing so it is estimated that the Government will save a substantial amount of money per annum, and proceedings against rogue directors will be faster, more efficient and cheaper. Contested disqualification proceedings can take up to four years. Under the new procedure, rogue directors will be removed from circulation more swiftly. From April to October 2001 there were around 400 undertakings accepted by the disqualification unit.[1]

1   See p.4 of the College of Law's leaflet on Company/Commercial Disqualification – shadow, de facto and nominee directors.

3.7   LANDLORD'S RIGHTS OF ACTION AND ADMINISTRATION

3.7.1   The right of a landlord to effect peaceable re-entry and seek to distrain over a tenant's goods is an ancient and highly useful self-help remedy available where a tenant is in default of rental payments. However this may conflict with attempts to rescue the company and may be at odds with the interests of all other creditors. The 1986 Act introduced a new administration procedure with ss.10 and 11 imposing a moratorium on creditors' actions against companies in administration without the court's permission. It was not immediately clear, however, whether these provisions encompassed a landlord's right to forfeit by peaceable re-entry or distrain for rent. Arguments evolved around whether peaceable re-entry fell under a step 'to enforce a security' within ss.10 (1)(b) and 11 (3)(c) of the 1986 Act or whether it fell within the scope of the phrase 'other proceedings . . . or other legal process' under ss.10(1) (c) and 11(3) (d) of the 1986 Act.[1]

1   For a detailed overview of the case law surrounding this redundant point, see: *Ezekiel v. Orakpo* [1977] QB 260 CA, *Razzaq v. Pala* [1997] 1 WLR 1336, and *Re Park Air Services Plc* [2000] 2 AC 172 for the 'enforcement of security argument'; and *Exchange Travel Agency v. Triton Property Trust Plc* [1991] BCC 341, *Re Olympia & York Canary Wharf* [1993] BCC 154 and *Clarence Café v. Comchester Properties* [1999] L & TR 303 for the 'other proceedings or legal process' argument.

3.7.2   However a number of court decisions established that where a tenant company was the subject of an administration order or petition, forfeiture by peaceable re-entry was not prevented by the 1986 Act. Effectively, s.9 of the 2000 Act closed this loophole by amending the 1986 Act to restrict a landlord's right to peaceable re-entry during a tenant's administration.[1] This section was implemented on 2 April 2001.

1   Note that similar provisions relate to a tenant's IVA and CVA as introduced by the Insolvency Act 2000.

3.7.3   As a result no landlord or other person to whom rent is payable may exercise any right of forfeiture by peaceable re-entry in relation to premises let to the company or re-enter to seek distraint over goods. This is despite the fact that the company may have failed to comply with any term or condition of its tenancy. If the landlord wishes to exercise its right of peaceable re-entry it must first obtain the court's permission which may be granted with or without conditions.

3.7.4   The 2000 Act does not outlaw the use of peaceable re-entry, it merely requires the landlord to obtain the court's consent or the administrator's approval before the remedy can be used. The factors which may influence a court's decision as to whether or not to grant peaceable re-entry may be those set out in *Re Atlantic Computers*.[1] In that decision the Court of Appeal set out a general approach to the court on applications. As a result of this reform, administrators will probably refuse consent to any landlord's action unless it can be shown that it is against the company's interests to retain the lease.

---

1   [1992] Ch.505, CA.

3.8   MISCELLANEOUS REFORMS MADE BY THE INSOLVENCY ACT 2000

The investigation and prosecution of malpractice by delinquent officers and members of companies

3.8.1   Section 10 of the 2000 Act amends the 1986 Act by changing the definition of the prosecuting authority from the Director of Public Prosecutions to the Secretary of State. Accordingly, a liquidator is to report suspicious or apparent criminal activity by past or present officers or members of a company to the Secretary of State.

Powers of compulsion

3.8.2   Section 11 of the 2000 Act amends s.219 of the 1986 Act by providing that answers given by an individual under a power of compulsion cannot be used against him, except in very limited circumstances, in subsequent criminal proceedings.[1]

---

1   See section 4.1 on human rights which explains why this amendment was necessary.

Powers of a trustee of a deceased insolvent's estate

3.8.3   The trustee may apply to court to recover the value of the deceased insolvent's former interest in a jointly owned property from the survivor of the benefit of the estate.[1]

---

1   Section 12 of the Insolvency Act 2000 inserts s.412A into the Insolvency Act 1986.

Bankruptcy – interest on sums held in insolvency services account

3.8.4   Section 13 of the 2000 Act enables the Lord Chancellor with the agreement of the Secretary of State to make rules relating to the investment of bankruptcy estate funds and the payment of interest. Further provisions are set out within the Enterprise Act 2002.

Cross-border insolvency

3.8.5   Section 14 of the 2000 Act allowed the Secretary of State to bring into effect the United Nations Commission on International Trade Law Model Law. (See section 4.5 for full commentary and analysis.)

General

3.8.6   Section 15 of the 2000 Act introduces Sched.5 which repeals various pieces of legislation. This section also amends s.356 of the Financial Services and Markets Act 2000 which relates to the Financial Services Authority's powers to participate in proceedings concerning CVAs.

3.9   WHEN DID IT COME INTO FORCE?

3.9.1   It was one of the more frustrating aspects of the 2000 Act that implementation was slow. Indeed, at the time of writing not all of the 2000 Act is yet in force. However:

- Section 14 (giving the Secretary of State power to give effect to the UNCITRAL model law) came into effect upon the 2000 Act obtaining Royal Assent on 30 November 2000.
- Most of the 2000 Act came into effect on 2 April 2001.
- The following came into force on 1 January 2003:
  - section 1 of the 2000 Act and Sched.1 (the moratorium provisions for small companies);
  - section 2 of the 2000 Act and Sched.2 (amendments to existing CVA procedures);
  - section 3 of the 2000 Act and Sched.3 (amendment to IVA procedures);
  - section 4 of the 2000 Act (changes to authorisation of nominees/ supervisors); and
  - section 15 of the 2000 Act and Sched.5 (minor amendments).

4 MAJOR LEGISLATION AFFECTING INSOLVENCY LAW AND PRACTICE

4.1 HUMAN RIGHTS ACT 1998

The pervasive effect of human rights on insolvency

4.1.1 Like it or not, European law has an ever-increasing influence on UK legislation. The option of making an application to the European Court of Human Rights in Strasbourg ('EctHR') in respect of an infringement of a human right has been available to a British citizen since 1951. However, by incorporating most of the European Convention for the Protection of Human Rights and Fundamental Freedoms[1] (the 'European Convention') directly into UK law, the Human Rights Act 1998 ('HRA 1998') has had a significant general impact on UK law and, in particular, introduced new considerations into insolvency law and practice. As a result, there has been a small flurry of human rights applications before the UK domestic courts, although not the deluge of human rights orientated claims that was originally feared.

---

1 The European Convention was ratified by the UK Government on 8 March 1951.

4.1.2 The HRA 1998 largely came into force on 2 October 2000[1] and it has a potentially far reaching retrospective effect.[2] The HRA 1998 has made it easier to bring claims for human rights infringements, as the claim can now be commenced in the UK courts (as opposed to the EctHR) thereby saving time and costs. However, it should be noted that applicants are subject to a short limitation period of one year within which to bring claims.

---

1 Sections 1–17 came into force on 2 October 2002.
2 Human Rights Act 1998, s.22(4).

4.1.3 Insolvency practitioners must now consider all their public functions in the light of the HRA 1998 or face the possibility of a claim. Many of the accepted customs and practices of insolvency practitioners, including those of the Official Receiver, have also been subject to review. Undoubtedly, the HRA 1998 has affected the insolvency practitioner's day-to-day administration of a case and the interpretation of his statutory powers. Indeed, where the court decides that the insolvency practitioner has infringed a human right protected by the HRA 1998, the insolvency practitioner can be held personally liable. That said, the impact of HRA 1998 on insolvency practice has to date been one of subtle changes in emphasis rather than a fundamental overhaul. Whether over time the HRA 1998 will have a more radical effect remains to be seen. Whilst the Enterprise Act 2002 has been signed off by the Secretary of State as being compliant with the HRA 1998, this will not prevent human rights lawyers developing arguments designed to set aside those provisions that might contravene their client's human rights.

4.1.4   This book will provide only a brief practical summary of the implications of the HRA 1998. The aim of this chapter is to summarise how the HRA 1998 has affected insolvency law and practice and examine those areas which have been most impacted by legal challenges. This chapter should therefore assist an insolvency practitioner in avoiding claims and also provide information to a victim of a breach of the HRA 1998 who is considering whether he has sufficient grounds for a successful claim.

Summary of the key protected human rights[1]

- right to life;[2]
- right not to be tortured or subjected to inhumane or degrading treatment;[3]
- right not to be enslaved or compelled to carry out forced labour;[4]
- right to a fair trial;[5]
- right to respect for private and family life, home and correspondence;[6]
- right to a remedy in the national courts if convention rights are infringed;[7]
- freedom from discrimination in respect of convention rights;[8] and
- a right to property.[9]

---

1 Human Rights Act 1998, Sched.1, Pt.1.
2 European Convention for the Protection of Human Rights and Fundamental Freedoms, Article 2.
3 European Convention for the Protection of Human Rights and Fundamental Freedoms, Article 3.
4 European Convention for the Protection of Human Rights and Fundamental Freedoms, Article 4.
5 European Convention for the Protection of Human Rights and Fundamental Freedoms, Article 6.
6 European Convention for the Protection of Human Rights and Fundamental Freedoms, Article 8.
7 European Convention for the Protection of Human Rights and Fundamental Freedoms, Article 13.
8 European Convention for the Protection of Human Rights and Fundamental Freedoms, Article 14.
9 European Convention for the Protection of Human Rights and Fundamental Freedoms, First Protocol.

4.1.5 An understanding of the general principles underpinning the European Convention is required to assess whether a specific course of action could give rise to a claim. The European Convention has long been described as a living instrument.[1] Therefore, the human rights protected by the European Convention (see summary box above) should be interpreted in the light of the socio-political conditions at the date of the interpretation (i.e. at the date when the case is heard by the court). This means that the EctHR's decisions are not strictly binding upon the English courts as the socio-political conditions at the date of the interpretation will change over time. Nevertheless, EctHR case law will undoubtedly have a persuasive effect on English judges and in the absence of proof that there has been a clear shift in the values of society as a whole, the protection of human rights afforded by the EctHR throughout the EU is likely to be largely followed by UK courts. Copies of the EctHR's judgments are to be made available online, although at the time of writing the web address has not yet been announced.

---

1 *Tyrer v. UK* (1979–80) 2 EHRR 1.

4.1.6 Pan-EU case law also indicates a general recognition within the European judiciary that the interpretation of the rights provided by the European Convention will vary not only over time, but also from state to state: i.e. there is a margin of appreciation[1] between individual EU states. However, it should be noted that the major reported cases that have considered the HRA 1998 within the UK have largely followed the EctHR's approach to human rights claims.

---

1 *Ireland v. United Kingdom* or *Lawless v. Ireland (No.3)* (1961) 1 EHRR 15, para.28.

4.1.7 The UK courts will consider both the substance and reality of a claim and will avoid an overly technical approach in determining a human rights application. This pragmatism explains why a significant number of applications brought to date under the HRA 1998 have been unsuccessful.

4.1.8 The UK judiciary's approach to human rights applications is exemplified in the case of *Daniels v. Walker*.[1] Lord Woolf (the Master of Rolls) stated, when dismissing a human rights application, that:

> It was essential that Counsel, and those who instructed Counsel, took a responsible attitude as to when it was right to raise arguments based on the Human Rights Act 1998 and judges should be robust in resisting inappropriate attempts to introduce such arguments.

---

1 17 May 2000, TLR, CA.

Principal obligations established by the HRA 1998

4.1.9 These can be summarised as the following:

- All UK legislation must be read and given effect to in a way that is compatible with the European Convention.[1]

- It is unlawful for a 'public authority' to act in a way that is incompatible with the European Convention.

---

1 Human Rights Act 1998, s.3. However, if the court decides that legislation is incompatible with the Human Rights Act 1998, this does not automatically affect the validity of the particular statutory provision. It simply alerts the government of the necessity to change the law. Human Rights Act 1998, s.4 introduces the new concept of incompatibility which indicates when legislation is not compliant with the Human Rights Act 1998. Where legislation is found incompatible, in very limited circumstances a victim may be able to secure compensation: see *H* v. *Mental Health Review Tribunal N & E London Region*, (2001) *The Times*, 4 April.

4.1.10 The latter obligation is more likely to affect insolvency practitioners. What amounts to a 'public authority' under the HRA 1998 has been consumed widely in case law.[1] The definition includes any person (for the purposes of this definition a 'person' includes a business) 'whose functions are functions of a public nature'.[2] Therefore, a public authority's acts will include most actions of an administrator, a trustee in bankruptcy, a compulsory liquidator, a provisional liquidator and a court appointed receiver, as all are officers of the court. Arguably, a liquidator of a voluntary liquidation,[3] a nominee/supervisor of a voluntary arrangement and an administrative receiver will not be regarded as 'public authorities' so long as they are not performing a public function.

---

1 For example, a privatised company carrying out public functions see: *Rights Brought Home* (Cm.3782, 1997), *DPP* v. *Manners* [1978] AC 43, HL.
2 Human Rights Act 1998, s.6 (3)(b).
3 Whether this view will change due to the provisions made for the registration of creditors voluntary liquidation appointments with the court (needed in order to comply with and make use of the European Regulation on Insolvency Proceedings) remains to be seen.

Requirements for commencing a claim

4.1.11 Notwithstanding the merits (or otherwise) of the legal case, the following conditions must be satisfied before a human rights based claim can be commenced:

- Only a victim of an unlawful course of action (i.e. a public authority's action which infringes a human right protected by the HRA 1998) can commence a claim.[1] What would amount to a victim is fairly widely construed by the courts and includes an individual, company, director, manager or even a shareholder of a company.
- The unlawful course of action must have been undertaken by a public authority[2] performing a public function.
- A victim must commence his claim within one year calculated from the date that the unlawful course of action took place.[3] Generally, this limitation period can be extended at the court's discretion having regard to all the circumstances.[4] However, the courts are now much more reluctant to extend deadlines (see para.4.1.19 on Article 6 of the European Convention).

---

1 Human Rights Act 1998, s.7 (1).

2   See definition of public authority at para.4.1.10.
3   Human Rights Act 1998, s.7 (5)(a).
1   Human Rights Act 1998, s.7 (5)(b) This general extension is subject to any rule imposing a stricter time limit in relation to the procedure in question.

Defending a claim

4.1.12   Although an insolvency practitioner could himself be a victim of an abuse of human rights and bring a claim in accordance with the HRA 1998, it is more likely that he will face a challenge from either a bankrupt, company, director and/or a shareholder alleging that a particular course of action under-taken was incompatible with the victim's human rights. Assuming that the victim is able to meet the general conditions for commencing a claim identified above, what factors will the courts consider when examining a claim under the HRA 1998?

4.1.13   The human rights protected by the European Convention are, save in specific instances,[1] qualified rights and are therefore potentially assailable. Following the EctHR's lead in taking a pragmatic view to cases brought under the European Convention, the UK courts have dismissed HRA 1998 claims where it was established by the defendant public authority that there was a *justifiable inter-ference* with the victim's human rights and as such the course of action taken was not unlawful. A justifiable interference with the victim's human rights can be shown where all of the following conditions are established:

- the interference by a public authority is otherwise lawful;
- it serves a legitimate purpose;
- it is necessary in a democratic society; and
- it is not discriminatory.[2]

1   For example, Article 2: Right to Life.
2   *Handyside* v. *UK* (1979–80) 1 EHRR 737 para.48; *Dudgeon* v. *UK* (1981) 3 EHRR 40 para.52.

4.1.14   Effectively, the court will consider whether the public authority's course of action was proportionate in the circumstances. There will be a weighing-up of the parties' competing interests with reference to the means employed by the pub-lic authority against the victim and the legitimate objectives pursued. An example of this is where a bankrupt's family home is at risk of being possessed and sold by the trustee in bankruptcy to pay off his creditors. Here there is potentially a breach of Article 8 of the European Convention (the right to respect of privacy and family life/home) as the bankrupt and his family may lose their home. However, the court is unlikely to prevent the sale of the family home by a trustee in bankruptcy on human rights grounds where there are creditors outstanding, as this is likely to be a justifiable interference with the bankrupt's human rights[1] (see para.4.3.19 for further analysis of this specific example). In summary, if the public authority's alleged 'unlawful' course of action is reasonable, serves a legitimate purpose and is in accordance with public policy, then a victim is unlikely to have a sustainable claim.

---

1   However, further statutory restrictions on the sale of the family home have been introduced (see section 4.3).

4.1.15   Accordingly, when exercising a public function, an insolvency practitioner must seek to avoid an infringement of any individual's human rights. In the event of a breach, it is still possible that a claim will fail if the insolvency practitioner can establish that his course of action was a justifiable interference with the victim's human rights. Further examples are considered later (see paras.4.1.18–4.1.31).

General effect upon the insolvency profession

4.1.16   Since the implementation of the HRA 1998 there have been a number of court cases where the compatibility of insolvency legislation with the European Convention has been tested. Where any part of the legislation is held by the court to be incompatible with the HRA 1998, the insolvency practitioner must be alert to consequential changes to the interpretation of the existing law or the introduction of new legislation. A misunderstanding of the current law is unlikely to be a sustainable defence when facing a damages claim.[1] For example, if under a mistake of law an insolvency practitioner distributes a bankrupt's pension proceeds to his creditors, those sums may be recoverable personally from the insolvency practitioner to compensate any victim (see section 4.2 for a detailed analysis of the statutory changes to the treatment of personal pensions). That said, the insolvency legislation has generally proved to be robust against most litigious attacks.

---

1   *Kleinwort Benson Limited* v. *Lincoln C.C.* [1998] 3 WLR 1095.

4.1.17   Where a claim is successfully brought against an insolvency practitioner under the HRA 1998, the court may grant 'such relief or remedy . . . as it considers just and appropriate'.[1] Each case will be decided on its own merits. The relief or remedy could include a compensatory award, damages, recovery of costs and/or the quashing of the public authority's decision. However, the courts have generally been reluctant to award damages[2] and the floodgates have not yet opened to speculative claimant victims seeking windfall financial rewards under the HRA 1998. For the foreseeable future, the critics' fears have largely been assuaged by the pragmatism of the UK courts.

---

1   Human Rights Act 1988, s.8.
2   In accordance with the limits set out in Human Rights Act 1998, s.8.

Specific examples of the application of the HRA 1998

4.1.18   This section examines a number of cases that have been decided with reference to the HRA 1998 and/or the European Convention and which relate to courses of action adopted by insolvency practitioners. This non-exhaustive list provides practical guidance to insolvency practitioners where public functions are being exercised. The examples refer to the particular extract from the Article of the European Convention set out within the following shaded boxes.

> 'Right to a fair trial': Article 6 provides that 'In the determination of his civil rights and obligations ... everyone is entitled to a fair and public hearing within a reasonable time by an independent and impartial tribunal established by law'.

Delay in completing an insolvency process

4.1.19 Liquidations and other insolvency processes may infringe an individual's human rights if they are not completed within a reasonable period of time. In such cases, the insolvency practitioner could face a legal claim based upon the alleged harm to the victim caused by the delays in concluding the insolvency process. When considering whether an insolvency process has been completed within a reasonable time period the court will take into account factors such as the complexity of the particular case and the conduct of the claimant victim. If the victim has caused the delays or is otherwise blameworthy it is unlikely that his compensation claim will be upheld. For example, in *GJ v. Luxembourg*[1] the EctHR held[2] that the six years spent in concluding an insolvency akin to the UK's compulsory liquidation procedure was unreasonable. In this case, the insolvency practitioner was found personally liable to pay damages to the company's shareholder plus costs. The claimant victim was also awarded financial compensation for the anxiety, distress and feelings of injustice caused by delays. It remains to be seen whether a UK court would be prepared to make a similar damages award if a comparable case came before it. A contrasting approach was seen in the case of *King v. Walden*[3] where it was held that a determination by the Inland Revenue's Commissioners which took 12 years to complete was reasonable (although the court conceded that it was very close to being unreasonable). In summary, for those insolvency practitioners who are efficient and follow best practice, Article 6 will be of little concern in this regard. However, where there is a long drawn-out insolvency process without reasonable excuse, insolvency practitioners should be aware of the risks.

1   [2000] BPIR 1021.
2   Overruling the Luxembourg Court's decision at first instance.
3   [2001] BPIR 1012.

Concurrent civil and criminal proceedings

4.1.20   A delay in proceeding with a cause of action pursuant to the 1986 Act (such as those contained in ss.238 and 239 of the 1986 Act) until criminal proceedings or CDDA 1986 proceedings are completed may expose the insolvency practitioner to the risk of a claim under the HRA 1998. As a consequence of the civil procedure reforms introduced by Lord Woolf (which were in part influenced by the provisions set out within the European Convention), the courts are now more reluctant to provide extensions of time to an applicant in connection with any court process particularly when deadlines are or may be missed. An insolvency practitioner is now less likely to obtain an adjournment of civil proceedings where there is a concurrent criminal action unless there is a real risk of serious prejudice to the criminal proceedings.[1] Where the court agrees to an adjournment of the civil trial, it is unlikely that a double jeopardy defence (preventing an insolvency practitioner from advancing the civil claim against the defendant after a criminal determination) would be successful.[2]

1   *Banke Geselleschaft Berlin International SA v. Zihnali* 2001 WL 753380.
2   *Re Cedarwood Properties Limited, Re Inter City Print and Finishing Ltd, the Secretary of State for Trade and Industry v. Rayna and Another*, 12 July 2001, TLR, CA.

The duty of utmost fairness

4.1.21   An insolvency practitioner must act with utmost fairness. Clearly, this means that he must avoid adopting a course of action which is tainted with fraud and/or bad faith. The insolvency practitioner must also be totally independent and impartial in his dealings with all creditors, and must not favour those who secured his appointment. If the insolvency practitioner complies with these principles, the court is unlikely to interfere with his day-to-day decision making.

Insolvency investigations and the right to silence

4.1.22   Particularly in the context of criminal proceedings, one interpretation of Article 6 is that an individual has a right to silence i.e. a right not to incriminate himself (although this right is not expressly provided for within Article 6).[1] This can cause a problem in relation to some insolvency legislation. For example, s.354 (3) of the 1986 Act provides that a bankrupt can face a criminal conviction for failing without reasonable excuse to account for a loss of a substantial part of his property, or provide a satisfactory explanation as to how that loss was incurred. In the light of Article 6 (although subject to the 'justifiable interference' defence) this appears to be contrary to the HRA 1998. This conflict, also found elsewhere within the 1986 Act,[2] has been considered by the courts.[3] The principles resulting from a number of the major decisions are summarised below.

1   Article 6, European Convention. Clause 2 goes on to state 'Everyone charged with a criminal offence shall be presumed innocent until proved guilty according to the law'.
2   For example, ss.236, 366 and 206 (4) of the 1986 Act.
3   Indeed, as a result of this conflict some of the bankrupt's restrictions have been repealed (see Chapter 9 and the analysis of the changes to the regime affecting bankrupts).

4.1.23   A victim's right to silence is a qualified right: i.e. the court will consider whether the insolvency practitioner's demand for information amounts to a justifiable interference[1] with the victim's human rights. Therefore, if the insolvency practitioner has acted reasonably and proportionately,[2] then the rights of the creditors to receive the requested information will prevail over the right of the bankrupt to remain silent. Thus the bankrupt should co-operate with the investigation carried out by his trustee in bankruptcy investigation, and indeed s.354 (3) of the 1986 Act has been upheld by the court as being compatible with Article 6.[3]

---

1   See para.4.1.13.
2   *Brown v. Stott* [2001] 2 WLR 817.
3   *R v. Kearns* (2002) EWCA Crim748.

4.1.24   An insolvency practitioner, when investigating a director or bankrupt's conduct and/or financial affairs, is unlikely to infringe the individual's human rights where the information is primarily sought and used for administrative purposes (i.e. so long as it is part of the general investigation of the individual's affairs). Therefore, the courts are likely to carefully examine the facts of the case to determine whether the office holder has strayed from these boundaries. However, the courts do not appear to be overly concerned with the fact that the information could be used in later civil or criminal proceedings.

4.1.25   The courts have found in favour of some victims. For example in the case of *R v. Carass*[1] the Court of Appeal held that the reversal of the legal burden of proof for an accused on a criminal charge brought under s.206 of the 1986 Act was not, on the facts of the case, a justifiable interference with the individual's rights. Therefore, when reading s.206 of the 1986 Act in the light of the HRA 1998, the prosecution is now obliged to prove its case on the criminal burden of proof standard. This case provides an example of how the HRA 1998 can force a reinterpretation of existing insolvency law.

---

1   [2002] BPIR 821.

4.1.26   In *Saunders v. UK*[1] the use in any subsequent proceedings of answers obtained under the DTI's compulsory powers was prohibited, in view of the manner in which they were obtained. However, the court made it clear that each case in the future will be determined on its own facts. As a result of the *Saunders* case, the Attorney General issued guidelines as to how to deal with such evidence.[2] The Court of Appeal decision in *R v. Frank Faryab*[3] confirms the applicability of the *Saunders v. UK* decision in the context of insolvency investigations. However, all is not lost for a persistent insolvency practitioner, as information that is in existence, independent of the will of the victim, can still be used in subsequent proceedings (*Saunders and the Attorney General's reference no. 7 of 2000*).[4]

---

1   [1998] 1 BCLC 362.
2   1998 Guidelines.
3   Unreported, 22 February 1999, Court of Appeal.
4   [2001] 1 WLR 1879.

Are insolvency fees reasonable?

4.1.27   Although a £250 deposit is required to be paid by an individual to bring his own bankruptcy petition, the court has held that the payment of this deposit is not contrary to Article 6.[1]

---

1   *Ex Parte Cleo Lightfoot* [2000] WLR 319.

The end of immunity for the official receiver?

4.1.28   The principle of immunity from claims brought by a claimant in negligence against professionals has gradually receded in other walks of life such as with Police Officers (*Osman* v. *UK*[1]) and for advocates (*Hall* v. *Simons*[2]). It is probable, subject to the facts of the particular case, that the Official Receiver's limited immunity to claims[3] will not survive a challenge under Article 6.

---

1   [2000] 29 EHRR 245.
2   [2000] 3 All ER 673.
3   See *Mond* v. *Hyde* [1998] 3 All ER 833 where it was held that the Official Receiver was immune to claims based on statements made within the scope of his powers and duties in the context of bankruptcy proceedings. Commentators have argued that the current immunity afforded to the Official Receiver is misplaced and therefore it is open to challenge. See John Murphy, '*Mond* v. *Hyde*: Negligence Immunity for the Official Receiver?' [1997] Insolv. L, Issue 5 (Sweet & Maxwell).

> **Article 8 provides that 'Everyone has the right to respect for his private . . . life, his home and correspondence'.**

Mail redirection orders

4.1.29   Article 8 was considered in *Foxley* v. *UK* which was a case concerning mail redirection orders[1] (s.371 of the 1986 Act). The EctHR held that this statutory power exercisable by a trustee in bankruptcy was a justifiable interference with the bankrupt's human rights, as it was of sufficient potential benefit to his creditors as a whole. However, the case set limits to this power by stating that the trustee in bankruptcy should neither read mail after the expiry of an order, nor should he read privileged correspondence passing between the bankrupt and his solicitor.

---

1   (2000) *The Times*, 4 July.

Some assets will not form part of the bankrupt's estate

4.1.30   Although *Haig* v. *Aitken*[1] was not decided on a claim brought under the HRA 1998, it is of relevance in this area as the court held that the private correspondence of the bankrupt (who was a former Government Cabinet Minister) did not form part of his estate.[2] Therefore, the bankrupt's personal correspondence cannot be sold by the trustee in bankruptcy on the open market to benefit the bankrupt's creditors. This case provides a good example of the pervasive influence of the HRA 1998 on the court's reasoning.

---

1 [2001] 3 All ER 80.
2 Section 306 of the 1986 Act; s.311 (1) of the 1998 Act was also considered.

4.1.31 See section 4.3 on the 'family home' in connection with the impact of the HRA 1998 upon the trustee in bankruptcy's ability to possess and sell the bankrupt's family home for the benefit of the bankrupt's creditors.

Conclusion

4.1.32 There have been surprisingly few claims under the HRA 1998 and of those made, few have been successful. That said, it is still relatively early days in the life of the HRA 1998. Arguably, the greatest direct influence of the European Convention in this area has been on the way the courts view the insolvency office-holder's exercise of his powers of investigation. More generally, judicial interpretation of insolvency legislation in the light of the HRA 1998 has tended to confirm its robustness. However, it is anticipated that in the future there will be many more HRA 1998 claims related to insolvency practice and procedure. Indeed, the Enterprise Act 2002 may provide fertile ground for such claims. Likely future claims include whether a public authority's course of action was actually of a public (i.e. covered by the HRA 1998) or private nature. There may also be claims in the context of a trustee in bankruptcy's attempt to sell the family home and even on claiming rights over the bankrupt's personal pension.

4.1.33 Only time will show whether the more controversial provisions introduced by the Enterprise Act 2002 survive an application under the HRA 1998. In the meantime, the insolvency practitioner should ensure that he is adequately insured against liability for potential HRA 1998 breaches, given that there remains a risk that he could face a claim for damages.

4.2 WELFARE REFORM AND PENSIONS ACT 1999

Pension benefits: an asset for creditors?

4.2.1 The encouragement of private pension provision to supplement and arguably eventually replace state pension benefits was a key feature of the Conservative Government's policy in this area during the 1980s. With tax advantages offered to individuals, companies offering occupational pension schemes and a booming stock market, individuals began to possess increasingly valuable private pension benefits.

4.2.2 Save for the matrimonial home (which is often heavily mortgaged), in the vast majority of cases, a bankrupt's pension is the only unencumbered major asset available for potential realisation by a trustee in bankruptcy. Given the sums which might be made available to creditors and the importance of a pension to the future financial security of the bankrupt and his immediate family, the question over the ownership of this important asset has been the subject of fierce litigation.

4.2.3   Over the course of the last 20 years there have been numerous shifts in both the courts' and the Government's approach to the vexed question of whether a bankrupt can retain his pension benefits or whether the benefits should be made available to his creditors. This chapter summarises how pensions have been dealt with in the past, the genesis of the recent statutory reforms and details of the provisions contained within the Welfare Reform and Pensions Act 1999. This is a complex area and in a work of this kind it is possible to give only a brief overview of the current position.

4.2.4   The key questions to be considered by a trustee in bankruptcy are:

■ *Do the pension benefits automatically vest within the bankrupt's estate?*[1] An affirmative reply means that pension benefits are available to the trustee in bankruptcy for distribution to the creditors.

■ A negative reply means that the trustee in bankruptcy will then need to ask: *can the pension benefits be otherwise drawn into the bankrupt's estate for distribution to creditors?* For example: the pension benefits could be drawn in by an application to the court for an income payments order or agreement[2] (see section 9.2).

In order to answer these questions, the date upon which an individual was declared bankrupt is critical. The implications of this are considered below.

1   Insolvency Act 1986, s.306.
2   Insolvency Act 1986, s.310.

Bankruptcies declared before the Insolvency Act 1986

4.2.5   An analysis of bankruptcy law preceding the implementation of the 1986 Act is not strictly within the scope of this book. However, the way in which the courts dealt with the retention of the bankrupt's pension benefits before 29 December 1986[1] may be relevant for a small number of individuals made bankrupt prior to the coming into force of the 1986 Act.

1   This being the commencement date of the 1986 Act.

4.2.6   The principal authority regarding the treatment of pensions for pre-1986 bankrupts is *Ex Parte Huggins*,[1] where the Court of Appeal held that the bankrupt's pension did not automatically vest in his trustee in bankruptcy. Although this case has been criticised by commentators as being wrongly decided, it remains good law. Therefore, pre-1986 bankrupts (who in the case of *Ex Parte Huggins* happened to be a retired Chief Justice of Sierra Leone) are permitted by the courts to retain their pension benefits.

1   (1882) 21 ChD 835.

4.2.7   In the event that one of these historic bankruptcies is encountered and there is a pension available, notwithstanding the *Ex Parte Huggins* decision, the trustee in bankruptcy can still apply to the court to exercise its discretion to make all or part of the pension benefits available to creditors. That said, pre-1986 the balance was very much in the bankrupt's favour at the expense of his creditors.

Bankruptcies declared during the 'intervening period'

4.2.8   For bankruptcies declared after the commencement of the 1986 Act (29 December 1986), but before the implementation of the Welfare Reform and Pensions Act 1999 (29 May 2000) (the 'intervening period'), the question as to whether the bankrupt retains pension benefits is answered by High Court's decision in *Re Landau*.[1] In this case, after reviewing the effect of the 1986 Act, the court confirmed that anyone declared bankrupt during the intervening period lost his unqualified right to receive his personal pension, even after the discharge of his bankruptcy.

---

1   [1998] Ch 233.

4.2.9   The reasoning underpinning this decision was that the bankrupt's right to receive private pension benefits under a retirement annuity contract constituted an existing 'property right'[1] and therefore it automatically formed part of the bankrupt's estate without the need of an express assignment. Furthermore, the court held that restrictions on alienation within the terms of the pension policy did not prevent this automatic transfer of pension benefits to the trustee in bankruptcy. The High Court concluded that it was not bound to follow the pre-1986 Act legal authority, as the 1986 Act amounted to a fundamental departure from the previous regime set out within the Bankruptcy Act 1914.

---

1   Insolvency Act 1986, s.436.

4.2.10   Understandably, bankrupts have been unhappy with this ruling as the balance during the intervening period had clearly swung in favour of creditors. Consequently, the *Re Landau* decision has been subjected to repeated litigious attacks. The important case law considering the bankrupt's pensions during the intervening period with reference to the different types of pension is considered below.

Personal pension schemes

4.2.11   The Court of Appeal's decisions in *Dennison* v. *Krasner* and *Lawrence* v. *Lesser*[1] upheld *Re Landau*, confirming the principles that:

- Personal pension rights automatically vest in the trustee in bankruptcy on bankruptcy and therefore applying for an income payments order[2] was unnecessary.

- The personal pension should be available to the trustee in bankruptcy even after the bankrupt's discharge in order to satisfy creditors.
- Attempts to forfeit a personal pension on bankruptcy (this was often a term within the pension policy) failed on public policy grounds.[3]

1   [2000] 3 All ER 234.
2   Insolvency Act 1986, s.310. For details of the new provisions for income payment orders see section 9.2.
3   *Dennison v. Krasner* [2000] 3 WLR 720, para.49.

4.2.12   Although leave to appeal the *Lawrence* v. *Lesser* decision to the House of Lords was obtained, the appeal was withdrawn, as a negotiated settlement was reached by the parties. Therefore, the Court of Appeal's decision remains good authority for the treatment of personal pensions during the intervening period. However, there remains the possibility that the House of Lords might determine the pension question in a different way. That said, given subsequent unsuccessful attempts to overturn these decisions, such an application appears to be increasingly unlikely. For example, the Court of Appeal in *Rowe* v. *Sanders*[1] more recently rejected the bankrupt's argument that the trustee in bankruptcy's attempts to seize his pension was incompatible with the first protocol, Article 1, of the European Convention[2] (see section 4.1 for further analysis of the Human Rights Act 1998). Leave to appeal this decision to the House of Lords was refused.

1   [2002] EWCA Civ242.
2   As now incorporated within English law by the HRA 1998. The First Protocol in summary states that no-one should be deprived of his possessions except for the public interest.

4.2.13   The final question to be considered is the enforceability of exclusion clauses[1] within the terms of the pension policy. In case there was any doubt, as from 6 April 2002 the Welfare Reform and Pensions Act 1999[2] provides that a person's rights under a personal pension scheme cannot be forfeited by reference to his bankruptcy. Therefore, any attempts to forfeit a pension on the basis of such an exclusion clause after 6 April 2002 is now prohibited by both statute and case law.[3]

1   For example: provisions prohibiting the alienation of the pension benefits.
2   Welfare Reform and Pensions Act 1999, s.14 inserts s.159A (1) into the Pension Schemes Act 1993.
3   For commentary on bankruptcies commenced after 29 May 2002 see para.4.2.21.

Occupational pension schemes

4.2.14   The court's decision in *Jones* v. *Patel*[1] confirmed the applicability of the *Re Landau* principles where a pension cash lump sum was payable (under a statutory occupational scheme) to an undischarged bankrupt following his redundancy. The court held that this sum fell within the bankrupt's estate[2] and was payable to his creditors.

1   [1999] BPIR 509.
2   Insolvency Act 1986, s.306.

4.2.15   However, this case is likely to be of limited applicability as the pension schemes of certain public sector employees and most private sector occupational schemes, generally include a provision to the effect that pension benefits cannot be paid to anyone other than the member. Unlike a similar provision in personal pensions, such a clause is not necessarily unenforceable. The rationale for this differing treatment is that with most occupational pension schemes employees have a *future* interest in the pension benefits: hence these do not automatically vest in the trustee in bankruptcy. Personal pensions generally provide for an unqualified right to the pension benefits, a distinction acknowledged in the decision of *Re Landau*.

4.2.16   The case of *Re Trusts of the Scientific Investment Pension Plan* upheld the enforceability of forfeiture clauses for such occupational pension schemes[1] notwithstanding the long established principle that parties are generally unable to contract out of the bankruptcy code.[2] Again in this case a distinction was drawn between present property rights (which are available to benefit creditors) and future rights (which can generally be withheld by pension trustees and transferred to a third party such as the bankrupt's spouse). Therefore, careful consideration of the terms of the pension scheme must be given to ascertain the bankrupt's rights under his particular scheme.

1   [1998] 3 All ER 154.
2   *British Eagle International Airlines Limited* v. *Compagnie National Air France* [1975] 2 All ER 390.

4.2.17   That said, the Welfare Reform and Pensions Act 1999[1] states that the previous statutory exception to the rule allowing forfeiture of rights under certain occupational schemes also ceases to have effect as from 6 April 2002. Therefore, for bankruptcies commenced after that date, such forfeiture clauses will generally be unenforceable. As these statutory provisions have time to bed down, the forfeiture clauses may become the focus of attack by trustees in bankruptcy[2] who may seek to recover the bankrupt's pension benefits on behalf of the creditors.

1   Welfare Reform and Pensions Act 1999, s.14 repeals Pensions Act 1995, s.92 (2)(*b*).
2   For commentary on bankruptcies commenced after 29 May 2000, see para.4.2.21.

State retirement pension and SERPs

4.2.18   A bankrupt receiving a state pension has no more than an entitlement to claim a weekly sum in state benefits. As no property vests in the bankrupt, there is nothing to automatically vest in his trustee in bankruptcy. However, the state pension benefit and indeed any other income payments received by the bankrupt may be recoverable for the creditors' benefit by means of a successful application for an income payments order or reaching an income payments agreement.[1]

1   Insolvency Act 1986, s.310 (see section 9.2).

The intervening period: concluding remarks

4.2.19 In view of the current legal authorities and subject to careful consideration of the terms of the pension scheme:

- In the absence of a valid forfeiture clause or court order (for a declaration as to the correct payee), pension providers should generally release the bankrupt's pension benefits to the bankrupt's trustee in bankruptcy where they are on notice of his interest.

- Trustees in bankruptcy should generally not refuse to pay out to creditors proceeds from a bankrupt's pension unless there is a distinguishing feature to one of the leading cases or one disputing party is willing to pursue a case to the House of Lords for definitive guidance. That said, in the light of the House of Lords' refusal to grant leave to appeal the *Rowe v. Sanders*[1] decision, there seems to be little appetite amongst the judiciary to set aside the Court of Appeal's view.

---

1 [2002] EWCA Civ242.

4.2.20 There remains the risk (albeit a small one) that if the House of Lords is asked to determine who should receive the pension benefits during the intervening period, a reversion to the pre-1986 position might be seen. In such circumstances, pension scheme trustees and the trustees in bankruptcy might be exposed to claims from aggrieved bankrupts (or their dependants), as money paid out under mistake of law can be recoverable.[1] As there were in excess of 200,000 bankruptcies commenced during the intervening period, such a decision could have a significant effect. It will therefore ultimately be a question for either the pension scheme trustees, a bankrupt or a trustee in bankruptcy to decide whether to take a risk and seek declaratory relief from the courts, or to ensure that the both the pension scheme trustees and the trustees in bankruptcy have adequate insurance in place.

---

1 *Kleinwort Benson Limited v. Lincoln City Council* [1998] 3 WLR 1095.

Bankruptcies commencing on or after 29 May 2000

4.2.21 Since 29 May 2000, the tide has now turned once again to favour bankrupts. The Court of Appeal's decisions on pensions during the intervening period prompted the Government to introduce the provisions set out within the Welfare Reform and Pensions Act 1999 so that 'approved'[1] and certain 'unapproved'[2] pension arrangements will now be retained by the bankrupt, subject to important statutory safeguards. The 1999 Act should be read in conjunction with the guidance notes provided by the Occupational and Personal Pension Schemes (Bankruptcy) Regulations 2002[3] (the 'OPPS Regs'). Importantly, as neither the 1999 Act nor the OPPS Regs have a retrospective effect, the preceding analysis is still relevant to a large number of bankruptcies.

---

1 Welfare Reform and Pensions Act 1999, s.11.

2   Welfare Reform and Pensions Act 1999, s.12.
3   SI 2002/427.

Approved pensions are generally excluded from the bankrupt's estate

4.2.22   The Welfare Reform and Pensions Act 1999 was implemented by the Government in piecemeal fashion. Section 11(1) provides that as from 29 May 2000 approved pension schemes (i.e. those approved by the Inland Revenue[1]) are excluded from the bankrupt's estate. Therefore, in most cases the bankrupt will retain his pension benefits. Surprisingly, the bulk of the statutory safeguards (for example, recouping excessive pension contributions for the benefit of creditors) were introduced almost two years later in April 2002. This delay in implementation is perhaps indicative of the Government's resolve to swiftly redress the perceived unfairness to the bankrupt and his family, while having less regard to safeguards for creditors (see para.4.2.27). Even so, the pension benefits payable to the bankrupt under an approved pension arrangement could have still been seized by the trustee in bankruptcy if an application was made for an income payments order.[2]

---

1   What amounts to an approved pension scheme is defined in Welfare Reform and Pensions Act 1999, s.11 (2). Please note that Inland Revenue approval can subsequently be withdrawn.
2   Insolvency Act 1986, s.310 (see section 9.2).

4.2.23   As a result of the new legislative reform, all approved pension schemes are protected from the bankrupt's creditors until pension payments are made to the bankrupt. Once pension payments are due, the trustee in bankruptcy can apply to the court for an income payments order to claim the sums (see section 9.2).

Unapproved pension arrangements can also be excluded from the bankrupt's estate

4.2.24   The OPPS Regs[1] allows certain unapproved pension schemes,[2] in limited circumstances, to be excluded from the bankrupt's estate so long as the following conditions are satisfied:

- it must be the bankrupt's sole or main pension arrangement (note that the State pension is not taken into account when considering this condition[3]); and
- subject to the conditions set out below, the exclusion (from the bankrupt's estate) is to be effected by either:

- the bankrupt's application to the court for an exclusion order; or
- a qualifying agreement reached between the bankrupt and his trustee in bankruptcy.

---

1 This regulation was introduced by Welfare Reform and Pensions Act 1999, s.12 (1) and came into force on 6 April 2002.
2 Regulation 3 of the Occupational and Personal Pension Schemes (Bankruptcy) Regulations 2002 sets out what amounts to be an unapproved pension scheme.
3 Regulation 3(c) of the Occupational and Personal Pension Schemes (Bankruptcy) Regulations 2002 states that a pension under Part II of the Social Security Contributions and Benefits Act 1992 (Contributory Benefits) is not taken into account when considering an unapproved pension arrangement.

Time limits

4.2.25 Such exclusions are subject to strict time limits. The bankrupt must commence a court application within 13 weeks, or conclude a qualifying agreement within nine weeks. Both time limits are calculated from the date when the bankrupt's estate or pension rights vested in the trustee in bankruptcy.[1] Furthermore, in the event that a qualifying agreement is made and then a trustee in bankruptcy serves on the bankrupt a valid notice of revocation[2] (for example on the grounds that the bankrupt has failed to disclose all material facts in respect of a pension arrangement), the bankrupt has a further 30 days (calculated from the effective date of revocation of the qualifying agreement) to apply to the court for an exclusion order. If these time limits are missed, the opportunity for the exclusion is lost, unless the bankrupt can persuade the court that there is 'good cause' to extend the deadlines. Whilst there is no reported case law at present which shows what constitutes 'good cause' if the court adopts the same approach as it does to the compliance with the Civil Procedure Rules deadlines, it is unlikely that substantial extensions of time will be generally provided to a bankrupt.

---

1 Insolvency Act 1986, s.306 or later if the scheme falls within reg.3 (1)(*a*) or (*b*) of the Occupational and Personal Pension Schemes (Bankruptcy) Regulations 2002.
2 Regulation 6 (4) of the Occupational and Personal Pension Schemes (Bankruptcy) Regulations 2002 states that a notice of revocation shall be:

1. dated;
2. in writing;
3. specify the reasons for revocation;
4. specify the date that the agreement shall be revoked which must be a date at least 30 days hence from the date of the notice; and
5. inform the bankrupt of his right to apply for an exclusion order within 30 days of the revocation date.

Once revoked the Trustee must inform the responsible person of the revocation: reg.6 (5) of the Occupational and Personal Pension Schemes (Bankruptcy) Regulations 2002. The responsible person is effectively the controlling individual or company who is the trustee, manager or provider of an unapproved pension arrangement.

Factors taken into account by the court on the bankrupt's application for an exclusion order

4.2.26   The court will consider the following factors when deciding whether to make an exclusion order:

- The future likely needs of the bankrupt and his family.
- Whether those needs can be adequately met by other pension benefits.

Whilst at the time of writing there is no reported case law on this specific provision, under other provisions of the 1986 Act the court has generally taken a wide view when considering what constitutes adequate needs for a bankrupt. For example in the case of *Rayatt*[1] it was held that private education could amount to reasonable domestic need. Although this case was considered under s.310 of the 1986 Act, it is likely that the court will consider that 'reasonable' needs are akin to 'adequate' needs. (For further consideration of this similar test, see section 9.2 on income payments orders.)

---

1   [1998] BPIR 495.

Can a trustee in bankruptcy seize a bankrupt's pension benefits? – a consideration of the statutory safeguards

4.2.27   These reforms have not provided carte blanche to bankrupts. In order to combat possible fraud and/or excessive pension contributions being made to avoid a more substantial distribution to the bankrupt's creditors, safeguard provisions have been introduced to allow a recovery of pension contributions by a trustee in bankruptcy in limited circumstances. These are considered below.

4.2.28   If the bankrupt makes excessive pension contributions into an approved or unapproved pension scheme, these can be seized by the trustee in bankruptcy upon application to the court for an excessive pension contributions order.[1] The court may make such an order if it considers that the bankrupt's pension contributions unfairly prejudice his creditors[2] and where it concludes that:

- any contribution was made for the purpose of putting assets beyond the reach of the bankrupt's creditors or any one of them; and
- the total amount of contributions are excessive in view of the individual circumstances when they were made.[3]

---

1   See Insolvency Act 1986, ss.342A to 342C inserted by Welfare Reform and Pensions Act 1999, s.15.
2   Welfare Reform and Pensions Act 1999, s.15 (2)(*b*).
3   Welfare Reform and Pensions Act 1999, s.15 (6).

4.2.29   The evidential burden placed on the trustee in bankruptcy is, however, onerous. The trustee has to file at court clear evidence to show that on a balance of probabilities, the bankrupt was attempting to defraud creditors by making excessive pension contributions. It is unlikely to be sufficient simply to rely on the fact that the bankrupt may have paid sums in excess of the limits set by the Inland Revenue to benefit from tax relief (i.e. the requisite percentage of an individual's income, set according to age). Each case will depend on the individual circumstances of the bankrupt. To date, there has been no reported case law on what amount of a pension contribution would be regarded as being excessive.

Further important provisions introduced by the Welfare Reform and Pensions Act 1999

4.2.30   The person responsible (i.e. the trustee, manager or provider) for an approved pension, unapproved pension arrangement or any other pension arrangements under which a bankrupt has at any time had rights, must on the bankrupt's trustee in bankruptcy's written request, provide such information about the pension arrangements and the bankrupt's rights as the trustee in bankruptcy may reasonably require. Such information (if available) will be required before the trustee in bankruptcy applies for an excessive contribution order.[1]

---

1   Welfare Reform and Pensions Act 1999, s.15 inserts s.342C (1) into the Insolvency Act 1986.

4.2.31   The forfeiture of pension benefits in accordance with the written terms of the personal pension schemes and also certain occupational schemes on bankruptcy will no longer be possible under statute.[1] In the event that a bankrupt is held by the court to have made an excessive pension contribution, then this 'culpable' behaviour will be a factor taken into account by the court where it considers whether it would be appropriate to impose a bankruptcy restriction order[2] on the bankrupt.[3]

---

1   Pension Schemes Act 1993, s.159A inserted by Welfare Reform and Pensions Act 1999, s.14 (1).
2   Section 257 of, and Sched.20 to, the Enterprise Act 2002 introduced Sched.4A into the Insolvency Act 1986.
3   See section 8.3 for more detailed analysis.

Conclusion

4.2.32   There is now a degree of certainty as to who receives pension benefits in respect of all bankruptcies commenced after 29 May 2000, although the legislation still remains largely untested and case law will need to define the limits of the exclusion and excessive contribution orders. However, there remains confusion over bankruptcies commenced prior to this date. Some commentators have expressed the view that Ex Parte Huggins was wrongly decided.[1] If the House of Lords confirms this view some pre-1986 bankruptcies may need to be re-examined where pension annuities are currently being paid to the bankrupt. For any bankruptcy commenced during the intervening period the position remains unsettled. At present, with pension benefits generally falling within the bankrupt's estate, creditors are more likely to receive an enhanced distribution, although as discussed this position may still be challenged in the House of Lords.

---

1   A. Deacock and D. Martin, *Insolvency Law & Practice*, Volume 16, No.4, 2000, p.130.

4.2.33   As a result of the legislative changes since the implementation of the Welfare Reform and Pensions Act 1999 the trustee in bankruptcy has lost a potentially significant asset for realisation to creditors. One may well conclude that this reform was born of political expediency and the wish to encourage the transition from reliance on state pension benefits to private and occupational pension provision. However, the result is that creditors are likely to receive significantly smaller distributions from bankruptcies unless the trustee in bankruptcy is able to successfully apply for an income payments order. We may also see a rise in the proportion of IVAs resulting from debtors offering all or part of their pension arrangements for the benefit of their creditors, which might not be available on bankruptcy. Experience will show whether this new law will lead to a more entrepreneurial culture where a businessman can take legitimate risks without fear of losing his pension, or whether there will simply be a rise in the number of consumer bankrupts who are confident that they can avoid paying over this major asset to their creditors.

4.3   THE FAMILY HOME

The bankrupt's family versus creditors' rights

4.3.1   The bankrupt's and his family's right to live in the family home when this asset could be realised to pay the bankrupt's creditors remains a hotly contested issue. Subject to any prior secured loan, the family home is likely to represent the only significant asset available for the benefit of creditors. One of the effects of the 'Thatcher years' was that home ownership within the UK rapidly increased. The percentage of home owners (as opposed to those who rent) within the UK is now higher than in most other European countries. In the light of this trend, it is perhaps not surprising that since 1986 the Government has increasingly bolstered the bankrupt's and his family's right to remain in occupation of their principal family home. This increased protection has culminated in the provisions introduced by the Enterprise Act 2002. The changes to the statutory regime, whilst obviously benefiting the bankrupt and his family, is detrimental to the bankrupt's creditors as, in many cases, there may be no other assets available for realisation.

4.3.2   In this chapter we review the facts that a trustee in bankruptcy is likely to need to consider before commencing legal proceedings, and the legislative and major court decisions since 1986 that have made it progressively more difficult for the trustee in bankruptcy to obtain an order to possess and sell the family home.[1]

---

1   For the sake of convenience we will assume the spouses' rights are those of a wife.

4.3.3   It should be borne in mind that save for HRA 1998 considerations, the legislative changes discussed here have only affected the trustee in bankruptcy's ability to realise the value in the family home. In the event that other property vests in the trustee in bankruptcy, the majority of the safeguards protecting the bankrupt and his family will not apply.

The factors to be considered by a trustee in bankruptcy

Assessing the value of the bankrupt's registered interest in the family home

4.3.4   The bankrupt's interest in the family home vests in the trustee in bankruptcy immediately on the trustee's appointment taking effect or, in the case of the Official Receiver, on the Official Receiver becoming the trustee.[1] Where the family home is registered in the sole name of the bankrupt, the trustee in bankruptcy is entitled to be registered as the sole proprietor.[2] Assuming that this registration is correctly completed, as the registered legal owner, the trustee in bankruptcy is entitled to sell the family home and (if necessary) apply to the court for an order for possession against the bankrupt. This scenario is relatively straightforward. Indeed, some commentators argue that where the home is solely owned and occupied by the bankrupt,[3] such a court order is unnecessary. However, to avoid the risk of being exposed to criminal liability in the event that the bankrupt does not voluntarily relinquish possession of his home, the trustee in bankruptcy will be well advised to seek an order for possession against the bankrupt.

---

1   Insolvency Act 1986, s.306.
2   Land Registration Act 1925, s.42 (1).
3   Berry, Bailey and Shaw Miller, *Personal Insolvency, Law and Practice*, 3rd Edn, (Butterworths Lexis Nexis), p.614.

Assessing the value of the bankrupt's interest in the family home where there are third party interests

4.3.5   Usually, there are third party interests which will affect whether the trustee in bankruptcy can sell the family home. For example, the property could be registered both in the name of the bankrupt and his spouse, or minors could also occupy the family home. Where there are two or more registered proprietors, the trustee in bankruptcy cannot usually register his interest on the legal title (as this interest is not severable upon an act of bankruptcy). Instead, a prudent trustee can either apply to register a restriction (if consent from the other registered proprietors is forthcoming) or a caution on the title. A caution will provide a degree of protection to the trustee in bankruptcy in the event that a third party attempts to sell or otherwise deal with the family home, as the Land Registry should provide prior notification of any attempt to deal in the family home. Even if the bankrupt is the sole registered proprietor, third parties (such as his spouse or children) may have rights of occupation in the family home which the trustee in bankruptcy must assess and if necessary, seek to extinguish before the family home can be sold. A trustee in bankruptcy must understand the impact that these third party interests have upon the realisable value of the bankrupt's share of the family home before deciding whether to proceed with a court application for possession and ultimately sale of the family home. The court might, in limited circumstances, allow the bankrupt and his family to remain in occupation within the family home for an extended period. These limited circumstances are considered at para.4.3.18.

Does the trustee in bankruptcy (i.e. did the bankrupt) actually have a beneficial interest in the family home?

4.3.6   As a matter of basic land law, a beneficial interest in property can be held by those with a beneficial entitlement as either joint tenants or as tenants in common. On bankruptcy the beneficial interest, if held as joint tenants, is automatically severed and is held as tenants in common. Accordingly, assessing the value of the respective shares when the family home is held as beneficial joint tenants is relatively easy, as it is an even split. For example, where the property is held by the bankrupt and his wife, the trustee in bankruptcy's share, subject to the other considerations listed below, is 50 per cent of the realisable value. However, where the beneficial interest in the family home was held immediately before the date of bankruptcy as tenants in common, particular attention must be paid by the trustee in bankruptcy to the terms of any trust deed which may set out the value of the respective shares. For example, if the family home had been gifted to the bankrupt's wife by her parents, the bankrupt might have only a nominal share in it. In that case, the trustee in bankruptcy's remaining option is to consider whether the trust deed can be unravelled (see para.4.3.8).

What is the value of the bankrupt's beneficial interest?

4.3.7   Subject to the above considerations as to how the beneficial interest was held, the factors to be taken into account when calculating the value of the bankrupt's (trustee in bankruptcy's) interest will include:

- Substantial capital improvements and/or capital payments solely funded by a third party (for example by the bankrupt's spouse). These may reduce the value of the trustee in bankruptcy's share in the family home.[1]
- Relative contributions to the purchase price.[2]
- Whether an issue such as undue influence or the equity of exoneration[3] apply. For example, in the event that the bankrupt persuades his spouse to agree to an increased secured loan on the family home to finance his ailing business and he then subsequently goes bankrupt, the loan might be capable of being set aside on the grounds of undue influence unless the House of Lords' guidelines (as set out within *Etridge*[4]) are complied with by the lender. Alternatively, the loan could be reassigned to the bankrupt's share of the beneficial interest of the family home, if his spouse successfully relies upon the principle of equity of exoneration.

- Any other valuable rights vesting in the trustee in bankruptcy relating to the land such as a right of pre-emption.[5]

---

1 *Re Gorman (A Bankrupt)* [1990] WLR 616.
2 *Re Pavlou (A Bankrupt)* [1993] WLR 1046.
3 *Re Pittoriou* [1985] 1 WLR 58.
4 The leading case on this point remains *Royal Bank of Scotland v. Etridge (No.2) and Others* [2001] UKHL 44.
5 *Dear v. Reeves* [2001] 3 WLR 469.

Can the trustee set aside the third party's interest?

4.3.8   Where a third party has a substantial beneficial interest in the family home, the following statutory provisions may provide the possibility of setting it aside:

- transactions at an undervalue;[1]
- preferences;[2]
- transactions defrauding creditors;[3] and/or
- failure to ratify a family proceedings property transfer order by the Bankruptcy Court.[4]

---

1 Insolvency Act 1986, s.339.
2 Insolvency Act 1986, s.340.
3 Insolvency Act 1986, s.423.
4 Insolvency Act 1986, s.284 (1).

General considerations

4.3.9   Before taking any final decision to commence legal proceedings, the trustee should assess the prospects of successfully obtaining orders for possession and sale in the event that an agreement cannot be achieved with the bankrupt and/or with any interested third parties. The trustee therefore needs to consider the statutory provisions protecting the family. These are dealt with in succession below, culminating with the further restrictions introduced by the Enterprise Act 2002.

4.3.10   In the event that court proceedings are necessary, the trustee in bankruptcy should consider applying for:

- An order compelling that third party to join the trustee in bankruptcy in selling the family home (with vacant possession) in the event that there is a legal proprietor other than the bankrupt.
- An order providing that the conduct of the sale be given to the trustee in bankruptcy and/or his solicitor.
- A declaration as to the value of the respective beneficial interests of the trustee in bankruptcy and any third parties.
- An order that the proceeds of sale be distributed between the trustee in bankruptcy and the third party in accordance with their respective beneficial interests once an appropriate deduction is made for all necessary expenses of sale and any valid secured charges have been redeemed.

- An order under the Family Law Act 1996[1] determining any matrimonial home rights or rights of occupation.[2]
- An order for possession.

---

1   Insolvency Act 1986, s.336.
2   Insolvency Act 1986, s.337(4).

Legislative reform since 1986 affecting the trustee in bankruptcy's position

The Family Law Act 1996

4.3.11   The Family Law Act 1996 ('FLA 1996') provides that a spouse (and/or any other family member including the bankrupt) without a proprietary interest in the family home can protect her right of occupation by registering her interest on the title of the family home. However, family home rights cannot be registered (and will therefore be enforceable) between the presentation of the bankruptcy petition and the vesting of the bankrupt's estate in the trustee in bankruptcy.[1] The effect of proper registration is limited as follows:

- If in occupation, it provides a spouse with a right not to be excluded from the family home without a court order.[2]
- If not in occupation, the spouse may seek the court's permission to enter and occupy the home.[3]

---

1   Insolvency Act 1986, s.336 (1).
2   *Re Gorman (A Bankrupt)* [1990] WLR 616.
3   Family Law Act 1996, s.33.

4.3.12   If such rights are enforceable then, in addition to seeking an order for possession, the trustee in bankruptcy must also apply for an order terminating the spouse's (and/or any other registered third parties') interest in the family home.

4.3.13   If such an application is not immediately successful (for example, if the court finds that the spouse's interest, and therefore her right of occupation, should subsist for a limited further period) the trustee in bankruptcy is still entitled to apply for a further order[1] to protect his interest in the family home. Such an order could oblige the spouse to:

- Ensure that repair and maintenance of the family home takes place.
- Discharge mortgage payments, other outgoings or make periodical payments in respect of occupation.

---

1   Family Law Act 1996, s.40.

4.3.14   Where the application is made within the first year of the bankruptcy, the court may make such order as it thinks is just and reasonable having regard to the following factors:

- The interests of the bankrupt's creditors.

- The conduct of a spouse or former spouse, so far as it may have contributed to the bankruptcy.
- The needs and financial resources of the spouse or former spouse, including the needs of any children.
- All the circumstances of the case other than the needs of the bankrupt.[1]

These are the same factors as apply when an order for sale is sought under s.335A of the 1986 Act (see para.4.3.16 for further analysis). The rights of cohabitees may be largely ignored (however, see para.4.3.19 on the pervasive effect of the HRA 1998).

---

1 Insolvency Act 1986, s.336 (4).

4.3.15   If an application for possession is commenced after the end of the first year in which the estate first vested the trustee in bankruptcy, the court will assume (unless there are exceptional circumstances[1]) that the interests of the creditors outweigh all other factors,[2] although the same considerations as above still apply. After a year has elapsed, it is likely that the trustee in bankruptcy will be able to secure possession and ultimately sell the family home, subject to the further statutory hurdles summarised in the following sections.

---

1 See more detailed analysis at para.4.3.18 on what could amount to 'exceptional circumstances'.
2 Insolvency Act 1986, s.336 (5).

Trustees of Land and Appointment of Trustees Act 1996

4.3.16   When comparing the old law applicable before 1 January 1997 (s.30 of the Law of Property Act 1925) with the new law, some commentators are of the view that when considering the trustee in bankruptcy's application for possession of the family home in accordance with the old law, the courts were more ready to accede and provide the required order.[1] Section 14 of the Trusts of Land and Appointment of Trustees Act 1996 ('TLTA 1996') (which inserted s.335A into the 1986 Act (see para.4.3.17)) sets out the factors that the court must take into account when considering whether to make an order for sale of the family home.[2] As its effect is retrospective, all applications for possession are covered by this provision.[3] The court with jurisdiction to hear the trustee in bankruptcy's application for possession etc. is that which has the conduct of the bankruptcy proceedings.

---

1 See Sealy & Milman, *Annotated Guide to the Insolvency Legislation*, 5th Edn, at p.387 (CCH Editions Limited).
2 Insolvency Act 1986, s.335A (2).
3 Insolvency Act 1986, s.335A (4).

4.3.17   Section 335A(2) of the 1986 Act states that:

On such an application the Court will make such an order [for the sale of the family home] as it thinks just and reasonable having regard to:

a. the interests of the bankrupt's creditors;
b. where the application is made in respect of a dwelling house which is or has been the home of a bankrupt or the bankrupt's spouse or former spouse:

(i)   the conduct of the spouse or former spouse, so far as contributing to the bankruptcy,

(ii)   the needs and financial resources of the spouse or former spouse, and

(iii)   the needs of any children; and

c.   all the circumstances of the case other than the needs of the bankrupt.

4.3.18   In the event that an application for possession is heard after one year of the family home vesting in the trustee in bankruptcy, the court will assume, unless there are exceptional circumstances, that the interests of the bankrupt's creditors outweigh all those considerations set out above.[1] Subject to human rights considerations (see para.4.3.19), only exceptional circumstances applicable to the bankrupt's spouse, former spouse and children will be considered by the court. Therefore, the needs of simple cohabitees are ignored. What amounts to exceptional circumstances? Some examples taken from case law are summarised below:

■   The illness of the bankrupt's wife can delay an application for sale in certain limited circumstances.[2] For example, where the illness was caused by the prospect of leaving the family home, the court postponed the sale.

■   Hardship caused to the bankrupt's wife and young children by a possession order are not exceptional circumstances, although it was said that a postponement of the sale of the family home might be ordered if it was highly unlikely that there could be resulting harm to creditors.[3]

■   That the sale of the family home might not immediately benefit creditors (as the proceeds were to be applied to meet the costs of the bankruptcy), was not of itself a sufficient reason to prevent the sale of the family home.[4] However, see commentary on the effect of the Enterprise Act 2002 (paras.4.3.21 to 4.3.29).

■   Protecting a child's educational needs would not necessarily amount to exceptional circumstances where the family could move to a different property within the school's catchment area, even if the child's public examinations were imminent.[5]

In summary, exceptional circumstances will only rarely arise. The burden of proof remains on the individual attempting to prevent the sale.

---

1   Insolvency Act 1986, s.335A (3).
2   *Judd v. Brown* [1997] BPIR 470.
3   *Re Citro* [1990] 3 All ER 952.
4   *Trustee of the Estate of Bowe (A Bankrupt) v. Bowe* [1997] BPIR 744.
5   *Re Bailey* [1977] 2 All ER 26.

Human Rights Act 1998

4.3.19   In summary, Article 8(1) of the European Convention provides that everybody has a right to respect for his home. Since the incorporation of the European Convention into UK law by the HRA 1998, a number of cases have been brought by bankrupts and their families challenging the trustee in bankruptcy's ability to take possession and sell the family home. Importantly, the courts have confirmed that Article 8 provides a right of respect for an individual's home, but not a right to an individual's home[1] and consequently such claims have failed. There is scope however for further cases to be brought under the HRA 1998, which may clarify whether the existing safeguards to protect the bankrupt's and his family's human rights are sufficient. That said, given the current state of the law, such applications are increasingly unlikely to be successful.

---

1   *Helen Mountney v. Stephen Treharno* [2002] EUCA 174.

4.3.20   The HRA 1998 is more likely to have an impact on increasing the level of protection afforded to co-habitees and other persons living in long-standing relationships outside marriage.[1] Currently, such individuals (whether in a heterosexual or homosexual relationship) do not receive the same level of protection as spouses.[2] As society's values change, successful applications to bring unmarried cohabitees' rights into line with married couples' should be expected.[3]

---

1   Article 8 and 14 of the European Convention for the Protection of Human Rights.
2   *Grant v. South West Trains Limited (Case G249/96)* [1998] CR 449; *Ghaidan v. Mendoza* (2002) *The Times*, 5 November.
3   For more general analysis on the effect of the Human Rights Act 1998, see section 4.1.

The Enterprise Act 2002

Why were the Enterprise Act reforms thought necessary?

4.3.21   The rise in the level of home ownership within the UK was abruptly interrupted by the collapse in property values during the recession of the late 1980s and early 1990s. The effect of this recession was that the bankrupt's family home was often in a 'negative equity' situation; i.e. the outstanding secured mort-gage exceeded its achievable sale price and therefore no value was available at that time to distribute to the bankrupt's creditors. As a result, proceedings by the trustee in bankruptcy were often left in abeyance.

4.3.22   Furthermore, for a number of different reasons (such as impecuniosity, the offer was not made or, more likely, the offer was ignored) often neither the bank-rupt nor the bankrupt's family were able or sought to buy out the trustee in bank-ruptcy's interest in the family home while the bankrupt remained undischarged. Where deals were struck, usually a nominal offer on behalf of the bankrupt was acceptable to his trustee in bankruptcy. However, for many bankruptcy cases no deal was concluded. On the bankrupt's discharge, the trustee in bankruptcy obtained his release, and where there had not been a 100 per cent distribution to unsecured creditors, the case went back to the Official Receiver to be filed. Some years later, the Insolvency Service's Protracted Realisations Unit reviewed its historic files and sent letters to those bankrupts inviting them to buy out the Official Receiver's interest registered on the title of their family home. These cases were often returned to the original trustee in bankruptcy and the trustee in bankruptcy would then seek to recover a significant proportion of the increased value of the family home on behalf of the creditors and to cover his own fees.

4.3.23   However, the available equity in the family home was often only present because the bankrupt and/or his family maintained the mortgage repayments whilst the file languished on the Official Receiver's shelves. Furthermore, it was perceived that there was an inconsistency in respective trustees' approaches to dealing with bankrupts' shares in their family homes.[1] Some trustees sold their interest (at a nominal value) back to the bankrupt's families at the time of the bankruptcy, whilst others did not. Bankrupts in the latter scenario were considered unlucky, as their creditors would probably have written off the debt years before. As a result, some critics have branded the pursuit of equity in family homes as merely a fee generation exercise for the trustee in bankruptcy. As a response to this situation, the Government has now implemented the radical reforms introduced by the Enterprise Act 2002.

1   See commentary at the Committee Stage of the Enterprise Act 2002 (16 May 2002).

The 'sunset provision'

4.3.24   In response to this perceived injustice, a late amendment to the Enterprise Act 2002, dubbed the 'sunset provision',[1] was introduced. This will affect how and when a trustee in bankruptcy seeks to secure possession of the family home. This new provision is aimed at avoiding a repetition of the inconsistent approaches adopted by different trustees in bankruptcy during the early 1990s and means that the discharged bankrupt and his family will not now live in fear of losing the family home.

1   The Minister Melanie Johnson's contribution to the debate on the family home when considered at the committee stage (16 May 2002).

4.3.25   Where the family home is the bankrupt's sole or principal residence, the trustee in bankruptcy's interest will after three years (calculated from the date of the bankruptcy) cease to form part of the bankrupt's estate and this interest in the family home will normally automatically revert to the bankrupt.[1] In the event that the family home reverts to the bankrupt, it will not be treated as 'after acquired property'.[2]

1   Insolvency Act 1986, s.238A (as introduced by s.261 of the Enterprise Act 2002).
2   Insolvency Act 1986, s.283A (4) (as introduced by the Enterprise Act 2002).

4.3.26   Once this reversion has taken place, the trustee in bankruptcy will be unable to realise any value in the family home for the benefit of the bankrupt's creditors. The exceptions to this general provision are set out below:

■   The automatic reversion will not apply in the event that within the three-year period the trustee in bankruptcy either:

- realises his interest in the family home;
- applies for an order for sale, order for possession or for a charge[1] on the bankrupt's family home; or
- reaches an agreement with the bankrupt where in return for a specified sum being paid to the bankrupt's estate the family home is in any event released from the bankrupt's estate.

■ In the event that the trustee in bankruptcy's application for either an order for sale or a charge on the family home is dismissed by the court then, unless the court orders otherwise, the trustee in bankruptcy's interest in the family home will cease to be comprised within the bankrupt's estate and will automatically revert to the bankrupt.[2] The trustee in bankruptcy must therefore take care to ensure that such an application is not dismissed, but merely adjourned if for example, the court provides the bankrupt and his family with a longer period to remain in the family home in accordance with the provisions set out within both the TLTA 1996 and the FLA 1996 (see paras.4.3.11 and 4.3.16).

■ In the event that the bankrupt fails to inform his trustee in bankruptcy/ Official Receiver of his interest in a property before the end of three months beginning with the date of bankruptcy, the three-year limitation period will not begin at the date of bankruptcy order, but will begin with the date on which the trustee in bankruptcy/Official Receiver first becomes aware of the bankrupt's interest.[3] It is anticipated that the time when the trustee in bankruptcy (or Official Receiver) first becomes aware of a bankrupt's property interest may be argued in the courts.

■ The court may either shorten, lengthen or disapply this three-year limitation period in certain prescribed circumstances. It is expected that these prescribed circumstances will be set out within the new Insolvency Rules which, at the time of writing, have not been published.[4]

1 I.e. an order under s.313 in Chapter IV of the 1986 Act.
2 Insolvency Act 1986, s.283A (4) (as introduced by s.261 of the Enterprise Act 2002).
3 Insolvency Act 1986, s.283A (5).
4 Insolvency Act 1986, s.283A (6), (7), (9).

The low value exception and minor provisions

4.3.27   The Enterprise Act 2002 also introduces additional amendments to the provisions in connection with the family home:

■ Minor amendments have been made to the process for obtaining a charge on the bankrupt's family home.[1]
■ A low value home exception has been introduced.[2] This arises where the beneficial interest in the family home (which was the bankrupt's, his spouse or former spouse's sole/principal residence) was at the date of the court hearing for a possession, sale or charging order, valued at below a prescribed amount. This prescribed amount will be set by a separate statutory instrument yet to be published. It is certainly the Government's intention that proceedings should only be commenced where value will pass to the creditors. In consequence, a

significant number of the applications advanced in the past by trustees in bankruptcy just to cover their costs may in the future be prohibited.

1 Insolvency Act 1986, s.283A (2) (as introduced by Enterprise Act 2002, s.261(2)) amends s.313 of the 1986 Act.
2 Insolvency Act 1986, s.313A (as introduced by Enterprise Act 2002, s.261(3)).

4.3.28 The new three-year limitation period also applies to bankruptcies which were commenced before s.283A of the 1986 Act came into force.[1] This is important for all historic bankruptcies as once the three-year period has elapsed (calculated from the date when s.283A came into force) the family home will automatically revert back to the bankrupt, subject to the exceptions to the general rule set out in para.4.3.26. A review of all historic bankruptcies should be undertaken by insolvency practitioners to ensure that any applications for possession are commenced within this time limit.

1 Insolvency Act 1986, s.283A (7)–(8) (as introduced by Enterprise Act 2002, s.261).

4.3.29 The sunset provision introduced by the Enterprise Act 2002 effectively provides further protection for most bankrupts, as the family home may be retained if his trustee in bankruptcy/Official Receiver fails to take sufficient steps to realise any value for the benefit of creditors within the limitation period. Therefore, if there is no beneficial value (equity) within the family home during the three years calculated from the commencement of the bankruptcy (from the commencement of the transitional provisions), the bankrupt's creditors may lose out on a significant potential asset within the bankruptcy. However, given that house prices tend to rise only gradually, it is likely that many creditors would have written the debt off after three years in any event and thus this may have only a limited effect on creditors. These provisions will however particularly affect creditors if a trustee in bankruptcy fails to advance the bankruptcy in an expeditious manner and fails to take steps to realise the potential value in the family home. Practitioners should make a careful note of the time limits in order to avoid being exposed to potential claims for failure to secure the family home for the creditor's benefit.

Conclusion

4.3.30 As has been noted in Chapter 1, calls for a so-called 'homestead exception' were made by interested parties during the reform process leading up to the Enterprise Act 2002. The proposals ranged from a complete protection from creditor action to the return to the bankrupt of a specified level of equity (e.g. £20,000) to assist in finding alternative housing. It was argued that such reforms would leave entrepreneurs free from the fear of losing their home, something recognised in the US as a major boon to a thriving entrepreneurial culture. The Government has retreated from introducing such radical reforms but has instead championed the sunset provision and the low value exception.

4.3.31 As a result, so long as the trustee in bankruptcy pays close regard to the considerations set out within this chapter (paying particular attention to the various time limits), if there is available value within the family home, it should be possible eventually to sell the family home. Whilst the legislative reforms since 1986 have made such an application more costly, there is, arguably, increased certainty as to whether the bankrupt and his family may remain in occupation. This in turn may discourage speculative actions and ultimately promote the desired entrepreneurial culture that lies at the heart of the Government's reforms.

4.4   EMPLOYMENT LAW REFORM

TUPE – a hindrance to a rescue culture?

4.4.1   The Transfer of Undertakings (Protection of Employment) Regulations 1981, SI 1981/1794[1] ('TUPE') are frequently accused of hampering the rescue of insolvent businesses.[2] Government research indicates that, at present, only 18 per cent of a total of 14,317 insolvent businesses are sold on as going concerns each year.[3]

---

1   As amended by the Transfer of Undertakings (Protection of Employment) (Amendment) Regulations 1987 (SI 1987/442), the Trade Union Reform and Employment Rights Act 1993 ('TURERA'), the Collective Redundancies and Transfer of Undertakings (Protection of Employment) (Amendment) Regulations 1995 (SI 1995/2587) and the Collective Redundancies and Transfer of Undertakings (Protection of Employment) (Amendment) Regulations 1999 (SI 1995/1925).
2   TUPE gives effect, under UK law, to the European Community Acquired Rights Directive 77/187 EEC as amended by 8221/00 EC ('the Acquired Rights Directive').
3   Preservation rates in 2000 were 18 per cent, 20 per cent in 1999 and 30 per cent in 1998. Transfer of Undertakings (Protection of Employment) Regulations 1981, Government Proposals for Reform, Detailed Background Paper, Employment Relations Directorate Department of Trade and Industry, September 2001.

4.4.2   The aim of TUPE is to safeguard employees' rights when a business changes hands. Essentially, the purchaser of an insolvent business (acquired by means of a disposal to an unconnected third party or an intra-group hive down) is deemed to step into the old employer's contractual shoes. Accordingly, the purchaser will inherit all accrued rights and liabilities connected with these employees' contracts of employment.

4.4.3   In insolvency situations, TUPE can therefore operate to increase the debts of an insolvent business and ultimately frustrate its rescue. The Government has, at long last, recognised this failing and, in September 2001, published a consultation paper setting out its proposed reforms to TUPE.[1] In this section we consider these proposals in light of the current regulations and take a brief look at the likely success of the reforms in achieving their stated aim of promoting the preservation or rescue of insolvent businesses.

---

1   The Government's proposed reforms implement the amendments made to the Acquired Rights Directive in 1998 and adopted in 2001 in the form of the Council Directive (2001/23/EC) ('the Revised Acquired Rights Directive').

The existing position

4.4.4   TUPE applies to the sale or transfer of an undertaking (which is defined widely)[1] situated immediately before the transfer in the UK [2] Currently, TUPE will apply where an insolvent business is sold on as a going concern. Whilst there is conflict between the application of TUPE and the Acquired Rights Directive,[3] it seems clear that TUPE does not apply where the business is liquidated to realise the value of its assets and all its employees dismissed. There are currently two TUPE provisions crucial to an insolvent business and its preservation:

---

1   Regulation 2 (1) of TUPE, as amended TURERA Pt.II, s.33 (2), defines 'Undertaking' as including any 'trade or business' and reg.2 (2) extends the definition to an undertaking or part of an undertaking.
2   Regulation 3(1) of the Transfer of Undertakings (Protection of Employment) Regulations 1981, SI 1981/1794.
3   TUPE gives effect, under UK law, to the European Community Acquired Rights Directive 77/187 EEC as amended by 8221/00 EC ('the Acquired Rights Directive').

(i)   Transfer of employees on existing terms and conditions

4.4.5   Under reg.5(1) of TUPE, contracts of employment are automatically novated to the purchaser of the employer's business. After the transfer, these employees will therefore continue in their jobs, with their existing terms and conditions (apart from occupational pension schemes[1]) and continuity of employment left intact.

---

1   Regulation 7 of the Transfer of Undertakings (Protection of Employment) Regulations 1981, SI 1981/1794 as amended by TURERA, Pt.II, s.33 (5).

4.4.6   The purchaser inherits all accrued rights and liabilities (contractual and statutory) associated with the transfer of the employees' contracts of employment.[1] The acts of the insolvent employer before the transfer in relation to these employees or their contracts are therefore deemed 'visited' on (or done by) the purchaser.[2] For example, liability for inter alia all forms of pre-transfer discrimination,[3] unfair dismissal,[4] personal injury, negligence or breach of a statutory duty,[5] will therefore pass to the purchaser. Compensation for unfair dismissal claims is currently limited to £52,600[6] and the absence of a statutory cap for discrimination awards,[7] means the risk of pre-transfer employment claims is a real deterrent to the sale of an insolvent business as a going concern.

---

1   Regulation 5 (2)(a) of the Transfer of Undertakings (Protection of Employment) Regulations 1981, SI 1981/1794.
2   Regulation 5 (2)(b) of the Transfer of Undertakings (Protection of Employment) Regulations 1981, SI 1981/1794.
3   Equal Pay Act 1970, Sex Discrimination Act 1975 or 1986, National Minimum Wage Act 1998, Race Relations Act 1976, Disability Discrimination Act 1995, Part-Time Workers (Prevention of Less Favourable Treatment) Regulations 2000 or Fixed-Term Workers (Prevention of Less Favourable Treatment) Regulations 2002.
4   Employment Rights Act 1996, s.94.

5 *Taylor* v. *(1) Serviceteam Ltd (2) London Borough of Waltham Forest* IDS December 1997, Brief 602.
6 Increased from £51,700 in February 2002 (s.124 (1)(b) of ERA as amended by SI 2002/10 (Employment Rights (Increase of Limits) Order 2002, Sched.1, para.1).
7 In a recent high profile sex discrimination and unfair dismissal claim (*Bower* v. *Schroder Securities Ltd* (3203104/1999) the tribunal awarded the applicant compensation of over £1.4 million.

4.4.7 Similarly, reg.5 of TUPE operates to prevent a purchaser changing employees' terms and conditions after the transfer either to reduce costs or to bring their contracts in line with those of its existing employees. Changes to terms and conditions can only be made if the variation is unrelated to the transfer[1] or if the employees are dismissed for an economic, technical or organisational reason and then re-employed on varied terms.[2] This is so, even if the changes are made with the consent of the employee in question.[3]

1 *Foreningen af Arbejdsledere i Danmark* v. *Daddy's Dance Hall A/S* [1988] IRLR 315.
2 *Wilson* v. *St Helens Borough Council* and *Meade and Baxendale* v. *British Fuels Limited* [1998] 4 All ER 609. In *Wilson*, Lord Slynn's obiter comments suggest that where a variation to terms and conditions is agreed for an economic or organisational reason, an employment tribunal is entitled to find that the changes were not related to the transfer and therefore not invalid under the principle established in *Foreningen af Arbejdsledere i Danmark* v. *Daddy's Dance Hall A/S* [1988] IRLR 315. However, these comments should be treated with caution as Lord Slynn did not preclude the possibility of a tribunal finding, on the facts, that despite the existence of an economic or organisational considerations, the principal reason for the variation was, nonetheless, the transfer itself.
3 *Foreningen af Arbejdsledere i Danmark* v. *Daddy's Dance Hall A/S* [1988] IRLR 315.

4.4.8 This principle has been blamed for frustrating the intended purpose behind TUPE i.e. safeguarding employees' jobs. Without having the flexibility to vary employees' contracts, the acquisition of an insolvent business will be less attractive to a purchaser and, ultimately, it becomes more likely that the business will be liquidated and its employees dismissed.

(ii)   Transfer-related dismissals

4.4.9 TUPE provides that if an employee is dismissed before or after the transfer by reason of or for a reason connected with the transfer,[1] that dismissal will be automatically unfair unless the employer can show an 'economic, technical, or organisational reason' for the dismissal, entailing a change in the workforce.[2]

1 The transfer or the reason connected with the transfer must be the reason or the principal reason for the dismissal. Transfer of Undertakings (Protection of Employment) Regulations 1981, SI 1981/1794, reg.8 (1).
2 Transfer of Undertakings (Protection of Employment) Regulations 1981, SI 1981/1794, reg.8 (2).

4.4.10 Assuming that a dismissed employee has acquired one year's continuous service with the insolvent employer, the employee would therefore be entitled to bring a claim for unfair dismissal against the new purchaser in an employment tribunal. Such claims must be brought within three months of the date of the dismissal.[1] If successful, the employee could be awarded compensation for his losses up to the maximum award for unfair dismissal, which is at present £52,600.

---

1   Employment Rights Act 1986, Pt.X.

TUPE reform

4.4.11   In September 2001, a public consultation process on the Department of Trade and Industry's (DTI) proposals for reforming TUPE was published. The process closed in December 2001 and the DTI's response to the consultation process and amended regulations are due to be published shortly. Draft regulations are expected to go before Parliament early next year. The proposals are, in part, intended to implement the revised Acquired Rights Directive. However, the proposals also make considerable headway in relaxing TUPE's application to insolvent businesses and promoting their rescue.

4.4.12   The consultation paper aims to bring UK law into line with existing European case law[1] by proposing that the TUPE safeguards will not apply where a business is the subject of formal insolvency proceedings,[2] i.e.:

■   compulsory winding up;
■   bankruptcy proceedings; or
■   (possibly) creditors' voluntary winding-up proceedings.

In addition, the paper recommends the following significant changes for businesses subject to all the differing insolvency regimes.[3]

---

1   *Abels v. Administrative Board of the Bedrijfsvereniging Voor de Metaal-industrie en de Electrotechnische Industrie* [1987] 2 CLMR 406.
2   Under the supervision of a competent public authority which may be an insolvency practitioner, determined by national law.
3   Including (in addition compulsory liquidation, creditors' voluntary liquidation and bankruptcy proceedings) administrations, company and individual voluntary arrangements and creditors' voluntary winding up.

(i)   Pre-existing debts

4.4.13   The consultation document proposes that an insolvent business' pre-existing debts to its employees will not pass to the transferee to the extent that these debts are guaranteed by the National Insurance Fund under the Employment Rights Act 1996, Part XII (i.e. claims for up to eight weeks' pay). For debts over and above these claims, the DTI proposes two options:

■   that they pass to the purchaser; or
■   that they remain with the insolvent business.

The first option undoubtedly offers employees a high degree of protection, whereas the second option comes down firmly on the side of the purchaser. The DTI have since confirmed that they favour the first option.

(ii)   Transfer-related changes to terms and conditions

4.4.14   In addition, the DTI recommends that insolvent businesses or their pur-
chasers should be free to negotiate transfer-related changes to terms and conditions, provided that the changes:

- are agreed between the insolvent business (or the new owner) and appropriate employee representatives;[1]
- are intended to ensure the survival of the business and preserve employment
  opportunities; and
- are not contrary to national law and practice (e.g. the Minimum Wage Act
  1998).

These proposals will certainly make the purchase of an insolvent business as a
going concern a more viable proposition and should ensure that the purchaser
can agree the removal or reduction in any overly generous terms and conditions.

---

1   The definition of appropriate representative will be consistent with that used for information and consultation purposes (Transfer of Undertakings (Protection of
Employment) Regulations 1981, SI 1984/1794, reg.10).

(iii)   Employee liability information

4.4.15   Another important change envisaged by the consultation document is
the obligation on insolvent businesses to provide the purchaser with employee
liability information. The proposals should go some way to increasing the
transparency of the transfer process. Ultimately, both the purchaser and the
transferring employees should know where they stand.

4.4.16   Written notification is to be given to the purchaser of all the rights
and obligations that the insolvent business owes to its transferring employees.
This should include: sickness, maternity, disciplinary and health and safety
records; equal opportunities monitoring; and details of any contractual and non-
contractual benefits. If an insolvent business complies with these provisions, it
should minimise the risk of unknown liabilities: for example, an undisclosed
employee on maternity leave exercising her right to return to her job six months
after a transfer.

4.4.17   The insolvent business is also obliged to update the transferee of any
changes to this information between initial notification and completion of the
transfer. This is intended to prevent any sharp practice by the transferring
business, such as increasing employees' salaries or benefits just before transfer.

4.4.18   The proposals state that information may be disclosed in instalments but
must be provided 'in good time'. If circumstances mean that this is not reasonably
practicable, disclosure should take place as soon reasonably practicable and in
any event no later than the completion of the transfer. What constitutes 'good
time' will vary according to the circumstances and the timescale of the individual
transfer. However, in general, these proposals should, where time permits, ensure
that the majority of potential liabilities are disclosed pre-transfer and that any
necessary reductions can be made to the purchase price.

4.4.19   The consultation paper proposes two possible remedies for failure to provide employee liability information:

- An award of damages against the insolvent employer. It is however recognised that the purchaser's loss would be difficult to quantify as liability for employees' claims would pass to the purchaser in any event. Also, there remains a question mark over the recoverability of any losses from what may well be a heavily insolvent employer.
- The ability of the purchaser to join the insolvent business as a party to any proceedings arising out of the breach. An employee could therefore issue proceedings against the insolvent business *and* the new owner and compensation would be apportioned between the entities on a just and equitable basis.

The Government has indicated that it favours the latter option.

Conclusions

4.4.20   The reforms are clearly intended to boost the 'rescue culture' and to promote the transfer of insolvent businesses as going concerns. Certainly, the draft regulations have ironed out uncertainty as to when and to what extent TUPE will apply to insolvent businesses. In addition, the information obligations make significant advances on the issue of businesses withholding or providing inadequate employee liability information. Finally, the proposals afford the purchaser the flexibility to reorganise the business following transfer by varying terms and conditions.

4.4.21   The regulations did not go as far as many employers would have liked: i.e. cancelling pre-transfer debts not guaranteed by the National Insurance Fund. The Government has been forced to strike a balance between its dual aims of protecting the transferring employees rights and promoting a rescue culture. The reforms remain far-reaching and, if they are adopted in this format, should have a beneficial effect on the UK economy. However, only experience will tell us whether the regulations will achieve their stated aim and until the regulations are finalised and introduced, practitioners will have to wait and see.

4.5   CROSS-BORDER INSOLVENCY

An overview

4.5.1   Corporate insolvency increasingly transcends international boundaries, yet there is no body of international law which governs insolvency with a cross-border dimension. Significant developments in cross-border insolvency have taken place since 1986. The need for such development has been highlighted by high profile international insolvencies such as BCCI, Polly Peck, Enron, Maxwell Communications and Barings Plc. Furthermore, in Europe, closer economic integration has increased the freedom of movement of goods, labour and capital and intensified the need for uniform measures to settle disputes and deal with cross border interests.

4.5.2   At common law it has long been established that the English courts will exercise their discretion to recognise the authority of officeholders appointed in a foreign jurisdiction; each case is assessed on its own facts. Consequently, a foreign appointed officeholder wishing to deal with assets of an insolvent company within the UK will find the outcome difficult to predict. In the majority of cases, to take control and manage a business operation including taking responsibility for employees, the officeholder will need to commence insolvency proceedings in the UK.

Section 426 of the Insolvency Act 1986

4.5.3   For those states which are 'relevant countries or territories' within the meaning of s.426 of the 1986 Act, recognition is somewhat easier.

4.5.4   A number of countries and territories were so designated by the Co-operation of Insolvency Courts (Designation of Relevant Countries and Territories) Order 1986[1] effective 29 December 1986. Further statutory instruments have added to the list of countries and territories, which now comprises:

- Anguilla
- Australia
- Bahamas
- Bermuda
- Botswana
- Brunei
- Canada
- Cayman Islands
- Falkland Islands
- Gibraltar
- Guernsey (including Alderney and Sark)
- Hong Kong
- Republic of Ireland
- Malaysia
- Montserrat
- New Zealand
- St Helena
- South Africa
- Turks and Caicos Islands
- Tuvalu
- Virgin Islands

---

1   SI 1986/2123.

4.5.5   The UK courts are obliged to assist officeholders appointed in these countries and territories. The courts may even allow the officeholders to exercise the powers conferred on UK officeholders under the 1986 Act, such as those powers of inquiry contained in s.236, should their own jurisdictions contain more restrictive powers.

4.5.6   Despite the statutory obligation, it took the courts some time to conclude that a request made by a foreign court under s.426 of the 1986 Act is one in which they have no alternative but to assist.[1]

---

1   See *Hughes v. Hannover-Rucksversicherungs AG* [1997] BCC 921; *Re Focus Insurance Co Limited* [1996] BCC 659; *Re J N Taylor Pty Limited* [1998] BRIR 347; *Southern Equities Corporation Ltd* (2000) 2 WLR 114.

EC Regulation on Insolvency Proceedings

4.5.7   For insolvency practitioners appointed within a member state of the European Union, the problem regarding recognition and ability to deal with assets in the UK has also eased. Work on a European convention for insolvency began in the early 1960s. After many drafts and varying degrees of enthusiasm for the project, the reform has recently been introduced.

4.5.8   The EC Regulation on Insolvency Proceedings[1] (the 'Regulation') came into effect throughout the EU (excluding Denmark) on 31 May 2002. Should greater political and economic harmonisation be implemented, the development of a pan-European insolvency code could result. In the meantime, the Regulation is limited to setting out how officeholders perform their functions in relation to companies with interests in more than one EU member state. The Regulation does not apply to insurance undertakings, credit institutions (banks) or investment undertakings which provide services involving the holding of funds or securities on behalf of third parties and collective investment undertakings (Article 1.2). Each instead has, or will have, their own EU regulation dealing with the case of insolvency for that particular type of company.[2]

---

1   Council Regulation (EC) No 1346/2000 of 29 May 2000.
2   EC Directive on the Re-organisation and Winding Up of Insurance Undertakings (Directive 2001/17/EC) adopted on 19 March 2001. EC Directive 2001/24/EC adopted 4 April 2001 deals with credit institutions.

4.5.9   Importantly, the Regulation does not aim to harmonise the insolvency laws of individual EU member states. The Regulation does however have important consequences for the manner in which cross-frontier issues are dealt with, in particular the question of the appropriate jurisdiction in which the insolvency proceedings should be commenced and the recognition of officeholders across the EU.

4.5.10   The Regulation applies to 'collective insolvency proceedings' (Article 1.1). In the UK these comprise:

- winding up by or subject to the supervision of the court;
- creditors' voluntary winding up (provided that the winding up is recognised by the court);
- administration;
- company and individual voluntary arrangements;
- bankruptcy and sequestration.

The Regulation does not therefore apply to non-insolvency proceedings such as members' voluntary liquidation, or winding up on the grounds of public interest.

4.5.11   The Regulation does not apply to any form of receivership, which is rightly not viewed as a collective insolvency procedure, but rather the realisation of security by an individual creditor. This means that if a UK company has an operation in another member state and an administrative receiver was appointed in the UK, the administrative receiver will not have the advantages of recognition afforded to, say, an administrator. This may have important practical consequences for any secured creditor currently able to appoint an administrative receiver, who may instead prefer to see an administrator appointed.

4.5.12   The Regulation distinguishes between 'main' and 'territorial' (or 'secondary') proceedings (Article 3). This distinction is vital as main proceedings will have 'universal scope' and 'aim at encompassing all of the debtor's assets'.[1] As we shall see, territorial/secondary proceedings are more limited in scope and subservient to the main proceedings.

---

1   Recital 12.

4.5.13   The Regulation provides that the main proceedings should be commenced (or in the wording of the Regulation 'opened') in the member state in which the debtor's 'main centre of interest' is situated. This term is not however expressly defined, although the recitals indicate this to be the place where the debtor conducts the administration of his interest on a regular basis. In the case of a company, there is a rebuttable presumption that this will mean the company's registered office.[1] The adoption of this definition straddles two concepts used to determine the issue of jurisdiction across Europe. In certain countries, including the UK, the place of incorporation of the corporate entity is deemed prima facie evidence to determine jurisdiction. In other countries, a 'real seat' doctrine has been adopted, whereby the courts consider where assets are held, business carried on, or decisions taken. The introduction of the concept of a debtor's 'main centre of interest' may therefore result in the courts of different countries applying their own national tests for determining jurisdiction. The opportunity for conflicting decisions when the same facts are presented to different courts is readily apparent. The decision of the European Court in *Centros Limited* v. *Erhvervs-og Selskabsstyrelsen*[2] has however been interpreted to mean that in the future the incorporation doctrine is to be favoured over the real seat doctrine. This could pave the way for a uniform approach in the future.

---

1   Article 3.1.
2   (1999) 1 ECR 1459.

4.5.14   Where main proceedings are opened, without the need for any further formality, the officeholder is recognised throughout all other EU member states. The officeholder must merely produce a certified copy of the decision appointing him or a certificate issued by his national court.[1]

---

1   Article 19.

4.5.15 Where a debtor does not have a main centre of interest, but merely 'an establishment' in a EU member state (i.e. a place of operations where non-transitory economic activity with human means or goods is carried out as defined in Article 2 (h)) 'territorial' insolvency proceedings may be commenced.[1] Where territorial proceedings are commenced *after* main proceedings have been opened they are termed 'secondary' proceedings and must be winding-up proceedings.[2]

1 Article 3.2.
2 Article 3.3.

4.5.16 The distinction between main and secondary/territorial insolvency proceedings is of great importance for the following reasons. This is because where main proceedings are commenced:

■ The applicable law governing the opening, conduct and closure of the insolvency will be that of the 'State of the opening of proceedings'.[1] The liquidator in the main proceedings may therefore exercise all powers conferred by the law of the EU member state opening the proceedings in any other EU member state. This right is conditional upon no other insolvency proceedings having been opened, as Articles 5 to 15 provide that the laws applicable to the following matters are those of the EU member state in which secondary proceedings are commenced:

  – security rights and other rights in rem;
  – rights of set-off;
  – reservation of title issues;
  – contracts relating to immovable property;
  – matters relating to payment systems and financial markets;
  – matters relating to contracts of employment;
  – rights of the debtor in immovable property, a ship or aircraft subject to registration in a public register;
  – matters concerning Community patents, trade marks or similar rights;
  – proceedings relating to acts detrimental to all of the creditors (e.g in the UK actions regarding preferences, transactions at an undervalue etc.);
  – disposition of immovable property, a ship or aircraft subject to registration in a public register, or securities whose existences presupposes registration by the debtor after the opening of insolvency proceedings;
  – matters concerning the effect of insolvency proceedings on pending actions.

■ The officeholder has the right to remove assets from other EU member states subject only to the rights of creditors with a proprietary interest in those assets (i.e. secured creditors or suppliers under a retention of title) from whom consent must be obtained.[2]

■ The officeholder has the right to commence legal actions in any other EU member state to set aside transactions in the interests of creditors.[3]

■ Secondary proceedings can only be commenced to deal with the assets of the company situated in the member state and can only be winding-up proceedings.

1   Article 4.
2   Article 18 (1).
3   Article 18 (2).

4.5.17 However, where territorial proceedings have been commenced prior to the main proceedings and are of a 'rescue' nature, the liquidator in the main proceedings may request that those proceedings are converted to winding-up proceedings.[1]

1   Article 37.

4.5.18 In addition, if territorial proceedings are of a winding up nature, the liquidator in the main proceedings may request a stay in those proceedings for up to three months and a stay will be granted unless manifestly not in the interests of the creditors in the main proceedings.[1] Officeholders in main and secondary/territorial proceedings are obliged to communicate relevant information and co-operate.[2]

1   Article 33 (1).
2   Article 31.

4.5.19 It should be remembered that the Regulation does not attempt to harmonise insolvency law across the EU, although there are moves to create a set of agreed principles in international insolvency. Further, most businesses operating across Europe do so through subsidiary companies established in each jurisdiction, rather than through branch offices. As such, main insolvency proceedings would need to be commenced for each company in each own jurisdiction. There is no express provision for co-operation in such circumstances. Furthermore, there is no ability to deal with companies within the group which may be solvent, nor does the Regulation introduce the US concept of 'substantive consolidation' which enables a number of related group companies to be treated as one for the purposes of Chapter 11 reconstruction. Consequently, in such instances the Regulation may be of little assistance.

Uncitral Model Law

4.5.20 The need for cross-border co-operation to deal with the insolvency of a multinational company is clearly not confined to the European Union. In close co-operation with the International Federation of Insolvency Practitioners (INSOL) the United Nations Commission on International Trade (UNCITRAL) undertook a review of international insolvency developments with a view to developing an international code of conduct. In doing so, UNCITRAL had the following objectives:

- To secure and foster greater co-operation between courts.
- To provide greater certainty for trade and investment.
- To ensure fairness and efficiency of insolvency procedures so as to protect all creditors and other interested persons, including the debtor.
- To protect and maximise the value of debtor's assets.
- Where possible to enable the rescue of businesses to protect investment and preserve employment.

4.5.21   The review led to the development of the UNCITRAL Model Law on Cross-Border Insolvency ('Model Law'), adopted on 30 May 1997. The Model Law is a 32-paragraph draft legislative text offered by UNCITRAL for adoption by the participant countries, i.e the 'Enacting States', and intended to encourage the Enacting States to co-operate and become 'efficient and achieve optimal results in the administration of cross-border insolvencies'.

4.5.22   Article 25(1) states that Enacting States shall 'co-operate to the maximum extent possible' with foreign courts and foreign representatives. The Model Law entitles those responsible for the administration of re-organisation or liquidation of the debtor's assets and affairs to communicate directly with foreign courts and foreign representatives. It ensures that no formal decision is required to 'recognise' that foreign representative. Whilst the English courts have long recognised the authority of a foreign liquidator to apply directly to the court, the Model Law places this on a statutory footing for all Enacting States.

4.5.23   The use of the Model Law is voluntary, and ultimately its success or otherwise will rest on the number of States which adopt and implement it. Section 14 of the Insolvency Act 2000 provides that the Model Law may be adopted by the UK and effected by statutory instrument, with or without modification (see para.3.8.5). The United States has also adopted the Model Law in Chapter 15 of the US Bankruptcy Code. However, it appears that widespread implementation of the Model Law by the international community is held in abeyance, while countries wait to see which others are willing to adopt it.[1]

---

1   With the Republican Party success in the Congressional Elections of November 2002 there is concern that bankruptcy law reform and therefore implementation of the UNCITRAL Model Law have been shelved.

4.5.24   It is however worth noting that the Model Law places great stress on the continued application of local laws. It does not seek to establish an international insolvency code applicable in all cases. This probably reflects the virtual impossibility of drafting a new globally applicable law on insolvency, due to differences in legal cultures, and the impact of economic and political considerations. In any event, even if such a code was developed it is doubtful that it would be capable of worldwide agreement. The hope is however that as the number of States which adopt the Model Law increases, greater co-operation between countries will lead to the establishment of generally accepted international insolvency principles.

4.5.25   UNCITRAL emphasises individual States' responsibility to review their own domestic legislation to determine if and how cross-border aspects are best dealt with. The Model Law provides a framework for resolving cross-border issues within the context of domestic legislation and is expressly drafted to be subservient to any Treaty or other obligation of the Enacting State. For instance, in the UK the EC Regulation on Insolvency Proceedings will have primacy. Like so much of the insolvency legislation, the Model Law is expressly stated to have no direct application to banks or insolvent insurance companies.

Recognition

4.5.26   The key to any efficient cross-border insolvency process is the recognition of a duly appointed insolvency practitioner to administer the organisation/liquidation of a debtor's assets or affairs.

4.5.27   The Model Law defines 'foreign proceedings' as being any collective judicial and/or administrative proceeding. In the UK this will include court supervised compulsory liquidations and administrations and most probably creditors' voluntary liquidations and company voluntary arrangements (as these are both collective procedures, recognised or capable of recognition by the court). It is clear that administrative receivership will not be covered.

4.5.28   A 'foreign representative' is defined as a person or body authorised in foreign proceedings to administer the reorganisation and/or liquidation of the debtor's assets or affairs.

4.5.29   As in the EC Regulation, the Model Law distinguishes between various types of insolvency proceedings. Foreign insolvency proceedings are deemed to be the 'main proceedings' if commenced in a state which the debtor has its 'centre of main interest'. Like the EC Regulation, this is not defined, but again in the case of a corporate debtor, the centre of main interest is presumed to be the registered office of the corporate debtor, unless proved to the contrary. Non-main proceedings take place in the State where the debtor has an 'establishment'. This is defined as any place of operations where the debtor carries out a non-transitory activity with human means, goods or services.[1]

---

1 See comparison to para.4.5.14.

4.5.30   The Model Law provides that a foreign representative is entitled to apply directly to the court of an Enacting State. No additional formality or legal process needs to be undertaken. Recognition of the foreign representative by the Enacting State remains a matter for the court's discretion and may not be granted if it would be manifestly contrary to the public policy of the Enacting State.

4.5.31   The foreign representative may also apply for insolvency proceedings to be commenced in the Enacting State, if this would be particularly useful to safeguard the assets of the debtors, in cases where there appears to be some risk of dissipation. The Model Law also provides a right for a foreign representative to intervene and/or participate in the domestic insolvency proceedings of the Enacting State.

Procedure for recognition

4.5.32   The Model Law provides that any application for recognition should be accompanied by a certified copy of the decision commencing the foreign proceedings and the necessary document appointing the foreign representative. This may be replaced by a certificate from a foreign court, or any other acceptable means of evidence for both the proceedings and the appointment.

4.5.33   There is no need for further authentication of the documents in any particular prescribed manner and each Enacting State is entitled to presume the authenticity of the documents provided. The Model Law also introduces a concept of 'mutual trust', such that the courts of the Enacting State will not look behind the decision which commenced the foreign proceedings and/or led to the appointment of the foreign representative.

The effect of recognition

4.5.34   The Model Law provides for the following:

- An automatic stay on the commencement or continuation of insolvency proceedings concerned with the debtor's assets. The Model Law however makes it clear that the stay is overridden by such powers as creditors may exercise by virtue of local domestic laws. For instance a receivership would not seem to be stayed due to 'main proceedings' being commenced in a foreign jurisdiction.
- Any party affected by any stay may apply to the court of the Enacting State for relief.
- The court of the Enacting State may grant appropriate relief to protect assets as requested by the foreign representative. This may include a stay on enforcement action being taken against any debtors' assets, examination of witnesses, or the entrusting of assets to the foreign representative.
- The court may permit the foreign representative to distribute assets located within the territory of the Enacting State.
- The foreign representative will have standing to initiate actions in the Enacting State; this will, however, be subject to any such applicable local laws.
- The foreign representative has a right to intervene in any proceedings in which the debtor is a party.

Pre-action relief

4.5.35   The Model Law also provides that where relief is 'urgently needed' the foreign representative can apply before recognition is determined if necessary to protect the debtors' assets and if it serves the interests of the creditors generally. The courts of the Enacting State have a discretion to make such orders as are necessary to protect and preserve asset values if it is believed that the assets are susceptible to devaluation, perishable or are otherwise in jeopardy.

Conclusion

4.5.36   The EC Regulation on Insolvency Proceedings has had an immediate impact on insolvency custom and practice. As practitioners become more used to the concepts behind the Regulation it is likely that we will see greater use of foreign courts in the collection of assets and/or restructuring of insolvent companies. This area is likely to be one of the fastest developing areas for insolvency law and practice during the next few years.

4.5.37   Given its important social and economic consequences for a country, domestic insolvency law is closely identified with a country's national interest. For this reason, progress to integrate insolvency regimes and produce an international code has been slow and difficult and is, perhaps, unachievable. However, this brief summary of international developments in insolvency since 1986 does show a desire for greater co-operation between respective jurisdictions. Increasing co-operation should lead to greater uniformity in insolvency which in turn will greatly assist the regulation of multi-national insolvencies.

4.6   INTERNATIONAL CORPORATE RECONSTRUCTION

Introduction

4.6.1   This book focuses principally on the statutory reforms affecting insolvency law since 1986. In Chapter 2, we looked at how differing methods of business rescue are used across the world and in section 4.5 we considered how legislative reforms are likely to influence cross-border insolvency. However, one area outside of the statutory framework, which is of great importance in the development of world wide corporate rescue models, is the informal work out.

4.6.2   The financial reconstruction of corporate vehicles outside of statutory confines defies categorisation. Informal arrangements can range from an individual creditor giving additional time for payment of an account, to major corporate restructuring involving debt for equity swops and distressed debt financing.

4.6.3   The advantage of informal work outs over a statutory corporate rescue procedure is that they are entirely flexible in both content and timescale. Furthermore, statutory rescue procedures in the UK are aimed at dealing with a single corporate vehicle, whereas informal work outs can apply to a whole group, spanning several countries and may include companies that are not necessarily insolvent.

The 'London Approach'

4.6.4   Unique amongst central banks, the Bank of England has a long tradition of involvement in corporate restructuring. Starting in the 1920s, the Bank adopted a 'hands on' approach in leading and formulating proposals for corporate restructuring. It did so where it was in the national interest, for instance if there were likely to be national economic consequences arising from the failure of any leading UK company or loss to a UK financial institution. The Bank's role was principally to co-ordinate the approach taken by high street (and other) banks and the money markets when dealing with a distressed company. The Bank facilitated discussions between lenders and debtors and acted as a peacemaker between various competing secured creditors.

4.6.5   This is a non-statutory role derived indirectly from its supervisory functions over the UK banking industry. However, in the early 1990s, the Bank increasingly moved away from direct involvement in the actual process of corporate reconstruction and instead issued a set of guidelines to assist work out proposals in multi-bank situations. These principles were derived from informal practices adopted in most multi-bank work outs and have become known as 'the London Approach'.

4.6.6   The key principles of the London Approach are:

■   Willingness by creditors to consider a non-statutory resolution to a company's financial difficulties, without recourse to individual creditors' enforcement action.

■   An independent review initiated by the banks and conducted by an independent investigative accountant. The review assesses the company's future viability, the present financial situation and the potential liabilities to the banks and other creditors in circumstances where the company would otherwise be liquidated.

■   While the review takes place the banks agree to withhold taking action and continue existing lines of credit to preserve suppliers and ensure customer confidence and the ongoing trade of the business.

■   Where an immediate requirement for additional funding exists, some or all of the existing lenders will act together in a syndicate, with each participating pro rata based on their exposure to the company. Often where proposals to restructure the insolvent business are eventually put forward, any new money introduced by the syndicate will be afforded 'priority security'. This is important, as it is not otherwise available within the UK statutory framework.

■   A single bank may be designated to lead the review process, to formulate proposals and hold discussions with the existing management of the debtor company. This 'lead bank' will generally be that with the largest exposure.

■   A committee will generally be formed, to whom the lead bank and the debtor company can report.

4.6.7   After the review process has been completed, a calculation of the loss that each bank may suffer on a theoretical liquidation will be made. An assessment of the seniority of claims will also take place with a view to sharing the loss between banks within the same category of lender. The long term viability of the distressed company will also be considered, with potential financial support (e.g. a creditors' interest holiday or the introduction of new money etc.) being granted in exchange for structural and managerial changes (e.g. the sale of an unprofitable part of the business or a change in management).

4.6.8   The London Approach potentially offers a higher rate of recovery for participating banks than would otherwise be available through statutory insolvency procedures. Importantly, it introduces a high degree of flexibility in negotiation between the banks and the distressed company. However, because the Bank of England no longer has a supervisory function over the UK banking industry (this is now exercised by the Financial Services Authority), the importance of the London Approach has diminished. As the Bank has become less involved in the process of restructuring, policing the London Approach has become more problematic. Other factors common to any forms of informal work out, which are explored later in this section, have also contributed to the Bank's decreasing role.

Development of global principles for multi-creditor work out

4.6.9   The globalisation of business and finance means that both domestic and foreign lenders have become more involved in major international corporate restructuring. This is one reason why the London Approach is of less importance to international reconstruction. Instead, organisations such as the International Monetary Fund, the World Bank and the United Nations have become increasingly concerned with this problem and sought to develop both statutory and non-statutory techniques for corporate rescue. At the forefront of the development of an international understanding in cross-border corporate reconstruction has been INSOL (the International Federation of Insolvency Professionals).

4.6.10   In October 2000, INSOL International published eight global principles for multi-creditor work outs. These principles, derived from the London Approach are as follows:

- Where appropriate, creditors should co-operate to ensure there is a stand still period from creditor action in which the debtor's financial difficulties can be evaluated and proposals formulated.
- During the stand still, creditors should expect that their position, as against other creditors, will not be prejudiced.
- During the stand still the debtors should not take any action which may adversely affect the creditors' position either collectively or individually.
- A creditors' committee should be formed to co-ordinate the creditors' response to the debtor's proposals.
- During the stand still, the debtor should provide the creditors, the committee and/or their professional advisers with all relevant information to enable them to make informed choices.
- Proposals should reflect applicable law and the relative positions of the creditors at the commencement of the stand still period.
- Information obtained by creditors in the course of the process should be treated as confidential unless it is already in the public domain.
- If funding is required either during the stand still period or as part of the restructuring plan, this should, if practical, be afforded priority status.

4.6.11   Together with this statement of principles, work is ongoing by the IMF and World Bank to instil efficient and worldwide standards of corporate reconstruction. It is however recognised that establishing worldwide standards in corporate reconstruction will be difficult owing to the differing cultures and approaches taken by countries to insolvency (explored in detail in Chapter 2).

The future of informal work out models

4.6.12   The development of complex financing agreements, the trade in distressed debt and the use of securitisation and derivatives have mitigated against an informal approach to work outs. This is because there is now a greater number of parties involved in the negotiation process during corporate reconstruction and the differing interests of each leads to greater conflict between these creditors. As the London Approach and the INSOL Model are based on unanimity, corporate work outs can be seriously delayed or become incapable of achievement.

4.6.13   Informal work out models commonly envisage a stand still period, but do not possess the necessary degree of compulsion that is available with a statutory moratorium. Interestingly, plans to introduce an enforceable moratorium in corporate work outs are being discussed, but it is more likely that individual countries will need to recognise the need for a robust but flexible statutory framework to assist this process.

4.6.14   Other disadvantages to the informal work out model include the excessive demand on management time for both the debtor and creditors. The need for professional advice for both the debtor and creditors means that they also tend to be immensely expensive. There is also a conflict between the position of secured creditors and ordinary trade creditors who may require immediate payment. These factors have emphasised the need for individual countries to develop statutory measures to ensure the continued use of international corporate reconstruction.

Schemes of arrangement

4.6.15   The use of schemes of arrangement in the UK as a means of corporate rescue has a long history. Schemes of arrangement were common in the late nineteenth Century and were used extensively during the years of pre-war depression. Their use has however declined recently as many of their uses in facilitating corporate rescue have been taken over by the statutory procedures introduced in the 1986 legislation.

4.6.16   Section 425 of the Companies Act 1985 gives the court power to sanction a scheme between a company and its creditors. The advantage of an approved scheme is that the court has the power to bind dissenting minority creditors. Importantly, the court can also bind those creditors who cannot be traced or ascertained, something that is not available when a company enters into a voluntary arrangement.

4.6.17   Schemes of arrangement have however been of particular use in the insurance industry, where the administration process was not available until 31 May 2002.[1] The particular need to deal with future claims makes schemes of arrangement a good vehicle for dealing with the potential and actual corporate insolvency of an insurer. This is because often an insurance company has liabilities running over many many years, yet cannot readily identify its potential creditors, or even if it can, it cannot accurately assess the level of claims that they may have in the future. Where the company is potentially insolvent, it is only right that there is some procedure to bring certainty to those creditors whose claims can be ascertained. The scheme of arrangement can therefore provide a procedure for dealing with claims in the future.

---

1   Pursuant to s.360 of the Financial Services and Markets Act 2000 and the Financial Services and Markets Act 2000 (Administration Orders relating to insurers) Order 2002, SI 2002/1242; the procedures relating to administration orders in the 1986 Act were made available to insurers.

4.6.18   There are however distinct disadvantages with the scheme of arrangement procedure. Different classes of creditors need to be represented at separate meetings and each class needs to vote by a requisite majority in favour of the scheme. It is the petitioner's responsibility to ascertain into which class interested parties fall. The preparation of schemes therefore can be slow, complicated and expensive. Previously, a further disadvantage was that the company needed to hold the class meetings of creditors prior to court approval being obtained, although this difficulty has in part been resolved by recent practice directions.

4.6.19   With readily accessible corporate rescue procedures being introduced by the Enterprise Act 2002, it is considered unlikely that there will be a revival of Company Act schemes of arrangement other than in specialist areas, where they remain of great use.

Financial Services and Markets Act 2000

4.6.20   The Financial Services Authority (the 'FSA') has considerable powers and rights to intervene and safeguard the position of investors, where a firm authorised by the FSA to carry out investment activity runs into financial difficulty. This is particularly relevant where that firm holds the investor's funds.

4.6.21   Part XXIV of the Financial Services and Markets Act 2000 (the 'FSMA 2000') deals with the FSA's powers of intervention with respect to an insolvent authorised firm. The provisions fall into the following categories:

■   Powers to initiate insolvency procedures.
■   Rights to intervene in insolvency proceedings commenced by third parties.
■   Special provisions dealing with the insolvency of insurers.

4.6.22   In particular, the FSA has the following specific powers:

■   Section 356 of the FSMA 2000 enables the FSA to participate in the CVA of a company which is an authorised person (i.e. regulated by the FSA) and the FSA may challenge the provisions of the CVA.

■   Section 359 of the FSMA 2000 provides that the FSA may present an administration petition in respect of a company which is or has been an authorised person, or which is or has been an authorised representative, or which is or has carried on a regulated activity in contravention of a general condition. The FSA is also entitled to be heard at an administration petition and an administrator is under a duty to inform the FSA without delay if the company has been carrying on an activity in contravention of a general provision of the FSMA 2000.

■   In the case of an administrative receivership, the FSA may apply to the court for directions and/or may be entitled to be heard at such an application.[1]

■   In the case of a voluntary winding up, the FSA may make an application to the court for directions.[2]

■   An insurer effecting or carrying on non-term insurance business may not be wound up voluntarily without the consent of the FSA.

■   The FSA may petition for the compulsory winding up of an authorised person or participate in the winding-up petition hearing.

■   A liquidator is under a duty to report to the FSA if the company is carrying on a regulated activity in contravention of any general prohibition.

1   Insolvency Act 1986, ss.35 and 41.
2   Insolvency Act 1986, s.112.

4.6.23   Consequently, in instances where an insolvency practitioner is advising an insolvent company which is or which may have been an 'authorised person' or 'authorised firm', the views and co-operation of the FSA are of great importance.

PART III ENTERPRISE ACT 2002 – CORPORATE INSOLVENCY REFORM

5 THE ABOLITION OF ADMINISTRATIVE RECEIVERSHIP?

5.1 RECEIVERSHIP

An historical perspective

5.1.1 Receivership is not, in reality, an insolvency procedure in that it lacks any collective approach to the problems that corporate insolvency poses for the company, its members and creditors. It remains a remedy open solely to a secured creditor and is generally used as a method of realising secured assets in settlement of a debt.

5.1.2 The roots of receivership lie in the equitable remedy created by the Court of Chancery in the sixteenth Century. In the case of *Hopkins* v. *Worcester and Birmingham Canal (Proprietors)*,[1] Gifford VC described the equitable remedy of appointing a receiver as 'one of the oldest remedies in this Court'.

---

1 (1868) LR 6 EQ 437.

5.1.3 In modern times receivership has almost exclusively been a matter of contractual agreement. This development arose from the practice of legal draftsmen in the nineteenth Century including provisions in charge documentation which permitted a lender to appoint a receiver without reference to the court. Private appointments therefore came to overtake the use of court appointed receivers.

5.1.4 Receivership is also a concept that is unrecognised in most other countries.

> The private receiver is a legal status unknown in the United States and research has disclosed no authority for any United States Court dealing with such an entity.[1]

It has however been adopted and developed in several Commonwealth jurisdictions, most notably Canada, New Zealand and Australia. Indeed the law in these jurisdictions has provided judicial guidance which has assisted the development of the UK's law in this area.

---

1 *Clarks & Co Limited* v. *Rockwell International Corp* (1977) 441 F.SUPP 792.

Receivership and administrative receivership distinguished

5.1.5 It is difficult to precisely define the term 'receiver' due to its historical antecedence and the common misuse of the term. In the case of *Re Manchester and Norford RLY Company*,[1] Sir George Jessell drew a distinction between a 'receiver' who was appointed to receive income and pay outgoings and a manager (or receiver and manager) who could buy and sell and carry on the trade and business. The terminology has however become blurred owing to the fact that a debenture holder appointing a 'receiver' is almost certainly appointing a receiver and manager, if not by name, then by virtue of the powers provided under the debenture. For the purpose of this text, any reference to a receiver will mean a receiver or manager rather than a statutory receiver.[2]

---

1 (1888) 14 ChD 641.
2 One appointed under Law of Property Act 1925 who has power only to receive income.

5.1.6 However, a distinction is drawn between a 'receiver' and an 'administrative receiver'. Such a distinction was recommended by the Cork Committee and is a major innovation of the 1986 Act. The definition of an administrative receiver is contained within s.29 of the 1986 Act and is as follows:

(a) a receiver or manager of the whole (or substantially the whole) of a company's property appointed by or on behalf of the holders of any debentures of the company secured by a charge which, as created, was a floating charge, or by such charge and one or more other securities; or

(b) a person would be such a receiver or manager, but for the appointment of some other person as the receiver of part of the company's property.

5.1.7 It is important to keep in mind that the provisions contained within Part III of the 1986 Act will remain in place and are unaffected by the reforms introduced by the Enterprise Act 2002. However, the Government has moved the control and limited the ability of secured creditors to use administrative receivership as a method of debt recovery. First, we shall examine why this has been done.

Why reform a successful procedure?

5.1.8 Despite the somewhat unique status of administrative receivership and the fact that it is not a true collective insolvency procedure, administrative receivership can be regarded as a highly successful tool to rescue businesses swiftly, efficiently and generally at significantly less cost than would be associated with a court appointed officeholder. This is perhaps somewhat at odds with the study undertaken by Julian Franks and Oren Sussman and published in April 2000[1] (sponsored by the DTI/Treasury Review Group on Company Rescue and

Business Reconstruction Mechanisms), which analysed the results obtained by companies and their creditors following administrative receivership.

---

1 'The Cycle of Corporate Distress, Rescue and Dissolution. A Study of Small and Medium Size UK Companies.' Institute of Finance and Accounting Working Paper 306–200.

5.1.9 The study was based on the private records of three UK clearing banks and examined all companies entering the banks' rescue units within a given period. These companies were then tracked for two years.

5.1.10 The research found that the banks' recovery rate averaged 77 per cent. Preferential creditors fared less well, recovering 27 per cent of their debts, but returns to trade creditors were negligible. The study also found that 44 per cent of administrative receiverships resulted in a sale of the business as a going concern. The report's authors conceded that this provided evidence that administrative receivers were prepared to continue to run businesses in order to achieve a sale as a going concern. This in turn saved jobs and in all likelihood increased the value of assets realised. The authors struck a note of caution by warning that these figures should be treated with some caution, as the definition of a 'going concern' was very loose.

5.1.11 The authors found that one quarter of the proceeds of an administrative receivership are taken up in costs, which was considered high. The authors attributed this to the fact that where a bank recovers its entire indebtedness, the costs of the administrative receivership will be effectively borne by the preferential and unsecured creditors. In such cases, the authors speculated that the secured creditor may have insufficient incentive to control costs. The study therefore provided ammunition for the joint Treasury/DTI Review Group to reach one of its key conclusions, namely that administrative receivership provided a poor return to unsecured creditors.[1]

---

1 'A Review of Company Rescue and Business Reconstruction Mechanisms', a Report by the Treasury/DTI Group May 2000.

5.1.12 During the consultation process, the banking industry lobbied hard, pointing to the successful use of administrative receivership in establishing a rescue culture and highlighting other pitfalls in removing administrative receivership. For instance, in response to a White Paper,[1] the British Bankers Association wrote:

> British Banking is highly based on rescue, unlike the American system, which is based on asset. By terminating administrative receivership, Banks are moved towards a system in which higher risk ventures, like independent start ups, will be shunned by lenders.

---

1 'Productivity and Enterprise: Insolvency – A Second Chance', Cm 5234, July 2001.

5.1.13   However, the reason for the ultimate demise of administrative receivership is perhaps a political one, engendered by concern over its legal nature. Throughout the reform consultation process, it was clear that the Government had misgivings regarding the limited duties that a receiver owes to any party other than his appointor and the subsequent disregard the receiver has to other creditors and stakeholders' interests. Why the Government reached this conclusion needs a little analysis.

5.1.14   Historically, the Court of Equity would impose stringent duties and responsibilities upon lenders when they took possession of property. A practice therefore evolved whereby the agreement between the parties would provide that the mortgagor would be required to appoint a receiver at the request of the mortgagee. The receiver would, however, be the agent of the mortgagor. This arrangement became a standard feature of company debentures from the nineteenth Century onwards and this practice was eventually recognised by statute.[1] The importance of the agency principle of receivership is that it limits the liability of both the receiver and the appointor, as an agent is not normally personally liable for contracts made on behalf of the principal. Furthermore, the appointor does not need to take account of the interest of other creditors.

1   Law of Property Act 1925, s.109(2) and Insolvency Act 1986, s.44(1).

5.1.15   In exercising the powers of appointment the receiver's duty is to realise assets to discharge the secured debt. The case of *Kennedy* v. *De Trafford*[1] is the leading authority for the proposition that the powers of the receiver in discharging this duty must be exercised in good faith.

1   [1897] AC 180.

5.1.16   The development of the receiver's duty is to be found in the leading authority of *Cuckmere Brick Co Limited* v. *Mutual Finance Limited*[1] in which the Court of Appeal held that a mortgagee exercising the power of sale must take reasonable care to ensure that the market value of the mortgage property is obtained. This case has become the accepted authority for the proposition that a receiver owes a similar duty to the mortgagor.

1   [1971] 2 All ER 633.

5.1.17   The courts however have been reluctant to extend this duty much further. In *China and South Seas Bank Limited* v. *Tan Soon Gin*,[1] the court was asked to determine if the receiver was under a duty to delay sale until market conditions improve. The court held that the receiver was under no duty to sell the secured property at any particular time or when market conditions were favourable.

1   [1990] 1 AC 536.

5.1.18   More recently in *Medforth* v. *Blake*,[1] the duties of a receiver were examined by Scott VC who remarked that the proposition that a receiver managing a mortgaged property owes no more than a duty of good faith offended commercial good sense. This case concerned a pig farm owner who argued that, in failing to limit the expenditure of the business by obtaining readily available pig feed at a discount, the appointed receiver was in breach of duty to him as mortgagor.

The court held:

- The receiver owed a duty in equity, including but not limited to that of good faith, to the mortgagor and any other party with an interest in the equity of redemption.
- When continuing to trade the business, the receiver owed a primary duty to create a situation whereby the interest on the secured debt could be paid and eventually the debt itself repaid.
- Subject to that primary duty, the receiver owed a duty to manage the property with due diligence.
- Whilst the receiver was not obliged to carry on the business previously carried on at the mortgage property, if he did so, the receiver owed a duty to take reasonable steps to ensure that the business traded profitably.

1   [1999] 3 All ER 97.

5.1.19   Despite this widening of the receiver's duties, the following criticism of the administrative receivership was contained in the report by the DTI/Treasury Review Group of May 2000.[1]

> It is clear that the mechanisms of the floating charge and the administrative receivership play a valuable role in the economy and it is important to ensure that as much as possible of this value is retained by any change that is made. Nevertheless we believe that the grounds of equity and efficiency are likely to favour the use of collective proceedings under which a duty of care is owed to **all** creditors, in which **all** creditors participate and which **all** creditors may look to an office holder for an account of the debtor's assets.

1   'A Review of Company Rescue and Business Reconstruction Mechanism' at p.21.

5.1.20   The conclusion of the Review Group may well have been influenced by the political pressure referred to in Chapter 1. The report of the Review Group however provided a clear indication that any reform to the 1986 Act would include a fundamental reassessment of the role of administrative receivership.

5.2   DEBENTURES ENTERED INTO PRIOR TO THE ENTERPRISE ACT 2002

The transitional period

5.2.1   On 9 November 2001 the Department of Trade and Industry issued a short statement by the Secretary of State, Patricia Hewitt,[1] confirming that whilst it was the Government's intention to abolish administrative receivership (sic), this would not apply to existing corporate lending agreements. This statement was heralded as a move to provide certainty for corporate lenders and borrowers.

---

1   DTI Press Notice (P/2001/629).

5.2.2   The relevant provisions contained in the Enterprise Act 2002[1] were therefore drafted to apply to floating charges created on or after the date of enactment and consequently it remains possible for a secured lender with both a loan contract and a floating charge created *before* the enactment of s.250 of the Enterprise Act 2002 to appoint an administrative receiver in exactly the same way as before.

---

1   Section 250 inserts in the 1986 Act a new Chapter IV prohibiting the appointment of administrative receiver save for certain specific exceptions. See Insolvency Act 1986, s.72A (4)(*a*).

Will administrative receiverships disappear?

5.2.3   Writing before the actual implementation of the Enterprise Act 2002, it is difficult to say if and how practice will alter in this regard. One can certainly foresee the possibility that the appointment of administrative receivers in respect of pre-Enterprise Act 2002 securities will continue for a considerable period of time: banks may be reluctant to renew their loan documentation and amend their procedures and practices until the new provisions have 'bedded down'. Furthermore, it is possible that refinancing companies will wish to take assignments of pre-Enterprise Act 2002 security, in addition to new security, in order to preserve the ability to appoint an administrative receiver.

5.2.4   A reluctance by lenders to change practice may however be countered by major creditors and bond holders insisting that old-style floating charges are discharged in favour of new-style charges. The reason being the more advantageous treatment of unsecured creditors under the new-style administration procedure. It is therefore possible that major creditors will refuse to trade with a company unless it discharges the old-style floating charge, or moves to another bank/lender who will have new-style documentation.

5.2.5   Further, banks may wish to court the Government's favour and will not (in all circumstances) rely on old loan documentation but may instead apply for an administration order under the new regime. Indeed there is some evidence to suggest that the decline in the use of administrative receivership, described earlier in this book, is as a result of a growing acceptance by the banks that use of the administration process (certainly prior to the Enterprise Act 2002) is both politically expedient and produces the necessary financial return. Indeed, it will be interesting to see if a major clearing bank will break rank and declare that it will not exercise its rights to appoint administrative receivers once the new procedure is in place. If this happens, it could spark similar moves by other lenders and the elimination of administrative receivership by major lenders almost overnight, rather than a gradual decline in use.

5.2.6 However, the use of the new administration process has some dangers for secured creditors:

- The administrator has wider duties to the creditors as a whole and, indeed, unsecured creditors have an enhanced right to sue the administrators for misfeasance. For example, a legal action could be commenced for furthering the secured creditors' interests to the detriment of the company and its unsecured creditors.
- The appointment of an administrator by a floating chargeholder is subject to challenge by the unsecured creditors. Such direct challenge is not available when an administrative receiver is appointed by a secured creditor.

It would be extremely unwise for an insolvency practitioner to take an appointment as an administrator and conduct it as if it were an administrative receivership.

5.2.7 Consequently, the appointed insolvency practitioner and the bank may conclude that administrative receivership remains preferable in respect of pre-Enterprise Act 2002 security. The 'abolition' of administrative receivership will therefore bring uncertainty, not perhaps as a result of legislative interpretation of the particular provision in the Enterprise Act 2002, but rather because it is difficult to predict the economic ramifications for secured and unsecured creditors and how the lending industry will react in the longer term to its loss. What is likely, however, is that insolvency practitioners will be required to have recourse to administration receivership practice and procedure for many years to come.

5.3   THE FUTURE OF SECURED LENDING POST-ENTERPRISE ACT 2002

The Enterprise Act 2002 reforms

5.3.1 The existing provisions dealing with receivership in the 1986 Act are being retained.[1] However, one of the most fundamental reforms introduced by the Enterprise Act 2002 is the reform of the administrative receivership process. This reform has been described as its abolition but, for reasons which are outlined below, this is perhaps an over-simplification of the position.

---

1 Insolvency Act 1986, Pt.III.

5.3.2   In the White Paper[1] preceding the Enterprise Act 2002, the Government confirmed that the creation of a floating charge and the right to appoint an administrative receiver played an important part in certain transactions in the capital markets. The Government's intention was therefore that administrative receivership would continue in cases where floating charges were granted in relation to such transactions. Interest groups involved in various project finance areas also lobbied the Government hard during the review process to ensure that other exemptions to the new provisions were included in the Enterprise Act 2002. We shall look briefly at each exemption but first it is necessary to explore how the amended 1986 Act seeks to control administrative receivership.

---

1 'Productivity and Enterprise: Insolvency – A Second Chance', Cm 5234, July 2001.

5.3.3   Section 250 of the Enterprise Act 2002 provides that ss.72A to 72G are inserted after Chapter III of Part III of the 1986 Act.

Section 72A (1) provides:

> The holder of a qualifying floating charge in respect of a company's property may not appoint an administrative receiver of the company.

5.3.4   The use of the words 'may not' is important but not entirely clear. Section 72A (1) does not prescribe any penalty in the event that an administrative receiver is appointed over a company. Is such an appointment therefore void or voidable?

5.3.5   It is arguable that any such appointment would take effect as a receivership and not an administrative receivership. In this case, the receivers would exercise such powers as are contained in the debenture. As has already been seen, receivership is a matter of contractual negotiation between lender and borrower; therefore could an extensive range of powers contained in the security document ensure that a receiver so appointed could carry out his duties as if he were acting as a pre-Enterprise Act 2002 administrative receiver? Is this a loophole which will be exploited by secured creditors and their legal draftsmen?

5.3.6   However, any attempt to circumvent the new legislation in this way would likely be to fail in light of the wording of s.72A (4)(b) which provides that s.72A (1) will apply:

> in spite of any provision of any agreement or instrument which purports to empower a person to appoint an administrative receiver (by whatever name).

The wording in the brackets appears to deal with the scenario outlined above. It will not however prevent attempts by legal draftsmen to reserve powers for the receiver which will be said to fall outside the definition of administrative receivership. For instance, will there be a cherry picking exercise, whereby lenders seek 'full' charges permitting the control and management of profitable parts of the company's assets but which nevertheless do not constitute the whole or substantially the whole of the company's property? This area is likely to be one that will result in significant legal debate, particularly if lenders became unhappy with the use and operation of the new administration procedures.

Exemptions to the new procedures

5.3.7   The Enterprise Act 2002 introduces new ss.72B to 72G into the 1986 Act which in turn detail the areas in which administrative receivership will continue. These exemptions apply to highly specialised forms of capital finance transactions where administrative receivership is required to maintain lender control and ensure continued cash-flow and/or operation. The Government feels that the continued operation of these capital financing methods is important to allow the City of London to compete on the international stage in specialist areas where there are significant advantages over conventional commercial lending.

5.3.8   Whilst a full exploration of these exceptions is outside the scope of this book, briefly the areas where there is an exemption to the use of the new administrative procedure are as follows.

First exception: capital market[1]

An agreement which is or forms part of a capital market arrangement if:

■   a party incurs or is expected to incur a debt of at least £50 million under the arrangement, and
■   the arrangement involves the issue of a capital market investment.[2]

---

1   Insolvency Act 1986, s.72B.
2   A 'capital market investment' is as defined by paras.2 and 3 of Sched.2A to the Insolvency Act 1986, e.g. debenture, debenture stock, loan stock, bond, certificate of deposit or other instrument creating or acknowledging indebtedness within the meaning of the Financial Services and Markets Act 2000 (Regulated Activities) Order 2001, SI 2001/544, art.77.

5.3.9   An arrangement is a 'capital market arrangement'[1] if:

■   it involves a grant of security to a person holding it as trustee for a person holding a capital market investment issued by a party to the arrangement;
■   at least one of the parties to the arrangement guarantees the obligations of another party to the arrangement;
■   at least one of the parties to the arrangement provides security in respect of the performance of the obligations of another party to the arrangement; or
■   the arrangement involves the issue of options, futures or contracts for differences.[2]

---

1   As defined in Insolvency Act 1986, Sched.2A, para.1.
2   Within the meaning of the Financial Services and Markets Act 2000 (Regulated Activities) Order 2001, SI 2001/544, arts.83–85.

5.3.10   The figure of £50 million is also worthy of note and was discussed at the Committee Stage of the Bill. Responding for the Government, the Minister, Douglas Alexander, explained that the figure had been reached after discussion between DTI officials and the City of London Law Society and was set at a level to avoid the use of this exemption by ordinary commercial lenders. This figure will, however, be reviewed and the Secretary of State has reserved powers to amend this section if thought necessary.

Second exception: public private partnership[1]

5.3.11   A project company[2] where the project is a public private partnership project and includes step-in rights.

1 Insolvency Act 1986, s.72C.
2 As defined in Insolvency Act 1986, Sched.2A, para.7.

5.3.12   A public private partnership project (PPP) is one where the resources (including funds, assets, skills, grant of a concession or franchise and other commercial resources) are provided at least partly by a public body[1] and partly by a private body, or are designed wholly or mainly to assist a public body in discharging its function.

1 As defined in Insolvency Act 1986, Sched.2A, para.9 and as specified by the Secretary of State.

5.3.13   It is interesting that where public money is at issue the Government seeks to preserve administrative receivership rather than use the new administration procedure. The Government's justification for this is that administrative receivership is required to protect public services and development, for example the building of a new hospital or school, which may otherwise be delayed by administration. It is also thought necessary in order to continue to attract financing from the private sector for public projects.

5.3.14   Step-in rights are those where the person providing the finance (including an indemnity) for a project has the right to take sole or principal contractual responsibility for carrying on all or part of the project upon the occurrence of certain agreed events or to make arrangements for the carrying out of all or part of the project e.g. the insolvency of the special purpose vehicle. There is no monetary threshold applicable to this exemption.

Third exception: utilities[1]

5.3.15   A project company, where the project is a utilities project and includes step-in rights. A utilities project is a project designated for the purposes of regulated business.[2] There is no monetary threshold applicable to this exception.

1 Insolvency Act 1986, s.72D.

2 Regulated business is as listed in Insolvency Act 1986, Sched.2A, para.10 and includes telecommunication services, gas supply, electricity, etc.

Fourth exception: project finance[1]

5.3.16 A project company where the project is a finance project and includes step-in rights. A 'finance project' is a project where a debt of at least £50 million is incurred or expected to be incurred for the purpose of carrying out the project. The section is therefore intended to cover large project finance development not otherwise covered in the PPP or utilities exceptions.

---

1 Insolvency Act 1986, s.73E.

5.3.17 The debt level of £50m is significant as this will exclude most major commercial property refurbishment, regeneration and development projects. Such projects are often financed with a company being set up as a special purpose vehicle to borrow the necessary funds, with the only assets of the company being the project which is being financed. It is vital for the investors providing the finance to be assured that in the event of financial difficulty they have the right to step in and immediately continue the project, so as to ensure that contractors do not leave the site and destroy any chance of completing the project. Administrative receivership enables speedy appointment, the continuation of the project with the minimum of disruption and the maximum degree of control for the property financiers.

5.3.18 The lack of administrative receivership as an available 'rescue' mechanism in this area may pose a grave danger for developers who may find that property financiers are discouraged from lending or seek a greater return for the additional risk incurred. The Commercial Property Industry therefore lobbied hard for this additional exemption and it was also mooted in the Parliamentary debates on the Enterprise Bill that the threshold should be lowered for property finance projects from £50 million to between £5 million and £10 million. This call was supported by the Association of Property Bankers, the Royal Institute of Chartered Surveyors and the British Bankers Association. Despite the weight behind these calls, the suggestions were rejected by the Government and we must wait to see if the area of small to mid-market commercial property development is adversely affected.

Fifth exception: financial markets[1]

5.3.19 A number of specific exemptions are made in relation to financial market operations:

- A company by virtue of a market charge within the meaning of s.173 of the Companies Act 1989.
- A system-charge within the meaning of the Financial Markets and Insolvency Regulations 1996, SI 1996/1469.

■   A collateral security charge within the meaning of the Financial Markets and Insolvency (Settlement of Finality) Regulations 1999, SI 1999/2979.

These exceptions followed successful lobbying from the City of London.

1   Insolvency Act 1986, s.72F (as amended).

Sixth exception: registered social landlords[1]

5.3.20   A registered social landlord[2] (generally meaning a housing association) is one that provides low cost housing, who have often taken over the Local Authority's responsibility for such housing. It is often difficult to attract lending in this sector.

1   Insolvency Act 1986, s.72G (as amended).
2   Defined in the Housing Act 1996, Pt.I.

5.3.21   There was therefore a widespread fear voiced by the Housing Corporation, National Housing Federation, Council of Mortgage Lenders and Housing Associations that financial institutions (who have lent approximately £25 billion to registered social landlords) would see the removal of administrative receivership as a major threat to their security, and would withdraw from this market and/or seek higher rates. Successful lobbying saw this as a late amendment to the Enterprise Bill and the creation of a further exception to s.72A (1) of the 1986 Act.

Powers to amend or vary the exceptions

5.3.22   The Enterprise Act 2002 provides[1] that the Secretary of State may:

■   Create additional exemptions.
■   Provide that an existing exemption will cease to have effect.
■   Vary or amend an exemption contained in ss.72B to 72G of the 1986 Act.
■   Amend Sched.2A to the 1986 Act.

1   Insolvency Act 1986, s.72H.

5.3.23   An Order of the Secretary of State to fulfil any of these purposes may be made by statutory instrument, although there is provision that if the Secretary of State exercises powers under this section, the order will be subject to possible annulment pursuant to a resolution of the Houses of Parliament.

5.3.24   The Secretary of State's ability to add, delete, vary or amend the exceptions to the general abolition of administrative receivership could, in theory, provide scope for the growth in the number of exemptions and a re-introduction of administrative receivership as a major tool for secured lenders. The 'return' of administrative receivership by statutory instrument must however be considered unlikely; the legislature has made it clear that administrative receivership is intended to be retained only in very limited circumstances and subject to the very special interests of the capital markets. This assumption will be turned on its head if s.72A (1) has no effective 'bite' and administrative receiverships develop in size and number.

Special administration regimes

5.3.25   Section 249 of the Enterprise Act 2002 makes clear that various special administration procedures applicable to certain types of company will continue to operate. Special administration regimes apply to:

- Water and sewage undertakers.[1]
- 'Protected' railway companies.[2]
- Air traffic control companies.[3]
- A London Underground public-private partnership company.[4]
- A building society.[5]

1 Holding an appointment under the Water Industry Act 1991.
2 Within the meaning of the Railways Act 1993 and companies involved in the Channel Rail Link.
3 Within the meaning of the Transport Act 2000.
4 Under the Greater London Authority Act 1999.
5 Within the meaning of the Building Societies Act 1986.

5.3.26   The provision in the Enterprise Act 2002 also goes on to give express power to the Secretary of State (and the Treasury in the case of building societies) to amend by statutory instrument the provisions relating to the respective special administration regimes.

Other special circumstances

5.3.27   Section 254 of the Enterprise Act 2002 allows the Secretary of State to apply insolvency legislation to foreign incorporated companies through secondary legislation (i.e. statutory instrument). The intention of this provision is to enable the rescue of such companies where there are assets available for creditors and employees in this country, making the new administration regime available to such companies, where at present the only option is to wind up the company by court order as an unregistered company. This must surely be intended to dovetail with the EU Regulations referred to in Chapter 4.

5.3.28   Section 255 of the Enterprise Act 2002 deals with industrial and friendly societies and provides the Secretary of State and the Treasury with wide powers to order by statutory instrument the application, amendment, variation or provision relating to company voluntary arrangements, administrations or schemes of arrangement, as they relate to industrial and friendly societies. Although this provision has been made, the Government has made clear that the Secretary of State's power will not be exercised without full consultation with all interested parties.

Secured lending post Enterprise Act 2002

5.3.29   There has been significant concerns voiced during the reform process that the restriction on the use of administrative receivership will adversely affect the commercial lending market. If secured creditors feel that they are losing effective control over corporate borrowers, they may become more conservative in their lending policy, increase rates or simply withdraw from providing general facilities. This could have catastrophic effects upon the UK economy.

5.3.30   Another consequence in the reduction of administrative receivership could be the greater proliferation of factors and asset based lenders who will be encouraged to fill any gap left in the commercial lending market. The increased number of secured creditors in the case of a corporate insolvency has been identified as a problem. On a practical basis, the insolvency practitioner will have more parties to deal with and may have very different economic considerations to take into account when viewing the collection of their debts. For instance, an asset based lender may simply be concerned to realise debts secured on that asset and have no regard to the general continuation of the company and its business.

5.3.31   The fears that there will be major disruption to the commercial lending market may yet prove to be misplaced. As we shall see, the reforms to the administration procedure introduced in the Enterprise Act 2002 have given the secured creditors a continued central role in corporate recovery. Despite this, however, there are several areas where restriction of an administrative receivership could prove costly, particularly in the area of project finance.

6 THE ABOLITION OF CROWN PREFERENCE

6.1 PREFERENTIAL DEBTS AND THE ENTERPRISE ACT 2002

What are preferential debts?

6.1.1 While a company remains solvent and free from any insolvency procedure, creditors are free to pursue the recovery of their debts as they consider appropriate. Creditors do not owe duties to one another and there is no collective responsibility in respect of the recovery of a debt; the first creditor in can take the spoils. The insolvency does not end this position per se. However, the adopted insolvency procedure, be that bankruptcy, individual or company voluntary arrangement, administration or liquidation, will affect and limit a creditor's rights of action and recovery. In the case of insolvency, however, creditors will also be treated in accordance with a prescribed order of priority, where certain classes of creditor are ascribed a 'preferential status'.

6.1.2 In this section we look at s.251 of the Enterprise Act which abolishes Crown preference[1] and which will have a dramatic impact upon the return that creditors will receive when a company's or individual's assets are realised.

---

1   Prior to the Enterprise Act 2002, Insolvency Act 1986, s.386 (1) (unamended) provided that:
    'A reference in this Act to the preferential debts of the company or an individual is to the debts listed in Schedule 6 to this Act (money owed to the Inland Revenue for income tax deducted at source, VAT, [insurance premium tax], [land fill tax], car tax, betting and gaming duties, [beer duty], [lottery duty], [air passenger duty], social security and pension scheme contributions, remuneration etc of employees, [levies on coal and steel production] and reference to preferential creditors to be read accordingly.' [The words in square brackets being later insertions by reason of Finance Acts 1991 to 1996.]

6.1.3 A return to creditors will occur on the liquidation of a company, when net realised assets are distributed to unsecured creditors on a rateable basis. This so called 'pari passu' principle is a central feature of UK insolvency law and is expressed in statutory form as follows:

Debts other than preferential debts rank equally between themselves in winding up.[1]

---

1   Insolvency Rules 1986, r.4.181 (1).

6.1.4   Preferential claims in insolvency have been recognised since the late nineteenth Century and imposed by the legislature for a variety of political and economic reasons. Legislation providing that certain debts should be classed as 'preferential debts' is thus an exception to the pari passu principle (although it should be remembered that preferential debts rank pari passu amongst themselves).

The reform process

6.1.5   Prior to the 1986 Act, the Crown enjoyed preferential status in respect of assessed taxes, namely income tax and corporation tax. The Cork Committee looked closely at the system of preferential debts, which was at that time seen as substantially hindering the prospects for recovery by unsecured creditors. However, the major reasons put forward for retaining Crown preferential status were twofold:

- The public benefit obtained in increasing tax collection; the Crown benefits from its preferential status to the tune of between £60 million and £90 million per year.[1]
- The Crown is, in effect, an involuntary creditor, which unlike other creditors has no choice in whether it contracts or enters into any legal relationship with the company. Companies are compelled to act as tax collectors for the Government and directors may feel the temptation to dip into Crown monies to overcome short-term cash flow difficulties.[2] Furthermore, unlike other creditors, the Crown has, in theory, no control over this process as only the directors of the company will be aware of the true state of the Crown's debt position.

1 'View of Company Rescue and Business Reconstruction Mechanisms' May 2000, p.24.
2 Such action by a director is conduct which may be regarded as rendering the individual unfit to be concerned in the control and management of a company and lead to directors disqualification proceedings. This sanction against abuse is still available and will remain unaffected by the abolition of Crown preference.

6.1.6   The Cork Committee concluded that they could see no good reason why individual creditors should suffer for the benefit of the public at large when that benefit was likely to be minimal and the loss to the individual creditors substantial. Whilst accepting that the Crown was in the position of an involuntary creditor, the Committee also noted that the Crown had remedies and powers available that many other creditors did not have.

6.1.7   Despite these conclusions, the Cork Committee recommended that Crown preference be retained for 'collected taxes', namely VAT, PAYE and National Insurance contributions. The justification for this was that the taxpayer had received or retained the tax due on behalf of the Crown. This method of collection was not only convenient for the Crown but also for the taxpayer and it would be wrong for general unsecured creditors to receive a benefit from this payment arrangement. It should however be noted that the courts have not regarded sums held and owing to the Crown as 'trust monies'; i.e. sums held by the company on behalf of the Crown. Calls to abolish the Crown preference entirely have continued since 1986 but in view of the Government's reluctance to forgo tax revenue, fundamental reform was considered unlikely.

6.1.8 In 'The Review of Company Rescue and Business Reconstruction Mechanisms', Report by the Review Group, The Department of Trade and Industry and HM Treasury published by the Insolvency Service in May 2000 it was suggested that there should once again be a review of the Crown's preferential status. However the review group concluded that ultimately the issue regarding Crown preference was one of political choice. The review group therefore concerned itself with simply putting forward a series of proposed measures which could improve company rescue, including the greater use of CVAs and the position that the Inland Revenue and Customs and Excise take when considering CVA proposals.[1]

---

1 This led to the formation of single specialist Voluntary Arrangement Service, combining Inland Revenue and Customs staff to assess all voluntary arrangements from April 2001.

6.1.9 It was not therefore until the publication of the White Paper 'Insolvency – A Second Chance' in July 2001, that the abolition of Crown preference was raised as a proposal. One can only speculate whether this was a sop to secured creditors who were threatened with a perceived loss of control and influence over their corporate borrowers.

Enterprise Act 2002 reform

6.1.10 Section 251 of the Enterprise Act 2002 abolishes Crown preference by removing from Sched.6 to the 1986 Act the following categories of preferential debts:

■ Those contained previously in paras.1 to 2 (debts due to the Inland Revenue);
■ Those contained previously in paras.3 to 5C (debts due to Customs and Excise);
■ Those contained previously in paras.6 to 7 (Social Security contributions).

In respect of these debts, the Crown will become an unsecured creditor.

6.1.11 Section 386 of the 1986 Act (as amended) will read:

A reference in this Act to the preferential debts of the company or an individual is to the debts listed in Schedule 6 to this Act (contributions to occupational pension schemes, remuneration of employees for the relevant period, levies on coal and steel production) and reference to preferential creditors to be read accordingly.

This section applies in respect of both corporate and individual insolvencies.

6.1.12   It should also be noted that preferential creditors do not disappear entirely; certain categories of preferential debt remain and those creditors will still enjoy priority over floating chargeholders and unsecured creditors.

6.1.13   One important exception to the general abolition of Crown preference is the Crown's (DTI) subrogated preferential rights in respect of salary and wage arrears payable under the Employment Rights Act 1986. Such subrogated preferential payments can be substantial. This exception has been retained because any amounts paid by the DTI are paid out of national insurance funds, with the DTI assuming the rights of all former employees and 'stepping into the shoes' of those employees in respect of their claims. In addition, Sched.17 removes s.198 (4) of the Employment Rights Act 1986. As a result, the DTI will no longer have priority over the preferential claims of former employees whose claims exceed the statutory maximum. Therefore, legislation has been retained which enables the DTI to step into the shoes of the employee, but the DTI now stands pari passu with other preferential creditors.

Crown debt post Enterprise Act

6.1.14   After the 1986 Act, legislative reform emanating from the Treasury widened the number and scope of debts deemed as preferential, moving away from the ethos espoused in the Cork Report. Will an increase in the classes of preferential claims post-Enterprise Act be similarly introduced by stealth? It is however recognised that the preferential status for occupational pension scheme contributions, employee claims[1] and the EU legislated levies on coal and steel production (referred to in Articles 49 and 50 of the ECSC Treaty[2]) will have much less impact on the realised sums available to unsecured creditors, than prior to the reform. The reform can therefore truly be regarded as radical.

---

1   i.e. Insolvency Act 1986, Sched.6.
  '9. So much of any amount which –
      (a) is owed by the debtor to a person who is or has been an employee of the debtor, and
      (b) is payable by way of remuneration in respect of the whole or any part of the period of 4 months next before the relevant date,
      as does not exceed so much as may be prescribed by order made by the Secretary of State. [As at 30 November 2002 being £800]
  10. An amount by way of accrued holiday remuneration, in respect of any period before the relevant date, to a person whose employment by the debtor has been terminated, whether before, on or after that date.
  11. So much of any sum owed in respect of money advanced for the purpose as has been applied for payment of a debt which, if it had not been paid, would have been a debt falling within paragraphs 9 or 10.'
2   Insolvency (ECSC Levy Debts) Regulations 1987, SI 1987/2093.

6.1.15   The abolition of Crown preference is a dramatic gesture by the Government to acknowledge that greater regard should be had to the interests of unsecured creditors and perhaps also an acknowledgement that the Crown is in a better position to absorb debt than small businesses. The Insolvency Service in summarising the responses to the White Paper indicated that the proposal had met with great favour, although a number of respondents including the Institute of Directors, Federation of Small Businesses and R3 expressed the hope that the abolition of Crown preference will not provoke the Inland Revenue or HM Customs & Excise to adopt harsher attitudes or claim money earlier than at present.[1] In light of the reform this must remain a concern.

1   In some jurisdictions the restriction of Crown and/or state preference, has been coun-
    tered by more stringent processes to ensure tax collection and in Australia by the
    widening of personal liabilities for directors.

6.2   OFFICEHOLDER'S PROCEEDINGS

The position after the 1986 Act

6.2.1   The White Paper[1] made clear that the Government's intention in abolishing Crown preference was not to give an unjustified windfall to chargeholders but to benefit unsecured creditors.

1   'Productivity and Enterprise: Insolvency – A Second Chance', Cm 5234, published July
    2001.

6.2.2   A proposal mooted in the Cork Report was to make a specified sum which would otherwise pass to the floating chargeholder, available to the liquidator. The liquidator could then use those monies to fund the collection of company debts or to exercise various rights of action contained within the 1986 Act so to seek recompense for loss occasioned to the company, namely:

■   Fraudulent trading (s.213).
■   Wrongful trading (s.214).
■   Transactions at an undervalue (s.238).
■   Preferences (s.239).
■   Transactions defrauding creditors (s.423).

6.2.3   Alternatively, the Cork Committee recommended that, as well as the liquidator, creditors could pursue these statutory rights of action at their own expense.

6.2.4   Neither recommendation was adopted; however, since the introduction of the 1986 Act there has been significant judicial debate as to the right of the liquidator to take such proceedings and, more importantly, how the costs incurred in doing so should be recovered.[1]

1   See *Re M C Bacon Limited (No.2)* [1990] BCC 430; *Katz v. McNally* [1997] BCC 784;
    Mond v. Hammond Suddards (No.2) [2000] Ch 40.

6.2.5   Case law since the nineteenth Century had established that a liability incurred by a liquidator was only considered as an expense of the liquidation where it was incurred in respect of a step taken with a view to benefit the estate. This principle was given statutory effect in the 1986 Act.[1] Furthermore, s.115 of the 1986 Act provides that liquidation expenses properly incurred by the liquidator are payable in priority to all other claims (and therefore rank in priority to the claims of the preferential creditors).

1   The liquidation expense principle has recently been reconsidered by the House of Lords in Re Toshoke Finance (UK) Plc [2002] UKHL 6, where it was held that the 'benefiit principle' was not a prerequisite of being a liquidation expense.

6.2.6   The Insolvency Rules 1986 provided that expenses properly chargeable or incurred by the Official Receiver or the liquidator in preserving, realising or getting in assets of the company[1] are payable out of the assets of the company in priority to any other expense of the liquidation.

1   Rule 4.218 (1)(a) of the Insolvency Rules 1986.

6.2.7   The Court of Appeal decision in *Re Floor Fourteen Limited; Lewis v. Commissioners of Inland Revenue & Others*[1] confirmed that the costs incurred in pursuing an action for wrongful trading were not incurred in 'preserving, realising or getting in assets of the company', and hence they were not recoverable expenses. The rationale for this was that liabilities will only be regarded as recoverable expenses where they are in the broadest sense incurred in realising the company's assets. Where a benefit is brought to the estate, it is only right that all creditors should bear the cost. However, in this case, an action pursuant to the liquidator's statutory right was not taken to realise the company's assets.

1   [2001] All ER 499.

6.2.8   The practical consequence of this decision was that liquidators required the consent of both unsecured and preferential creditors to recover from the undistributed reserves in the estate the expenses of taking action, irrespective of the benefits a successful action would bring the estate. However preferential creditors were sceptical of giving consent because the liquidator's costs and expenses in pursuing the action would be taken from distributions that would have otherwise passed to them. In the absence of the support of the preferential creditors, liquidators were effectively risking their own money if they took recovery action on the creditors' behalf.

6.2.9   As an alternative, a liquidator could have recourse to s.156 of the 1986 Act, which entitles the court, in the event of their being insufficient assets to satisfy liabilities, to order a payment out of assets in such priority as it thinks fit.

The courts have been very reluctant to exercise this discretion where a liquidator has sought to ensure payment of his expenses in pursuing a statutory right of action. A court hearing a s.156 application will not seek to second guess the court which would hear the claim pursuant to the statutory right of action. Hence this remedy has been of little use to the liquidator.

6.2.10   Unsurprisingly, and certainly not unreasonably, there was therefore a marked reluctance on the part of liquidators to bring proceedings. The *Floor Fourteen* decision therefore had the regrettable effect of discouraging the commencement of recovery actions intended to swell the funds available to creditors. This has only partially been addressed by the advent of conditional fee arrangements and 'after the event' insurance products.

Section 253 of the Enterprise Act 2002

6.2.11   Section 253 of the Enterprise Act 2002 represents a welcome attempt to restore the effectiveness of the insolvency legislation aimed at curbing 'misconduct'. This section inserts into Part 1 of Sched.4 to the 1986 Act a new para.3A which provides that a liquidator may only bring legal proceedings under ss.213, 214, 238, 239 or 423 of the 1986 Act with the following sanction:

- In the case of a member's voluntary winding up, with the sanction of an extraordinary resolution of the company.
- In the case of a creditor's voluntary or compulsory winding up, with the sanction of the court or the liquidation committee (or if no committee, a meeting of the creditors).[1]

Both conditions put into statutory effect what was in reality good practice.

---

1   Insolvency Act 1986, ss.165, 167.

6.2.12   During the passage of the Enterprise Bill through Parliament, it was pointed out that mere consent would still not overcome the problem that those costs and expenses incurred in pursuing the statutory rights of action were not treated as expenses of the liquidator. It will therefore come as some relief to the insolvency profession to know that the Government intends to amend the Insolvency Rules to take account of this problem, thereby making the commencement of recovery proceedings attractive once again.

6.3   THE RING-FENCED SUM

Section 252 of the Enterprise Act 2002

6.3.1   It is perhaps to be regretted that the reforms of the Enterprise Act 2002 did not go further and follow the Cork Committee's recommendation to make some part of floating charge realisations available to the liquidator. However, the new provisions contained in the Enterprise Act provide that, in relation to a floating charge created after the coming into force of the legislation, the benefit of the abolition of Crown preferential status will pass (at least in part) to the unsecured creditors, not the liquidator.

6.3.2   The Act inserts a new s.176A into the 1986 Act.[1] The effect of s.176A is that where a company is in liquidation, administration, provisional liquidation or receivership and has granted a floating charge, the office holder will make a 'prescribed part' of the company's 'net property' available to unsecured creditors.

---

1   Enterprise Act 2002, s.252.

6.3.3   The 'prescribed part' will be a percentage of the company's net property as set by the Secretary of State by statutory instrument. In Germany similar provisions impose a 9 per cent levy on the realisations of the secured creditors' collateral. It was indicated during the Committee stage of the Enterprise Bill's progress through Parliament that the ring-fenced sum may be on a sliding scale with a de minimis level, e.g.:

- 50 per cent on the first £10,000.
- 10 per cent on realisations between £10,000 and £1,000,000.
- 5 per cent on realisations over £1,000,000.

6.3.4   'Net property' is defined as the amount of any property available after the discharge of:

- sums secured pursuant to a fixed charge;
- the cost of realising the company's assets;
- preferential claims.

6.3.5   During the passage of the Enterprise Bill through Parliament a question was also raised as to whether net property also included any trading losses incurred by the officeholder. Douglas Alexander, the Minister reporting to the Committee confirmed that this would fall within the definition of a cost of realisation, so setting at rest the Opposition's fears that the officeholder would be precluded from carrying on the business with the prospect of selling it as a going concern.

Limitations on the new provision

6.3.6   The officeholder will not however be required to call for a prescribed part of the company's net property to be made available to unsecured creditors if:

- the company's net property is less than the prescribed minimum; and
- the liquidator, administrator or receiver thinks that the cost of making a distribution to unsecured creditors would be disproportionate to the benefits.[1]

The 'prescribed minimum' level has yet to be settled at the time of writing, although at committee stage, the Minister indicated that a level of £5,000 seemed probable.

---

1 Insolvency Act 1986, s.176A(3).

6.3.7   It should also be noted that if the sum available is less than the prescribed minimum, the officeholder is still required to consider whether a distribution would be disproportionate to the benefits. For instance, if there are only a few creditors, it may be assumed that the cost of distribution would be small and would justify the officeholder in reserving a sum for the unsecured creditors. Guidance on this issue will be required in the new Insolvency Rules and consultation on these proposals are, at the time of writing, taking place and should be concluded by the end of 2002.

6.3.8   This reform clearly intends to tackle the concern voiced during the reform process that liquidations resulted in a poor return to unsecured creditors. The ring-fenced sum may increase returns to unsecured creditors, but there must be a fear that chargeholders will seek wider fixed charges over the company's assets meaning that little falls into the floating charge, so circumventing the intention behind these provisions.

6.3.9   The most significant issue upon which the Enterprise Act 2002 is silent, and which was not dealt with in the Parliamentary debate, is the situation where there is more than one floating chargeholder. Will the prescribed sum be deducted from the first floating chargeholder's realisations? If so, this will have a potential significant impact on any subsequent chargeholder. Will the prescribed sum be calculated and then deducted in proportionate shares from each chargeholder? We must hope that guidance is provided in the amended Insolvency Rules.

7 THE NEW ADMINISTRATION PROCEDURE

7.1 INTRODUCTION TO THE ENTERPRISE ACT 2002 REFORMS

7.1.1 Restrictions introduced by the Enterprise Act 2002 on the use of administrative receivership are accompanied by radical reform to the administration procedure contained within the 1986 Act. As shown earlier, it was acknowledged during the reform process, that administration was an important tool in facilitating corporate rescue, but the procedure could be legalistic, cumbersome, inflexible, overly complex and costly. For these reasons, administration was criticised as an unattractive option for small companies. Concern was also voiced that secured creditors had an effective veto over the whole process.

7.1.2 Therefore, the Government's intention in reforming the administration procedure was to create an efficient, less costly and streamlined process:

- With a clearer focus on company rescue.
- To secure a better return to creditors as a whole where company rescue is not practicable.
- With a clearer timescale to ensure that administration is not drawn out at the expense of creditors.
- To ensure that an administrator owes wider duties to the creditors as a whole.[1]

---

1 Lord Sainsbury Parliamentary Under-Secretary of State of Trade Industry outlined these objectives in the House of Lords on the second reading of the Enterprise Bill (2 July 2002).

7.1.3 The reforms see administration as the main gateway to corporate rescue, replacing in the most part administrative receivership and being designed to decrease liquidations. Unlike the German models of corporate rescue (see section 2.3), it is not, however, a single gateway to corporate rescue. Interestingly one of the most radical reforms, namely the introduction of a non-court route for the appointment of an administrator, was a relatively late development in the reform process. Indeed, the provisions dealing with this particular innovation seem to have been greatly influenced by the banking and lending community whose interests, as we shall see, have received greater protection than was initially proposed.

7.1.4   Part II of the 1986 Act has been replaced in its entirety; with s.248 of and Sched.16 to the Enterprise Act 2002 introducing a new s.8 and a new Sched.B1 into the 1986 Act. Schedule B1 sets out the new administration procedure and is broken down into the following sections.

- The nature and purpose of the administration procedure – paras.1 to 9.
- Who can appoint an administrator – paras.10 to 39.
- The effect of administration – paras.40 to 45.
- Procedures and steps to be taken during administration – paras.46 to 58.
- The duties of an administrator – paras.59 to 75.
- The ending of administration – paras.76 to 86.
- Procedures for replacing an administrator – paras.87 to 99.
- Miscellaneous provisions – paras.100 to 116.

In this chapter we explore in detail the new provisions and speculate on how the new procedures will work in practice.

7.2   THE PURPOSE OF ADMINISTRATION

7.2.1   The four statutory purposes of administration previously found at s.8 (3) of the 1986 Act[1] have been replaced by a greatly simplified single statutory purpose intended to place greater emphasis on company rescue.

---

1 Namely:

  (i) The survival of the company, and the whole or part of its undertaking, as a going concern.
  (ii) Approval of a voluntary arrangement.
  (iii) The sanctioning of a scheme of arrangement.
  (iv) The more advantageous realisation of company assets than would be effected on winding up.

7.2.2   This single overriding purpose for administration is contained in para.3 (1) of Sched.B1 and will apply in every administration irrespective of by whom and by what method the administrator was appointed.

  3(1)   An administrator of a company must perform his functions with the objective of –

    (a) rescuing the company as a going concern, or
    (b) achieving a better result for the company's creditors as a whole than would be likely if the company were wound up (without first being in administration), or
    (c) realising property in order to make a distribution to one or more secured or preferential creditors.

7.2.3   The administrator must perform his functions in the interests of the company's creditors as a whole[1] (save in the limited circumstances where the administrator is realising property in order to make a distribution to one or more secured or preferential creditors; in these circumstances the administrator must not unnecessarily harm the interests of the creditors as a whole).

---

1   Insolvency Act 1986, Sched.B1, para.3(2).

7.2.4   Paragraph 3 of Schedule B1 then goes on to provide that the administrator must also perform his function with the objective of rescuing the company as a going concern[1] unless he thinks either:

- That it is not reasonably practicable to achieve this objective.
- That realising the company property (with a view to obtaining a better result than on winding up and therefore presumably effecting a sale on a break-up basis) would achieve a better result for the company's creditors as a whole.

---

1   Insolvency Act 1986, Sched.B1, para.3(3).

7.2.5   Interestingly, this section of the Enterprise Act 2002 went through significant debate and amendment during the passage of the Bill through Parliament. The resulting amendments have both clarified the uncertainty caused by the initial draft but also placed a great deal of responsibility for assessing the course of the administration upon the administrator. It should be noted that it is dependent upon the administrator's judgement as to whether the company is sold as a going concern, on a break-up basis, or whether he is in office purely to realise property for the secured or preferential creditors. In exercising this judgement, he must have the interests of the creditors as a whole as his paramount concern. The formulation of this provision does not, however, leave his decisions entirely free from attack (see para.7.2.12).

Rescuing the company as a going concern

7.2.6   The administrator of a company must perform his functions with the objective of rescuing the company as a going concern, if this is reasonably practicable or unless he considers the creditors' interests as a whole are better served by another means. The originally proposed wording for this section did not include the words 'as a going concern'. It should also be remembered that the former s.8 (3)(i) of the 1986 Act referred to the 'whole or part of the undertaking as a going concern'. The addition of the words 'as a going concern' is significant; not only does it suggest that the administrator could seek to rescue the company by trading through its difficulties, but it also seems to allow the administrator to sell the company (and its business) as a going concern.

7.2.7   A company is nothing more than the legal entity that owns the business. The business of the company is made up of its goodwill, its employees, and its tangible and intangible assets. It is in the business that any value is held. As the majority of pre-Enterprise Act 2002 administrations resulted in the sale of the business, there would appear to be little use in rescuing the corporate vessel. Indeed, the generally accepted presumption in UK insolvency law before the reforms brought in by the Enterprise Act 2002 was to ensure the continuation of the business, preserving its goodwill and value for the benefit of the company's creditors and saving the jobs of its employees.

7.2.0   Furthermore, the continued operation of a company or purchase of the company by a third party controlled by its failed management/stakeholders may be at odds with the interests of the creditors. Short-term rescue of the company may hide the structural difficulties faced by the business. The company may in reality have no long-term future as its customers and suppliers move elsewhere. Rescuing such a company cannot be in the long-term interest of creditors or employees. The rescue of the company may also only have been achieved by a substantial debt write off, which may be prejudicial to the interests of creditors who would have obtained a better return if the business were sold.

7.2.9   During the committee stage of the Enterprise Bill's progress through Parliament, the Minister for E-commerce and Competitiveness, Douglas Alexander, attempted to give comfort to the committee by outlining the Government's thinking behind the statutory wording:

> The first objective of administration would be to rescue the company and the whole or part of its business (sic). We recognise that there is no use at all in making the administrator try to rescue companies that are . . . merely empty shells, at the expense of rescuing viable businesses. The purpose 'to rescue the company' evidently means to rescue it as a going concern, with the whole or much of its business intact. We are confident that the Courts will interpret the purpose that way.

7.2.10   The late amendments to this section have had the effect of blurring the distinctions between the rescue of the company and saving its business, and as the administrator can take the course which bests serves the interests of the creditors as a whole, the distinction may have little consequence in practice. The Government, however, wished to make it clear that company rescue should be the first consideration of the administrator as this will act as a motivation for owner/managers to use the administration procedure. A perceived problem in the past is that there was little incentive for directors/shareholders to put the company into administration, given that ultimately they would probably lose control of their business. As one of the principal reasons behind the streamlining of the administration procedure is to encourage its use by small companies, the Government felt that if the primary purpose of administration was to rescue the company, this would encourage the director/shareholder to use the procedure. This argument is perhaps another nod towards the US and the wish to encourage an entrepreneurial culture and increase the number of owner-run businesses.

A better result than winding up

7.2.11   Where the administrator considers that the rescue of the company as a going concern is not reasonably practicable or considers it is not in the interest of the creditors as a whole, the administrator must perform his functions with the objective of achieving a better result for the company's creditors as a whole than would be likely if the company were wound up. This is most likely to occur on a sale of the whole or, more often, part of the 'business' as a going concern, or the sale of the business on a break-up basis, providing this is more advantageous than winding up. It should also be noted that the determination of whether company rescue is reasonably practicable, as a matter of both economic value and timescale, is one for the commercial judgement of the administrator. The decision of the administrator is to be viewed on a subjective basis, i.e. what the administrator actually 'thinks' is achievable as opposed to what a reasonable administrator ought to have thought.

7.2.12   During the course of the Enterprise Bill through Parliament, the Government emphasised that where a sale of the company's business (as a going concern or on a break-up basis) would result in a better return to creditors, the administrator's overriding duty to act in the interests of all creditors as a whole would mean that rather than rescue the company, the administrator should follow the option of sale. The situation the Government wished to deal with in the new legislation was where the results of sale, or rescue, may be of equal benefit to the creditors. In such cases, it was considered that there should be an obligation on the administrator to rescue the company rather than to break it up. Furthermore, the Government made clear that it did not wish to leave the administrator totally free from criticism from creditors or stakeholders, who should retain a right of challenge in cases of bad faith and/or negligence on the part of the administrator.

7.2.13   Under the pre-Enterprise Act 2002 administration regime, the courts were reluctant to intervene and/or seek to criticise the exercise of the administrator's commercial judgement, except in cases where bad faith had been established or a decision had been taken negligently, i.e. one which no reasonable administrator would have taken.[1] It can be reasonably expected that this practice will continue.

---

1   *T & D Industries Plc (In Administration)* [2000] 1 BCLC 471.

Realisation of property for purposes of secured or preferential creditors

7.2.14   Where company rescue as a going concern is possible and the business cannot be sold, an administration order may be granted for the purposes of realising the company's remaining assets and making a distribution to secured and/or preferential creditors.

7.2.15   For floating chargeholders using the route of non-court appointment, this section gives an alternative to receivership and provides a fall-back position for the administrator if the sale of the business as a going concern proves to be unattainable. In such circumstances the administrator will not need to apply to discharge the administration order and can continue to act; the purpose of the administration will be achieved even if the realisation of the company's assets only enables a payment to the company's secured or preferential creditors.

7.2.16   However, it is important to note that notwithstanding the chargeholder's ability to make the appointment, the administrator must first have regard to rescuing the company as a going concern. If this is not a realistic option or it is not in the best interests of the creditors, he can consider selling the business in order to achieve a better result than on winding up. It is only in the absence of any reasonable possibility of these results that the administrator can act solely for the purposes of realising assets for the chargeholder.

7.2.17   When the company is placed into administration, it is not always clear what the likely result of the administration will be (i.e. whether corporate rescue of the company or sale of the whole or part of the business of the company is capable of achievement). For example, are there any potential buyers? As the administrator's primary regard is to rescue the company, this may lead to disputes between the administrator and the various different creditors' interest groups who may prefer to see the business sold immediately (on a break-up basis) rather than waiting to see if a buyer can be found for the company and its business as a going concern.

7.2.18   Importantly, however, if the administrator is to realise property for the purposes of one or more secured creditors only, he must not unnecessarily harm the interests of the creditors as a whole. It would, therefore, be extremely unwise for an administrator to act as if he were an administrative receiver and simply realise the assets for the floating chargeholder without regard to other creditors' interests. There is now also a duty on the administrator to perform his functions as quickly and effectively as reasonably practicable.[1] This is a late and novel amendment to the Enterprise Act 2002 and it will be interesting to see how the courts will interpret this section and in what context. It may, perhaps, be used to discourage unmerited applications to extend the period of the administration. We shall deal with the appointment of an administrator by floating chargeholders by a non-court route in more detail later in this Chapter.

1   Insolvency Act 1986, Sched.B1, para.3 (4).

Status of the administrator

7.2.19   Paragraph 5 of Schedule B1 makes it clear that an administrator is an officer of the court whether or not appointed by the court. This retains the pre-Enterprise Act 2002 status of administrators.

7.2.20   Like any officer of the court, the administrator must act fairly and honourably in dealing with persons who have adverse claims to his own and must not merely stand on his rights at law or in equity. Furthermore, the court can exercise control over administrators as officers of the court and can give directions accordingly.[1]

1   *Re Mirror Group (Holdings) Limited* [1993] BCLC 538.

Restrictions on the use of administration

7.2.21   Paragraphs 6 to 9 of Schedule B1 sets out provisions to ensure that an administrator (who must be a qualified insolvency practitioner) may only be appointed:

■   where the company is already in administration: if the administrator is appointed to replace an existing administrator;
■   where the company is in creditors' voluntary winding up: if the liquidator makes an application for administration;[1]
■   where the company is in compulsory winding up: if the liquidator makes an application for administration, or the holder of a qualifying floating charge makes an application for administration.

---

1   Insolvency Act 1986, Sched.B1, para.38.

The appointment of an administrator

7.2.22   An administrator of a company may be appointed by:

■   order of the court;
■   the holder of a floating charge;
■   a company or its directors.

In the next section of this Chapter, we shall look at each alternative in turn. It should be noted at this point that any act of an administrator is valid despite any defect in his appointment or qualification.[1]

---

1   Insolvency Act 1986, Sched.B1, para.104.

7.3   APPOINTMENT OF AN ADMINISTRATOR BY THE COURT

Pre-conditions before appointment

7.3.1   The court may make an administration order in relation to a company only if satisfied that:

■   the company is or is likely to be unable to pay its debts;[1] and
■   the administration order is reasonably likely to achieve the purposes of the administration.

---

1 Where an administration application is made by the holder of a qualifying floating charge, the court may make an administration order whether satisfied or not that the company is or is likely to become unable to pay its debts: Sched.1B, para.35 (1).

7.3.2   These pre-conditions are similar to the provisions previously contained in the former s.8 (1)(*a*) and (*b*) of the 1986 Act, although two changes should be noted.

7.3.3   First, the former s.8 (1)(*a*) provided that the court may make an administration order if satisfied that the 'company is or is likely to be unable to pay its debts (within the meaning given to that expression by section 123 of this Act)'. Section 123 provides a number of instances where there is a statutory presumption that the company will be unable to pay its debts. These include:

- failure to comply with a statutory demand;
- unsatisfied execution, etc. on a judgment debt;
- where it is proved to the satisfaction of the court the company is unable to pay its debts.

These are generally regarded as the 'cash flow' tests of insolvency.

7.3.4   Section 123 also states that a company is deemed to be unable to pay its debts if it is proved to the satisfaction of the court that the value of the company's assets is less than the amount of its liabilities, taking into account its contingent and prospective liabilities. This is the so-called 'balance sheet test' for insolvency.

7.3.5   It is unlikely to be significant that the new section[1] when stating that a company is or is unlikely to be 'unable to pay its debts' does not also go on to state that this definition is by reference to s.123. The reason for this is that the question as to whether a company is able to pay its debts has always ultimately been a question of fact for the court. Section 123 simply provides a number of statutory presumptions. It is probable that in assessing whether or not a company is unable to pay its debts the court will continue to follow the presumptions set out in s.123.

---

1   Insolvency Act 1986, Sched.B1, para.11.

7.3.6   The second difference between the former and new procedures is that in granting an administration order under the new procedure, the court need only be satisfied that it is 'reasonably likely to achieve the purpose of the administration'. The judiciary traditionally paid very close regard to the former Rule 2.2 Report in assessing whether the purposes of administration were 'likely' to be achieved. The word 'reasonably' is a new addition and this, it is suggested, is intended to provide a less vigorous test for the court to apply when determining whether an administration order should be granted. Together with the abolition of the strict requirements imposed by former Insolvency Rule 2.2, this particular provision evidences the Government's intention to make the obtaining of an administration order by court application, a simpler and easier procedure. The publication of the new Insolvency Rules must be awaited to see what requirements are placed on a proposed administrator and/or the application in discharging this provision.

Who may apply to court?

7.3.7   An administration application to court may only be made by:

- the company;
- the directors of the company;
- one or more creditors of the company (including both contingent and prospective creditors[1]);
- the Justice and Chief Executive of the Magistrates' Court in the exercise of the powers conferred by s.87(A) of the Magistrates' Court Act 1980 (i.e. fines imposed on a company); or
- a combination of persons listed above.

---

1   Insolvency Act 1986, Sched.B1, para.12 (4).

7.3.8   The category of party who may seek an administration order in respect of the company, therefore, remains unaltered from the pre-Enterprise Act 2002 position, and thus members of the company remain excluded from this process.

7.3.9   As a creditor of the company, a floating chargeholder may apply to court for an administration order and may do so even if there is doubt as to the validity of the floating charge, or where there are company assets abroad and the floating chargeholder wishes the appointed administrator to benefit from the provisions within the EC Regulation on Insolvency Proceedings that are not available to administrative receivers (see para.4.5.7).

Notice provisions

7.3.10   As soon as reasonably practicable after the making of an administration application the applicant must notify any person:

- Who has appointed an administrator receiver of the company.
- Who is entitled to appoint an administrative receiver of the company.
- Who is entitled to appoint an administrator under para.14.
- Who may be prescribed.[1]

---

1   We must await the new Insolvency Rules for details.

The position of the floating charge holder

7.3.11   The applicant is therefore compelled to provide notice to any floating chargeholder who holds pre or post-Enterprise Act 2002 security. As we have seen, any security created before the Act will still entitle the holder to appoint an administrative receiver. Any security created after the Enterprise Act 2002 will generally only entitle the floating chargeholder to appoint an administrator under the procedure set out above. If a floating chargeholder objects to the proposed appointment, he has the ability either to apply to court for the appointment of a specified person as administrator (and not the person specified by the applicant seeking the administration order[1]) or request that the court makes an alternative order.[2] The court will give effect to the floating chargeholder's request to appoint a specified person unless the particular circumstances of the case warrant a refusal of the application. Floating chargeholders will therefore be able to block the administration by placing the company into administrative receivership in respect of a pre-Enterprise Act 2002 security or by appointing their own nominated administrator (subject to the court's overriding consent).

1 Insolvency Act 1986, Sched.B1, para.36.
2 Insolvency Act 1986, Sched.B1, para.13 (1). On the hearing of an administration application the court may make or dismiss the application, adjourn the hearing, treat the
   application as a winding-up petition or make such order as it thinks fit.

7.3.12   We will have to wait for a body of case law to develop before assessing when the court will consider it right to refuse the floating chargeholder's applica-tion. We can however speculate that this may be in circumstances where the float-ing chargeholder's interests are minimal (and will be sufficiently protected) when compared to other creditors, or alternatively if the court thinks a certain person may be too 'secured creditor friendly' and will not have regard to the interests of creditors as a whole. However, as the administrator clearly owes wider duties to the creditors as a whole, it is difficult to conceive of instances where the profes-sional integrity of the potential appointee is so open to doubt as to cause the court to reject the floating chargeholder's nomination.

7.3.13   The legislation also ensures that where an administrative receiver is in place, an administrator cannot be appointed unless the floating chargeholder con-sents to the appointment and has agreed to vacate the receivership.[1] It is clearly undesirable for an administrator and administrative receiver holding similar pow-ers of control and company management to be in office simultaneously, save in exceptional circumstances.

1 Insolvency Act 1986, Sched.B1, para.39 (1)(a).

7.3.14   Former Rule 2.7 of the Insolvency Rules 1986 provides that notice must be given to a floating chargeholder at least five days before the hearing of the administration petition. At the time of writing, clarification (which will be pro-vided in the new Insolvency Rules) is awaited as to what period of notice will be required in the future.

7.3.15   Where an administrative receiver of a company is already in place, under the new procedure, the court must dismiss the administration application unless:

■   The person who appointed the receiver consents to the making of the administration order.
■   The Court considers the security may be invalidated under ss.238 to 240 of the 1986 Act (i.e. provisions related to transactions at undervalue and preferences).
■   The court considers the security under which the receiver was appointed may be invalidated under s.245 of the 1986 Act (i.e. provisions related to the avoidance of a floating charge).

7.3.16   These provisions are identical to the pre-Enterprise Act 2002 provisions and therefore continue to raise the practical difficulty that the validity of the security can often only be fully examined during the course of the administration. It is unlikely that all the evidence which would be available to an administrator would be apparent to any applicant challenging the security. Consequently, a challenge may be difficult to mount at the time when an application for administration is made.

7.3.17   Pre-Enterprise Act 2002, the usual practice in the vast majority of potential administrations was to ascertain from the floating chargeholders whether they would be likely to consent to the appointment of an administrator prior to petition. This procedure had much to commend it as it avoided the applicant incurring the costs of the preparation of an expensive Insolvency Rule 2.2 Report, the drafting of the petition and collating supporting evidence without first discovering whether key creditors were likely to object.

7.3.18   Although the new procedures will make it easier for an application to be made speedily and at less cost (for instance it has been indicated that no report similar to an Insolvency Rule 2.2 Report will be required), it will probably remain good practice to obtain the consent of floating chargeholders before making the administration application. This is particularly the case where an expedited hearing of the administration order is required and the requirement for giving five days' notice to floating chargeholders may prejudice the chances of successful corporate rescue. It is often essential that an administration order is obtained as a matter of urgency (in order to prevent creditors' action) and consequently, any delay, even as little as five days, can be vital. Obtaining the floating chargeholders' agreement to an administration before the issue of the administration petition can therefore significantly improve the likelihood of a successful rescue.

7.3.19   The effective continued right of veto for a chargeholder is an important concession in the final draft of the Enterprise Act 2002. During the reform process, the chargeholder's veto was criticised and appeared to be under threat. Although there has been an attempt to achieve a better balance between the interests of secured creditors and those of other parties, the requirement for prior notice and therefore the effective need for consent from the floating chargeholder is a vital concession obtained by the banking industry. As has been discussed, the other important concession has been the right of a floating chargeholder to choose the identity of the administrator (subject to the court's overriding consent), where an administration application is brought by any other party.

The application before court

7.3.20   On hearing the application, the court may make an administration order, dismiss or adjourn (conditionally or unconditionally) the application or make an interim order or any other order as it thinks fit. An interim order may be ordered by the court, for example where the company's property is considered to be in immediate jeopardy. In such cases, the court may appoint an appropriate person (who may or may not be the intended administrator) to take control of the company's property and manage its affairs pending determination of the substantive matter.

7.3.21 An interesting provision in the new procedures is that the court can treat the administration application as a winding-up petition and make an order under s.125 of the 1986 Act. This provision has been criticised, in that it confers an element of uncertainty for any party making an administration application and introduces an unwarranted degree of judicial intervention. However, it is likely that this procedure will be used extremely sparingly, i.e. in cases where the company is clearly insolvent and the administration has no prospect of success. In those circumstances, it might seem preferable to immediately wind up the company rather than to allow a period of further uncertainty.[1]

---

1   Insolvency Act 1986, Sched.B1, para.13 (1)(e).

7.3.22 A liquidator of a company,[1] or the holder of a qualifying floating charge[2] can apply for an administration order when the company is in liquidation. In either case if the court grants the administration order the winding-up order will be discharged and the court will make such provision as to how the administrator may perform his functions and in respect of what property as deemed appropriate.

---

1   Insolvency Act 1986, Sched.B1, para.38.
2   Insolvency Act 1986, Sched.B1, para.37.

7.3.23 Just as pre-Enterprise Act 2002, the administration application may not be withdrawn without permission of the court. The courts have been consistent in their attempts to dissuade creditors from using insolvency procedures as a means of debt collection. This provision continues the court's regulation of the administration procedure and is designed to discourage improper applications.

7.4   APPOINTMENT BY FLOATING CHARGEHOLDER

7.4.1 The most significant change in respect of administration procedure is the introduction of two new 'out of court' routes for the appointment of an administrator. This marks a radical departure from the proposals put forward in the White Paper[1] which had included the following proposals:

- A floating chargeholder would be entitled to petition the court for an administration order. As a concession, unlike other petitions for an administration order, no Insolvency Rule 2.2 Report would be required.
- In cases of urgency, a specific power to petition without notice would be reserved for floating chargeholders and this would lead to the appointment of an interim administrator.

---

1   'Productivity and Enterprise: Insolvency – A Second Chance' Cm 5234, July 2001.

COMPANY/DIRECTORS

- Company has not been in administration, instigated by company or directors in previous 12 months
- Not subject to moratorium in respect of unsuccessful CVA in previous 12 months
- Not subject to widening up petition or liquidation
- Administrative receiver not in office

FLOATING CHARGEHOLDER

- Must have qualifying floating charge/s
- Charge/s must be enforceable on date of appointment
- Company not in liquidation and no provisional liquidator appointed
- Administrative receiver not in office

Company is or is likely to become unable to pay its debts

Has qualifying and enforceable floating charge and wishes to appoint administrator

If no floating chargeholder	If floating chargeholder

Notice of appointment filed at court with statutory decleration and statement from administrator consenting to appointment and stating that in his/her opinion the purpose of administration is reasonably likely to be achieved

(MORATORIUM TAKES EFFECT)

Statutory declaration filed with court with notice of intention to appoint.

Notice of intention to appoint sent to floating chargeholders and others entitled to notice

(MORATORIUM TAKES EFFECT)

Floating chargeholder content with appointment

Not content with appointment

Either responds within 5 business days or does not respond; implied agreement

Identifies alternative administrator

Confirmation Statutory Declaration

Notice of appointment filed at court with statement from administrator consenting to appointment and stating that in his/her opinion the purpose of administration is reasonably likely to be achieved

Gives notice to holders of qualifying floating charges, with priority over their charge, notifying them of intention to appoint

Prior floating chargeholder either responds within 2 business days or does not respond; implied agreement

Notice to appoint administrator filed at court with statutory declaration confirming that they hold an enforceable qualifying floating charge. Accompanying this will be statement from administrator consenting to appointment and stating that in his/her opinion the purpose of administration is reasonably likely to be achieved

APPOINTMENT COMMENCES		APPOINTMENT COMMENCES

Figure 7.1 Administration, appointments out of court

■   Detailed provisions were set out as to the role of such an interim administrator.

7.4.2   These proposals were heavily criticised by the lending community during the consultation process. This resulted in a Government rethink and radically different proposals were put forward in the Enterprise Bill. Following publication of the Bill, however, further consultation was minimal, although the Government has argued that the resulting Act has taken account of the criticisms made.

7.4.3   What has emerged in the Enterprise Act 2002 is a procedure whereby a floating chargeholder can appoint an administrator of their choice without court application and without notice to the company. The difference between this form of administration and the ability of a floating chargeholder to appoint an administrative receiver is slight and far from as radical as anticipated by the original White Paper. Indeed, arguably a system of administrative receivership has been retained by the back door.

Pre-conditions before appointment

7.4.4   A floating chargeholder may appoint an administrator of its choice provided that:

■   the floating chargeholder holds a 'qualifying floating charge';[1] and
■   the debenture (or charge or other form of security)[2] relates to the whole or substantially the whole of the company's property.

---

1   As defined in Insolvency Act 1986, Sched.B1, para.14 (2) (i.e. the instrument contains the appropriate power of appointment).
2   Where the potential appointor holds more than one debenture, charge or other form of security, the assets secured thereunder must together relate to the whole or substantially the whole of the company property and at least one instrument must be a 'qualifying' floating charge: Sched.B1, para.14 (3)(*c*).

7.4.5   Section 29 (2) of the 1986 Act provides that an administrative receiver is defined as 'a receiver or manager of the whole or substantially the whole of the company's property'. This remains a question of fact determined by reference to the total value of the company's property. The holder of a charge over only part of the company's property is therefore entitled to appoint a receiver, but not an administrative receiver. Similar restrictions apply to floating chargeholders and as to whether they can appoint an administrator under the new procedure. As we have seen in previous sections, any creditor is entitled to apply to court for the appointment of an administrator. Consequently a secured creditor could take this route if there was any doubt as to whether the debenture covered 'the whole or substantially the whole of the company's property'.

Restrictions on appointment

7.4.6   A person may not be appointed as an administrator by a floating chargeholder in the following situations:

- Without two clear days' written notice to the holder of any prior floating charge in circumstances where the holder of that prior[1] floating charge has an entitlement to appoint an administrator. Alternatively, the prior floating chargeholder may give consent, thereby dispensing with the need for the two-day notice period to expire.[2]
- Where the floating charge is not enforceable.
- Where the company is in liquidation (see floating chargeholder powers referred to below).
- Where a provisional liquidator of the company has been appointed under section s.135 of the 1986 Act.
- Where an administrative receiver of the company is in office.
- Where an administrator is already in office.

---

1 A charge is to be considered as 'prior' if created first or it has priority in accordance with any agreement between the floating chargeholders. Insolvency Act 1986, Sched.B1, para.15 (2).
2 Insolvency Act 1986, Sched.B1, para.15 (1)(b).

7.4.7   It should be noted that these restrictions do not include any reference to the company's ability or inability to pay its debts as they fall due. This important concession in the legislation entitles the floating chargeholder to appoint in any given circumstance (subject only to the power of appointment arising under the floating charge). This makes the new procedure very similar indeed to the powers that a floating chargeholder has in appointing an administrative receiver.

7.4.8   Where the company is in liquidation, the new procedures entitle the floating chargeholder to apply to court for an administration order. If the administration order is made, the winding up order shall be discharged and the court may make such provision as to how the administrator shall perform his functions and in respect of what property as it deems necessary.[1]

---

1 Insolvency Act 1986, Sched.B1, para.37 (3).

7.4.9   Also of note is the restriction that the administrator will not be appointed where the floating charge upon which the appointment is made is unenforceable. The proposed administrator must scrutinise the security to the same degree as when taking an appointment as an administrative receiver. The checks which need to be carried out include:

- Does the company have the requisite capacity to borrow and create the debenture?
- Do the company's directors have the requisite power to execute the debenture?
- Was the debenture validly executed?
- Was the debenture registered within the 21-day time limit requirement as set out in the Companies Act 1985, s.395?
- Does the debenture secure the whole or substantially the whole of the company's property?

- Has the power to appoint an administrator under the debenture arisen?
- Is the debenture capable of attack by any party (primarily a liquidator appointed at the relevant time) on any of the following grounds:

  - as a transaction at an undervalue;[1]
  - as a preference;[2]
  - as an extortionate credit transaction;[3]
  - where the floating charge was created to secure past indebtedness within 12 or 24 months (depending on whether it was granted to a connected person) from the onset of insolvency;[4]
  - as the transaction was entered into at an undervalue with the intention of putting assets beyond the reach of a person who was making a claim or who might otherwise make a claim, or where such transaction prejudiced that party's position.[5]

---

1 Insolvency Act 1986, s.238.
2 Insolvency Act 1986, s.239.
3 Insolvency Act 1986, s.244.
4 Insolvency Act 1986, s.245.
5 Insolvency Act 1986, s.423.

7.4.10   Often it will not be clear that the debenture is unenforceable when the insolvency practitioner takes the appointment, since matters which cast doubt on the validity of the debenture may only come to light some time after the appointment has been taken. This is particularly so in the case where the company eventually enters into liquidation and the liquidator challenges the validity of the security. To cover this particular problem, Sched.B1, para.21 to the 1986 Act (as amended) provides that where an appointment is discovered to be invalid, the court may order the appointor to indemnify the person appointed against any liability arising solely by reason of the appointment's invalidity. This mirrors the provisions contained within s.34 of the 1986 Act which apply to cases where a receiver or manager's appointment is invalid.

Notice of appointment

7.4.11   The appointment of the administrator takes effect when the person has filed at court the following:

- A notice of appointment identifying the administrator in the prescribed form.
- A statement by the administrator that he consents to the appointment.
- A statement by the administrator that in his opinion, the purpose of the administration is reasonably likely to be achieved.[1]
- A statutory declaration by the person appointing the administrator made within a prescribed period providing that:

  - he holds a qualifying floating charge over the whole or substantially the whole of the company's property;

- this was enforceable at the date of the appointment; and
- that the appointment was in accordance with the schedules.

---

1 And such further information as is prescribed in the new Insolvency Rules. At the time of writing, these Rules have yet to be released, although it is anticipated that the requirements will not be as onerous as the former Rule 2.2.

7.4.12   When filing a statement, the administrator is entitled to rely on information supplied by the company's directors, unless he has a reason to doubt its accuracy. The extent to which the proposed administrator is prepared to rely on the directors' information before deciding to undertake his own investigations is a matter of his own professional judgement. He will take into account when exercising that judgement the fact that any person making a statutory declaration is guilty of an offence if he makes any statement which is false and does so without reason of believing it to be true. Nevertheless caution must be exercised by the proposed administrator to avoid later criticism or even legal action.

7.4.13   The fact that the appointment of the administrator takes effect on the filing of the specified documents at court has led to concern that in urgent cases (where an appointment may need to be made outside court hours, perhaps at weekends or on bank holidays), valuable time might be lost. Indeed, delay caused by the inability to file documents at court may prejudice the possibility of a successful administration. During the passage of the Bill through Parliament, the Government gave assurances that the possibility of filing papers outside normal court hours would be investigated. Details of the Government's proposals have not been made available at the time of writing.

7.4.14   As soon as reasonably practicable, the appointor must notify the administrator and any other prescribed persons of the appointment. An offence is committed if the appointor fails without reasonable excuse to comply with this requirement.

7.5   APPOINTMENT BY COMPANY OR ITS DIRECTORS

Introduction – initiating the procedure

7.5.1   If the introduction of a non-court route for appointment of an administrator by floating chargeholders was the result of lobbying by the banking industry, it is more difficult to ascertain the genesis of the introduction of the new non-court route of appointment available to the company or its directors. The procedure does have similarities with the Australian voluntary administration procedure referred to earlier (see section 2.4) and is a radical step in introducing a cheaper, less complex administration system. However, there is real doubt that this new route offers the necessary degree of speed for a successful appointment. Furthermore, as the protection given to floating chargeholders within the procedure ensures their effective control of the process, it may be a less attractive option for the company and less used than first anticipated.

7.5.2   The process by which a company may commence this procedure will depend upon its articles of association, i.e. a special resolution of the members may be required to initiate any insolvency proceedings. Usually, however, the directors will be empowered to act in the name of the company and will consequently be able to commence this procedure in the name of the company without recourse to its members. As a result, some companies may wish to amend their articles of association to take account of this new insolvency procedure.

7.5.3   It should be noted that directors have their own separate power to appoint an administrator, distinct from that provided to the company. Previous case law stated that where the directors determined the company was insolvent and should be placed in administration they should do so unanimously.[1] However, the new legislation specifically provides that any decision to appoint an administrator can be taken by the majority of directors.[2]

1   *Re Instrumentation Electrical Services Limited* [1998] 4 BCC 301.
2   Insolvency Act 1986, Sched.B1, para.105.

Restrictions on appointment

7.5.4   A company or its directors may only appoint an administrator if:

■   An administrator has not been appointed by the company or its directors, nor was the company subject to a moratorium in respect of a voluntary arrangement (under Sched.1A to the 1986 Act) in the previous 12 months.
■   The company is or is likely to be unable to pay its debts.
■   No petition for winding up nor any administration application has been presented and is outstanding in respect of the company.
■   The company is not in liquidation or provisional liquidation.
■   No administrator is already in office.
■   No administrative receiver is in office.

7.5.5   The imposition of a 12-month prohibition on the commencement of an administration in circumstances where there has been an appointment of an administrator or a CVA within that period is designed to prevent unscrupulous companies and directors making serial use of the moratorium procedures to the detriment of their creditors. There is of course nothing to prevent the company or its directors making an administration application to court during the 12-month period, but it is clearly the intention of the Government that in these circumstances the court should closely scrutinise such an application.

Notice provisions

Notice of intention to appoint

7.5.6   One of the most important controls over the appointment of an administrator by a company or its directors is the requirement that at least five business days' notice of the proposed appointment should be given to any floating chargeholder entitled to appoint an administrative receiver and/or an administrator under the new procedure (and any other prescribed persons).[1] This notice gives the floating chargeholder an effective veto over the choice of administrator and/or may lead to the appointment of an administrative receiver in cases where the debenture holder has an appropriate form of security.

1   The further prescribed persons are likely to be detailed in the new Insolvency Rules which are unavailable at the time of writing.

7.5.7   As soon as reasonably practical after giving the required notice, the appointor must file at court:

- The notice identifying the proposed administrator in a prescribed form.
- A statutory declaration in the prescribed form and within a prescribed period, by or on behalf of the appointor, stating that:
  - the company is or is unlikely to be unable to pay its debts;
  - the company is not in liquidation;
  - as far as the person making the statement can ascertain, there is no restriction in making the appointment; and
  - such further information as may be prescribed.[1]

1   Details of this and the other prescribed forms, time periods and other information will be set out in the new Insolvency Rules which are unavailable at the time of writing.

7.5.8   Having been served with the notice of intention to appoint, the floating chargeholder must either agree to the appointment or appoint its own choice of administrator (or administrative receiver in the case of a pre-Enterprise Act 2002 security). To take this latter course, however, the floating chargeholder must carefully consider whether an event of default has arisen. In the case of a pre-Enterprise Act 2002 security, the mere giving of the notice under the new procedure may not necessarily constitute an event of default.

7.5.9   If the floating chargeholder consents, or does not respond within five business days, the appointor must make the appointment of the administrator no later than 10 business days after filing of the notice of intention. If no notice of appointment is filed within this 10-day period, the interim moratorium will cease (the effect of the moratorium is explained in para.7.6.10 onwards) and an administrator cannot thereafter be appointed pursuant to the notice of intention. In the case where there is no floating chargeholder, the appointor can proceed directly to the filing of a notice of appointment at court.

Notice of appointment

7.5.10   The appointment of the administrator by a company or its directors takes effect on the filing of the following:

- A notice of appointment identifying the administrator in the prescribed form.
- A statement by the administrator that he consents to the appointment and that in his opinion the purpose of administration are reasonably likely to be achieved and providing such further information or opinion as may be prescribed.[1]
- a statutory declaration stating that:

  - the appointor is entitled to appoint (under Sched.B1, para.22 to the 1986 Act, as amended);
  - the appointment is in accordance with the requisite Schedule; and

so far as the person providing the statutory declaration is able to ascertain, the statements and information contained in the statutory declaration filed with the notice of intention remain accurate.

---

1   To be detailed in the new Insolvency Rules (as above).

7.5.11   For the purpose of making the above statement, the administrator is entitled to rely on information supplied by the directors or company (unless he has reason to doubt its accuracy). A person commits an offence if he makes a statutory declaration containing a statement which is false and which he has no reasonable belief to be true.

7.5.12   As soon as reasonably practicable after the filing of the notice of appointment, the appointer must notify the administrator and any other prescribed persons of the administrator's appointment.

7.5.13   If for any reason the administrator appointed under this section is later discovered to have been invalidly appointed, the court may order that the person who made the appointment indemnifies the administrator against liability arising by reason of the appointment's invalidity.

7.5.14   The new provisions provide that if the administration order or an appointment of an administrator by a floating chargeholder takes place before the appointer has filed the notice of appointment, any appointment purportedly made under this section will have no effect.

7.5.15   The control exercised by a floating chargeholder over the appointment of administrator by a company or its directors significantly undermines the radical nature of the original proposals for director and company appointment. The requirement to provide five business days' notice to floating chargeholders also presents practical difficulties. As we have previously explored, any delay in the commencement of the administration procedure can be significant. Frequently a troubled company requires immediate protection from creditors' actions to avoid the value of the business as a going concern being quickly dissipated. The five-day delay may be fatal to company's future survival. To counter this problem, the new procedure provides for an interim moratorium which at least gives the company protection from enforcement measures, even if the administrator cannot act swiftly in disposing of the business. The interim moratorium is explored at para.7.6.18.

7.6   THE EFFECT OF ADMINISTRATION

Winding-up petition

7.6.1   If an administration order is made, any current outstanding winding-up petitions against the company will be dismissed.[1] Any applicant seeking an administration order should therefore ensure that any court application is heard before or at the same time as the winding-up petition.

---

1   Insolvency Act 1986, Sched.B1, para.40(1).

7.6.2   The position is different where there is a non-court route appointment made by a floating chargeholder.[1] In this case, the winding-up petition will be suspended during the course of the appointment.[2]

---

1   Under Sched.B1 para.14 to the 1986 Act.
2   This provision does not apply to a petition presented under s.124A (public interest) or s.367 of the Financial Services and Markets Act 2000 (petitioned by the FSA). Where an administrator becomes aware that such a petition has been presented during the course of appointment, he must apply to court for directions under para.63 (Sched.B1, para.40 (2) and (3).

7.6.3   There is no similar provision when dealing with the non-court route appointment of an administrator by the company or its directors. The justification for this is that the company or its directors should not be able to block a creditor's winding-up petition by appointing an administrator. Instead, the company or its directors must apply to court for an administration order. Where the company or its directors applies to court it will be necessary for the court to scrutinise the application for administration and weigh up the company's interests against those of the petitioning creditor.

7.6.4   This is another example of the ability of floating chargeholders to control the insolvency process and signifies the continued prominent role of secured creditors in UK insolvency legislation. This contrasts strongly with insolvency legislation in other jurisdictions, for instance the Chapter 11 procedure in the USA (discussed at section 2.2).

Receivership

7.6.5   On the making of an administration order, any administrative receiver must vacate office.[1] However, as we have already seen, the new procedure[2] provides that the court must dismiss any administration application unless:

■   the appointee of the administrative receiver consents to the administration order; or

■   the court thinks that the security under which the appointment of the administrative receiver has been made may be released or discharged under ss.238 to 240 or avoided under s.245 of the 1986 Act.

1   Insolvency Act 1986, Sched.B1, para.41 (1).
2   Insolvency Act 1986, Sched.B1, para.39.

7.6.6   Consequently, administration cannot be used to regain control and management of the company from an administrative receiver, save where the validity of the security is in doubt. Again this marks the dominance of secured creditors' interests over other creditors' interests.

7.6.7   Where a secured creditor has appointed a receiver over any part of the company's property, the administrator may require that receiver to vacate office.[1] There is no automatic vacation of office by the receiver, rather he will remain in office at the discretion of the administrator. The powers exercised by such a receiver are strictly controlled, however, as any step to enforce security over the company requires the consent of the administrator or permission of the court. We shall explore this provision in more detail later at paras.7.8.1 onwards. It is also noteworthy that the control over the receiver (as opposed to the administrative receiver) is exercisable by the administrator by whichever manner he was appointed, i.e. by court order, by floating chargeholder or by the company and/or its directors.

1   Insolvency Act 1986, Sched.B1, para.41 (2).

7.6.8   On the vacation of office, either where an administration order is made, or where required to do so by the administrator, the receiver's right to remuneration[1] is secured and paid (ahead of the claim by the security holder appointing him) from any property in his custody or control immediately before he vacates office. However, the receiver can only receive payment after obtaining the consent of the administrator or permission of the court.

1   Remuneration includes expenses properly incurred and the administrative receiver or receiver is entitled to be indemnified for such sums out of the assets of the company: Insolvency Act 1986, Sched.B1, para.41 (4)(*a*).

7.6.9   Neither an administrative receiver nor any other form of receiver is required to take any further steps under ss.40 or 59 of the 1986 Act once he is released from his appointment. These provisions require a receiver appointed under a floating charge to pay preferential debts 'out of the assets coming into his hands'.

Moratorium

7.6.10   Prior to the commencement of any insolvency procedure, it is open to any of the company's creditors to pursue their claims and enforce any judgements they have obtained. When a company is in financial difficulty, speed of action is often vital to gain an advantage over other creditors and obtain payment and/or gain security over the company's property.

7.6.11   The moratorium against legal action afforded by administration is thus the essential feature of the procedure. It provides the administrator with a window of opportunity to assess the viability of the business and steady the ship in order to retain key suppliers and employees. Thereafter the administrator can take measures to restore the company to profitability and/or preserve the valuable parts of the business to enable a sale as a going concern. In performing this function, it is vital that the administrator is free from attempts by creditors to enforce their claims.

7.6.12   The benefits of a moratorium have increasingly been recognised by floating chargeholders who, rather than appoint an administrative receiver (who does not enjoy the benefit of a moratorium), have encouraged companies to enter into administration. It should be noted, however, that where an administrative receiver is in office prior to the issue of an administration application, the moratorium which would otherwise be enjoyed when the administration order is made only takes effect when the administrative receiver's appointer consents to the making of the order.[1]

---

1   Insolvency Act 1986, Sched.B1, para.44 (4).

7.6.13   Once the company is in administration, the following steps cannot be taken without consent of the administrator or permission of the court:

- Enforcement of security over the company's property.
- Repossession of goods in the company's possession held under a hire purchase agreement.[1]
- Forfeiture by peaceable re-entry by the landlord (including any person to whom rent is payable).
- Commencement or continuation of any legal process, including legal proceedings, execution or distress.

---

1   *On Demand Information Plc* v. *Michael Gerson (Finance) Plc* [2001] 1 WLR 155, CA held that this extended to finance leases.

7.6.14   Where the court gives a creditor permission to take any one of the above steps, it may impose such conditions or requirements in connection with that permission as thought fit. It should be noted that the the aim is not to destroy the rights of creditors, but merely to control the exercise of their rights.

7.6.15   The principal authority giving guidance on how the courts will assess whether to grant permission to a creditor to continue enforcement action is the case of *Re Atlantic Computers System Plc*.[1] In this case, the Court of Appeal made it clear that whilst the court should always have regard to the full facts in every case and not stick too closely to any rigid rules of automatic application, there were certain guiding principles which should be considered when granting leave. These are summarised as follows:

- It is for the person seeking permission of the court to make out a case
- If the granting of permission to the owner of land or goods (the lessor) to repossess their property is likely to impede the purpose of the administration, permission should not normally be granted.
- In any other case, the court should balance the interests of the lessor against the company's other creditors and consider whether the refusal to grant permission would be inequitable.
- In carrying out the balancing exercise, greater weight should be given to the lessor's proprietary or secured interest. The benefits occasioned to unsecured creditors should not be detrimental to those interests except where limited and unavoidable.
- If significant loss would result to the lessor, it would not normally be appropriate to grant permission. However, permission may be granted in a case where the loss caused to other creditors substantially outweighs the loss caused to the lessor.
- In considering the likely losses to both the lessor and other creditors, the court should have regard to, inter alia:
  - the financial position of the company;
  - the company's ability to pay interest, charges or arrears to the lessor;
  - the administrator's proposals and prospect of success for the administration;
  - the period during which the administration has already run and what period is left to run;
  - the conduct of the parties; and
  - the effect on all parties should permission be granted.
- After considering all of the above, the court may impose such terms or conditions upon the exercise of the lessor's right as thought fit. The court may also impose conditions on the administrator if permission is refused.
- The court will not seek to adjudicate any dispute over security unless it is a short point of law and convenient to do so.

---

1 [1990] BCC 859.

7.6.16   On a practical level, when an administrator takes office he must pay close regard to the landlord and other lessors' interests. It is important that he quickly assesses whether any equipment and premises held by the company are required for the continuation of the company's business or whether their retention is uneconomic and they should be returned to the lessor immediately. The administrator should also take into account whether the premises and equipment are necessary for the sale of the business and whether they are likely to be transferred to any potential purchaser. Careful negotiation with the landlord of the premises and lessors of equipment is essential once a potential purchaser of the business has been identified.

7.6.17   The administrator must ensure that the landlord and lessors of equipment are not prejudiced by the administration. This normally involves agreeing that sums due during the course of administration (although not always the arrears) are paid. In these circumstances, rather than applying to court for permission to re-possess, the landlord or lessor will probably wait to see what proposals are put forward and whether negotiations with a potential new tenant or lessee are possible.

Interim moratorium

7.6.18   An interim moratorium will be effected where:

- An administration application has been issued but not heard.
- An administration application has been granted, but the administration order has yet to take effect.
- Notice of intention to appoint an administrator has been filed at court.

7.6.19   An interim moratorium will not take effect where an administrative receiver is in office until the appointor of the administrative receiver has consented to the administration order.

7.6.20   The interim moratorium has the same effect as the moratorium outlined above, but does not stop certain specified actions, namely:

- The presentation of public interest winding-up petitions (pursuant to s.124A of the 1986 Act or s.367 of the FSMA 2000.
- The appointment of an administrator by a floating chargeholder.
- The appointment of an administrative receiver.
- The carrying out by the administrative receiver of his functions whenever so appointed.

Requirements for publicity

7.6.21   While a company is in administration, the administrator must ensure that every business document including invoices and orders issued by or on behalf of the company bears:

- the identity of the administrator; and
- a statement that the affairs, business and property of the company are being managed by him.[1]

---

1   Insolvency Act 1986, Sched.B1, para.45 (1).

7.6.22   An administrator, an officer of the court and the company commits an offence if, without reasonable excuse, it permits a contravention of this section. This follows the pre-Enterprise Act 2002 legislation, where the penalty for non-compliance was on summary conviction a fine of up to a maximum of one fifth of the statutory maximum[1] (presently £1,000).

---

1   Insolvency Act 1986, Sched.B1, para.45 (2).

7.7   THE PROCESS OF ADMINISTRATION

Notice of appointment

7.7.1   As soon as reasonably practicable after his appointment the administrator must:[1]

- Send notice of his appointment to the company;[2]
- Publish notice of his appointment (i.e. advertise in both the *London Gazette* and an appropriate newspaper).
- Obtain a list of the company's creditors and send notice to each creditor of whose claim and address he is aware.
- Send notice of appointment to the Registrar of Companies; this must in any event be within seven days of his appointment.
- Send notice to one or more relevant persons[3] requiring the person(s) to provide a statement of affairs of the company.
- Send notice to such other persons as prescribed within the required time.[4]

---

1 Insolvency Act 1986, Sched.B1, para.46.
2 Notice is required to be sent to the company in every given circumstance, even if the company has appointed the administrator. This avoids any possibility that the company's appointment has been made without appropriate authority.
3 A relevant person is a person who is or was an officer of the company (which includes a director, manager or secretary) or employee (which includes those employed under a contract of service, and therefore could arguably include a company's professionals, e.g. its accountants, solicitors and bankers) or any other person who took part in the formation of the company, within one year of the company entering into administration.
4 At the time of writing, the new Insolvency Rules have not been published. This requirement will presumably be dealt with in the new Rules.

7.7.2   An administrator commits an offence if he fails to comply without reasonable excuse with these requirements. A fine of one fifth of the statutory maximum and a daily fine of one fiftieth of the statutory maximum can be imposed (presently £1,000 and £100 respectively).[1]

---

1 Insolvency Act 1986, Sched.B1, para.46 (9).

7.7.3   The time limits for compliance with the requirements for providing notice contained in the 1986 Act have been amended:

- The administrator previously had 28 days in which to send notice to creditors. The new legislation provides that notice must be sent 'as soon as reasonably practicable'. This implies a much shorter time period. Under the revised legislation the court may however direct that notice may be dispensed with altogether, or apply a different time period.
- The time period in which to send notice to the Registrar of Companies has been reduced from 14 to seven days.

Statement of affairs

7.7.4   A person providing a statement of affairs to the administrator must verify it by providing a statement of truth. A person providing a statement of truth in which he has no reasonable belief commits an offence.

7.7.5   The statement of affairs must be in a prescribed form, containing the following information:

■   Details of the company's property.
■   The company's debts and liabilities.
■   The names and addresses of the company's creditors.
■   Details of any security held by any creditor.

7.7.6   A person on whom notice is served must provide the statement of affairs within 11 days, unless the administrator agrees or the court orders otherwise. This is a reduction from the previous time limit of 21 days and provides another example of the intention to speed up the administration process. Any person failing to comply with the notice is liable on summary conviction for a fine of up to the statutory maximum (at present £5,000) and on indictment to an unlimited fine.[1]

---

1   Insolvency Act 1986, Sched.B1, para.48 (4).

Administrator's proposals for the administration

7.7.7   Having taken over the control and management of the company, considered the statement of affairs and conducted his own investigations, the administrator must do one of the following:

■   Set out his proposals for achieving the purpose of administration.
■   Explain why he does not consider it reasonable and practicable for the company to be rescued and, if appropriate, why it is not reasonably practicable for the company's creditors as a whole to achieve a better result than if the company were to be wound up.[1]

---

1   Insolvency Act 1986, Sched.B1, para.49.

7.7.8   These provisions ensure that not only must the administrator have regard to company rescue as the pre-eminent purpose of the administration, but also that he must justify to the creditors why he considers it cannot be achieved, if that is the case. It is likely that the new Insolvency Rules will also prescribe that the administrator provides further information with the proposal, such as the statement of affairs and a list of creditors.

7.7.9   The administrator may propose either a CVA or a scheme of arrangement (one of the two previous purposes of administration) for the company. This is a logical amendment as both are methods of achieving the purpose of administration (rather than purposes in their own right) and both methods offer an opportunity for company rescue and/or a higher return to creditors.

7.7.10   The administrator's proposals may not however include any action which would:

- Affect the right of a secured creditor to enforce his security.
- Result in a preferential debt being paid otherwise than in priority to non-preferential debts.
- Result in one preferential creditor being paid a smaller proportion of his debt than another.[1]

The administrator's proposals may, however, provide for any of the above eventualities if the relevant creditor's approval is first obtained, or the proposal involves the company entering either a CVA[2] or a scheme of arrangement.

---

1   Insolvency Act 1986, Sched.B1, para.74 (1).
2   Although in any event, a CVA cannot affect the rights of a secured creditor to enforce his security, except with concurrence of the secured creditor.

7.7.11   Unlike the previous report required by s.23 of the 1986 Act (which had to be provided within three months) the administrator's statement of proposals must be sent as soon as reasonably practicable and in any event within eight weeks to:[1]

- the Registrar of Companies;
- the company's creditors; and
- every member of the company (although this obligation can be fulfilled by publication of a notice advising the members that a copy of the statement is available free of charge for their inspection).

The eight-week time limit may be extended by permission of the court or by creditors' agreement[2] obtained in writing or at a creditors' meeting.

---

1   Insolvency Act 1986, Sched.B1, para.49 (5).
2   Creditors' agreement means the consent of each secured creditor and if the administrator considers that a distribution may be made to preferential creditors, the consent of the secured creditors and at least 50 per cent (in terms of value) of the preferential creditors.

7.7.12   An extension obtained by creditors' consent:[1]

- can be agreed only once;
- must not be for more than 28 days;
- must not be used to extend a court deadline; and
- may not be used to extend a period after expiry.

---

1   Insolvency Act 1986, Sched.B1, para.105.

7.7.13   In other instances where an extension of time is required, an application to court will be required. On a court application, an extension can be obtained more than once and after expiry. This ensures that for simpler cases the administrator's proposals will be received within 12 weeks (after consent to an extension has been obtained), but in more complex cases, where longer than 12 weeks may be required to formulate a proposal, any extension of time will require court approval. These provisions constitute a further tightening of time limits and evidences the Government's wish for greater court control of the administration process.

7.7.14   There has been criticism from insolvency practitioners that an eight-week time limit is insufficient. In the first few weeks of an administration, the administrator's key concern is to stabilise the business. In complex cases, therefore, administrators will only have had the opportunity to carry out a perfunctory assessment of the company's affairs and it may not be possible to formulate a full strategy. There is also a concern that the short time period would encourage 'template' type proposals, reducing an important part of the administration process to a brief, vague, general report to creditors. If a proposal cannot be formulated within three months an application to the court will be required, which may mean that the administrator becomes bound to successive extension applications. This will increase costs and possibly result in excessive legal intervention in the administration process. These criticisms led to amendments being suggested during the passage of the Bill through Parliament. However, the Government rebutted the proposals by pointing to the Australian system of voluntary administration where proposals must be put within 21 days and it is reported that the benefit of tight timescales outweighs the costs.

7.7.15   It is an offence for an administrator to fail to comply with the requirements of these provisions without reasonable excuse. The penalty is a fine of one fifth of the statutory maximum, with a possible further daily rate fine of one fiftieth of the statutory maximum[1] (at present £1,000 and £100 respectively).

---

1   Insolvency Act 1986, Sched.B1, para.71 (6).

Sale of business prior to creditors' approval of proposals

7.7.16   Previously, in cases where the administrator concluded that a quick sale of the business was necessary in order to produce the best return to creditors after his appointment, the administrator faced a difficult decision. Should he proceed with the sale without creditors' approval or await the creditors' meeting three months after his appointment and risk allegations that an opportunity was missed to maximise the return for creditors? In order to minimise personal exposure, the administrator would usually apply to court for consent or ratification of a sale which was to take place prior to the creditors' meeting.

7.7.17   The use of this practice was always open to some doubt[1] and was finally rejected by the courts in *T & D Industries Plc.*[2] In this case the court reminded the administrator that the powers of control and management of the company included rights of disposal. Furthermore, as the administrator was left with a wide discretion in commercial matters, the court would not act as a 'bomb shelter' from creditor criticism. The courts would however always be slow to disturb a decision of an administrator if taken with reasonable commercial judgement.

If they were not thought fit to make commercial decisions without the Court's sanction that would normally be a sign that the Court had no confidence in them.[3]

Consequently, if the administrator took the decision to sell part of the business
without creditor approval, he did so at his own risk.

1   *Re Consumers & Industrial Press Limited (No.2)* [1998] BCC 72 where Peter Gibson J
    refused to approve a sale as this would deprive the creditors' meeting of any purpose.
2   [2000] 1 WLR 646.
3   *MTI Trading Systems Limited* v. *Winter* [1998] BCC 591, per Neuberger J.

7.7.18   Shortening the timescale for preparing the statement of proposals from
three months to eight weeks, may mean that fewer sales will need to be concluded
prior to a creditors' meeting. However this will not always be the case and the
explanatory notes to the Enterprise Bill (which are of course of non-binding
effect) state that in the event that a sale takes place prior to the creditors' meeting, the circumstances of the sale should be outlined in the proposals. This is a
tacit acknowledgement that the practice of sale prior to creditors' meeting will
continue, if considered by the administrator to be essential to achieve a better
realisation for the creditors. It should also be noted that the administrator is
empowered to do anything 'necessary and expedient' for the management of the
company's affairs[1]. This appears wider than the previous powers contained in the
1986 Act[2] and it is likely that the guidelines set out in recent case law will
continue to be followed.

1   Insolvency Act 1986, Sched.B1, para.53 (1).
2   Insolvency Act 1986, s.14 (1).

Initial creditors' meeting

7.7.19   A copy of the statement of proposals sent to all creditors must be accompanied by an invitation to the initial creditors' meeting. This meeting must be held
as soon as reasonably practicable and in any event within ten weeks of appointment. This time limit can only be extended on a court application or with creditors'
approval (subject to the same provisos as apply to creditors' consent to extend the
eight-week time limit to send the statement of proposals and notice of meeting).

7.7.20   An administrator will not be required to hold an initial creditors'
meeting if he thinks:

- The company has sufficient property to enable each creditor to be paid in full.
- The only distribution to unsecured creditors will be the 'ring fenced sum
  realisation from the floating charge'.[1]
- The company cannot be rescued, nor will the realisations obtained be greater
  than those obtained on winding up.

1   Insolvency Act 1986, s.176A (2)(*a*).

7.7.21   The test the administrator has to apply is whether he 'thinks' that these results will be achieved. This formulation is used throughout much of the new procedure and contrasts with other formulations such as 'reasonably believes', 'in his opinion' or 'considers' which imply varying degrees of subjectivity or objectivity. The Government has favoured the word 'thinks' as this implies that the administrator has taken a considered view. It would be wrong however to apply a completely subjective test. Hence the decision of an administrator would be subject to a rationality test and could be challenged if it were shown that no reasonable administrator would have acted in such a way in those particular circumstances. This test also discourages challenges to the bona fide commercial judgement exercised by the administrator; as we have seen, the courts will not second guess the administrator[1] in this regard.

---

1   *T & D Industries Plc* [2002] WLR 646.

7.7.22   It should also be noted that an initial creditors' meeting will be held in any event if called by creditors holding at least one tenth of the total debt.[1] This is considered by the Government to be a sufficient safeguard to ensure than an administrator cannot avoid holding an initial creditors' meeting where there is sufficient creditor interest. The Government also made clear that the administrator should only involve creditors with a financial interest. To call a meeting of unsecured creditors (who would have no financial interest in the administration) would increase the burden and costs of the administrator and reduce the return to creditors who would have a financial interest. Whether this will be given effect in the new Insolvency Rules remains to be seen. It is also unclear whether a meeting called by creditors will be at the administrator's or the creditors' expense; this, again, may be dealt with in the new Insolvency Rules.

---

1   Insolvency Act 1986, Sched.B1, para.52 (2).

7.7.23   It is a lacuna of the new legislation that whilst secured creditors do not have the right to vote on the administrator's proposal, unsecured creditors can vote (and veto) proposals even if the only likely outcome is a distribution to secured creditors. This is particularly relevant when the issue of the payment of the administrator's professional fees is considered. In the case of an administrative receivership, fees are generally agreed between the potential appointee and the floating chargeholder, often prior to appointment. In practice, this agreement over fees is seldom revisited by other creditors. Under the new regime who will agree the fees? It seems ludicrous to suppose that unsecured creditors will be called upon to agree fees when the appointment has been made out of court at the behest of the floating chargeholder and where they have no potential interest. Will the fees need to be approved by the court? There was no debate on this crucial issue during the progress of the Enterprise Bill through Parliament. Another problem is that even if an administrator did not consider it appropriate to call a creditors' meeting, he could still be compelled to do so by unsecured creditors with no potential financial interest. One answer may be to make it a pre-condition that a creditor has a probable financial interest, but this remains an area where it is to be hoped that adequate guidance will be provided in the new Insolvency Rules.

7.7.21   The statement of proposals will be put to the creditors who may approve, modify with the administrator's consent, or reject the proposals. If the administrator's proposals are rejected, the court can order that the administrator's appointment will cease to have effect, adjourn the hearing conditionally or unconditionally, make an interim order on a suspended winding-up petition, or make any other order as it sees fit.

7.7.25   Once the proposals have been agreed, the administrator cannot make any substantial amendment without first obtaining the creditors' consent (by holding a further creditors' meeting on providing proper notice etc.). The administrator's duty thereafter is to follow the actions outlined in the proposals, although he may take any other 'insubstantial actions' without the creditors' consent.

7.7.26   During the course of the meeting, a creditors' committee may be established. This committee will have the ability to require the administrator to attend before the committee and to provide such information to the committee as is necessary to perform its function within seven days.

7.7.27   At the conclusion of the initial creditors' meeting (or any other further meeting called to reconsider any revised proposals), the administrator shall as soon as reasonably practical report the decision to:

- the court;
- the Registrar of Companies; and
- any other prescribed persons.[1]

---

1   At the time of writing, the new Insolvency Rules are not available. This requirement will be dealt with in the new Rules.

7.7.28   It should be noted that new and novel provisions have been introduced which state that anything that could be done by or at the creditors' meeting may be conducted by correspondence in accordance with the Rules.[1] This is said to include correspondence by e-mail, fax or even telephone. This will significantly alter previous practice and enable swift and effective decision making during the administration.

---

1   Insolvency Act 1986, Sched.B1, para.58.

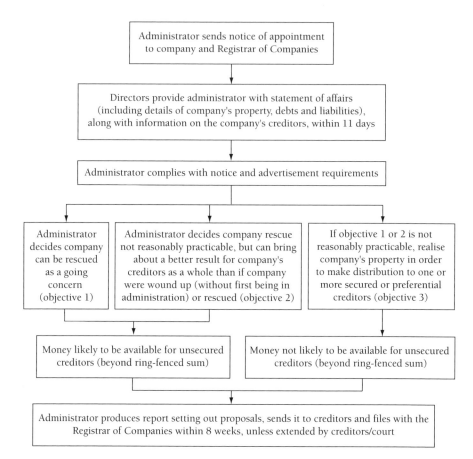

Figure 7.2 Process of administration

7.8   THE FUNCTIONS OF AN ADMINISTRATOR

The powers of an administrator

7.8.1   The administrator may do anything 'necessarily expedient' for the management of the affairs, business and property of the company.[1] This replaces former s.14 (1)(a) of the 1986 Act which, interestingly, did not contain the word 'expedient'. This emphasises still further the wide powers of management granted to an administrator; e.g. an ability to sell the business prior to creditor approval if expedient to do so.

1 Insolvency Act 1986, Sched.B1, para.59 (1).

7.8.2   Generally the administrator will exercise those powers previously enjoyed by the directors prior to the administration and the specific powers detailed in Sched.1 to the 1986 Act.

7.8.3 Any person dealing with the administrator in good faith and for value need not enquire whether the administrator is acting within his powers.[1] The administrator acts as an agent of the company.[2] As such the third party will receive adequate protection through the rules of agency, either as a result of the administrator's actual or unlimited ostensible authority.

1 Insolvency Act 1986, Sched.B1, para.59 (3).
1 Insolvency Act 1986, Sched.B1, para.70 (3).

7.8.4 Without prejudice to the general powers of management, the revised legislation provides the administrator with the following specific powers:

- To remove or appoint a director;
- To call a meeting of members or creditors;
- To apply to court for directions regarding the carrying out of his functions.
- Subject to his obligations under s.175 of the 1986 Act (i.e. payment of preferential debts) to make payment to:

  – a secured or preferential creditor without permission of the court;
  – an unsecured creditor either:

    (a) with the permission of the court, or
    (b) if the administrator thinks it is likely to assist the achievement of the purpose of the administration.

7.8.5 The ability to pay secured, preferential and even unsecured creditors is a useful new power. It may curtail problems which previously arose regarding the wish, and sometimes the necessity, to make certain distributions during the course of administration; i.e. when an unsecured creditor/supplier demanded payment of pre-administration debts before recommencing supplies to the business.

7.8.6 The court may give directions as to the administrator's management of the company's business and affairs,[1] but may only do so if one of the following applies:[2]

- No proposals have been approved.
- The directions sought are consistent with the proposals or agreed revised proposals.
- The court considers that directions are necessary to reflect a change in circumstances since the approval by the creditors of the proposal or agreed revised proposals.
- The court considers directions are desirable to give effect to a misunderstanding in the proposals or the agreed revised proposals.

1 On the administrator's application pursuant to Sched.B1 para.63 of the 1986 Act (as amended).
2 Insolvency Act 1986, Sched.B1, para.68 (3).

7.8.7 The powers of the administrator supersede any powers of the company officers exercisable under statute or the company's articles of association.

Although the directors remain in office (unless removed by the administrator), their powers of management are therefore restricted to instances where the administrator consents or delegates authority and/or where the directors' actions will not interfere with the administrator's powers. It should however be noted that directors are not released from their statutory or common law duties, such as the requirement to file annual returns and prepare accounts.

The duties of an administrator

7.8.8   The administrator acts as agent of the company. He therefore owes fiduciary duties to the company and is entitled to an indemnity from the company for obligations incurred on its behalf. The administrator will not generally incur personal liabilities for any obligations entered into on behalf of the company.

7.8.9   On appointment, the administrator takes custody and control of the property to which he thinks the company is entitled. This will include secured property or property owned by a third party in which the company has an interest (e.g. property held subject to a hire purchase agreement).

7.8.10   The new procedure evidences the primacy of the creditors' role in administration proceedings by ensuring that the administrator manages and controls the company in accordance with the proposals, the revised proposals, or where the revisions to the proposals are not thought by him to be substantial.[1] The administrator's power to carry out actions outside the proposals which are considered insubstantial may lead to a potential conflict with creditors and a challenge.[2] The creditor or members may apply to court claiming that the administrator is acting, has acted or proposes to act in a manner which will unfairly harm the interests of the applicant (whether alone or in common with some or all other members and creditors (see further para.7.9.1 onwards).

1   Insolvency Act 1986, Sched.B1, para.68 (1)(*b*).
2   Insolvency Act 1986, Sched.B1, para.75.

Administrator's power to deal with charged property

7.8.11   The administrator may dispose of property subject to a floating charge as if the property were unencumbered. The floating chargeholder will however continue to enjoy such rights of priority over the proceeds of sale or other acquired property as previously existed.

7.8.12   The court may grant the administrator power to deal with property subject to a fixed charge as if the property were unencumbered and will do so where the disposal of the property is likely to promote the purposes of the administration. An order granting the administration power to deal with fixed charge security will only be made by the court on condition that:

■   The net proceeds of sale will be available to meet the sums secured.
■   If there is a shortfall, additional sums be paid to the secured creditor to

produce a total return to the secured creditor which is equal to the sale price of the secured property at market value.

7.8.13   This provision ensures that the secured creditor is not financially prejudiced by the court's approval of the administrator's proposal to dispose of their secured property. The administrator can (and usually will) act in conjunction with the secured creditor and obtain the relevant consent or release before dealing with the property. However this provision covers the situation where the administrator believes that the disposal of the secured property is an essential component to the sale of the business as a going concern but the secured creditor is unwilling to co-operate. This section mirrors former s.15 of the 1986 Act upon which significant case law has grown up regarding the court's approach.[1] In essence, the court will weigh up the interests of the secured creditor against the likelihood of success of the administrator's proposals and the benefit to creditors as a whole. In order to ensure that the secured creditor is not prejudiced by the administrator's sale, the court will require proper valuation evidence before undertaking this exercise.

---

1   *Re ARV Aviation Limited* [1998] 4 BCC 708; *Re Consumer and Industrial Press Limited (No.2)* [1998] 4 BCC 72.

7.8.14   Where the court makes an order under this section, the administrator is required to send a copy of the order to the Registrar of Companies within 14 days. Failure without reasonable excuse to file the order is punishable by a fine of up to one fifth of the statutory maximum with a daily default rate of one fiftieth (at present being £1,000 and £100 respectively).

Administrator's power to deal with property subject to a hire-purchase agreement

7.8.15   The court may grant the administrator power to dispose of property subject to a hire charge agreement as if the property were owned by the company. The court will do so where the disposal of the property is likely to promote the purpose of the administration.

7.8.16   During the passage of the Enterprise Bill through Parliament, amendments were proposed to compel the administrator to pay for goods held under hire-purchase agreements. It was argued that the requirement for the lessor to apply to court for relief was inappropriate as it was disproportionately costly in relation to low value goods such as photocopiers, IT equipment, etc. These amendments were rejected by the Government, who remained of the view that the courts are best able to balance the various competing interests as in *Re Atlantic Computer Systems Plc.*[1]

---

1   [2000] Ch 505.

7.8.17   An order made in respect of property held under a hire-purchase agreement is subject to the same conditions as would apply to a sale of property subject to a fixed charge. Thus, there are identical requirements regarding the filing of the order with the Registrar of Companies. In the case of secured assets, filing at Companies House enables those persons searching the Register of Charges to be kept appraised of secured interests over company property. There would seem little reason, however, for this requirement where title to property remains with third parties.

7.9   CHALLENGE REGARDING AN ADMINISTRATOR'S CONDUCT

Pre-conditions for challenge

7.9.1   Any creditor or member of a company in administration may apply to court if the administrator has acted or proposes to act in a way which has harmed, or which will harm, his interests. The applicant must show that his interest either alone or in common with some or other creditors or members has or will be harmed.[1]

---

1   Insolvency Act 1986, Sched.B1, para.74 (1) (as amended).

7.9.2   This right replaces former s.27 of the 1986 Act which provided that a creditor or member may be petition for an order on the grounds that:

> the company's affairs, business and property are being or have been managed by the administrator in a manner which is unfairly prejudicial to their interests.

7.9.3   The differences to note between the provisions are twofold:

- The new section is not confined to the actual management of the company by the administrator, but includes any conduct of the administrator. This will open up the administrator to a wider degree of challenge.[1] A challenge will be available even where the administrator is acting within the scope of the powers of management and control provided by the 1986 Act, or in reliance on a court order permitting the administrator to deal with secured property or property held under a hire-purchase agreement.
- The new section provides that the applicant must show *unfair harm* to his interest rather than *unfair prejudice*. The Oxford English dictionary definition of prejudice is 'harm or injury to a person that results or may result from a judgement or action, especially one where his or her rights are disregarded'. This contrasts with the definition of harm, which is 'hurt, injury, damage, mischief'. Prejudice therefore tends to denote a loss of rights or interest which may or may not be accompanied by actual loss. Harm however suggests that actual injury, damage or loss must be suffered. Consequently where a creditor or member wishes to challenge an administrator's actions he will

need to go further than he did under former s.27 of the 1986 Act, and will probably now have to show that in addition to a loss of rights he has suffered actual harm, loss or damage. This may therefore restrict the number of challenges.

---

1   See *Re Charnley Davies (No.2)* [1990] BCC 605 which discusses in detail the scope and limitations of s.27 of the 1986 Act.

The court's powers

7.9.4   On application by any creditor or member of the company the court can:

■   grant relief;
■   dismiss the application;
■   adjourn the hearing conditionally or unconditionally;
■   make an interim order;
■   regulate how the administrator will exercise his functions;
■   compel the administrator to take or refrain from taking an action or course of conduct;
■   compel the calling of a meeting of creditors for a specific purpose;
■   remove the administrator from office; or
■   make any other order or consequential provision as deemed appropriate.

7.9.5   An order will not be made by the court if it would impede or prevent the implementation of:

■   an approved CVA;
■   a sanctioned scheme of arrangement; or
■   an approved administrator's proposal, if the challenge is not made within 28 days after approval.

7.9.6   This prevents creditors and/or members circumventing existing rights of challenge or seeking to overturn a CVA and/or scheme of arrangement. The right to challenge the administrator's agreed proposals is limited to a 28-day period.

7.9.7   Furthermore, the court may examine the conduct of an administrator[1] or purported administrator on the application of:

■   the Official Receiver;
■   the administrator (in the case of a purported administrator);
■   a liquidator;
■   a creditor; or
■   a contributory of the company.

---

1   This includes an administrator who has obtained discharge under para.98, but only with permission of the court: Sched.B1, para.75 (6).

7.9.8   This leaves open the possibility that an administrator invalidly appointed by a floating chargeholder and/or the company or directors could subsequently be pursued under this section by the eventually appointed administrator. The grounds for the application are:

■ misapplication or retention of money or other property of the company;
■ failure to account for money or other property of the company;
■ breach of fiduciary or other duty; and/or
■ misfeasance.

7.9.9   On examining the conduct of the administration, the court may order the repayment of monies and interest and/or an account for monies and, in cases of misfeasance, order a compensatory sum to be paid to the company.

7.9.10   Although these new provisions apply to breaches of duty towards the company, they do not give a creditor or member a direct right of action against the administrator for any loss that he has suffered.

7.9.11   It is highly likely that case law will develop to establish the precise nature and extent of the fiduciary and other duties owed by the administrator to the company. What is clear, however, is that although an administrator will owe duties similar to those that a director owes to the company, the respective duties are not identical.

7.10   ENDING THE ADMINISTRATION

The one-year limitation period

7.10.1   One of the most severely criticised aspects of the proposed new administration procedure by the insolvency profession was that the administrator would automatically vacate office three months after the date that the administration commenced. This was amended to 12 months late in the Enterprise Bill's progress through Parliament.[1] However, allied to the requirement that the administrator's proposals be laid before creditors within eight weeks, this reform still provides clear evidence that the Government wishes to speed up the administration process and ensure that longer more complex cases are regulated by the courts. In doing so, the Government has taken on board criticisms received during the consultation process that the administration process was too slow and there was little certainty as to when creditors would receive payment. Another possible motive was the wish to reassure the lending community that the replacement of administrative receivership by administration would not prejudice their interests and that recovery would not be unjustifiably delayed.

1   Insolvency Act 1986, Sched.B1, para.76.

7.10.2   However, it may prove to be the case that in practice, save for straightforward cases, an avalanche of applications to the courts for an extension of time may result. This in turn will increase costs and legal interference in the administration process.

7.10.3   Interestingly during the committee stage of the Enterprise Bill's passage through Parliament[1] the Government made clear that the timescales were set particularly tight to encourage small scale administrations, leaving larger cases to undergo court scrutiny, possibly on successive adjournment applications. Scrutiny is required to review the administrator's performance and ensure that the purpose of administration is still capable of achievement. It was recognised that sometimes administration continues during the course of a CVA (so an administrator may exercise rights of action not enjoyed by the supervisor, e.g. ss.238 to 239 of the 1986 Act), and it was in committee stage accepted that this practice could continue with the court granting longer periods of extension.

1   Standing Committee B, 15th Sitting (9 May 2002).

Extension of time

7.10.4   The one-year period can be extended[1] by:

■   court order (for as long as the court thinks necessary); or
■   consent from the appropriate creditors (for a period not exceeding six months).

1   Insolvency Act 1986, Sched.B1, para.76 (2).

7.10.5   It is important to note that consent to an extension of time cannot be obtained after expiry of the initial term. After the expiry of the initial term, an application for an extension of the administration must be made to the court, which is expected to look unfavourably on an administrator who has, without reasonable excuse, failed to obtain consent from the creditors or an order from the court extending the term of administration. The court will perform a balancing act, weighing up whether the purposes of the administration are still capable of being achieved against creditors' interest.

7.10.6   It will be interesting to see how the courts will approach this new level of scrutiny over the administration process. At the very least, it is likely that all the information supplied to creditors will need to be put before the court and further assurances (evidence?) from the administrator that the purpose of the administration is still reasonably likely to be achieved will be required.

7.10.7   Consent by creditors for an extension of time can be obtained only once and for no longer than a further six-month period. It cannot be obtained after the expiry of a court approved extension, nor after the expiry of the initial 12-month period. The consent of all secured creditors and creditors holding 50 per cent of the total unsecured debt is required.

7.10.8   However, in cases where the administrator has provided a statement[1] that:

■   the company has sufficient property to pay all creditors;

- unsecured creditors will receive no payment, or payment only under the 'ring fence' provisions;[2] or
- the only possible objective for the administration capable of being achieved will be to make a distribution to secured creditors,

consent may be obtained from all secured creditors and, if an appropriate distribution is to be made, the consent of the preferential creditors holding at least 50 per cent of the total debts. Consent may be obtained in writing or at a creditors' meeting.

1   Pursuant to Insolvency Act 1986, Sched.B1, para.52.
2   Insolvency Act 1986, s.176A (2)(a).

7.10.9   As soon as reasonably practicable after the extension order is obtained from the court or the consent of the creditors has been obtained, the administrator must notify the Registrar of Companies.[1] The administrator commits an offence if he fails to do so without reasonable excuse. This is punishable by a fine of one fifth of the statutory maximum and a daily rate fine of one fiftieth of the statutory maximum (at present £1,000 and £100 respectively).

1   Insolvency Act 1986, Sched.B1, para.77 (3).

Cessation of appointment by administrator

7.10.10   The administrator is required to apply to court to end the appointment:[1]

- if he thinks the purpose of the administration cannot be achieved;
- if he thinks the company should not have entered into administration;
- if required to do so by the creditors at a creditors' meeting; or
- in the case of court appointment only, if the purpose of the administration has been sufficiently achieved.

1   Insolvency Act 1986, Sched.B1, para.79 (2).

7.10.11   On the application, the court may: order the appointment of the administrator to cease at a specified time; adjourn the hearing conditionally or unconditionally; dismiss the application; or make such interim order or other order as thought necessary. Where the court decides the appointment should come to an end, the court will discharge the administration order and the administrator must send a copy of the order to the Registrar of Companies within 14 days, beginning with the date of the order.[1]

1   Insolvency Act 1986, Sched.B1, para.86.

7.10.12   An administrator commits an offence if without reasonable excuse he fails to comply with this provision and can be fined one fifth of the statutory maximum with a daily fine of one fiftieth of the statutory maximum (at present £1,000 and £100 respectively).

7.10.13   In cases where he has been appointed by a floating chargeholder or by the company/its directors, if the administrator thinks the purposes of the administration have been sufficiently achieved, he may file a notice in the prescribed form with:

- the court; and
- the Registrar of Companies.[1]

---

1   Insolvency Act 1986, Sched.B1, para.80 (2).

7.10.14   Within a further prescribed period (to be set out in the new Insolvency Rules), the administrator will be required to send copies of these notices to all the company's creditors of whom he is aware, although he may be entitled to notify the creditors in some other manner (e.g. by advertisement) that they have the opportunity to request copies of the notice.[1] An administrator commits an offence if he fails to comply with this provision and will be liable to a fine of one fifth of the statutory maximum and daily rate fine of one fiftieth[2] of the statutory maximum (at present £1,000 and £100 respectively).

---

1   Insolvency Act 1986, Sched.B1, para.80 (5). The detailed provisions regarding this section are likely to be provided in the new Insolvency Rules, when published.
2   Insolvency Act 1986, Sched.B1, para.80 (6).

7.10.15   The administration appointment ends on the filing of the requisite notices with the court and the Registrar of Companies. Interestingly, the notice does not need to be sent to the company or its directors. During the committee stage of the Enterprise Bill's passage through Parliament, the Government pointed out that as the administrator's overriding duty is to the company's creditors, it is therefore to the creditors that that notice should be sent. In any event, the normal working practice of the administrator will be to inform the company and directors of his future intention regarding the administration. For this reason the Government rejected several suggested amendments.

Cessation of appointment on creditors' application

7.10.16   An interesting provision in the new legislation allows a creditor to apply to end the appointment of the administrator if the creditor considers the appointment was made for an improper motive.[1]

---

1   Insolvency Act 1986, Sched.B1, para.81.

7.10.17   This right contrasts with the creditors' right to claim that they have suffered unfair harm as a result of the administrator's conduct.[1] The ability to bring the administration to an end is not aimed at policing the administrator's conduct and preventing harm or otherwise to creditors, but is squarely aimed to provide a means to attack the motive behind the appointment. As a consequence, it does not appear necessary to show that the creditor must have actually suffered harm as a result of the appointment or that the administrator has or proposes to act improperly.

---

1 Insolvency Act 1986, Sched.B1, para.74 (as amended).

7.10.18   The legislation does not provide a definition of 'improper motive' and case law will clearly need to develop in order to establish its meaning. We can speculate that it would involve an element of bad faith on the part of the appointor, possibly motivated by commercial reasons, perhaps with the intention that the appointment would lead to the failure of the business. However, it is unlikely that a floating chargeholder's motivation could be challenged on the basis of irrationality or that its decision lacked commercial sense, so long as the decision is made in good faith. It is possible that the legislation is seeking to prevent company directors from using the administration process to avoid paying creditors and setting up 'phoenix companies', stripping the company of its assets. Certainly, the safeguard is thought necessary owing to the introduction of a non-court appointment route and constitutes a warning to potential appointors and the administrator acting on their instructions. On application, the court may make such order as it thinks fit.

Cessation of appointment on public interest winding-up petition

7.10.19   An administrator's appointment will cease on the court order (or alternatively the administrator's powers will be varied and/or limited) where a winding-up order is made or a provisional liquidator appointed under:

■ s.124A of the 1986 Act (a public interest petition); or
■ s.367 of the FSMA 2000 (FSA petition).

Consequences of cessation of appointment

7.10.20   An administrator's appointment generally ceases as a result of either the success or failure of the administration (i.e. where either the purpose of administration has been fulfilled or is no longer capable of being achieved).

7.10.21   If the company has been rescued, the control of the management of the company would normally pass back to its directors and shareholders. In the past, this has not been a common consequence of administration. Now that the pre-eminent purpose of administration is the rescue of the company, it will be interesting to see whether practice accords with the theory of the new legislation.

7.10.22   In the past it has been usual for the business and assets of the company to be sold by the administrator during the course of the administration. This created a 'cash pile' which could be passed to creditors to discharge all the company's outstanding debts or, more likely, to pay a proportion of the total debt.

7.10.23 As we have seen, an administrator may now make distributions to secured and preferential creditors during the course of the administration. With permission of the court, the administrator may also make payments to unsecured creditors and will do so where the payment is likely to assist the achievement of the purposes of the administration. It should be noted, however, that this provision does not entitle the administrator to make a distribution to unsecured creditors *after* the purpose of the administration has been achieved. Distributions to unsecured creditors has not and will not be a role for the administrator. Payments to unsecured creditors during the course of administration will only occur if it will further the purpose of the administration generally. For example, it may be necessary in order to cover payment to ransom creditors (i.e. suppliers who will withdraw essential supplies without payment of existing debts).

7.10.24 Methods to distribute funds to creditors include the use of a CVA or a scheme of arrangement. Both have the advantage of securing the future of the corporate vehicle, but may be inappropriate if actions are being considered against the directors that cannot be pursued by a supervisor of a Voluntary Arrangement.[1] It is also often the case that where the business and assets are being transferred away from the company, there is no wish to retain the corporate vehicle. In these circumstances, the appropriate method to distribute assets is via liquidation.

---

1 Certain statutory rights of action can only be taken by the liquidator, e.g. ss.238, 239.

7.10.25 On application to discharge an administration order, the administrator has the ability to petition for the compulsory winding up of the company. In this case, the 'relevant date' for the purposes of determining the existence and amount of a preferential debt has been deemed to be the date of the making of the administration order. There are however significant disadvantages in putting a company into compulsory liquidation as opposed to voluntary liquidation; namely the need to use the Insolvency Service account by the liquidator and the imposition of an *ad valorem* fee starting at 15 per cent of the monies paid into the account. This increases the costs of the liquidation and decreases the return to creditors. It is generally considered preferable for the company to enter into voluntary liquidation, as this avoids the *ad valorem* fee, provided that a distribution is made within six months.

7.10.26 However, under the previous procedure, after the conclusion of an administration there was particular difficulty and uncertainty as to how the company could move from an administration to voluntary liquidation efficiently and without loss to preferential creditors. The problems are:

- A moratorium during administration prevents the passing of the necessary resolution.
- The relevant date for the purposes of ascertaining whether a debt was preferential would mean that the date of the administration order was the date of the resolution.

■   A hiatus period between the administration order and the voluntary liquidation might allow directors to take control of the company and, in the interim, misappropriate funds accumulated by the administrator.

7.10.27   Techniques were developed to avoid these problems, including passing a conditional resolution to wind up the company and agree with the preferential creditors that they would be treated as if the winding up were a compulsory one (i.e. an earlier relevant date arises). Significant case law on this area emerged, as doubt was cast on these techniques.[1]

---

1   *Re Powerstore (Trading) Limited* [1998] 1 BCLC 90; *Re Mark One (Oxford Street) Plc* [1998] BCC 984; *Re Philip Alexander Securities and Futures* [1998] BCC 819; *Re Novditrack (UK) Limited* [2000] 1 WLR 343; *Re UCT (UK) Limited* [2001] 2 All ER 186.

7.10.28   The new legislation has ended this problem by entitling an administrator to move from administration into voluntary winding up without any intervening period.[1] Where the administrator considers that the secured creditors have been paid in full and are likely to receive no further payment (consequently, any preferential creditors will also have been paid in full), but it is likely that money will be available to unsecured creditors, the administrator may file with the Registrar of Companies a notice stating that Sched.B1 para.83 applies. On the filing of this notice, the administrator's appointment ends and the company will immediately enter into a creditors' voluntary liquidation, as if an appropriate resolution had been passed on that date. This not only overcomes the problem of the hiatus period and need for conditional resolutions, but also ensures that the issue of the relevant date becomes irrelevant as the preferential creditors are likely to have been discharged already.

---

1   Insolvency Act 1986, Sched.B1, para.83.

7.10.29   The liquidator of the company will be the former administrator, unless the creditors appoint an alternative liquidator (in a manner and within a time period prescribed by the new Insolvency Rules). As soon as reasonably practicable, the former administrator is required to file a notice of application of this paragraph at court and send a notice to every creditor.

Dissolution following administration

7.10.30   Where the administrator thinks that there will be no distribution to unsecured creditors, he must file a notice to that effect with the Registrar of Companies.[1] A copy of this notice must be served as soon as reasonably practicable on the court and to each creditor. Thereafter, the company will be deemed to be dissolved within three months after the date of filing. It is however open to the court, the administrator or any interested party to extend, suspend or apply that the dissolution should not take place. In such cases, the administrator must file a notice with the Registrar of Companies.

---

1   Insolvency Act 1986, Sched.B1, para.84 (1).

7.10.31   This clears up the exit route from administration in circumstances where there are assets left to distribute, there is no future for the insolvent corporate shell and where liquidation is inappropriate.

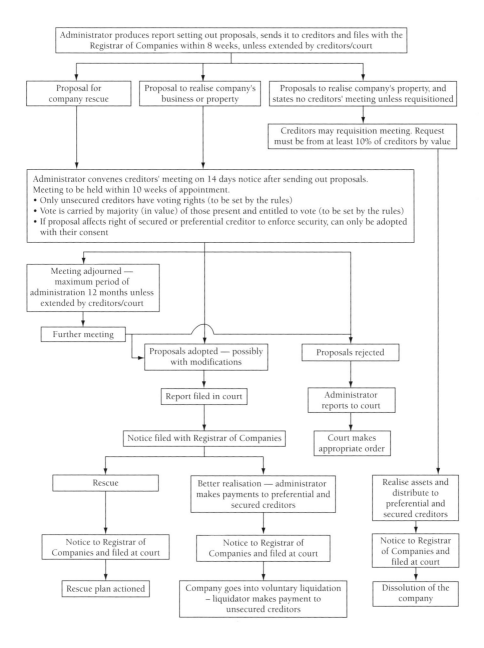

Figure 7.3 Conclusions to administration

7.11 REPLACING AN ADMINISTRATOR

Circumstances where an administrator maybe removed

7.11.1   The administrator will be removed from office by the following methods:

- Court order.[1] The court may remove an administrator from office at any time.
- Resignation.[2] An administrator may resign by providing written notice to:
  - the court, if appointed by a court order;
  - the floating chargeholder, if appointed pursuant to para.12; or
  - the company or its directors, if appointed pursuant to para.20.

- On ceasing to be appropriately qualified.[3] Where an administrator ceases to be qualified as an insolvency practitioner, he must give notice to the court, the floating chargeholder or the company or its directors (as appropriate), of his vacation of office. The administrator commits an offence if he fails to take this step.

1   Insolvency Act 1986, Sched.B1, para. 88.
2   Insolvency Act 1986, Sched.B1, para. 87.
3   Insolvency Act 1986, Sched.B1, para. 89.

Replacement of an administration

7.11.2   Where an administrator dies, resigns, is removed by a court order, or vacates office after ceasing to be qualified, he may be replaced. Where the administrator was appointed by court order, the administrator may only be replaced on application by:

- the creditors' committee; or
- any remaining administrator still in office.

7.11.3   Where there is no creditors' committee, an application can be made by the company, its directors, or one or more creditors. The court will only grant an order on such an application if it considers that any other party entitled to replace the administrator is not taking reasonable steps to do so, or if it is right for the court to so order.[1]

1   Insolvency Act 1986, Sched.B1, paras.91 and 95.

7.11.4   Where the administrator was appointed by a floating chargeholder, the appointor retains the power to replace the administrator.[1] If the holder of a prior qualifying floating charge (i.e. one created first or granted priority by agreement) objects to the person nominated as the replacement, that party may apply to court for an order appointing their own nominee.

1   Insolvency Act 1986, Sched.B1, paras.92 and 96.

7.11.5   Where the administrator was appointed by the company or its directors, the appointer can only replace the administrator if:

- any creditor holding a qualifying floating charge consents; or
- if consent is withheld, the court grants permission.[1]

1   Insolvency Act 1986, Sched.B1, paras.94 and 97.

7.11.6   Where there is no qualifying floating charge, the administrator may be replaced by resolution of the creditors' committee.

The effect of vacation of office

7.11.7   Where a person ceases to be an administrator of a company, he is discharged from liability in respect of any action taken as administrator.[1] This discharge takes effect at a time specified by the court, or in the case of an administrator dying, on the filing at court of his notice of death. The discharge of the administrator is without prejudice to the court's right to examine the conduct of the former administrator in respect of any potential misfeasance.

1   Insolvency Act 1986, Sched.B1, para.98 (4).

Charges and liabilities

7.11.8   The former administrator's remuneration, expenses and any sum due to him as a result of any contract he has entered into in connection with his appointment will be:

- charged on and payable out of the property of which the former administrator had custody and control of immediately prior to the time when he ceased to be the company's administrator;
- payable in priority to the claims of any creditor whose debts are secured by floating charge.[1]

1   Insolvency Act 1986, Sched.B1, para.98 (4).

7.11.9   These provisions follow former ss.19 (4) and 19 (5) of the 1986 Act. Section 19 was extensively amended by the Insolvency Act 1994, which was hurriedly introduced to cover the problems that had resulted from the decision of the Court of Appeal in *Powdrill v. Watson; Re Paramount Airways Limited (No. 3)*.[1]

1   [1994] 2 All ER 513.

7.11.10   In that case, the Court of Appeal[1] held that:

- A contract of employment for an employee of the insolvent company is either adopted as a whole or not. It is not open for the administrator to 'cherry pick' those parts of the contract to which he wishes to be bound.

■   A contract of employment is inevitably adopted if the administrator causes the company to continue the employment of the employee after appointment.

■   The practice that administrators had assumed of writing to employees within the first 14 days to state that the administrator did not incur any personal liability in respect of the adoption of contracts was of no effect.

---

1   The case was heard by the House of Lords after the introduction of the Insolvency Act 1994, which held that the administrator's liabilities were limited to those incurred during his tenure.

7.11.11   This decision meant that an administrator's claim for his own remuneration and expenses was subordinated to a wide range of claims by employees and former employees. The Insolvency Act 1994 has no retrospective effect and consequently contracts of employment adopted by the administrator before 15 March 1994 are still governed by previous case law.

7.11.12   The Insolvency Act 1994 introduced revisions to s.19 of the 1986 Act (which are mirrored in the new legislation[1]) which ensure that an administrator will not be liable under any adopted contract of employment for any liabilities arising under that contract and for that purpose:

■   Any action taken within 14 days of appointment shall not be taken into account or be said to have contributed to the adoption of the contract.
■   No account shall be taken of any liability which arose or incurred before the adoption of the contract.
■   No account shall be taken of a liability to make payment other than of wages or salary.

---

1   Insolvency Act 1986, Sched.B1, para.99 (5).

7.11.13   It should of course be noted that the making of an administration order does not automatically bring to an end employees' contracts of employment, or indeed any other contractual liability. However, for contracts of employment adopted on or after 15 March 1994, the administrator is only liable for 'wages and salaries'. This means:

■   holiday pay;
■   sickness pay;
■   sums payable in lieu of holiday; and
■   contributions to occupational pension schemes.

PART IV ENTERPRISE ACT 2002 – PERSONAL INSOLVENCY REFORM

8 THE NEW BANKRUPTCY REGIME

8.1 THE DURATION OF THE BANKRUPTCY ORDER

Introduction

8.1.1   The Government's White Paper preceding the Enterprise Act 2002 was entitled 'Insolvency – A Second Chance'. The White Paper re-emphasised the Government's commitment to the reform process and in particular a desire that business and individuals could have a 'second chance' after business failure:

> Government must help create an ambitious business culture, which enables people from all walks of life to realise their creativity, innovative ability and entrepreneurial potential. We must help any person with the will and the ability to create and grow a successful business. An honest business failure should not mean that you cannot have another go.[1]

---

1   Opportunity For All In A World of Change, DTI/DFEE White Paper, February 2001, Chapter 5.2.

8.1.2   The Government hopes that the Enterprise Act 2002 reforms will create a dynamic entrepreneurial culture in which individuals shall no longer be discouraged from taking risks due to the fear of financial failure. In doing so they hope to create more entrepreneurs who will develop dynamic small businesses, the life blood to any successful economy. The reforms to the bankruptcy regime are designed to encourage this by reducing (or in some cases removing) the stigma of bankruptcy and the restrictions and disabilities of bankruptcy. Central to this is reform to the duration of the bankruptcy period.

8.1.3   The length of the bankruptcy is important to both the bankrupt and his creditors, as the restrictions upon the bankrupt's conduct and affairs will generally end once the bankrupt is discharged from his bankruptcy (see section 9.4 on the reforms to the restrictions imposed on a bankrupt). This section considers the major reform introduced by the Enterprise Act 2002, which will have the effect of reducing the duration of most bankruptcies. Consequential reforms such as the introduction of new creditor safeguards, which include the bankruptcy restrictions order ('BRO') and the bankruptcy restrictions undertaking ('BRU') are also examined. Finally, we will also consider whether the proposed new creditor safeguards will be effective.

Duration under the former bankruptcy regime

8.1.4   Under the old law as set out within the unamended 1986 Act, most bankruptcies lasted for a maximum of three years. The exceptions to this being:

- Where there were low-value estates falling within the summary administration procedure, the duration of the bankruptcy was limited to a maximum of two years.
- In the case of either a 'criminal' bankrupt[1] or a 'repeat' bankrupt (i.e. someone who had previously been made bankrupt within the preceding 15 years), an application could be made to the court by the trustee in bankruptcy (or the Official Receiver) for an extension to the normal duration of the bankruptcy.

---

1   i.e. An individual made bankrupt in accordance with s.264 (1)(d) of the 1986 Act.

Duration under the new bankruptcy regime

8.1.5   In the majority of cases, a bankrupt will, at the latest, be discharged at the end of the first year calculated from the date on which the bankruptcy commenced.[1] Furthermore, the Enterprise Act 2002 reforms have gone further, as the Official Receiver may file at court a notice stating that the bankrupt is to be discharged even earlier than the expiry of this new one-year limitation period. Such a notice may be filed where:

- The Official Receiver considers that an investigation of the bankrupt's conduct and affairs is unnecessary (or it has been effectively concluded).
- No restrictions on the bankrupt's conduct need to be imposed (see section 9.1 on the reforms to the investigatory role of the Official Receiver).

---

1   Insolvency Act 1986, s.279 (as amended) as substituted by Enterprise Act 2002, s.256.

8.1.6   In view of the radical shortening of the duration of most bankruptcies, references to the summary administration procedure have been removed from the 1986 Act in their entirety.[1]

---

1   Section 269 of the Enterprise Act 2002 introduces Sched.23 making minor and consequential amendments to amongst other matters the removal of references to the summary administration procedure within the 1986 Act.

8.1.7   The general reduction in the period of bankruptcy is clearly influenced by the US system with its mechanism for early release (see section 2.2 for further detail). It is, however, worth noting that the initial proposal in the Enterprise Bill was for a six-month maximum period. After significant criticism regarding this proposal, a relatively late amendment to the Enterprise Act 2002 was allowed. That said, it is anticipated that the vast majority of bankrupts will be discharged by no later than the end of the first anniversary of their bankruptcy and could be within six to eight weeks.

8.1.8   Before considering the creditors safeguards introduced by the Enterprise Act 2002 reforms, it is worth examining the principal concerns to this reform, which are twofold:

- The first major concern over the reduced duration of most bankruptcies is its potentially adverse impact upon the ability of the bankruptcy regime to regulate the economy. For example, a bankrupt discharged within weeks could potentially quickly re-enter into debt. Creditors may lose confidence in the ability of the regime to regulate financial behaviour and may not use bankruptcy proceedings, knowing its limited impact. Actual and potential creditors' exposure and loss to repeated financial failure may be met with greater restrictions on credit and an increase in prices. The effect on the economy as a whole will swiftly multiply. This concern has, in part, been addressed by the increased creditor safeguards which form part of the amended restrictions regime, but the question remains of whether such safeguards will be sufficient. The Government has concluded that the possible detrimental effect on the economy caused by abuse of this relaxation of the bankruptcy regime is worth the risk, as the beneficial effect of providing a second chance to entrepreneurs should provide greater benefits to the economy as a whole.
- The second major concern is that the Official Receiver's office appears to be receiving neither significant additional funding nor additional personnel to meet its substantial new obligations to protect creditors from 'culpable'[1] bankrupts. Therefore, there is a risk that, at the very least in the short term, a full and proper investigation of the bankrupt's affairs and conduct may not be completed within the one-year period of most bankruptcies or if it is, that it will be of poor quality due to the lack of available resources. If the Official Receiver's investigations cannot be completed both effectively and in good time then some culpable bankrupts may slip through the safety net and avoid being subjected to the amended restrictions regime.

---

1   See section 8.3 on BROs for a full discussion on the concept of 'culpable bankrupts'.

The new law: suspension of the bankruptcy period

8.1.9   Upon an application by the trustee in bankruptcy (or the Official Receiver), the court may order that the calculation of time attributable to working out the one year limitation period of the bankruptcy will cease to run. Such an order will be made where the court is satisfied that the bankrupt has failed or is failing to comply with his statutory obligations as set out within the 1986 Act. For example, a bankrupt may have failed to provide complete disclosure of assets. Where the court has ordered that such a suspension of time should take effect, the form of the order will be that the calculation of time attributable to working out the one-year limitation period will cease to run until either:

- the end of a specified period (which will inevitably be a period of time causing the bankruptcy to last longer than one year); or
- the fulfilment of a specified condition. A 'condition' is defined within the Enterprise Act 2002 as 'a condition requiring that the Court be satisfied of something'. For example, the condition could be a requirement imposed on the bankrupt to particularise all his creditors and his assets before such a suspension of time is lifted.

8.1.10   The court's power to annul (as opposed to discharge) the bankruptcy order is unaffected by the existence of any order suspending the bankruptcy period.[1] The effect of an annulment of the bankruptcy remains unchanged by the Enterprise Act 2002.[2] Therefore, any dispositions of property, etc. carried out by the trustee in bankruptcy are valid, although the court can order the revesting of property back to the bankrupt or to any third party.

1   Section 279 (7) of the 1986 Act as inserted by s.256 of the Enterprise Act 2002. For example, an annulment may be provided if an IVA is approved by qualifying creditors (see section 9.3 on IVAs).
2   I.e. as set out within s.282 (4) of the 1986 Act.

8.1.11   The law applying to a 'criminal'[1] bankrupt remains largely unchanged in that he will still need to apply to court for a discharge from his bankruptcy.[2] However, there has been a change to the procedure applying to a repeat bankrupt. The new law provides that where an individual has previously been made bankrupt within the last six years,[3] either the Secretary or State or the Official Receiver (acting under the direction of the Secretary of State) may apply to court for a bankruptcy restriction order ('BRO') or seek to obtain a bankruptcy restriction undertaking ('BRU') from the bankrupt (see sections 8.3 and 8.4).

1   i.e. An individual made bankrupt in accordance with s.264 (1)(d) of the 1986 Act.
2   Section 279 (6) of the 1986 Act as inserted by s.256 of the Enterprise Act 2002. A minor amendment has been introduced by s.269 of the Enterprise Act 2002 which introduces changes by Sched.23, para.3 to s.280 (1) of the 1986 Act to take into effect amendments elsewhere.
3   Time is calculated from the period of six years ending with the date of the current bankruptcy. This contrasts with the old law where a repeat bankrupt who had been bankrupt within the preceding 15 years would remain an undischarged bankrupt for a minimum of five years. Schedule 4A, para.3 to the 1986 Act, as inserted by the Enterprise Act 2002.

8.2   THE TRANSITIONAL PROVISIONS

Introduction

8.2.1   The Enterprise Act 2002 sets out in detail the transitional provisions that are to apply to all undischarged bankrupts who were made bankrupt before the commencement of the Enterprise Act 2002 (the 'pre-commencement bankrupt').[1] The effect of the transitional provisions is to apply to the pre-commencement bankrupt a mix of the old provisions set out within the unamended 1986 Act, together with some of the new provisions introduced by the Enterprise Act 2002. Unamended copies of the 1986 Act should be retained, as some provisions will continue to apply to these transitional bankruptcies. This section considers in detail how the various transitional provisions are to be applied to the pre-commencement bankrupt.

---

1   Schedule 19 to the Enterprise Act 2002.

The general transitional provisions

8.2.2   Upon the commencement of s.256 of the Enterprise Act 2002, neither the old law, nor the new law as contained within s.279[1] of the 1986 Act (which refers to the duration of the bankruptcy) will apply.[2] Rather, the transitional provisions provide that the pre-commencement bankrupt will be discharged from his bankruptcy at whichever is the earlier of either:

- The end of the period of one year calculated from the commencement date of the relevant provision within the Enterprise Act 2002.[3]
- The end of the relevant statutory discharge period applicable to the bankrupt as it had effect immediately before the commencement of the relevant provision of the Enterprise Act 2002.[4] Therefore, the bankrupt can still be automatically discharged in accordance with the earlier expiry of any of the historic time limits provided for under the old provisions of the 1986 Act.[5]

---

1   Inserted by Enterprise Act 2002, s.256.
2   Schedule 19, para.3 to the Enterprise Act 2002.
3   i.e. Enterprise Act 2002, s.256.
4   Section 279 (1)(b) of the 1986 Act (unamended by the Enterprise Act 2002).
5   For example s.279 of the 1986 Act (unamended) which sets out the discharge periods in detail.

8.2.3   Some of the now largely historic safeguards protecting creditors from 'culpable'[1] bankrupts have also been retained. For example, where under the old law a court order was obtained to suspend the calculation of time attributable to working out the duration of the bankruptcy, then the terms of that suspension order will generally remain in force.[2] Therefore, notwithstanding the general transitional provisions set out above, the suspension order will remain in force until either the expiry of the time period set out within the court order, or until the fulfilment of such conditions as may be specified within that order. Such an order may have been sought by the Official Receiver where the bankrupt has failed or is failing to comply with his obligations under the 1986 Act[3] to disclose all his assets. Therefore, until all of the bankrupt's assets are disclosed, he will remain an undischarged bankrupt. That said, such an order may be varied or revoked after the commencement of the relevant provision of the Enterprise Act 2002 upon an application to the court by the trustee in bankruptcy (or the Official Receiver) in accordance with the new law.[4]

1   See section 8.3 for a full discussion of the concept of 'culpable bankrupts'.
2   Insolvency Act 1986, s.279 (3) (unamended).
3   Insolvency Act 1986, s.279 (3) (unamended).
4   Insolvency Act 1986, s.279 (3) as amended by s.256 of the Enterprise Act 2002: Enterprise Act 2002, Sched.19, para.4 (2).

8.2.4   For any pre-commencement bankrupt affected by these general transitional provisions, s.279 (3)–(5) of the amended 1986 Act will also apply. Therefore, notwithstanding the absence of any historic suspension order in place in accordance with the old law, the trustee in bankruptcy (or the Official Receiver) specifically has the power to apply to the court for an order suspending the calculation of time attributable to working out the duration of the bankruptcy (for commentary on when such an order might be sought, see para.8.1.9).

Criminal pre-commencement bankruptcy

8.2.5   In the event that a pre-commencement bankrupt was adjudged as a 'criminal' bankrupt[1] he will not be discharged from his bankruptcy in accordance with the general transitional provisions set out above. However, he may still be discharged upon his application to the court seeking an order for his discharge[2] in accordance with s.280 of the 1986 Act.

1   In accordance with Insolvency Act 1986, s.264 (1)(d).
2   This provision is set out within Enterprise Act 2002, Sched.19, para.6. Section 280 of the 1986 Act is also amended by Sched.23, para.3 of the Enterprise Act 2002.

The 'repeat' pre-commencement bankrupt

8.2.6   Where the pre-commencement bankrupt has previously been an undischarged bankrupt at some time during the preceding 15 years (ending with the day before the date on which the pre-commencement bankruptcy commenced), the pre-commencement 'repeat' bankrupt shall not be discharged from his current bankruptcy in accordance with the general transitional provisions set out above. The applicable provisions are detailed below.

8.2.7   The Enterprise Act 2002 provides that any court order which remains in force relating to the bankrupt's absolute or conditional discharge shall continue to have effect after the commencement of the relevant provision of the Enterprise

Act 2002.[1] Subject to the terms of any of such orders, a pre-commencement repeat bankrupt will not receive an automatic early discharge in accordance with the general transitional provisions, rather he will be discharged at either:

- The end of a period of five years beginning with the commencement of the relevant provision of the Enterprise Act 2002.[2]
- Such earlier date as the court may specifically order. Such an order will only be made following a court application (usually commenced by the bankrupt) seeking to discharge the order.[3]

---

1   See s.280 (2)(b) or (c) and s.280 (3) of the 1986 Act (unamended) provides for where the court can place conditions upon a bankrupt. The relevant provision of the Enterprise Act 2002 is s.256.
2   Enterprise Act 2002, s.256.
3   Such an application to be made in accordance with s.280 of the 1986 Act.

8.2.8   For example, an individual made bankrupt for the second time one year before the commencement of the relevant provision would be eligible to apply to court for his discharge four years after the commencement of the relevant provision. If no application is made then the bankruptcy is automatically discharged five years after the relevant provision was commenced.

8.2.9   Furthermore, as with the general transitional provisions, a pre-commencement repeat bankrupt is also subject to s.279 (3)–(5) of the amended 1986 Act.[1] Therefore, notwithstanding the absence of any order imposing restrictions, the trustee in bankruptcy (or the Official Receiver) specifically has the power to apply to the court for an order suspending the calculation of time attributable to working out the duration of the bankruptcy (for commentary on when such an order might be sought, see para.8.1.9).

---

1   As substituted by Enterprise Act 2002, s.256.

8.2.10   Finally, it is worth noting that these specific transitional provisions will not apply to any repeat pre-commencement bankrupt if the previous bankruptcy (or the previous bankruptcies) has been annulled by the court.[1]

---

1   In accordance with Insolvency Act 1986, s.282.

The effect on any bankruptcy restrictions order ('BRO')

8.2.11   In the event that an individual is discharged from his bankruptcy pursuant to any of the various transitional provisions set out above, then any BRO (or interim BRO or BRU) which may be made in relation to that individual or a bankruptcy restrictions undertaking entered into by that individual will remain in force.[1] Therefore, a pre-commencement bankrupt could find himself subject to the new restrictions introduced by the Enterprise Act 2002.

---

1   Enterprise Act 2002, Sched.19, para.8.

8.3   BANKRUPTCY RESTRICTIONS ORDERS ('BROs')

Introduction

8.3.1   The BRO is a safeguard provision introduced by the Enterprise Act 2002 aimed at penalising certain 'culpable'[1] bankrupts where their conduct is such that some form of sanction is considered by the court as being appropriate. Examples of culpable bankrupts will include those individuals who are perceived to be abusing the system, are dishonest or are otherwise blameworthy for their financial position. This reform provides a counterpoint to the significant liberalisation of the bankruptcy regime within England and Wales considered elsewhere in this book. Individual bankrupts are now distinguished for the first time in the modern bankruptcy regime according to the degree of personal 'culpability' for their bankruptcy. This reform is central to the Government thinking on this area, namely that the vast majority of bankrupts are non-culpable (i.e. simply unlucky) and therefore should be treated more favourably. Therefore, the majority deserves a 'second chance' to become the kind of entrepreneurial, dynamic and risk-taking individuals beloved by the Government. However, where in the minority of cases, the blame for the cause of the bankruptcy is attributed to the individual culpable bankrupt, then a BRO should be imposed. A BRO not only acts as a restriction on the individual bankrupt, but may also act as a deterrent to possible misconduct by others. Therefore, a BRO has the potential to be a useful measure in policing the bankrupt's conduct during the bankruptcy process. As we shall see, it has great similarities to the present system of director disqualification.

---

1   The Government's White Paper 'Introduction to Bankruptcy Proposals' distinguished between the 'culpable' and 'non-culpable' bankrupt. The former category could include those who, for example, repeatedly become bankrupt or where gambling caused the bankruptcy, etc. Extracts from the White Paper which provides an insight to the Government's policy are as follows: 'We propose the following changes to the personal insolvency regime . . . Providing for a tougher regime of restrictions on bankrupts whose conduct has been irresponsible, reckless or otherwise culpable . . . The Government will legislate to provide for robust and effective remedies against the small minority who have acted recklessly, irresponsibly or dishonestly.'

The grounds for making a BRO

8.3.2   A BRO may be made by the court on the application by the Secretary of State or the Official Receiver. The court has a wide discretion as to whether such an order should be made and can have regard to the conduct of the bankrupt either before or after the making of the bankruptcy order. The court will, in particular, take into account the following kinds of behaviour on the part of the bankrupt when considering whether it is appropriate to make a BRO:

■   Where the bankrupt was an undischarged bankrupt at some time during the period of six years ending with the date of the bankruptcy to which the application relates. It is considered that this provision will also apply to a pre-commencement bankrupt.

- Failing to keep records which account for a loss of property by the bankrupt, or by a business carried on by him, where the loss occurred in the period beginning two years before petition and ending with the date of the application.[1]
- Failing to produce records of that kind on demand by the Official Receiver or the trustee in bankruptcy.[2]
- Entering into a transaction at an undervalue.[3]
- Giving a preference.[4]
- Making an excessive pension contribution.[5] (See section 4.2 for further analysis on how the bankrupt's pension is treated under the new bankruptcy regime.)
- A failure to supply goods or services which were wholly or partly paid for which gave rise to a claim provable in the bankruptcy.
- Trading at a time before the commencement of the bankruptcy when the bankrupt knew or ought to have known that he was unable to pay his debts. This kind of behaviour will be considered by the court on an objective basis. Therefore, the court will determine whether either the bankrupt should have known even if he professes that he did not, was wilfully turning a blind eye to his increasingly poor financial position or was being negligent with his finances. If so, any such conduct may attract the court's displeasure and therefore a BRO. The boundaries to this objective test may well be tested within the courts over time. It is anticipated that the case law considering the analogous wrongful trading provision within s.214 of the 1986 Act (applicable to directors in a corporate insolvency situation) may provide guidance as to how the court will consider this element of the bankrupt's behaviour.
- Incurring, before the commencement of the bankruptcy, a debt which the bankrupt had no reasonable expectation of being able to pay.
- Failing to account satisfactorily to the court, the Official Receiver or the trustee in bankruptcy for a loss of property or for an insufficiency of property to meet bankruptcy debts.
- Carrying on any gambling, rash or hazardous speculation or unreasonable extravagance which may have materially contributed to or increased the extent of the bankruptcy, or which took place between presentation of the petition and commencement of the bankruptcy. This has been included as the criminal offence of causing bankruptcy by gambling has now been repealed (see section 9.4 on the changes to the bankruptcy restrictions regime).
- Neglect of business affairs of a kind which may have materially contributed to or increased the extent of the bankruptcy.
- Fraud or fraudulent breach of trust.
- Failing to cooperate with the Official Receiver or the trustee in bankruptcy.[6]

---

1   Insolvency Act 1986, Sched.4A, para.2 (2) inserted by s.257 of the Enterprise Act 2002.
2   For example, s.268 of the Enterprise Act 2002 by Sched.23 substitutes s.291 (4) of the 1986 Act by providing that the bankrupt must give the Official Receiver such inventory

of his estate and such other information and attend the Official Receiver as the Official Receiver may require in connection with the making of a BRO.
3 Insolvency Act 1986, s.339.
4 Insolvency Act 1986, s.340.
5 Insolvency Act 1986, s.342A.
6 Insolvency Act 1986, Sched.4A, para.2 inserted by s.257 of the Enterprise Act 2002 sets out all the factors save for the first one.

8.3.3   An application for a BRO must be made before the end of the expiry of first year of the bankruptcy calculated from the date on which the bankruptcy commences. If the Secretary of State or the Official Receiver (acting on the direction of the Secretary of State) wishes to make an application after this one-year limitation period has expired then they will need the court's permission. The court is unlikely to provide permission to extend time limits unless there is good reason for the delay (see section 4.1 on the pervasive effect of the HRA 1998). The calculation of time attributable to this one-year limitation period will be automatically extended if there is for example, a court order in place suspending the time attributable to calculating the duration of bankruptcy.[1]

1 Such an application would be brought pursuant to Insolvency Act 1986, s.279 (3)–(5) (as amended).

8.3.4   The calculation of the BRO's duration is simple as it comes into effect on the date it is made by the court and will cease to have an effect at the end of the date specified within the BRO. In addition, the BRO must continue for a minimum of two and a maximum of 15 years, calculated with reference to the date upon which the BRO was made. Again, the close correlation between BROs and directors disqualification proceedings is exemplified. The effect of a BRO is to extend the restrictions and disabilities imposed on a bankrupt for the duration of the BRO (see section 9.4 for further commentary on the changes to the restrictions regime).

Interim BRO

8.3.5   It may prove to be the case that a substantive hearing of a BRO application cannot be heard prior to the bankrupt's discharge. This is particularly true where the BRO is contested. Therefore, an interim BRO may be made by the court on the basis of either public interest or where there are prima facie grounds to suggest that an application for a BRO will be successful. The Secretary of State or the Official Receiver (acting on the direction of the Secretary of State) may only apply to the court for an interim BRO where an application for a BRO has already been issued at court, but before it has been heard by the court.

8.3.6   An interim BRO will have the same effect as a BRO and it will come into force when it is made. However, the interim order will cease to have effect in the following circumstances:

- On the determination of the application for the BRO.
- On the acceptance of a bankruptcy restrictions undertaking (BRU) offered by the bankrupt.
- If the court discharges the interim BRO on the application of either the bankrupt or the original applicant.

8.3.7   In the event that a BRO is subsequently made by the court, its commencement date is backdated to the date that the interim BRO commenced.[1]

---

1   Insolvency Act 1986, Sched.4A, para.6 as inserted by s.257 of the Enterprise Act 2002.

8.4   BANKRUPTCY RESTRICTIONS UNDERTAKING ('BRU')

Introduction

8.4.1   The Insolvency Act 2000 reformed the directors disqualification regime by enabling directors facing disqualification proceedings to provide undertakings which would have the same effect as if a court order had been made on like terms. This reform was introduced to improve the speed and efficiency of the system, allowing those directors who would have 'pleaded guilty' to avoid the cost and expense of a trial and to increase use of the system. It also put on a statutory footing the procedure[1] which had been formulated to deal with the summary disposal of applications which were uncontested. The Enterprise Act 2002 reforms of the personal insolvency regime and the introduction of BROs posed similar issues as the original Company Directors Disqualification Act 1986, i.e. what if the individual would consent to an order being made? To avoid the necessity and associated cost of a court hearing, the bankrupt may offer a bankruptcy restrictions undertaking ('BRU') to the Secretary of State. The Secretary of State will consider whether accepting a BRU is appropriate, having regard to the kind of behaviour considered by the court when making a BRO as specified in Sched.4A, para.2 (2) and (3) to the 1986 Act[2] (see para.8.3.2).

---

1   *Re Carecraft Construction Co Ltd* [1994] 1 WLR 172.
2   As inserted by Enterprise Act 2002, s.257.

The nature of a BRU

8.4.2   The nature of a BRU:

- A BRU has the same effect as a BRO.
- It will come into force once it is accepted by the Secretary of State and will cease to have effect at the end of the date specified within the BRU.
- It is subject to the same restrictions on its duration as the BRO, i.e. it must last not less than two and not more than 15 years (as calculated from the date when the BRU is accepted by the Secretary of State).

- The bankrupt may subsequently apply to the court for an order to annul the BRU or to shorten its duration.[1]
- Any reference within the Enterprise Act 2002 to an individual being subject to a BRO should also be taken to include a reference to a BRU.

1   Insolvency Act 1986, Sched.4A, para.7.

8.5   THE EFFECT OF ANNULMENT ON A BRO OR BRU

8.5.1   During the passage of the Enterprise Bill through Parliament, one possible problem which was identified with the new BRO regime was its interplay with post-bankruptcy IVAs (see section 9.3). On an IVA being accepted, the bankruptcy order would be annulled. Whilst this procedure offers a clear encouragement to debtor rehabilitation and may ensure a greater return to creditors, it could potentially have been exploited by the unscrupulous bankrupt to avoid the restriction of a BRO. Firstly, he could propose an IVA in circumstances where he felt that a BRO might be imposed. Secondly, if BRO proceedings were successful he could nullify its effect by applying for an IVA. Amendments to the Enterprise Bill have partially addressed these concerns.

8.5.2   In general, on the annulment of most bankruptcy orders[1] any BROs, interim BROs or BRUs which remain in force will be automatically annulled. Also, no new BROs or interim BROs may be made or BRUs entered into after the annulment. This provision only refers to an annulment of the bankruptcy order on the grounds that at the time when the bankruptcy order was made it ought not to have been made, or where a criminal bankruptcy order has been rescinded as a consequence of a successful appeal.

1   i.e. Any annulment in accordance with Insolvency Act 1986, s.282 (1)(*a*) or (2).

8.5.3   However, where the bankruptcy debts are purportedly paid off in full, or where there is an annulment on different grounds[1] such as pursuant to an IVA being approved then:

- An annulment shall not affect the BRO, interim BRO or BRU that may apply to the bankrupt.
- The court may still make a BRO in relation to the bankrupt on an application instituted before such an annulment.
- The Secretary of State may still accept a BRU offered before such an annulment.

1   i.e. Any annulment in accordance with Insolvency Act 1986, ss.261, 263D or 262 (1)(*b*).

8.5.4   However, an application for a BRO or an interim BRO in respect of the bankrupt may not be instituted after such an annulment. Therefore the Official

Receiver must ensure that an application for a BRO has been commenced (if appropriate) before any annulment is ordered by the court. This therefore means that within the first 28 days of bankruptcy (i.e. before an IVA can be proposed), the Official Receiver must have completed his investigation and concluded that he is satisfied that BRO proceedings should not be initiated and instead, agree that an IVA may be proposed (see section 9.3 for further details of this procedure). If this is not the case, then the IVA arrangement should not be recommended to the bankrupt's creditors as this would risk allowing a 'culpable' bankrupt to avoid being subjected to this new restriction regime.

8.6   WILL THE NEW REGIME WORK?

8.6.1   The Secretary of State will maintain a register of all BROs, interim BROs and BRUs.[1] It is anticipated that this will be open for public viewing, as is the Register of Disqualified Directors. The DTI has set up a telephone hot-line for people to report their suspicions that a disqualified director is concerned in the promotion, management and/or control of a company. It remains to be seen whether the DTI makes similar provisions regarding reporting on the conduct of individuals subject to BROs, interim BROs or BRUs. The rules in this regard are at the date of writing still to be released.

---

1   Section 269 of the Enterprise Act 2002 introduces various minor amendments to the insolvency regime included within Sched.23, para.16 (3). This inserts minor provisions at Sched.9, para.29A to the 1986 Act which includes centralising the registers. The details of these procedures have not yet been announced.

8.6.2   It would appear from reading the Enterprise Act 2002 that a pre-commencement undischarged bankrupt could be subjected to either a BRO, an interim BRO or offer a BRU. Importantly, this view is in accordance with the Official Receiver's understanding of the new provisions.

8.6.3   It is anticipated that this new regime will be relatively cost effective. There remains a question mark over whether the costs of a contested BRO or interim BRO court application will be recoverable. It is expected that this point will be covered within the accompanying rules which have yet to be published by the Government. The Official Receiver does not intend to generally use solicitors to assist and it is hoped that most 'culpable' bankrupts will enter into BRUs and as a result the implementation of this procedure should, in theory, be neither costly nor time consuming.

8.6.4   It is clear that the BRO and BRU regime has significant similarities with the disqualification of company directors under the Company Directors Dis-qualification Act 1986.[1] The Enterprise Act 2002 does not specify all the circum-stances in which such an order can be made but sets out particular examples of the kind of conduct which would be relevant to the court's determination. This obviously provides the court with flexibility to make an order against a 'culpable' bankrupt in respect of conduct not included on the list of which it disapproves. However, in the early years after the implementation of the new provision, it will be difficult to advise individuals with complete certainty as to what particular activities may attract the wrath of the court and where the BROs could be imposed. This lack of certainty could reduce the impact of these proposals in deterring recalcitrant bankrupts.

1   Company Directors Disqualification Act 1986, s.1A.

8.6.5   Furthermore, in assessing the possible duration of a BRO, the Enterprise Act 2002 provides no guidance. Therefore, it is expected that the analogy with the Company Directors Disqualification Act may mean that the courts follow the general principles set out within the case of *Re Sevenoaks Stationers (Retail) Limited.*[1]

> the most serious cases, attracting a period of disqualification within this suggested top bracket of 10 to 15 years, will include cases of deceit and fraud. To draw the line between cases which should fall within the suggested bottom bracket (2–5 or 6 years) and the middle bracket (5 or 6 to 10 years) is more difficult. However, possible areas of distinction are (a) whether the serious failures came about deliberately or with knowledge of the potential result and harm they would cause, or innocently and through lack of knowledge or incompetence and (b) whether the failure were 'one off' or part of a pattern.

1   [1991] Ch 164 at 171 C–E, CA.

8.6.6   The Insolvency Service estimate that between 7 and 12 per cent of all bankruptcies are culpable bankruptcies. With on average 25,000 bankruptcies per year (and this figure may increase if economic conditions deteriorate), there are likely to be between 1,750 to 3,000 potential BROs or BRUs per year. Conversely, over 20,000 bankrupts will be released annually within a year of their bankruptcy. It remains to be seen whether the safeguards will be effective or mere window dressing. If this safeguard system fails to have the desired effect, it is likely that the number of bankruptcies will snowball and this will have a wider detrimental effect upon the national economy.

8.6.7   As the BRO can only be made by the Secretary of State or the Official Receiver, the implementation and application of this regime will be dependent upon the policies adopted by the DTI, the availability of effective manpower and also funding.[1] This means that there may be a natural inclination to focus upon straightforward cases as opposed to larger, more complex cases where the 'culpable' bankrupts might have the resources to fight their position. Therefore, whilst these changes are welcomed, the questions over the lack of funding and available resources for the new system remain a concern. It is also hoped that the Government will not decide to introduce the reforms in a piecemeal fashion (as they did with the Welfare Reform and Pension Schemes Act 1999: see section 4.3) as the liberalisation of the bankruptcy regime by way of a reduction in the period of bankruptcy needs to be introduced at the same time as appropriate creditor safeguards. Time will tell whether these safeguards will indeed act as an effective deterrent to recalcitrant bankrupts or whether commentators will look back with longing to the old regime.

1 Section 269 of the Enterprise Act 2002 inserts s.415A into the 1986 Act and a new general fee order. It is expected that once published, the new Insolvency Rules will provide further background to the amendments to the funding regime.

9 FURTHER REFORMS TO PERSONAL INSOLVENCY LAW

9.1 INVESTIGATORY DUTIES OF THE OFFICIAL RECEIVER

The duty to investigate

9.1.1 The investigatory duties imposed upon the Official Receiver have been reformulated by the Enterprise Act 2002. Section 289 of the 1986 Act has been replaced in its entirety by the new provisions introduced by the 2002 Act.[1]

---

1 Enterprise Act 2002, s.258.

9.1.2 The Enterprise Act 2002 provides that the Official Receiver will investigate the conduct and affairs of each bankrupt.[1] The nature of the investigation will include a consideration of the bankrupt's conduct and affairs both before and after the making of the bankruptcy order. Once the investigation has been completed, the Official Receiver may in the exercise of his discretion report his findings to the court. The Enterprise Act 2002 therefore introduces no substantive change to the nature of the general investigations to be undertaken by the Official Receiver.

---

1 Insolvency Act 1986, s.289 (1).

9.1.3 However, a major change to the usual procedure occurs if the Official Receiver considers that an investigation of the bankrupt's conduct and affairs is unnecessary. In these circumstances, an investigation need not be undertaken[1] and the Official Receiver will thereafter usually file at court a notice stating that the bankrupt should be discharged from his bankruptcy (see section 8.1 on the duration of the bankruptcy). The introduction of such a discretion has been welcomed by some commentators.[2] However, whilst ensuring that only serious cases are investigated may have the advantage of reducing the burdens on the Official Receiver's office, there must be some concern that this measure is principally driven by a desire to cut costs and that some 'culpable'[3] bankrupts may avoid sanction. At the very least, the fact that in the past bankrupts would have been in every case automatically investigated by the Official Receiver may have been, in itself, a deterrent to some bankrupts. The Chief Executive of the Insolvency Service, Desmond Flynn, in his paper of 8 November 2002[4] stated that it was the intention to interview all bankrupts and after this initial inquiry the Official Receiver will report to the creditors. He went on to suggest that a creditor should have 28 days in which to object to a proposal for early discharge. If no objection was received, then notice would be automatically filed at court, effecting discharge. The process could be over within a matter of weeks and therefore the majority of bankrupts would be released within say six to eight weeks.

1   Insolvency Act 1986, s.289 (2).
2   See editorial to [2002] *Insolvency Lawyer*, Issue 4 (Sweet & Maxwell).
3   'Introduction to Bankruptcy Proposals' distinguished between the 'culpable' and 'non-culpable' bankrupt. See further comment in Chapter 8.
4   www.insolvency.gov.uk/eactindiv.htm.

Obligation to report on discharge of bankruptcy

9.1.4   Where a bankrupt makes an application to the court for his bankruptcy to be discharged,[1] the Official Receiver will make a report to the court about such matters as may be prescribed.[2] The court will consider the Official Receiver's report before determining the discharge application. Any report completed by the Official Receiver will in any legal proceedings be prima facie evidence of the facts stated within it. This avoids the necessity of the Official Receiver attending court to prove his report.[3]

1   Such an application is made under Insolvency Act 1986, s.280.
2   The Enterprise Act 2002 does not set out what these prescribed matters are. It is likely that they will be set out within the revised Insolvency Rules which will probably mean an update of the existing Rule 6.218. At the time of writing, these updates have not yet been published.
3   Insolvency Act 1986, s.289 (3)–(4).

Powers of the trustee in bankruptcy

9.1.5   In the event that the Official Receiver or trustee in bankruptcy intends to bring legal proceedings in connection with transactions at an undervalue,[1] preferences,[2] or other transactions defrauding creditors,[3] prior sanction from the bankrupt's creditor is required. These provisions bring into line best practice and the sanction requirements required for liquidators (see para.6.2.11).[4]

1   Insolvency Act 1986, s.339.
2   Insolvency Act 1986, s.340.
3   Insolvency Act 1986, s.423.
4   Section 262 of the Enterprise Act 2002 introduces para.2A to Pt.1, Sched.5 to the 1986 Act.

The concealment and falsification of records by the bankrupt

9.1.6   Under the Enterprise Act 2002, the requirement for the bankrupt to deliver up possession to the Official Receiver (or the trustee in bankruptcy) of all his books, papers and other records of which he has possession or control and which relate to the estate or his affairs remains largely unchanged. If the bankrupt fails to do this, he could be guilty of an offence under the 1986 Act.[1] A minor amendment to this provision is the extension of the following deadlines from 12 months to two years. The bankrupt is guilty of an offence if:

- in the *two years* before the date of the bankruptcy petition or in the initial period[2] he conceals, destroys, mutilates or falsifies, or causes or permits the concealment, destruction, mutilation or falsification of any books, papers or other records relating to his estate or affairs or he makes, causes or permits the making of any false entries in any book, document or record relating to the estate or affairs; or
- in the *two years* before the bankruptcy petition or in the initial period he does anything which prevents the production of any books, papers or records relating to his estate or the affairs.

---

1 Insolvency Act 1986, s.355.
2 'Initial period' is the period of time falling between the date of the bankruptcy petition and the date of the bankruptcy order.

9.1.7 This extension from twelve months to two years only applies to the bankrupt's 'trading records'.[1] A trading record is defined within the Enterprise Act 2002 as a book, document or record which shows or explains the transactions or financial position of a person's business, including:

- A periodic record of cash paid and received.
- A statement of periodic stocktaking.
- In the case of goods sold by way of retail trade, a record of goods sold and purchased which identifies the buyer or enables the buyer to be identified.

---

1 Section 355 (5) of the 1986 Act, inserted by s.269 of the Enterprise Act 2002 (Sched.23, para.13).

9.1.8 Where the Official Receiver (or the trustee in bankruptcy) wishes to investigate the conduct and affairs of the bankrupt in more detail, this amendment should encourage fuller disclosure by the bankrupt of the pertinent financial records. If the bankrupt acts in bad faith and fails to comply with his obligations, an offence is committed. The reforms are clearly intended to apply to tackle the problem of misconduct by the bankrupt during the investigation process and ensure proper scrutiny where the culpability of the bankrupt is suspected.

9.1.9 Experience of the new investigatory regime will show what effect this streamlined procedure will have on ensuring that culpable bankrupts do not escape appropriate sanction, such as the BROs. The main benefit of this reform is the freeing up of the Official Receiver, which should allow him to reallocate resources to meet the onerous new duties imposed upon his office by the other reforms, such as the proposals for income payment orders, post-bankruptcy IVAs and the BRO regime. That said, in practice, the Official Receiver will need to at the very least conduct a preliminary investigation of all bankrupts in order to determine whether a full investigation is necessary. Whether this summary investigation will be any less vigorous than the present investigations carried out of all bankrupts remains to be seen. There may be added pressure on the Official Receiver to investigate the bankrupt where the Government imposes targets to achieve a certain number of BROs, BRUs or IVAs. It could well be the case that this reform may not lead to the expected cost and time savings after all.

9.2   INCOME PAYMENTS ORDERS/AGREEMENTS

Background to the reforms

9.2.1   Save for a limited list of basic necessities (tools of trade, household effects, etc.[1]), the vast majority of the assets within the bankrupt's estate vest in the trustee in bankruptcy immediately upon the appointment taking effect or, in the case of the Official Receiver, on his becoming the trustee.[2] The 1986 Act (and its predecessor the Bankruptcy Act 1914) treat after-acquired property[3] and subsequently earned income in a different manner and these automatic vesting provisions do not apply. The Bankruptcy Act 1914, however, failed to contain any effective method to ensure that income earned by the bankrupt prior to his discharge could be obtained for the benefit of the creditors. This was in part remedied by the introduction of the income payments order procedure within the 1986 Act which, subject to certain statutory safeguards protecting the bankrupt, enabled the trustee in bankruptcy to secure the bankrupt's income for the benefit of his creditors upon an application to the court.

1   See s.283 (2) of the 1986 Act which is subject to s.308 of the 1986 Act.
2   Insolvency Act 1986, s.306.
3   Insolvency Act 1986, s.307.

9.2.2   However, since the introduction of the 1986 Act, on the basis of the limited evidence available, it appears that the income payments order procedure has generally been underutilised by trustees in bankruptcy.[1] A poor take-up rate may be largely explained by the fact that often the bankrupt's income is insufficient to make such an application to the court worthwhile, as the costs of bringing a contested application may be high. The Enterprise Act 2002 has reformed this area of the law by introducing a revised income payments order procedure with the intention of reducing overall costs and maximising the returns to creditors.

1   Gareth Miller, 'Income Payments Orders' [2002] *Insolvency Law & Practice*, Volume 18, No.2.

9.2.3   When an income payment order had been obtained by a trustee in bankruptcy in accordance with the unamended 1986 Act procedure, the order generally ended upon the discharge of the bankruptcy (see para.8.1.5).[1] As the Enterprise Act 2002 reforms have the effect of shortening the duration of a bankruptcy,[2] concerns were raised during the consultation process that if the existing income payment order procedure had remained unamended, it would have undoubtedly resulted in even less of the bankrupt's income being made available to creditors. The reforms introduced in the Enterprise Act 2002 in part address these concerns,[3] by providing that an income payments order can end after the discharge of the bankruptcy. Furthermore, in a move to save costs, settlement can be effected by means of an income payments agreement (i.e. an agreement reached between the bankrupt and his trustee in bankruptcy) which will be enforceable by the court as if it were an income payments order. These provisions are examined in detail below.

1   Insolvency Act 1986, s.310 (6).
2   Section 279 of the 1986 Act (as amended) introduced by s.256 of the Enterprise Act 2002.
3   Section 259 of the Enterprise Act 2002 amends s.310 (1) and (6) of the 1986 Act. Section 260 of the Enterprise Act 2002 inserts a new s.310A into the 1986 Act.

The new procedure: the income payments order

9.2.4   The amendments to the existing income payments order procedure can be summarised as follows:

- A court application for an income payments order can only be commenced by the trustee in bankruptcy before the bankrupt's discharge.[1]
- The income payments order must specify the period of duration and it:
  - *may* end after the bankrupt's discharge; but
  - *must* end before the expiry of three years beginning with the date on which the order is made.[2]
- Subject to the prescribed three-year limitation period, any income payments order may be varied by the court upon an application brought by either the trustee in bankruptcy or the bankrupt. Such an application can be made either before or after the bankrupt's discharge.[3]

1   Insolvency Act 1986, s.310 (1) (as amended).
2   Insolvency Act 1986, s.310 (6) (as amended).
3   Insolvency Act 1986, s.310 (6A) (as amended).

9.2.5   Since the introduction of the 1986 Act, due to the effects of other legislative changes, the realisation of a bankrupt's assets for the benefit of creditors has become increasingly more limited (see sections 4.2 and 4.3). This trend, when examined in the light of the substantial reduction in the duration of the bankruptcy, may lead some creditors to insist that the trustees in bankruptcy take steps to obtain some level of income stream from the bankrupt. However, the relatively minor procedural reforms introduced in the Enterprise Act 2002 are not in themselves likely to lead to a substantial increase in the number of income payments orders obtained by trustees in bankruptcy, as the reforms do not address the core problems of the former procedure, i.e. the associated costs resulting from a contested hearing and the bankrupt's lack of any significant sources of income. That said, the reforms will provide creditors with some degree of comfort, given the potential availability of an income stream for a period of up to three years from the bankrupt. Finally, it is worth noting that the wide statutory definition of the bankrupt's 'income' has been maintained,[1] although this is subject to the statutory protection considered in para.9.2.9 onwards.

---

1   Insolvency Act 1986, s.310 (7) (as amended).

The new procedure: the income payments agreement

9.2.6   The newly introduced income payments agreement procedure is akin to the director disqualification undertaking procedure introduced by the Insolvency Act 2000[1] and the bankruptcy restrictions undertaking (see commentary section 8.4).

---

1   Company Directors Disqualification Act 1986, s.1A (as amended).

9.2.7   The important principles of the new income payments agreements regime are summarised below:

- A written agreement must be made between the bankrupt and his trustee in bankruptcy (or the Official Receiver).[1]
- This agreement can provide that either the bankrupt or a third party (who might have originally been obliged to make an income payment to the bankrupt, e.g. an employer) must pay to the trustee in bankruptcy (or to the Official Receiver) an amount equal to a specified or proportion of the bankrupt's income for a specified period.[2] It would appear that whilst a third party need not be a signatory to this agreement, he may be bound by its terms.
- In the event that a valid agreement is reached, then the terms can be enforced as if they were a provision of an income payments order.[3]
- The agreement may be varied in writing by the parties (in accordance with the normal principles of contract law) or by the court on an application made by either the bankrupt or his trustee in bankruptcy (or the Official Receiver). However, any variation must:
  - not extend the duration of the agreement beyond the three-year limitation period[4] (see below);
  - not include a provision of a kind which could not be included within an income payments order;[5] and
  - allow the bankrupt to retain such sufficient sums as are necessary to meet the reasonable domestic needs of both the bankrupt and his family.[6]
- During the course of the agreement, the court may also on the application of a bankrupt or his trustee in bankruptcy (or the Official Receiver), discharge

or vary an attachment of earnings order that may be in force to secure payments by the bankrupt for the benefit of his creditors.[7]

■ Any monetary sum received by the trustee in bankruptcy (or the Official Receiver) pursuant to such an agreement will form part of the bankrupt's estate.[8]

■ The meaning of 'income' remains unchanged (currently defined in s.310 (7) to (9) of the 1986 Act[9]).

■ As with an income payments order, the agreement must specify the period of duration and it:

– *may* end after the bankrupt's discharge; but
– *must* end before three years beginning with the date on which the order is made.[10]

---

1   Insolvency Act 1986, s.310A (1) and (1)(b).
2   Insolvency Act 1986, s.310A (1)(a). Such a specified period is subject to the three-year limitation period (Insolvency Act 1986, s.310A (5) (as amended)).
3   Insolvency Act 1986, s.310A (2).
4   Insolvency Act 1986, s.310A (6).
5   Insolvency Act 1986, s.310A (7)(a).
6   Insolvency Act 1986, s.310A (7).
7   Insolvency Act 1986, s.310A (3).
8   Insolvency Act 1986, s.310A (4)(a).
9   Insolvency Act 1986, s.310A (4)(b).
10 Insolvency Act 1986, s.310A (5).

9.2.8   It is probable that income payments agreements will be utilised more often than income payments orders given that both the costs and time involved in securing such an agreement should be significantly less. This view is supported by the analysis within the Government's insolvency reform consultation document 'Bankruptcy: A Fresh Start' where it was shown that nearly all of the income payments orders obtained by the Official Receiver in the year up to March 2000 were obtained with the bankrupt's consent. It is likely that the agreements will be widely sought by trustees in bankruptcy to avoid the risk of an adverse costs order.[1]

---

1   Civil Procedure Rules: Rule 1.1 – the overriding objective.

The bankrupt's statutory protection

9.2.9   Despite bankruptcy, the bankrupt may still continue to earn income and may remain the family's major breadwinner, responsible for the financial welfare of himself and his family. There is therefore a conflict between the interests of the creditors who would wish to obtain most or all of the bankrupt's funds and those of the bankrupt and his family. The 1986 Act resolves this conflict by providing that an income payments order shall not be made by the court where the effect of the order would reduce the bankrupt's income below what would appear to the court to be necessary to meet the 'reasonable domestic needs' of the bankrupt and his family.[1] As a consequence, if the trustee in bankruptcy (or the Official

Receiver) cannot persuade the court that the bankrupt receives income over a level exceeding reasonable domestic needs, then the application will be dismissed.

1   Insolvency Act 1986, s.310 (2).

9.2.10   The key question is therefore what amounts to the bankrupt's (and his family's) reasonable domestic needs? This has been considered by the courts and the important principles that can be distilled are as follows:

- Each case will depend on its own facts. It is therefore not possible to advise precisely how much income a bankrupt may retain, either in terms of an amount or as a percentage. What is reasonable for the bankrupt (and his family) are judged according to that family's particular needs.
- In the case of *Re Rayatt (A Bankrupt)*,[1] Mr Michael Hart QC (sitting as a High Court Judge) stated that the object of s.310 of the 1986 Act was not to make the bankrupt 'a slave to his creditors'. He went on to explain that the test was not what was necessary to enable the bankrupt to live on, but what is necessary for meeting the *reasonable* domestic needs of the bankrupt *and* his family. The court therefore decided that expenditure by the bankrupt on private schooling for his child was reasonable as there was evidence before that court to indicate that the bankrupt's daughter would be seriously disadvantaged if she were moved at that precise juncture from her present school. Accordingly, the income payments order was discharged.
- In the subsequent case of *Malcolm v. Official Receiver*,[2] Rattee J held that it was unreasonable for a bankrupt to live in the family home on his own where it required him to make payments of £820 per month to meet his mortgage instalments, out of a monthly income of £1,100. That said, the variation of the income payments order was postponed in this case until the bankrupt had been given a reasonable opportunity to find alternative accommodation.

1   [1998] 2 FLR 264.
2   [1999] BPIR 97.

9.2.11   In addition, the trustee in bankruptcy's power to obtain an income payments order must be considered in the light of the HRA 1998 (see section 4.1). Whilst an income payments order is likely to amount to a 'justifiable interference' to an individual's human rights, the HRA 1998 will have a further persuasive effect in ensuring that the courts will seek to protect the bankrupt's income from creditors if there is a reasonable justification for it to be withheld to maintain the bankrupt's level of expenditure.

After-acquired property

9.2.12   Some after-acquired property (which could include a new income stream) which is obtained by the bankrupt during the course of the bankruptcy could potentially be seized by the trustee in bankruptcy on behalf of the creditors.[1]

The bankrupt remains under a duty to notify the trustee in bankruptcy (Official Receiver) in the event that any new income streams are secured during this period.[2] The law on this point remains unchanged by the Enterprise Act 2002 reforms. However, as the duration of most bankruptcies has now been reduced (see section 8.1), the possibility of a creditor 'windfall' from such after-acquired property has therefore diminished.[3] This issue was raised during the course of the Bill through Parliament and although it was conceded by the Government that this was a legitimate concern, it was felt that the windfall of 'after-acquired property' only occurred in rare cases. The loss to creditors as a whole was therefore small and was outweighed by the advantages of shortening the period of bankruptcy.

---

1   Section 307 of the 1986 Act does not cover income. Therefore, if the bankrupt has no contractual right for the income it cannot be seized.
2   Insolvency Act 1986, s.333 (2).
3   An income payments order can only be obtained prior to discharge of the bankruptcy.

The transitional provisions

9.2.13   Where a pre-commencement bankrupt (i.e. an individual who was made bankrupt before the commencement of the Enterprise Act 2002) has not been discharged from his bankruptcy, then, if an income payments order remains in force, it will continue to have effect until the expiry date stated within that order has lapsed.[1] That said, the court may, upon an application brought by the bankrupt, vary the income payments order or provide that the income payments order should cease to have effect before the date set out within the order. It is worth noting that this provision does not state on what grounds the court may agree to a variation and it does not allow either the trustee in bankruptcy (or the Official Receiver) to apply to the court to extend the period of an existing income payments order. Further information on this provision may be forthcoming when the Government publishes the new Insolvency Rules. It is likely that such an order will be subjected to the three-year limitation period applicable to income payment orders secured in accordance with the provisions introduced by the Enterprise Act 2002.

---

1   Schedule 19, para.7 to the Enterprise Act 2002.

The bankrupt's pension

9.2.14   A detailed analysis regarding the bankrupt's pension is given in section 4.2. If a trustee in bankruptcy (or the Official Receiver) seeks to seize pension payments under the income payments order procedure, the statutory safeguards protecting the bankrupt's income will still apply.[1]

---

1   Amendments to this procedure have been introduced at s.310 (8) and (9) of the 1986 Act by the Pensions Act 1995 (Sched.3, para.15). It is more likely that a trustee in bankruptcy might seek an excessive contributions order which is available in certain circumstances: Welfare Reform and Pensions Act 1999, s.15.

Will the new procedures work?

9.2.15   As we have examined, the balance between the competing interests of the creditor and bankrupt has remained largely unchanged, despite the reforms to this area introduced by the Enterprise Act 2002. The reforms have essentially been confined to ensuring a continuing place for income payment orders and to encouraging their use despite the reduction in the duration of bankruptcy. Interestingly, this in itself could be seen as a discouragement to debtor rehabilitation, which may mitigate against the entrepreneurial culture espoused in the Enterprise Act 2002 given that the bankrupt may have to forgo a sizeable share of his income to his creditors for up to three years. Furthermore, in view of the fact that since the 1986 Act the value of the return to creditors from a significant number of important assets has been reduced, creditors may increasingly put pressure on the trustee in bankruptcy (or the Official Receiver) to seize the bankrupt's income stream to increase the prospect of some form of distribution. This often neglected area may therefore assume greater importance in the future.

9.3   FAST-TRACK INDIVIDUAL VOLUNTARY ARRANGEMENTS

Background to the reforms – the nationalisation of IVAs?

9.3.1   One of the most radical proposals ultimately incorporated within the Enterprise Act 2002 is the Official Receiver's new ability to act as both the nominee and supervisor of Individual Voluntary Arrangements ('IVAs').[1] The amendment of the IVA procedures to increase their use by bankrupts is a central feature of the reform to the personal insolvency regime,[2] as the Government perceives IVAs to be one of the major successes of the 1986 Act[3] and hopes that post-bankruptcy IVAs will encourage greater debtor rehabilitation. The Government points to statistical data which shows that IVAs generally provide a higher rate of return to creditors and enjoy associated lower costs when compared to bankruptcy. Currently, there are around 7,000 IVAs made each year, of which a very small minority are entered into after a bankruptcy order has been made. The Government has also looked further afield by examining the bankruptcy regime of the US. In the US, post-bankruptcy IVAs supervised by the US equivalent of the Official Receiver have been shown to generate substantial economies of scale, which has had the beneficial effect of lowering costs and thereby increasing distributions to creditors. However, the question remains: can the UK also benefit from a similar IVA procedure largely run by a 'nationalised' nominee and supervisor service?

1   Insolvency Act 1986, s.389B introduced by Enterprise Act 2002, Sched.22.
2   Section 261 of the 1986 Act has been replaced in its entirety by the provisions set out within Sched.22. That said, the general procedure in respect of IVAs has only been amended in minor detail.
3   Keith Pond [2002] *Insolvency Law & Practice*, Vol 18, No.1 states that since 1986 there has been a steady annual rise in the incidence and acceptance of IVAs.

9.3.2   The introduction of a new 'fast-track' IVA whereby the bankrupt may submit his proposed IVA to the Official Receiver when on the point of bankruptcy may prove to be a quick and cost-efficient method for the bankrupt to settle his debts. If successful, these reforms will have the combined effect of providing creditors with an increased level of distribution and also allowing the bankrupt an opportunity to rebuild his business life afresh in a relatively short period of time without being shackled by the stigma and disabilities of bankruptcy. However, a number of concerns have been expressed by critics as to whether this particular reform can be implemented effectively. The aim of this section is to consider how the new IVA procedure will work in practice and indeed whether it will be used. It will also analyse whether the Official Receiver is ready to meet the new demands imposed by the reforms, particularly given the introduction of the 'fast-track' IVAs.

The effect of an IVA: annulment of the bankruptcy order

9.3.3   Where a creditors' meeting (which is correctly summoned[1]) approves the proposed IVA (with or without modifications) and the debtor is an undischarged bankrupt, then the court will annul the bankruptcy order. For such an annulment to be ordered, an application to the court should be commenced by the bankrupt. If the bankrupt has not issued a court application within the prescribed period (see para.9.3.4 below), then the application may be commenced outside of that period by the Official Receiver.[2]

---

1   In accordance with s.257 of the 1986 Act.
2   This section does not define whether a bankrupt will be prevented from commencing an application outside the prescribed period. We will have to wait to see whether the new Insolvency Rules provide guidance on this point.

9.3.4   The limitations upon the bankrupt commencing an application for an annulment are set out below. An application cannot be commenced in any of the following circumstances.

- Within 28 days[1] beginning with the day on which the report of the creditors' meeting was first made to the court.[2] Thus an application for an annulment cannot be commenced during the time period within which the creditors' meeting's decision can be challenged.
- Where an application to challenge the decision of the creditors' meeting is pending.
- While an appeal in respect of a court's judgment over a challenge to the decision of the creditors' meeting is pending or may be brought.[3] Although the Enterprise Act 2002 does not set out to what extent a creditor will need to establish to the court that an appeal 'may be brought', it is likely that the court will generally agree to an annulment once the time limit for the filing of the notice of appeal has expired.[4] Further guidance may be contained within the new Insolvency Rules which are yet to be published.

If an application for an annulment is brought in contravention of the above statutory limitations, it is likely that it will be dismissed with the applicant being ordered to pay any objecting party's costs.

1 This refers to the 28-day period specified in s.262 (3)(*a*) of the 1986 Act which is the period of time during which the decision of the creditors' meeting can be challenged by an application to the court made in accordance with the specific provisions set out within s.262 of the 1986 Act.
2 i.e. In accordance with the existing reporting obligations upon the chairman of the creditors' meeting set out within s.259 of the 1986 Act.
3 Insolvency Act 1986, s.262.
4 Civil Procedure Rules, Rule 52.4. The general time limit for filing an appeal application is 14 days after the date of the court's decision, unless the court will agree to extend this deadline. However, the courts are generally reluctant to vary such deadlines unless there is a very good reason for non-compliance. (See section 4.1 on the Human Rights Act 1998 and the impact of Article 6 of the European Convention on Human Rights.) This interpretation is in line with the wording set out within the previous version of s.261 of the 1986 Act.

9.3.5 Subject to the above provisions, the court may give such directions about the conduct of the bankruptcy and the administration of the bankrupt's estate as it considers appropriate in order to facilitate the implementation of the approved IVA. In summary, the minor amendments to the IVA procedure preserve the existing statutory safeguards to ensure that an annulment will not be ordered by the court whilst a challenge to the creditors' meeting's decision remains extant or is pending. It remains to be seen whether the new Insolvency Rules will impose any additional restriction upon a bankrupt's ability to seek an annulment once an IVA has been finalised.

The fast-track IVA procedure

9.3.6 The introduction of the fast-track IVA procedure is one of the more controversial and far-reaching reforms contained within the Enterprise Act. The fast-track IVA procedure is available to any undischarged bankrupt (debtor) who intends to make a proposal to his creditors for an IVA, where the Official Receiver will act as the nominee of the IVA. It can be applied for immediately after a bankruptcy order is made. It is termed 'fast-track' as it will be processed by the Official Receiver in accordance with the streamlined procedure set out below. However, the fast-track IVA procedure is not available if an interim order has already been applied for.[1] There are also no provisions for the private sector insolvency practitioner to be the nominee of a fast-track IVA. Therefore, the Official Receiver is the monopoly provider of this service to debtors.

1 Section 253 of the 1986 Act states that an application for an interim order can be made by the bankrupt, his trustee in bankruptcy or the Official Receiver.

9.3.7 On the assumption that the bankrupt's (debtor's) proposal complies with the above basic criteria, an application for a fast-track IVA is commenced by the debtor (bankrupt) by submitting to the Official Receiver both of the following:

- A document setting out the terms of the debtor's IVA proposal.
- A statement of the debtor's affairs containing such particulars as may be prescribed (which will include details of his creditors, debts, other liabilities and assets, etc.). It is expected that the details of these requirements will be set out within the new Insolvency Rules.

9.3.8   The Official Receiver will review the proposal, but will only invite the debtor's creditors to consider the debtor's IVA proposal, if he considers that the proposal has a reasonable prospect of being both approved and implemented. If the Official Receiver agrees to proceed with the debtor's proposal:

- Each 'creditor' (the definition of a creditor for this section is defined within the Enterprise Act)[1] will be provided with a copy of the proposed IVA.
- Each creditor must be provided with information about the criteria to be used by the Official Receiver to determine whether the qualifying creditors approve or reject the proposed IVA.

---

1   Insolvency Act 1986, s.263B. A creditor for this purpose is a creditor of the debtor in respect of a bankruptcy debt and of whom the Official Receiver is aware.

9.3.9   The creditors will not generally be provided with an opportunity to make or suggest modifications to the proposed IVA.[1] This provision will help to initially speed up the process. It has been indicated that creditors will be sent a written proposal and simply asked to accept or reject the proposal within a prescribed time.[2] If the opportunity of making or suggesting modifications is not generally available to creditors, there may be a greater number of challenges to the eventual IVA. This may in turn cause some fast-track IVAs to become effectively 'paralysed' (see para.9.3.13).

---

1   Insolvency Act 1986, s.263B (4).
2   See Explanatory notes to the Enterprise Bill, HL Bill 92–EN.

9.3.10   Once the debtor has submitted his IVA proposal to the Official Receiver, no application can be made for an interim order[1] until the Official Receiver has either completed the creditor notification arrangements (as described above) or informed the debtor that he does not intend to proceed and make such arrangements. Where the Official Receiver declines to act (for example where he does not consider that the IVA has a reasonable prospect of being approved or implemented), the debtor's bankruptcy will proceed in the usual way and/or the bankrupt may consider a traditional (non fast-track) IVA procedure supervised by an insolvency practitioner from the private sector.

---

1   Insolvency Act 1986, s.253.

9.3.11   Upon the completion of the creditor notification arrangements, the Official Receiver must as soon as is reasonably practicable report to the court whether the proposed IVA has been approved or rejected by the creditors.[1] The majority required for approval remains unchanged by these reforms.[2] Where the

Official Receiver reports to the court that the proposed IVA is approved, the IVA will take effect and will bind the creditor and every person who was entitled to participate within the creditor notification arrangement (see section 3.3). The court will also annul the bankruptcy order on an application made by the Official Receiver.[3] However, as with standard IVAs, such an application for an annulment of the bankruptcy order is subject to limitations and it may not be made:

■ Until 28 days have elapsed, calculated from the date that the Official Receiver first made his report to the court[4] (and therefore an application for an annulment cannot be made within the time period in which the creditors' meeting's decision may be challenged at court).

■ Where an application for the revocation of the fast-track IVA is pending.

■ Where an appeal (in respect of the court's decision over whether or not the fast-track IVA should be revoked) is either pending or may be brought.[5]

---

1   Insolvency Act 1986, s.263C.
2   Insolvency Rules, Rule 5.18.
3   Section 269 of the Enterprise Act introduces Sched.23 which provides minor and consequential amendment to the 1986 Act. Accordingly, s.282 of the 1986 Act has been amended so that where the court annuls a bankruptcy order as a result of a fast-track IVA, then:
      (1)   any sale or disposition of property, payment made or other thing duly done, under any provision within the 1986 Act or under the authority of the Official Receiver or a trustee in bankruptcy of a bankrupt's estate or by the court is valid; but
      (2)   if any of the bankrupt's estate is then vested, under any such provision within the 1986 Act, in such a trustee in bankruptcy, it shall vest in such person as the court may appoint or, if the court fails to appoint, revert to the bankrupt on such terms (if any) as the court may direct.
4   An annulment cannot be made until the 28-day deadline has expired for the commencement of an application to the court seeking the revocation of a fast-track IVA in accordance with s.263F of the 1986 Act.
5   Insolvency Act 1986, s.263D (4) (see note at para.9.3.4 where the interpretation of these phrases is considered).

9.3.12   The Enterprise Act also introduces some further incidental provisions relating to fast-track IVAs, namely:

■ The court may make such additional directions about the conduct of the bankruptcy and the administration of the bankrupt's estate as it thinks is appropriate for facilitating the implementation of the approved IVA.

■ The Deeds of Arrangement Act 1914 (c.47) does not apply.[1]

■ Any statutory provisions described elsewhere within the 1986 Act for the implementation and supervision of standard approved IVAs will apply also to fast-track IVAs.[2]

---

1   This is in accordance with s.260 (3) of the 1986 Act which applies to standard IVAs.
2   Insolvency Act 1986, s.263D (7).

The revocation of a fast-track IVA

9.3.13   Given that the Official Receiver is not obliged to provide creditors with the opportunity to suggest or make modifications to the debtor's proposed IVA, it is expected that disgruntled creditors may more readily challenge the IVA if they consider that the approved fast-track IVA prejudices them.

9.3.14   The Court may make an order revoking a fast-track IVA on either of the following grounds:

- It unfairly prejudices the interests of one of the debtor's creditors.
- A material irregularity occurred in relation to the creditor notification arrangements undertaken by the Official Receiver.[1]

---

1   Insolvency Act 1986, s.263F (1) as introduced by the Enterprise Act 2002.

9.3.15   An application for a revocation order can only be commenced by either:

- the debtor;
- a person who was entitled to participate in the arrangements, i.e. a creditor with a bankruptcy debt of whom the Official Receiver has been provided notice;[1] or
- the trustee in bankruptcy (or the Official Receiver).

---

1   Insolvency Act 1986, s.263B (3).

9.3.16   Such an application must be commenced before the expiry of the 28-day period beginning with the date on which the Official Receiver first makes his report to the court[1] on whether the IVA proposal is approved.[2] This time limit is automatically extended where a creditor (who was not made aware of the proposed IVA) becomes aware of the IVA. In those circumstances, that creditor may make an application for a revocation order within 28 days, beginning on the date on which he first becomes aware of the fast-track IVA. In order to avoid applications for a revocation order being commenced at a late stage, the Official Receiver will need to ensure that all the qualifying creditors are properly notified of the IVA proposal in accordance with the provisions within the Enterprise Act 2002.

---

1   Insolvency Act 1986, s.263C.
2   Insolvency Act 1986, s.263F (3).

Alternatives to the fast-track IVA

9.3.17   In the event that the Official Receiver does not accept the bankrupt's proposed fast-track IVA, then the bankrupt still has the option of seeking creditor approval for a 'standard IVA' run by a private sector nominee/supervisor and he can still apply for an interim order. The significant downside of a such an IVA will probably be higher costs, as the private sector will not be able to benefit from the economies of scale expected to be generated by the Official Receiver's statutory monopoly. Time will tell whether these reforms will effectively lead to a 'cheap and cheerful' IVA process proposed by most bankrupts and approved by their creditors or whether due to lack of resources at the Official Receiver's office, the procedure becomes unworkable.

9.3.18 In addition, there remains a very large question mark over why a 'non-culpable' bankrupt would want to propose a fast-track IVA. As set out previously (see section 9.1) it is expected that approximately 90 per cent of bankrupts will be discharged within a matter of weeks. Will a bankrupt be concerned as to whether he receives annulment rather than discharge? Will most understand the distinction? Certainly in the context of a consumer bankrupt, the major disability of bankruptcy is a bad credit rating. Will credit reference agencies distinguish between discharge or annulment? There is certainly a greater risk for the bankrupt in entering an IVA, as if he is in breach of the terms of the IVA, a bankruptcy order will follow and this will be a second bankruptcy. In such cases, the bankrupt will not receive early release and a BRO may be imposed or a BRU sought. Why would a bankrupt take such a risk when an income payments order procedure is available? There is therefore a significant possibility that this procedure will not be widely used.

Fast-track IVAs and BROs

9.3.19 One of the major concerns during the consultation process in respect of fast-track IVAs, was expressed by the Insolvency Lawyers Association who stated that:

> We believe that the biggest single inducement to propose a post-bankruptcy IVA is likely to be the avoidance of a BRO. In the interests of the protection of the public, consideration needs to be given as to whether the annulment of the bankruptcy, consequential upon the approval of an IVA, should preclude either the institution of proceedings for, or the making of, a BRO.[1]

1 Christopher Brougham QC and John Briggs, 'Current Issues in Insolvency – Bankruptcy Reform Proposals', *Insolvency Intelligence*, March 2002.

9.3.20 This concern has been addressed within the Enterprise Act 2002. Therefore, the annulment of the bankruptcy as a consequence of a fast-track (or standard[1]) IVA approved by qualifying creditors, will not affect:

- any existing BRO or BRU (see sections 8.3 and 8.4); or
- preclude the court from making a BRO upon an application by the Official Receiver commenced *before* the annulment, or the Secretary of State from accepting a BRU offered *before* the annulment.[2]

1 i.e. Where a bankrupt seeks an annulment of a bankruptcy order in accordance with s.261 of the 1986 Act.
2 Insolvency Act 1986, Sched.4A, para.11.

9.3.21 If the Official Receiver has a genuine belief that the bankrupt is only making an IVA proposal to avoid a BRO or BRU, he has the discretion not to recommend an IVA to the creditors in the first place. That said, there remains an unanswered question over whether the Official Receiver will have had sufficient time to investigate thoroughly the circumstances of the bankruptcy before putting a fast-track IVA proposal to the creditors. Perhaps insufficient time to conduct a proper investigation may prove to be a reason why the Official Receiver will decline to put proposals to creditors. However, this is very much a matter which will be resolved in light of adopted practice and procedure.

Will the new procedures work?

9.3.22 The other major question mark hanging over the effectiveness of the new fast-track IVAs procedure is whether the Official Receiver's office will be sufficiently funded and will have the available personnel to meet the new obligations being placed upon it.[1] In the absence of sufficient funding or trained personnel, there is a substantial risk that the fast-track IVA process will drag on for a disproportionate amount of time, or that the proposals will not receive proper consideration before presentation to the creditors. In either event, such IVAs may be open to a creditor's challenge due to procedural defects. If this scenario were to happen, then the Government's aim of encouraging a more entrepreneurial culture within the UK by enabling bankrupts to recover from a financial set-back as quickly as possible could begin to founder. This concern may be addressed if the Government allows private sector insolvency practitioners to act as both nominees and supervisors of fast-track IVAs.

---

1 Section 269 of the Enterprise Act introduces Sched.23 which provides a minor consequential amendment to the 1986 Act. These include at para.16 provisions on the Official Receiver acting as a nominee or supervisor in relation to voluntary arrangement. It does not set out in detail the provisions with respect to remuneration and the terms of appointment and these are expected to be contained within the new Insolvency Rules when published.

9.3.23 The Enterprise Act 2002 has proposed that some form of alternative funding for the Insolvency Service may be introduced at an unspecified time in the future. Details of these proposals have not been published at the time of writing. These changes may be an opportunity to address the concerns over the lack of funding.

9.3.24 Experience will show whether these reforms will have the desired effect (as in the US) or will degenerate into a farce. Some research indicates that the IVA cases dealt with by the centralised Official Receiver in the US tend to encounter greater problems than arrangement procedures.[1] Therefore, if there are problems in the US and this is reflected in England and Wales, there is a substantial risk that the expected benefits of a reduction in costs through centralisation of the IVA system and the resulting economies of scale will not be delivered.

---

1 Keith Pond [2002], 'New Rules and New Roles for the Individual Voluntary Arrangement' *Insolvency Law and Practice*, Volume 18, No.1.

9.3.25   Furthermore, it is likely that in more complex cases (i.e. a trader or professional) expert professional advice will be required by the debtor. Indeed, it is expected that the fast-track IVAs will be more attractive to those bankrupts who wish to trade. Accordingly, the services of a private sector supervisor may need to be obtained, as the Official Receiver may not be prepared (or have the time or expertise) to provide the required detailed advice. It will also be interesting to see whether creditors are willing to accept fast-track IVA proposals or want the assurance that the matter has received proper investigation and professional input.

9.3.26   As discussed, there is also significant doubt whether this procedure will be attractive to bankrupts. In the vast majority of cases, why should the bankrupt be concerned to receive an annulment (and take on the risk and burden of an IVA) when he will be discharged within weeks? Even if the bankrupt wishes to proceed with a fast-track IVA, will creditors approve them? It is likely that creditors will be faced with a proposal on a 'take it or leave it basis' which they cannot modify and therefore there may be an increased tendency to reject proposals where a modification would have been requested.

9.3.27   If these reforms do not achieve the desired result, one of the key aims of the bankruptcy reforms (i.e. keeping costs down for small value IVAs) and therefore encouraging the greater use of IVAs in bankruptcy will have failed.

9.4   BANKRUPTCY RESTRICTIONS

Introduction

9.4.1   The Government has used the Enterprise Act 2002 as an opportunity to review the restrictions imposed upon the bankrupt's conduct and affairs during the course of his bankruptcy. The importance of this is to send a clear message that financial failure should no longer bear a stigma and, in turn, that responsible risk taking should be encouraged. Despite the reforms, it has been estimated[1] that there are over 230 bankruptcy restrictions still in place (including disqualification from certain professions). This section considers the major amendments to some of the restrictions imposed upon a bankrupt contained within the 1986 Act and examines how the amendments fit in within the context of the other reforms of the bankruptcy regime. It should also be remembered that an individual could be guilty of bankruptcy offences during the course of either a BRO and BRU, despite the fact that he may have been discharged.[2]

---

1   Estimate is reportedly provided by the Insolvency Service.
2   Section 350 (3A) of the 1986 Act (as amended); Schedule 21 of the Enterprise Act.

The new restrictions

A Justice of the Peace may remain in office upon his bankruptcy

9.4.2   An individual may now remain as a Justice of the Peace or be appointed as a Justice of the Peace, despite the fact that he has been made bankrupt.[1] Previously, a bankrupt was disqualified from either maintaining such office or becoming a Justice of the Peace until after either the discharge or annulment of his bankruptcy. However, the removal of a bankrupt Justice of the Peace is still possible in accordance with the Lord Chancellor's discretionary power where it is thought appropriate.

---

1   Section 264 of the Enterprise Act 2002 repeals s.65 of the Justices of the Peace Act 1997.

Disqualification from office: Parliament

9.4.3   A detailed examination of these provisions is beyond the scope of this book, given that these reforms will have only a limited applicability to a small number of bankrupts. It is however interesting to note the large amount of Parliamentary time spent debating these provisions. The key provisions are as follows:

- An individual is no longer disqualified from membership of Parliament by reason of bankruptcy commenced in England or Wales.
- Where a BRO or a BRU[1] applies, an individual is automatically disqualified from membership of the House of Commons, from sitting or voting in the House of Lords and from sitting or voting in a committee of the House of Lords or the joint committees of both Houses. As a result, either the bankrupt's House of Common's seat will be vacated or where the bankrupt is a member of the House of Lords, no attendance writ or summons will be issued. Therefore, on bankruptcy only 'culpable' peers and MPs will be disqualified from Parliament. Similar provisions have been introduced for the devolved regional assemblies.
- On the making of either a BRO or an interim BRO, the court should notify the speaker of the relevant House. The same notification obligation is placed upon the Secretary of State where the bankrupt's BRU is accepted.[2]
- The effect of parliamentary privilege is irrelevant to the extent that it contravenes the bankruptcy restriction provisions set out within the Enterprise Act 2002.[3] Further details of the mechanics of the restrictions are likely to be set out within the new Insolvency Rules, when these are published.

---

1   Section 257 of, and Sched.20 to, the Enterprise Act 2002 insert Sched.4A into the Insolvency Act 1986.
2   Similar notification provisions also apply where there is a BRO, interim BRO in force or a BRU has been accepted if the bankrupt is a member of the devolved assemblies which include the Scottish Parliament, Northern Ireland Assembly and the National Assembly for Wales. See Insolvency Act 1986, s.426A inserted by Enterprise Act 2002, s.266.
3   Insolvency Act 1986, s.426B, inserted by Enterprise Act 2002, s.266.

Disqualification from office: local government

9.4.4   In most cases, an individual may now be elected for and hold on to his office as a member of a local authority despite the fact that he has been made bankrupt, unless he remains subject to either a BRO, interim BRO or a BRU.[1]

---

1   Section 267 of the Enterprise Act substitutes s.80 (1)(*b*) and repeals s.81 (1) and (2) of the Local Government Act 1972.

Disqualification from office: generally

9.4.5   The Secretary of State now has the power to order a 'disqualification provision' which if ordered can impose further disqualifying restrictions on an individual or group of individuals whether permanently, temporarily and/or absolutely or conditionally from:

- being elected or appointed to a public office or position;
- holding a public office or position; or
- becoming or remaining a member of a body (for example, Parliament or some other legislative body) or group.

9.4.6   This provision effectively allows the Secretary of State to introduce a procedure where the bankruptcy restrictions regime on public officeholders can be either strengthened or weakened. Further details are expected to be provided within the new Insolvency Rules.

Restriction on the bankrupt acting as a receiver or manager

9.4.7   This historic restriction is amended to take into account the effect of either a BRO or a BRU. Therefore, an individual commits an offence if he acts as a receiver or manager of the property of a company on behalf of debenture holders whilst he is an undischarged bankrupt or where either a BRO or BRU applies to him. A person guilty of such an offence will be liable to face imprisonment and/or a fine. However, this restriction does not apply where the receiver or manager has been appointed by the court.[1]

---

1   Section 31 of the 1986 Act has been substituted by this provision.

Disqualification from acting as an insolvency practitioner

9.4.8   An individual cannot act as an insolvency practitioner whilst either a BRO or BRU remains in force.[1]

---

1   Section 275(3) of the Enterprise Act 2002 implements Sched.21, para.4 which makes an addition to s.390 of the 1986 Act.

General bankruptcy offences after discharge

9.4.9   In the event that either a BRO or BRU applies to a bankrupt, then the individual remains subject to existing and new bankruptcy restrictions and could face legal proceedings brought by the Secretary or State (by or with the consent of the DPP) during the course of the BRO or BRU[1] if he contravenes the restrictions. In addition, the restriction on a bankrupt obtaining credit and engaging in business, as set out within s.360 of the 1986 Act, has been extended to last throughout the course of a BRO.[2]

1   Insolvency Act 1986, s.350(3A) as inserted by Sched.21, para.2 of the Enterprise Act 2002.
2   Insolvency Act 1986, s.360 (5)–(6) as amended by Sched.21, para.3 of the Enterprise Act 2002.

Prohibition against involvement in a company and restrictions on a bankrupt's business

9.4.10   It is an offence for an individual to act as a director of a company or directly or indirectly take part or be concerned in the promotion, formation or management of a company, without the permission of the court when he is either an undischarged bankrupt or a BRO or BRU remains in force.[1] Similar provisions also prevent a bankrupt from trading a name other than that under which a person was made bankrupt whilst a BRO or BRU remains in force.[2]

1   Section 256 of the Enterprise Act 2002 implements Sched.21, para.5 which replaces s.11(1) of the Company Directors Disqualification Act 1986 in its entirety.
2   Section 257 of the Enterprise Act 2002 amends s.360 of the 1986 Act.

Disabilities on the revocation of an administration order against an individual

9.4.11   The time limit for the applicability of this provision has been reduced from two years to one year.[1] This provision refers to County Court Administration Orders, which fall outside the insolvency regime.

1   Insolvency Act 1986, s.429 (2)(b) (as amended).

The repeal of certain bankruptcy offences

9.4.12   The Enterprise Act has repealed two offences, namely failure to keep proper accounts[1] and gambling.[2] There has been a question mark over these offences, given that they had a retrospective nature and therefore could have been subject to challenge under the HRA 1998 (see section 4.1). Such misconduct on the part of the bankrupt is therefore decriminalised, but will be relevant when the court considers whether a BRO should be made (see section 8.3).

1   Insolvency Act 1986, s.361 (unamended).
2   Insolvency Act 1986, s.362 (unamended).

Further reform

9.4.13   A bankrupt must disclose the fact of his bankruptcy if he wishes to obtain credit in excess of £25. Whilst there was some discussion on this point at the Bill stage, an amendment has not been made to the Enterprise Act 2002. Such a reform may yet be introduced when the new Insolvency Rules are published.[1] However, in view of the anticipated reduction of the duration of approximately 90 per cent of all bankruptcies to a few weeks, this provision has largely lost its effectiveness for all but the 'culpable' bankrupts. Finally, there is also a minor amendment introduced by the Enterprise Act 2002 preventing, in certain cir-cumstances, obtaining credit above the prescribed limit without first disclosing that the bankrupt is subject to a BRO.[2]

1   See amendments (if any) to the Insolvency Proceedings (Marketing Limits) Order 1986.
2   Enterprise Act 2002, s.257 amends Insolvency Act 1986, s.360.

9.4.14   There have been only minor amendments to the restrictions regime and therefore the historic regime remains largely unchanged. The amendments intro-duced are mainly there to ensure that the stigma associated with bankruptcy is reduced and that 'culpable' bankrupts are appropriately caught by the amended restrictions regime.

PART V CONCLUSIONS

10 INTO THE FUTURE

10.1 THE FUTURE OF CORPORATE INSOLVENCY

The beginning of further reform?

10.1.1 The reform of insolvency law and practice has never in the past been regarded as a 'sexy' topic. It is hardly likely to be a substantial vote winner and a Government that is seen to be overly concerned with the consequences of business failure may feel it is sending out the wrong message, namely that it takes a pessimistic view of the country's economic prospects. However, the view of insolvency and the acknowledgment of its importance to the economy has changed dramatically over the last 20 years. The 1986 Act was the first major reform of corporate and personal insolvency in over 70 years. It represented a fundamental root and branch reform of the law, putting to centrestage the importance of corporate rescue, introducing as it did new procedures to assist business recovery. If anything, the 1986 Act appears to have whetted the appetite of Parliament and has set on course a string of further changes to insolvency law and practice which have culminated in the Enterprise Act 2002 reforms. It is a sign of the growing importance of insolvency law in fostering a vibrant and successful economy that it has thrust its way into this major part of the Government's legislative programme.

10.1.2 A successful and efficient insolvency regime is now recognised as being crucial to the development of a dynamic and competitive culture, which in turn is the central aim of the Enterprise Act 2002. To encourage this, businesses and individuals should be afforded a second chance after financial failure: again an overriding theme of the Enterprise Act 2002 reforms. It will be interesting to see whether this sates the appetite for insolvency law reform or whether it will encourage yet further change.

The role of the secured creditor

10.1.3 What changes to practice are we likely to see in the years following the introduction of the Enterprise Act 2002 reforms? Certainly the most heralded change to corporate insolvency law reform has been the abolition of administrative receivership and its replacement by a streamlined multi-purpose administration procedure. This has been seen as an attack on the predominant position of secured creditors in the insolvency process, who have in the past been criticised for their role in creating a spiralling recessionary down-turn through premature and overenthusiastic reliance on administrative receivership. However, if the detail of the new administration procedure is reviewed, the reforms are perhaps not as radical as they first appear. Importantly, the transitional provisions ensure that a security created prior to the commencement of the Enterprise Act 2002 will continue to remain effective and that secured creditors will have the right to appoint an administrative receiver arising from existing security. Some commentators have suggested that bondholders and unsecured creditors (who maintain essential supplies to a business), will demand that companies with whom they have dealings obtain agreement with their secured lenders to relinquish their post-Enterprise Act 2002 security. Whilst there is some force in this argument, it remains likely that in the early years of the new administration procedures and certainly, while the new system beds down, secured creditors are more likely to rely on well used pre-Enterprise Act 2002 security and procedures and therefore continue to appoint administrative receivers. It is only when secured creditors feel fully comfortable with the appointment of administrators that a sea-change may occur.

10.1.4   Importantly, however, the central role of the secured creditor in the insolvency process in this country, which is acknowledged as being one of the most secured creditor friendly countries in the world, will continue. The Enterprise Act 2002 reforms provide that the secured creditor will effectively have an ability to appoint the insolvency practitioner of its choice as administrator and at a time of its choosing (subject only to the powers contained in the charge documentation, which are certain to remain widely drawn). A secured creditor is also left with an effective veto over any nominated appointee of the company or its directors, subject only to the court's overriding 'policing' of this veto. However, real change may eventually be seen due to the overriding requirement that an administrator should act in the interests of the creditors as a whole rather than solely in the interests of his appointer. This will certainly act as a discouragement to the unscrupulous administrator who feels that he can act as if he were simply an administrative receiver. The real engine to change in the way that corporate insolvency is approached may therefore not be the abolition of administrative receivership, but may rather be a result of how insolvency practitioners view their new duties and the role they must fulfil to the creditors as a whole.

10.1.5   As well as introducing a new administration procedure, the Enterprise Act 2002 marks the potential demise of the administrative receiver and this in turn will have a profound effect upon the position of secured lenders in the UK. Any discussion regarding the future for secured lending must also consider briefly the impact of recent case law. In this area, there has also been a perceived attack on the powers of secured creditors, particularly over the secured creditor's ability to create a fixed charge over book debts. Much has been written since the Privy Council decision on 5 June 2001 in *Agnew and Bearsley v. Inland Revenue*

Commissioner (Brumark Investments Limited) ('*Brumark*').[1] The first point to note is that *Brumark* is a Privy Council decision and is technically non-binding in England. However, the Privy Council is comprised of senior Law Lords and it is highly unlikely that Law Lords sitting as the Privy Council would reach any different conclusion if sitting as Law Lords hearing an English case. Furthermore, in November 2001 in the case of *Re Coslett Contractors Limited*,[2] the House of Lords without directly approving *Brumark* cited the case in reaching its decision on the question of determining the nature of the charge.

1   [2001] 1 BCLC 353.
2   [2001] 3 WLR 1347.

10.1.6   Commentators on *Brumark* have rightly focused on the conclusion reached by the Privy Council, namely that the case of *Re New Bullas Trading Limited*[1] was wrongly decided. This case (determined in 1994) was authority for the proposition that fixed charges could exist over book debts, whilst the floating charge could exist over their proceeds. Subsequent to the *New Bullas* decision, this type of clause (and distinction) was widely adopted. The Privy Council however felt that while the debts and its proceeds may have been said to form two separate assets, the latter was merely a traceable proceed of the former, simply representing its value. Any attempt to distinguish the two made no commercial sense. The Privy Council stated that the approach taken by the Court of Appeal in *New Bullas*, of engaging in a process 'simply of construction' such that 'unless unlawful, the intention of the parties to be gathered from the terms of the debenture' must prevail, was fundamentally mistaken. Instead, in determining whether a charge was fixed or floating, the court should be engaged in a two-stage process:

■   It must construe the instrument of charge and seek to ascertain the intentions of parties from the language that they have used. The object is not to discover whether the parties intended to create a fixed or floating charge, it is to ascertain the rights and obligations which the parties intended to grant each other in respect of the charged assets.
■   Once determined, the court should categorise the charge by reference to those rights and obligations, not by reference to what the parties may or may not have intended. Consequently, if the parties had granted the borrowers' rights which were inconsistent with the nature of the fixed charge, then the charge cannot be fixed, however so described.

1   [1994] 2 WLR 197.

10.1.7   As a result, in order to establish whether the charge is effective as a fixed charge over book debts, it will be necessary to establish the extent to which the company was left free to deal with the book debts and the proceeds of such book debts, if and when they were collected. A number of clearing banks have referred to the 1979 decision of *Siebe Gorman*;[1] where Slade J made an assumption, that if there had been a credit balance at the time on the account, the bank would have been entitled to prevent the company from using the proceeds. Clearing banks have used this in support of an argument that once the proceeds of charged receivables are paid into the company's account with the bank, nothing more is needed, as the bank could 'prevent withdrawals even if the account was in credit'. During *Brumark*, it was argued that if the proceeds were paid into such an account and they were not made available for the company's disposal, then the charge would be fixed. However in his *Brumark* judgement, Millett LJ stated that 'their lordships would wish to make it clear that it is not enough to provide in the debenture that the account is a blocked account, if it had not operated as one in fact'. Whilst the *Siebe Gorman* type charge was not expressly dealt with in the *Brumark* decision, it would be surprising if there emerged a lower standard required to create a fixed charge for clearing banks and a higher standard to create such a charge in favour of non-clearers.

---

1   [1979] 2 Lloyd's Rep 142.

10.1.8   The Privy Council in *Brumark* made it clear that the availability of book debts of the company as a source of cash flow is inconsistent with the existence of a fixed charge. To ascertain what would be sufficient control to achieve a finding that the charge is fixed, further case law must be awaited for a definitive answer. The following general principles may however provide useful guidance:

- An arrangement requiring book debts and proceeds to be paid into an account upon which the company has an unfettered right to draw is unlikely to constitute sufficient control. To constitute sufficient control, the proceeds should be paid into a designated account upon which the company is not free to draw, or cannot draw without specific authority of the bank.
- Where a designated account is used to fund a current account upon which the company is free to draw, the authority and basis for the transfers between the designated account and the current account will need to be established.
- If the transfers require some positive act or decision-making process from the chargeholder, then this is likely to constitute sufficient control.
- If the transfers require no action, nor a decision-making process on the part of the chargeholder and/or the company has the right to request and obtain the transfer, it is unlikely that sufficient control will be deemed to exist.

10.1.9   We can speculate as to whether the 'decision-making process' must be one which must be explained in each individual case or whether it can be fixed by standard policy, whether it can be automatically operated (say by a computer program) and/or whether it applies where the company is free to draw up to a maximum level from the account without specific authority. These are all questions which will probably need to await further determination by the courts.

10.1.10   The attack on the banks and the secured creditors' ability to process a fixed charge over book debts is of major practical implication. It may significantly reduce the return to secured creditors and encourage the proliferation of other lenders such as asset based financiers and factors who will be willing to provide alternative capital requirements for companies. As we have explored, an increased number of creditors with secured interests may make corporate rescue more difficult to achieve in the future. The practical implications of *Brumark* will probably decrease over the coming years due to the Enterprise Act 2002 reform, following the abolition of Crown preference. As a result, the significance of preferential creditors in any liquidation will significantly decrease and, consequently, the conflict between the floating chargeholder and preferential creditors will be less acute.

10.1.11   In its place will be a new conflict between floating chargeholders and unsecured creditors over the 'ring fenced sum'. At the time of writing, there is also an unresolved conflict as to how a company with multiple floating charges will be dealt with under s.176A of the 1986 Act.[1] This move was introduced by the Government to increase the role of the unsecured creditors in the insolvency process to ensure that at least some return is made to them. Whilst this sum has not been made available to the liquidator in order to fund statutory based actions,[2] there has been reform promised in this area as well; it has been stated by the Government that the Insolvency Rules will be amended to ensure that liquidators' actions based on statutory rights of action are recoverable as expenses of the liquidation, even if those actions are unsuccessful. As a pre-condition, any such actions will need to be sanctioned by the unsecured creditors. The purpose of this reform is to ensure the more effective policing (on behalf of the unsecured creditors) by liquidators of directors' misconduct and to increase the involvement of the unsecured creditor in the insolvency process. As unsecured creditors become more included in the process, they may have a more positive contribution to play in corporate rescue.

1   See section 6.3 and in particular para.6.3.9.
2   For example, Insolvency Act 1986, ss.238 and 239.

The new administration regime

10.1.12   The introduction of the new streamlined procedure is also heralded as one capable of being used worldwide and may challenge the predominant use of US Chapter 11 procedures. However, the potential value of the new administration procedure has been diminished by the rejection of two radical proposals.

- The first issue is the continued overriding role of the administrator in the UK procedure. One of the most difficult issues for any company's management in facing financial difficulty is to admit defeat and hand control of the company over to a third party. Insolvency proceedings are therefore misinterpreted as an end, not a chance for a new beginning. In the US, Chapter 11 procedures generally ensure that the control and management of the company remains within the existing management (so-called 'debtor in possession'). This in turn means that companies are more likely to seek the protection afforded by legislation. Indeed, it is the very willingness of companies and individuals to use insolvency procedures which has been criticised in the US as an overused means of avoiding creditor payment. At the other end of the spectrum, in the UK the control or management of the company is handed over entirely to the administrator, who will only retain the existing management if it is of use to him in discharging his duties (this is particularly relevant if the company is to trade as a going concern). It is usual, however, for the administrator to place a team from his office into the company and they will carry out the necessary statutory obligations and trade the business, while the administrator formulates a proposal for creditors. This in turn has significant impact upon the costs of the administration procedure and makes it less attractive and sometimes out of reach for smaller companies. This issue has not been addressed in the Enterprise Act 2002 and, consequently, there must remain some doubt that the new administration procedure offers an attractive proposition for smaller companies.

■ The second issue which has not been tackled is the funding of the administration process. One major drawback to the use of the administration process is its costs and the fact that during the administration process, the administrator may well require funding to pay the ongoing expenses of the company (e.g. wages and essential supplies). It may be that the business of the company can be continued and that trading profits will cover the overheads of the administration, but this is not often the case. Furthermore, essential suppliers to a business may withhold goods and services until any arrears have been paid and they may change their terms of supply (for example, by demanding cash on delivery). Employees may also require incentives to continue in service. As a consequence, the costs of running the business may increase at a time when cash flow is often restricted. This means that additional funding of the business is often essential, particularly to retain any possibility of the business being sold as a going concern. Such funding might be obtained in the case of small to medium sized businesses where the owner or managers seek to purchase the whole or part of the business back from the administrator. In these circumstances, it is often in their interests to see the business continuing as a going concern and they may be willing to provide unsecured funds. However, such offers are not always available, as the personal financial position of the existing owner or managers may well have deteriorated along with that of the business. Whilst in the case of large-scale insolvencies and multi-bank workouts, there may be a unanimous agreement between any number of secured creditors over the funding arrangement and agreement that funds provided during the insolvency process will enjoy 'super-priority', this is not often available in the context of the insolvency of a small to medium company. The absence of super-priority funding during the administration process will continue to be a serious handicap in facilitating corporate rescue in the UK.[1]

---

1 Any attempt to introduce priority funding in the UK would need to tackle the concept of the floating charge. It is regretted that the recent discussions and consultation on the registration of securities has not dealt with this problem.

10.1.13 One further problem with the new regime is the current uncertainty over how agreement can be reached as to the administrator's fees when unsecured creditors have no financial interests in the administration. This issue must be dealt with in the forthcoming Insolvency Rules, or the resulting mischief which could be caused will make the new procedure unattractive to insolvency practitioners.

The international challenge

10.1.14 In respect of international corporate reconstruction, one major problem has been the increased number of interested parties involved in the insolvency process. The trade in international distressed debt has led to a proliferation of the 'vulture' capital vehicles who seek to recover bad debt through the aggressive use of domestic insolvency procedures. These companies will buy bad debt from creditors and seek to obtain a return on their investment; consequently their interests are not necessarily compatible with corporate rescue. This can lead to a particular conflict between their interests and those of the company and its other creditors. Such companies may be particularly averse to plans which include the debtor company continuing to trade, with company rescue being the primary aim. It will be interesting to see how an administrator appointed under the new procedures (in the light of the overriding purpose of administration) will deal with this conflict. In any event, the emergence of international insolvency procedures and the observance of international protocols will be of extreme importance in the coming years if this problem is to be globally tackled.

Will it work?

10.1.15 Corporate insolvency reforms since 1986 have placed an immense amount of power and influence in the hands of insolvency practitioners. The Government in looking to administration as the key route to corporate rescue follows this trend. The reforms are designed to maintain the value of existing businesses, where there is a valuable service or commodity being produced, but at the same time ensuring that creditors as a whole benefit from the procedure. Will we see a statistical improvement in business rescue? Are we about to undergo a fundamental shift in the approach to corporate rescue, moving away from the dormant role played by secured creditors, to one where the interests of creditors as a whole are paramount? Only time will tell. At this stage, what we can say is that the reforms introduced by the Enterprise Act 2002 are not as radical as the Government would like us to think and many of the more far-reaching proposals envisaged during the consultation process have been watered down. Whilst the corporate practice in the UK has undoubtedly significantly altered since 1986, it may take some years to actually establish the state we are now in.[1]

---

1   With apologies to Anthony Trollope.

10.2   THE FUTURE OF PERSONAL INSOLVENCY

Liberalisation – the effects?

10.2.1   We have moved a long way from the quasi-criminal penalties imposed on an individual who suffers financial misfortune. Bankruptcy laws in the UK have increasingly become more liberal, surprisingly at a time when the rates of bankruptcy have continued to rise. Whilst it is unlikely that the rise in bankruptcy levels is a direct result of such liberalisation, clearly the stigma arising from bankruptcy is on the wane. This has been given official sanction by the Government in the Enterprise Act 2002 reforms.

10.2.2   In attempting to encourage responsible risk-taking and therefore a dynamic entrepreneurial economy, the Government has introduced a set of reforms to redress the perceived harshness of the UK bankruptcy system. Furthermore, because the Government has concluded that the vast majority of bankruptcies are caused by reasons beyond the control of the individual and that the conduct of most bankrupts in relation to their finance and their creditors is fair and above board, it believes that the vast majority of bankrupts should be quickly rehabilitated and given a second chance. The reduction in the period of bankruptcy for the vast majority, from a three-year period to no more than 12 months is a clear signal of this intent.

10.2.3   However, equally significant is the introduction into the modern UK insolvency regime of a two-tier system in which the treatment of culpable and non-culpable bankrupts will differ.[1] A distinction between the blameworthy and innocent is however something of an oversimplification. Risk is something which by its very nature will entail the chance of disaster or loss. A responsible risk-taker takes account of the possibility of loss in calculating the reward and benefit. Important in calculating this risk is the recognition that there may be unforeseen circumstances which come into play and, as a result, contingencies or reserves should be factored into any decision taken. As a result, far from being dishonest, an individual failure can be caused by an inability to calculate this risk due to recklessness, naivety or foolishness. However, this needs to be viewed in a wider perspective, for as well as losing his own money, a bankrupt has taken a risk at the cost of someone else's money. As a consequence, although the reasons for financial failure may be numerous and often due to circumstances beyond the control of the individual, this does not necessarily lead to the inevitable conclusion that the individual is not in some way 'responsible' for his bankruptcy. It is doubtful in view of the direction taken in the consultation process, White Paper and the progress of the Enterprise Bill through Parliament that the courts will be inundated with applications for BROs in cases where the individual has simply failed to take adequate account of risk. What appears more likely is that BROs will be confined purely to exceptional cases.

---

1   Pre-1914 Bankruptcy Act, there was provision for the release from bankruptcy on the issuance of a certificate of misfortune. This was issued by the courts in circumstances

where the bankruptcy was caused through no fault of the bankrupt. It was however a stringent regime and certificates were only issued in limited circumstances.

10.2.4   A bankruptcy regime should aim to fulfil the following functions:

- To regulate a fair and equitable means of distribution of available assets to creditors.
- A means of encouraging and facilitating financial rehabilitation, allowing the bankrupt after a suitable period of time to recommence trade or business unfettered by previous debts.
- To restrict individuals from undertaking certain activities during bankruptcy.
- To act as a deterrent to reckless debtors, ensuring that individuals who have lost other people's money share some sense of responsibility for the loss they have caused to others. A period of introspection and possibly financial education may help to ensure that it does not occur again.

10.2.5   Arguably the reforms introduced by the Enterprise Act 2002 will mean that the UK system no longer fulfils this last criteria, as the majority of bankrupts will be released from bankruptcy within 12 months. Importantly, however, if the Official Receiver has concluded his investigations into the individual's conduct, the individual may be released from bankruptcy much earlier. Indeed, the Official Receiver can conclude that investigations are not even required. It is only in the small number of cases where an individual is found by reason of his conduct to be worthy of further restrictions that the period of bankruptcy will exceed 12 months. Is this in any way a deterrent? Will creditors lose confidence in the bankruptcy regime?

10.2.6   There are great similarities in the BRO procedure to the present Company Directors Disqualification Act 1986 proceedings. There must therefore be some concern that the process may be irregularly used, that it may not be applied uniformly and that those bankrupts who by their very nature are dishonest may have both the inclination and money to defend any proceedings. With the limited resources of the Insolvency Service, there may be a temptation to pick on easier targets. Without substantial funding being made available to ensure proper and full investigations, there must be some doubt as to whether the BRO regime will be an effective method of policing the conduct of debtors.

10.2.7   In light of the Enterprise Act 2002 reforms, there may well be a rise in the number of bankruptcies. Traditionally, in the UK the majority of individuals facing bankruptcy do so due to business failure. This compares with the US system, where approximately 98 per cent of all bankruptcies are consumer related. If one can be released so easily from bankruptcy debt, will there be a greater incentive to take excessive credit? Will there be a rise in consumer related debt? The cost of bankruptcy to the economy however is high. A loss to a small creditor may have a serious implications to the potential survival of that creditor's business, while on the larger scale, lenders and utility companies may lose payments from bankrupts and may ultimately pass on these losses to their customers through increases in price. Lenders may also feel the need to protect themselves by raising rates for borrowers and possibly requiring additional security. The potential increase in the use of security is in itself a potential disincentive to an entrepreneurial culture. In the more liberal regime of the US, commentators have estimated that this has led to a substantial rise in the number of bankruptcies with a cost to every US citizen of $400. Indeed, closer to home, in Scotland, the Scottish Law Commission envisaged that liberalisation of the bankruptcy regime in Scotland would lead to an increase in the number of sequestrations to 150. In fact, annual sequestrations rose to around 14,000 with a resulting substantial increase in cost. Currently in England and Wales, individual insolvencies stand at just under 25,000 and are on an upward trend.[1] Could this rise be repeated in the UK? As a result, will consumer credit become so expensive that it will dry up, or will there be effectively a market divergence with 'vulture lenders' offering credit to bankrupts immediately upon their discharge? There must be a significant danger[2] that when UK consumers appreciate that there is an early release available and a reduced stigma associated with bankruptcy that the number of bankruptcies will surge. As a consequence of a further rise in bankruptcy levels, it is possible that the main aim of the Enterprise Act 2002 reforms, i.e. the development of a dynamic economy, may be scuppered.

1   DTI statistical press release, 15 November 2002.
2   Recent research warns of a 50 per cent increase in personal bankruptcies as a result of these reforms (report by Centre for Economics and Business Research).

The creditor's position

10.2.8   One of the key features of personal insolvency since 1986, has been the move to provide bankrupts with greater protection from asset recovery by creditors, e.g. in the area of pensions and the family home. It should be remembered that the Enterprise Act 2002 reforms do not directly alter this position; the property of the bankrupt will still vest in the trustee in bankruptcy. However, with quicker investigations and an early release, a full asset recovery to benefit creditors may be imperilled.

10.2.9   A late amendment to the Enterprise Act 2002 was the introduction of the 'sunset provision' regarding the bankrupt's family home. This provision will ensure that generally trustees in bankruptcy only have a period of three years from the date of the bankruptcy order to take steps to realise the bankrupt's interest in the family home. As a result of the property crash of the early 1990s, which coincided with a peak in the number of annual bankruptcies,[1] often a bankrupt's interest in property was not pursued because of problems of negative equity. Many of these cases were referred to the Insolvency Services protracted realisation unit; as at the beginning of August 2002 the protracted realisation unit had 14,325 cases which involved a bankrupt or discharged bankrupt's interest in a property. Due to the sharp increase in property prices in more recent years, the position may now have dramatically changed. The resulting windfall to creditors many years after discharge is seen as potentially unfair to the bankrupt and his family and a major disincentive to rehabilitation. Whilst this may be true, the introduction of this sunset provision will have the effect of limiting creditors' recovery. In the short term however, as a result of this reform, there will be a significant rise in the number of proceedings commenced by trustees in bankruptcy to realise their interests in family homes, as old cases are cleared out.

---

1   1992: 32,106.

10.2.10   One proposal made during the consultation process was that the UK should follow the US example and make discrimination against individuals solely on the ground of their bankruptcy unlawful. Former bankrupts, despite discharge, will continue to encounter significant problems in obtaining credit in the future. In the UK most individuals have become highly dependent upon credit and the continuing existence of a bad credit reference will make successful rehabilitation difficult. From a creditor's point of view, the fact that an individual has in the past been subject to a bankruptcy order is important in considering whether to grant credit or enter into any contract with that individual. To remove the creditor's right to refuse credit due to past bankruptcy would seem unfair, and the rejection of this proposal seems reasonable.

The new bankruptcy regime: will it work?

10.2.11   In the coming years, there would also appear to be an increased role and importance for income payments orders. The reason for this is that despite early discharge, an income payments order can continue for a period of three years. As realisations are squeezed in other areas, this may be a route for creditor recovery, in particular if relatively cost-effective income payment agreements are entered into with ease and regularity.

10.2.12   One further consequence of the reform of the individual bankruptcy regime is also likely to be the decrease in use of pre-bankruptcy IVAs. The IVA has been one of the most successful procedures introduced by the 1986 Act and consistently shows a greater return to creditors than bankruptcy. If the duration of bankruptcy is short and financial rehabilitation swiftly achieved, there seems little incentive for an individual to go through the rigours of an IVA and effectively work for his creditors. Post-bankruptcy fast-track IVAs are, however, a new introduction and will be run by the Insolvency Service, a reform intended to encourage financial rehabilitation. As was discussed (in section 9.3), the fear must be that a bankrupt proposing a fast-track IVA and seeking an annulment of the bankruptcy, will do so less to benefit the creditors, but more to avoid potential sanctions such as a BRO. The time provided for the Official Receiver to consider the bankruptcy and the IVA proposal is limited and the creditors may similarly have little knowledge of any misconduct. Indeed, misconduct is often identified only after full investigation. Will creditors be fully informed of the true position when considering a post-bankruptcy IVA? Will they be able to weigh up the potential returns that could result from proceedings being commenced by a trustee in bankruptcy[1] against the proposed return under the IVA? In any event, what is clear is that this reform can only proceed if the Official Receiver's office has sufficient funding and expertise within its personnel to handle this procedure.

---

1   i.e. Preference/transactions of an undervalue proceedings to recover the assets falling with the bankruptcy estate?

10.2.13   At the risk of providing a downbeat final word, there must be a fear that the Enterprise Act 2002 reforms will cause a rise in bankruptcy levels, that the BRO regime will be little and inconsistently used and returns to creditors will be restricted. If these factors coincide, then significant damage to the economy as a whole may be suffered and we may find that the Government seeks to bring in tighter restrictions and introduce new penalties in the not too distant future.

10.3   WHEN DO THE ENTERPRISE ACT 2002 REFORMS COME INTO FORCE?

10.3.1   The implementation of the Enterprise Act 2002 will require secondary legislation, and as we have discussed at various points throughout this book, significant changes to the Insolvency Rules. At the time of writing (November 2002) the Insolvency Service was consulting with interested parties before placing the matter in the hands of the Insolvency Rules Committee.

10.3.2   It is therefore difficult to state with any degree of certainty when the Act will be implemented, although the early indications are as follows:

- Crown preference will be abolished as at the end of the current financial year (5 April 2003).
- Corporate insolvency provisions will come into effect soon thereafter: it is anticipated that this will be sometime in June or July 2003. Any period between the abolition of Crown preference and the introduction of s.176A of the 1986 Act (as amended) would see a windfall to floating chargeholders.
- The personal insolvency provisions and changes to the financial regime at the Insolvency Service are anticipated to come into effect in the early part of the financial year beginning April 2004.

10.3.3   The delay in implementing the changes to the personal insolvency regime is necessary as the Insolvency Service will need to undertake a substantial programme of staff training and re-organisation to deal with the new systems of investigation, BROs and post-bankruptcy IVAs.

10.3.4   Useful sources for further information on the implementation of the Enterprise Act 2002 can be found on the Insolvency Service website: **www.insolvency.gov.uk** and the DTI's Enterprise Act 2002 website: **www.dti.gov.uk**.

Appendix 1
INSOLVENCY ACT 2000

2000 CHAPTER 39

An Act to amend the law about insolvency; to amend the Company Directors Disqualification Act 1986; and for connected purposes.   [30th November 2000]

BE IT ENACTED by the Queen's most Excellent Majesty, by and with the advice and consent of the Lords Spiritual and Temporal, and Commons, in this present Parliament assembled, and by the authority of the same, as follows:

Voluntary arrangements

1 Moratorium where directors propose voluntary arrangement

Schedule 1 (which –

- (a) enables the directors of a company to obtain an initial moratorium for the company where they propose a voluntary arrangement under Part I of the Insolvency Act 1986,
- (b) makes provision about the approval and implementation of such a voluntary arrangement where a moratorium is obtained, and
- (c) makes consequential amendments),

is to have effect.

2 Company voluntary arrangements

Schedule 2 (which –

- (a) amends the provisions about company voluntary arrangements under Part I of the Insolvency Act 1986, and
- (b) in consequence of Schedule 1 and those amendments, makes amendments of the Building Societies Act 1986),

is to have effect.

3 Individual voluntary arrangements

Schedule 3 (which enables the procedure for the approval of individual voluntary arrangements under Part VIII of the Insolvency Act 1986 to be started without an initial moratorium for the insolvent debtor and makes other amendments of the provisions about individual voluntary arrangements) is to have effect.

4 Qualification or authorisation of nominees and supervisors

(1) Part XIII of the Insolvency Act 1986 (insolvency practitioners and their qualification) is amended as follows.

(2) In section 388 (meaning of 'act as insolvency practitioner') –

- (a) for subsection (1)(b) there is substituted –
  - '(b) where a voluntary arrangement in relation to the company is proposed or approved under Part I, as nominee or supervisor',

(b)   for subsection (2)(c) there is substituted –

'(c)   where a voluntary arrangement in relation to the individual is proposed or approved under Part VIII, as nominee or supervisor', and

(c)   after subsection (2A) there is inserted –

'(2B) In relation to a voluntary arrangement proposed under Part I or VIII, a person acts as nominee if he performs any of the functions conferred on nominees under the Part in question.'

(3)   In section 389 (acting without qualification an offence), after subsection (1) there is inserted –

'(1A) This section is subject to section 389A.'

(4)   After that section there is inserted –

'389A. Authorisation of nominees and supervisors.

(1)   Section 389 does not apply to a person acting, in relation to a voluntary arrangement proposed or approved under Part I or Part VIII, as nominee or supervisor if he is authorised so to act.

(2)   For the purposes of subsection (1) and those Parts, an individual to whom subsection (3) does not apply is authorised to act as nominee or supervisor in relation to such an arrangement if –

(a)   he is a member of a body recognised for the purpose by the Secretary of State, and

(b)   there is in force security (in Scotland, caution) for the proper performance of his functions and that security or caution meets the prescribed requirements with respect to his so acting in relation to the arrangement.

(3)   This subsection applies to a person if –

(a)   he has been adjudged bankrupt or sequestration of his estate has been awarded and (in either case) he has not been discharged,

(b)   he is subject to a disqualification order made or a disqualification undertaking accepted under the Company Directors Disqualification Act 1986 or to a disqualification order made under Part II of the Companies (Northern Ireland) Order 1989, or

(c)   he is a patient within the meaning of Part VII of the Mental Health Act 1983 or section 125(1) of the Mental Health (Scotland) Act 1984.

(4)   The Secretary of State may by order declare a body which appears to him to fall within subsection (5) to be a recognised body for the purposes of subsection (2)(a).

(5)   A body may be recognised if it maintains and enforces rules for securing that its members –

(a)   are fit and proper persons to act as nominees or supervisors, and

(b)   meet acceptable requirements as to education and practical training and experience.

(6)   For the purposes of this section, a person is a member of a body only if he is subject to its rules when acting as nominee or supervisor (whether or not he is in fact a member of the body).

(7)   An order made under subsection (4) in relation to a body may be revoked by a further order if it appears to the Secretary of State that the body no longer falls within subsection (5).

(8)   An order of the Secretary of State under this section has effect from such date as is specified in the order; and any such order revoking a previous order may make provision for members of the body in question to continue to be treated as members of a recognised body for a specified period after the revocation takes effect.'

Disqualification of company directors etc.

5 Disqualification orders

(1) In section 1 of the Company Directors Disqualification Act 1986 (disqualification orders: general), in subsection (1), for the words following 'an order that' there is substituted 'for a period specified in the order –

    (a) he shall not be a director of a company, act as receiver of a company's property or in any way, whether directly or indirectly, be concerned or take part in the promotion, formation or management of a company unless (in each case) he has the leave of the court, and

    (b) he shall not act as an insolvency practitioner.'

(2) At the end of subsection (2) of that section there is inserted 'and, unless the court otherwise orders, the period of disqualification so imposed shall begin at the end of the period of 21 days beginning with the date of the order'.

(3) In section 22 of that Act (interpretation), at the end there is inserted –

'(10) Any reference to acting as receiver –

    (a)   includes acting as manager or as both receiver and manager, but

    (b)   does not include acting as administrative receiver;

and "receivership" is to be read accordingly.'

6 Disqualification undertakings

(1) The Company Directors Disqualification Act 1986 is amended in accordance with this section.

(2) After section 1 there is inserted –

'1A. Disqualification undertakings: general

(1) In the circumstances specified in sections 7 and 8 the Secretary of State may accept a disqualification undertaking, that is to say an undertaking by any person that, for a period specified in the undertaking, the person –

    (a)   will not be a director of a company, act as receiver of a company's property or in any way, whether directly or indirectly, be concerned or take part in the promotion, formation or management of a company unless (in each case) he has the leave of a court, and

    (b)   will not act as an insolvency practitioner.

(2) The maximum period which may be specified in a disqualification undertaking is 15 years; and the minimum period which may be specified in a disqualification undertaking under section 7 is two years.

(3) Where a disqualification undertaking by a person who is already subject to such an undertaking or to a disqualification order is accepted, the periods specified in those undertakings or (as the case may be) the undertaking and the order shall run concurrently.

(4) In determining whether to accept a disqualification undertaking by any person, the Secretary of State may take account of matters other than criminal convictions, notwithstanding that the person may be criminally liable in respect of those matters.'

(3) In section 7 (applications to court under section 6; reporting provisions), after subsection (2) there is inserted –

'(2A) If it appears to the Secretary of State that the conditions mentioned in section 6(1) are satisfied as respects any person who has offered to give him a disqualification undertaking, he may accept the undertaking if it appears to him that it is expedient in the public interest that he should do so (instead of applying, or proceeding with an application, for a disqualification order).'

(4) In section 8 (disqualification after investigation of company), after subsection (2) there is inserted –

'(2A) Where it appears to the Secretary of State from such report, information or documents that, in the case of a person who has offered to give him a disqualification undertaking –

(a) the conduct of the person in relation to a company of which the person is or has been a director or shadow director makes him unfit to be concerned in the management of a company, and

(b) it is expedient in the public interest that he should accept the undertaking (instead of applying, or proceeding with an application, for a disqualification order),

he may accept the undertaking.'

(5) After that section there is inserted –

'8A. Variation etc. of disqualification undertaking

(1) The court may, on the application of a person who is subject to a disqualification undertaking –

(a) reduce the period for which the undertaking is to be in force, or

(b) provide for it to cease to be in force.

(2) On the hearing of an application under subsection (1), the Secretary of State shall appear and call the attention of the court to any matters which seem to him to be relevant, and may himself give evidence or call witnesses.

(3) In this section "the court" has the same meaning as in section 7(2) or (as the case may be) 8.'

(6) In section 9 (matters for determining unfitness of directors), after subsection (1) there is inserted –

'(1A) In determining whether he may accept a disqualification undertaking from any person the Secretary of State shall, as respects the person's conduct as a director of any company concerned, have regard in particular –

(a) to the matters mentioned in Part I of Schedule 1 to this Act, and

(b) where the company has become insolvent, to the matters mentioned in Part II of that Schedule;

and references in that Schedule to the director and the company are to be read accordingly.'

7 Effect of Northern Irish disqualifications

(1) After section 12 of the Company Directors Disqualification Act 1986 there is inserted –

'12A Northern Irish disqualification orders.

A person subject to a disqualification order under Part II of the Companies (Northern Ireland) Order 1989 –

(a) shall not be a director of a company, act as receiver of a company's property or in any way, whether directly or indirectly, be concerned or take part in the promotion, formation or management of a company unless (in each case) he has the leave of the High Court of Northern Ireland, and

(b) shall not act as an insolvency practitioner.'

(2) If provision is made in relation to Northern Ireland for undertakings corresponding to the disqualification undertakings provided for by section 6, the Secretary of State may by order made by statutory instrument make any modifications of the Company Directors Disqualification Act 1986, or any enactment amended by Part II of Schedule 4, which he considers necessary or expedient to give effect to those undertakings in relation to Great Britain.

(3) A statutory instrument containing an order under this section is to be subject to annulment in pursuance of a resolution of either House of Parliament.

8 Amendments

Schedule 4 (which makes minor and consequential amendments about the disqualification of company directors, etc.) is to have effect.

Miscellaneous

9 Administration orders

(1) Part II of the Insolvency Act 1986 (administration orders) is amended as follows.

(2) In section 10 (effect of application), after paragraph (a) of subsection (1) there is inserted –

'(aa) no landlord or other person to whom rent is payable may exercise any right of forfeiture by peaceable re-entry in relation to premises let to the company in respect of a failure by the company to comply with any term or condition of its tenancy of such premises, except with the leave of the court and subject to such terms as the court may impose'.

(3) In section 11 (effect of order), after paragraph (b) of subsection (3) there is inserted –

'(ba) no landlord or other person to whom rent is payable may exercise any right of forfeiture by peaceable re-entry in relation to premises let to the company in respect of a failure by the company to comply with any term or condition of its tenancy of such premises, except with the consent of the administrator or the leave of the court and subject (where the court gives leave) to such terms as the court may impose'.

10 Investigation and prosecution of malpractice

(1) Section 218 of the Insolvency Act 1986 (prosecution of delinquent officers and members of company) is amended as follows.

(2) In subsection (1), for 'to the prosecuting authority' there is substituted –

(a) in the case of a winding up in England and Wales, to the Secretary of State, and

(b) in the case of a winding up in Scotland, to the Lord Advocate'.

(3) Subsection (2) is omitted.

(4) In subsection (4) –

(a) for the words from the beginning of paragraph (a) to 'that authority' in paragraph (b) there is substituted 'forthwith report the matter –

(a) in the case of a winding up in England and Wales, to the Secretary of State, and

(b) in the case of a winding up in Scotland, to the Lord Advocate,

and shall furnish to the Secretary of State or (as the case may be) the Lord Advocate',

(b) for 'the authority' there is substituted 'the Secretary of State or (as the case may be) the Lord Advocate'.

(5) For subsection (5) there is substituted –

'(5) Where a report is made to the Secretary of State under subsection (4) he may, for the purpose of investigating the matter reported to him and such other matters relating to the affairs of the company as appear to him to require investigation, exercise any of the powers which are exercisable by inspectors appointed under section 431 or 432 of the Companies Act to investigate a company's affairs.'

(6) In subsection (6)(b), 'to the prosecuting authority' is omitted.

(7) In section 219 of that Act (obligations arising under section 218) –

    (a) in subsection (1), for 'under section 218(5)' there is substituted 'in consequence of a report made to him under section 218(4)' and for 'that subsection' there is substituted 'section 218(5)',

    (b) in subsection (3), for 'the prosecuting authority' and 'that authority' there is substituted 'the Director of Public Prosecutions, the Lord Advocate',

    (c) in subsection (4), for 'prosecuting authority' there is substituted 'Director of Public Prosecutions, the Lord Advocate'.

11 Restriction on use of answers obtained under compulsion

In section 219 of the Insolvency Act 1986, after subsection (2) (answers given by a person pursuant to powers conferred by section 218 may be used in evidence against him) there is inserted –

    '(2A) However, in criminal proceedings in which that person is charged with an offence to which this subsection applies –

        (a) no evidence relating to the answer may be adduced, and

        (b) no question relating to it may be asked,

    by or on behalf of the prosecution, unless evidence relating to it is adduced, or a question relating to it is asked, in the proceedings by or on behalf of that person.

    (2B) Subsection (2A) applies to any offence other than –

        (a) an offence under section 2 or 5 of the Perjury Act 1911 (false statements made on oath otherwise than in judicial proceedings or made otherwise than on oath), or

        (b) an offence under section 44(1) or (2) of the Criminal Law (Consolidation) (Scotland) Act 1995 (false statements made on oath or otherwise than on oath).'

12 Insolvent estates of deceased persons

(1) After section 421 of the Insolvency Act 1986 (power to apply provisions of Act to insolvent estates of deceased persons) there is inserted –

'421A Insolvent estates: joint tenancies –

(1) This section applies where –

    (a) an insolvency administration order has been made in respect of the insolvent estate of a deceased person,

    (b) the petition for the order was presented after the commencement of this section and within the period of five years beginning with the day on which he died, and

    (c) immediately before his death he was beneficially entitled to an interest in any property as joint tenant.

(2) For the purpose of securing that debts and other liabilities to which the estate is subject are met, the court may, on an application by the trustee appointed pursuant to the insolvency administration order, make an order under this section requiring the survivor to pay to the trustee an amount not exceeding the value lost to the estate.

(3) In determining whether to make an order under this section, and the terms of such an order, the court must have regard to all the circumstances of the case, including the interests of the deceased's creditors and of the survivor; but, unless the circumstances are exceptional, the court must assume that the interests of the deceased's creditors outweigh all other considerations.

(4) The order may be made on such terms and conditions as the court thinks fit.

(5)   Any sums required to be paid to the trustee in accordance with an order under this section shall be comprised in the estate.

(6)   The modifications of this Act which may be made by an order under section 421 include any modifications which are necessary or expedient in consequence of this section.

(7)   In this section, 'survivor' means the person who, immediately before the death, was beneficially entitled as joint tenant with the deceased or, if the person who was so entitled dies after the making of the insolvency administration order, his personal representatives.

(8)   If there is more than one survivor –

   (a)   an order under this section may be made against all or any of them, but
   (b)   no survivor shall be required to pay more than so much of the value lost to the estate as is properly attributable to him.

(9)   In this section –

   "insolvency administration order" has the same meaning as in any order under section 421 having effect for the time being,
   "value lost to the estate" means the amount which, if paid to the trustee, would in the court's opinion restore the position to what it would have been if the deceased had been adjudged bankrupt immediately before his death.'

(2)   In subsection (1) of section 421, after 'apply' there is inserted 'in relation'.

13 Bankruptcy: interest on sums held in Insolvency Services Account

(1)   In Schedule 9 to the Insolvency Act 1986 (individual insolvency rules), in paragraph 21, for 'handled' there is substituted 'invested or otherwise handled and with respect to the payment of interest on sums which, in pursuance of rules made by virtue of this paragraph, have been paid into the Insolvency Services Account'.

(2)   In section 406 of that Act (interest on money received by liquidators and invested) –

   (a)   for 'a company' there is substituted 'or paragraph 21 of Schedule 9 to this Act (investment of money received by trustee in bankruptcy) a company or a bankrupt's estate',
   (b)   for the sidenote there is substituted 'Interest on money received by liquidators or trustees in bankruptcy and invested'.

14 Model law on cross-border insolvency

(1)   The Secretary of State may by regulations make any provision which he considers necessary or expedient for the purpose of giving effect, with or without modifications, to the model law on cross-border insolvency.

(2)   In particular, the regulations may –

   (a)   apply any provision of insolvency law in relation to foreign proceedings (whether begun before or after the regulations come into force),
   (b)   modify the application of insolvency law (whether in relation to foreign proceedings or otherwise),
   (c)   amend any provision of section 426 of the Insolvency Act 1986 (co-operation between courts),

   and may apply or, as the case may be, modify the application of insolvency law in relation to the Crown.

(3)   The regulations may make different provision for different purposes and may make –

   (a)   any supplementary, incidental or consequential provision, or
   (b)   any transitory, transitional or saving provision,

   which the Secretary of State considers necessary or expedient.

(4)   In this section –

   'foreign proceedings' has the same meaning as in the model law on cross-border insolvency,

'insolvency law' has the same meaning as in section 426(10)(a) and (b) of the Insolvency Act 1986,

'the model law on cross-border insolvency' means the model law contained in Annex I of the report of the 30th session of UNCITRAL.

(5) Regulations under this section are to be made by statutory instrument and may only be made if a draft has been laid before and approved by resolution of each House of Parliament.

(6) Making regulations under this section requires the agreement –

(a) if they extend to England and Wales, of the Lord Chancellor,

(b) if they extend to Scotland, of the Scottish Ministers.

General

15 Amendments of Financial Services and Markets Act 2000 and repeals

(1) The enactments mentioned in Schedule 5 are repealed to the extent specified.

(2) For the purposes of the Financial Services and Markets Act 2000, the functions conferred on the Financial Services Authority by virtue of Schedules 1 and 2 are to be treated as conferred by that Act.

(3) Section 356 of that Act (Authority's powers to participate in proceedings: company voluntary arrangements) is amended as follows –

(a) for subsection (1), there is substituted –

'(1) Where a voluntary arrangement has effect under Part I of the 1986 Act in respect of a company or insolvent partnership which is an authorised person, the Authority may apply to the court under section 6 or 7 of that Act.',

(b) for subsection (2), there is substituted –

'(2) Where a voluntary arrangement has been approved under Part II of the 1989 Order in respect of a company or insolvent partnership which is an authorised person, the Authority may apply to the court under Article 19 or 20 of that Order.',

(c) in subsection (3), for 'either' there is substituted 'any'.

16 Commencement

(1) The preceding provisions of this Act (including the Schedules) are to come into force on such day as the Secretary of State may by order made by statutory instrument appoint.

(2) Subsection (1) does not apply to section 14 (which accordingly comes into force on the day on which this Act is passed).

(3) An order under this section may make different provision for different purposes and may make –

(a) any supplementary, incidental or consequential provision, and

(b) any transitory, transitional or saving provision,

which the Secretary of State considers necessary or expedient.

17 Extent

This Act, except section 15(3), Part II of Schedule 2 and paragraphs 16(3) and 22 of Schedule 4, does not extend to Northern Ireland.

18 Short title

This Act may be cited as the Insolvency Act 2000.

SCHEDULES

SCHEDULE 1   MORATORIUM WHERE DIRECTORS PROPOSE VOLUNTARY ARRANGEMENT

AMENDMENTS OF THE INSOLVENCY ACT 1986

1   The Insolvency Act 1986 is amended as provided in this Schedule.

2   After section 1 there is inserted –

'1A. Moratorium

(1)   Where the directors of an eligible company intend to make a proposal for a voluntary arrangement, they may take steps to obtain a moratorium for the company.

(2)   The provisions of Schedule A1 to this Act have effect with respect to –

(a)   companies eligible for a moratorium under this section,

(b)   the procedure for obtaining such a moratorium,

(c)   the effects of such a moratorium, and

(d)   the procedure applicable (in place of sections 2 to 6 and 7) in relation to the approval and implementation of a voluntary arrangement where such a moratorium is or has been in force.'

3   In section 2(1) (procedure where nominee is not the liquidator or administrator), at the end there is added 'and the directors do not propose to take steps to obtain a moratorium under section 1A for the company'.

4   Before Schedule 1 there is inserted –

'SCHEDULE A1   MORATORIUM WHERE DIRECTORS PROPOSE VOLUNTARY ARRANGEMENT

PART I   INTRODUCTORY

Interpretation

1   In this Schedule –

"the beginning of the moratorium" has the meaning given by paragraph 8(1),

"the date of filing" means the date on which the documents for the time being referred to in paragraph 7(1) are filed or lodged with the court,

"hire-purchase agreement" includes a conditional sale agreement, a chattel leasing agreement and a retention of title agreement,

"market contract" and "market charge:" have the meanings given by Part VII of the Companies Act 1989,

"money market contract" and "money market charge" have the meanings given by the Financial Markets and Insolvency (Money Market) Regulations 1995 ("the 1995 regulations"),

"moratorium" means a moratorium under section 1A,

"the nominee" includes any person for the time being carrying out the functions of a nominee under this Schedule,

"related contract" has the meaning given by the 1995 regulations,

"the settlement finality regulations" means the Financial Markets and Insolvency (Settlement Finality) Regulations 1999,

"system-charge" has the meaning given by the Financial Markets and Insolvency Regulations 1996.

Eligible companies

2   (1)   A company is eligible for a moratorium if it meets the requirements of paragraph 3, unless –

        (a)   it is excluded from being eligible by virtue of paragraph 4, or

        (b)   it falls within sub-paragraph (2).

    (2)   A company falls within this sub-paragraph if –

        (a)   it is an insurance company within the meaning of the Insurance Companies Act 1982,

        (b)   it is an authorised institution or former authorised institution within the meaning of the Banking Act 1987,

        (c)   it is a party to a market contract, a money market contract or a related contract or any of its property is subject to a market charge, a money market charge or a system-charge, or

        (d)   it is a participant (within the meaning of the settlement finality regulations) or any of its property is subject to a collateral security charge (within the meaning of those regulations).

3   (1)   A company meets the requirements of this paragraph if the qualifying conditions are met –

        (a)   in the year ending with the date of filing, or

        (b)   in the financial year of the company which ended last before that date.

    (2)   For the purposes of sub-paragraph (1) –

        (a)   the qualifying conditions are met by a company in a period if, in that period, it satisfies two or more of the requirements for being a small company specified for the time being in section 247(3) of the Companies Act 1985, and

        (b)   a company's financial year is to be determined in accordance with that Act.

    (3)   Subsections (4), (5) and (6) of section 247 of that Act apply for the purposes of this paragraph as they apply for the purposes of that section.

4   (1)   A company is excluded from being eligible for a moratorium if, on the date of filing –

        (a)   an administration order is in force in relation to the company,

        (b)   the company is being wound up,

        (c)   there is an administrative receiver of the company,

        (d)   a voluntary arrangement has effect in relation to the company,

        (e)   there is a provisional liquidator of the company,

        (f)   a moratorium has been in force for the company at any time during the period of 12 months ending with the date of filing and –

            (i)   no voluntary arrangement had effect at the time at which the moratorium came to an end, or

            (ii)   a voluntary arrangement which had effect at any time in that period has come to an end prematurely, or

        (g)   a voluntary arrangement in relation to the company which had effect in pursuance of a proposal under section 1(3) has come to an end prematurely and, during the period of 12 months ending with the date of filing, an order under section 5(3)(a) has been made.

    (2)   Sub-paragraph (1)(b) does not apply to a company which, by reason of a winding-up order made after the date of filing, is treated as being wound up on that date.

5   The Secretary of State may by regulations modify the qualifications for eligibility of a company for a moratorium.

PART II   OBTAINING A MORATORIUM

Nominee's statement

6   (1) Where the directors of a company wish to obtain a moratorium, they shall submit to the nominee –

   (a) a document setting out the terms of the proposed voluntary arrangement,
   (b) a statement of the company's affairs containing –

   (i) such particulars of its creditors and of its debts and other liabilities and of its assets as may be prescribed, and
   (ii) such other information as may be prescribed, and

   (c) any other information necessary to enable the nominee to comply with sub-paragraph (2) which he requests from them.

   (2) The nominee shall submit to the directors a statement in the prescribed form indicating whether or not, in his opinion –

   (a) the proposed voluntary arrangement has a reasonable prospect of being approved and implemented,
   (b) the company is likely to have sufficient funds available to it during the proposed moratorium to enable it to carry on its business, and
   (c) meetings of the company and its creditors should be summoned to consider the proposed voluntary arrangement.

   (3) In forming his opinion on the matters mentioned in sub-paragraph (2), the nominee is entitled to rely on the information submitted to him under sub-paragraph (1) unless he has reason to doubt its accuracy.

   (4) The reference in sub-paragraph (2)(b) to the company's business is to that business as the company proposes to carry it on during the moratorium.

Documents to be submitted to court

7   (1) To obtain a moratorium the directors of a company must file (in Scotland, lodge) with the court –

   (a) a document setting out the terms of the proposed voluntary arrangement,
   (b) a statement of the company's affairs containing –

   (i) such particulars of its creditors and of its debts and other liabilities and of its assets as may be prescribed, and
   (ii) such other information as may be prescribed,

   (c) a statement that the company is eligible for a moratorium,
   (d) a statement from the nominee that he has given his consent to act, and
   (e) a statement from the nominee that, in his opinion –

   (i) the proposed voluntary arrangement has a reasonable prospect of being approved and implemented,
   (ii) the company is likely to have sufficient funds available to it during the proposed moratorium to enable it to carry on its business, and
   (iii) meetings of the company and its creditors should be summoned to consider the proposed voluntary arrangement.

   (2) Each of the statements mentioned in sub-paragraph (1)(b) to (e), except so far as it contains the particulars referred to in paragraph (b)(i), must be in the prescribed form.

(3)   The reference in sub-paragraph (1)(e)(ii) to the company's business is to that business as the company proposes to carry it on during the moratorium.

(4)   The Secretary of State may by regulations modify the requirements of this paragraph as to the documents required to be filed (in Scotland, lodged) with the court in order to obtain a moratorium.

Duration of moratorium

8   (1)   A moratorium comes into force when the documents for the time being referred to in paragraph 7(1) are filed or lodged with the court and references in this Schedule to "the beginning of the moratorium" shall be construed accordingly.

(2)   A moratorium ends at the end of the day on which the meetings summoned under paragraph 29(1) are first held (or, if the meetings are held on different days, the later of those days), unless it is extended under paragraph 32.

(3)   If either of those meetings has not first met before the end of the period of 28 days beginning with the day on which the moratorium comes into force, the moratorium ends at the end of the day on which those meetings were to be held (or, if those meetings were summoned to be held on different days, the later of those days), unless it is extended under paragraph 32.

(4)   If the nominee fails to summon either meeting within the period required by paragraph 29(1), the moratorium ends at the end of the last day of that period.

(5)   If the moratorium is extended (or further extended) under paragraph 32, it ends at the end of the day to which it is extended (or further extended).

(6)   Sub-paragraphs (2) to (5) do not apply if the moratorium comes to an end before the time concerned by virtue of –

(a)   paragraph 25(4) (effect of withdrawal by nominee of consent to act),

(b)   an order under paragraph 26(3), 27(3) or 40 (challenge of actions of nominee or directors), or

(c)   a decision of one or both of the meetings summoned under paragraph 29.

(7)   If the moratorium has not previously come to an end in accordance with sub-paragraphs (2) to (6), it ends at the end of the day on which a decision under paragraph 31 to approve a voluntary arrangement takes effect under paragraph 36.

(8)   The Secretary of State may by order increase or reduce the period for the time being specified in sub-paragraph (3).

Notification of beginning of moratorium

9   (1)   When a moratorium comes into force, the directors shall notify the nominee of that fact forthwith.

(2)   If the directors without reasonable excuse fail to comply with sub-paragraph (1), each of them is liable to imprisonment or a fine, or both.

10   (1)   When a moratorium comes into force, the nominee shall, in accordance with the rules –

(a)   advertise that fact forthwith, and

(b)   notify the registrar of companies, the company and any petitioning creditor of the company of whose claim he is aware of that fact.

(2) In sub-paragraph (1)(b), "petitioning creditor" means a creditor by whom a winding-up petition has been presented before the beginning of the moratorium, as long as the petition has not been dismissed or withdrawn.

(3) If the nominee without reasonable excuse fails to comply with sub paragraph (1)(a) or (b), he is liable to a fine.

Notification of end of moratorium

11 (1) When a moratorium comes to an end, the nominee shall, in accordance with the rules –

(a) advertise that fact forthwith, and

(b) notify the court, the registrar of companies, the company and any creditor of the company of whose claim he is aware of that fact.

(2) If the nominee without reasonable excuse fails to comply with sub-paragraph (1)(a) or (b), he is liable to a fine.

PART III   EFFECTS OF MORATORIUM

Effect on creditors, etc.

12 (1) During the period for which a moratorium is in force for a company –

(a) no petition may be presented for the winding up of the company,

(b) no meeting of the company may be called or requisitioned except with the consent of the nominee or the leave of the court and subject (where the court gives leave) to such terms as the court may impose,

(c) no resolution may be passed or order made for the winding up of the company,

(d) no petition for an administration order in relation to the company may be presented,

(e) no administrative receiver of the company may be appointed,

(f) no landlord or other person to whom rent is payable may exercise any right of forfeiture by peaceable re-entry in relation to premises let to the company in respect of a failure by the company to comply with any term or condition of its tenancy of such premises, except with the leave of the court and subject to such terms as the court may impose,

(g) no other steps may be taken to enforce any security over the company's property, or to repossess goods in the company's possession under any hire-purchase agreement, except with the leave of the court and subject to such terms as the court may impose, and

(h) no other proceedings and no execution or other legal process may be commenced or continued, and no distress may be levied, against the company or its property except with the leave of the court and subject to such terms as the court may impose.

(2) Where a petition, other than an excepted petition, for the winding up of the company has been presented before the beginning of the moratorium, section 127 shall not apply in relation to any disposition of property, transfer of shares or alteration in status made during the moratorium or at a time mentioned in paragraph 37(5)(a).

(3) In the application of sub-paragraph (1)(h) to Scotland, the reference to execution being commenced or continued includes a reference to diligence being carried out or continued, and the reference to distress being levied is omitted.

(4) Paragraph (a) of sub-paragraph (1) does not apply to an excepted petition and, where such a petition has been presented before the beginning of the moratorium or is presented during the moratorium, paragraphs (b) and (c) of that sub-paragraph do not apply in relation to proceedings on the petition.

(5) For the purposes of this paragraph, "excepted petition" means a petition under –

 (a)   section 124A of this Act,

 (b)   section 72 of the Financial Services Act 1986 on the ground mentioned in subsection (1)(b) of that section, or

 (c)   section 92 of the Banking Act 1987 on the ground mentioned in sub-section (1)(b) of that section.

13 (1) This paragraph applies where there is an uncrystallised floating charge on the property of a company for which a moratorium is in force.

 (2) If the conditions for the holder of the charge to give a notice having the effect mentioned in sub-paragraph (4) are met at any time, the notice may not be given at that time but may instead be given as soon as practicable after the moratorium has come to an end.

 (3) If any other event occurs at any time which (apart from this sub-paragraph) would have the effect mentioned in sub-paragraph (4), then –

 (a)   the event shall not have the effect in question at that time, but

 (b)   if notice of the event is given to the company by the holder of the charge as soon as is practicable after the moratorium has come to an end, the event is to be treated as if it had occurred when the notice was given.

 (4) The effect referred to in sub-paragraphs (2) and (3) is –

 (a)   causing the crystallisation of the floating charge, or

 (b)   causing the imposition, by virtue of provision in the instrument creating the charge, of any restriction on the disposal of any property of the company.

 (5) Application may not be made for leave under paragraph 12(1)(g) or (h) with a view to obtaining –

 (a)   the crystallisation of the floating charge, or

 (b)   the imposition, by virtue of provision in the instrument creating the charge, of any restriction on the disposal of any property of the company.

14 Security granted by a company at a time when a moratorium is in force in relation to the company may only be enforced if, at that time, there were reasonable grounds for believing that it would benefit the company.

Effect on company

15 (1) Paragraphs 16 to 23 apply in relation to a company for which a moratorium is in force.

 (2) The fact that a company enters into a transaction in contravention of any of paragraphs 16 to 22 does not –

 (a)   make the transaction void, or

 (b)   make it to any extent unenforceable against the company.

Company invoices, etc.

16 (1) Every invoice, order for goods or business letter which –

(a)   is issued by or on behalf of the company, and

(b)   on or in which the company's name appears,

shall also contain the nominee's name and a statement that the moratorium is in force for the company.

(2)   If default is made in complying with sub-paragraph (1), the company and (subject to sub-paragraph (3)) any officer of the company is liable to a fine.

(3)   An officer of the company is only liable under sub-paragraph (2) if, without reasonable excuse, he authorises or permits the default.

Obtaining credit during moratorium

17   (1)   The company may not obtain credit to the extent of £250 or more from a person who has not been informed that a moratorium is in force in relation to the company.

(2)   The reference to the company obtaining credit includes the following cases –

(a)   where goods are bailed (in Scotland, hired) to the company under a hire-purchase agreement, or agreed to be sold to the company under a conditional sale agreement, and

(b)   where the company is paid in advance (whether in money or otherwise) for the supply of goods or services.

(3)   Where the company obtains credit in contravention of sub-paragraph (1) –

(a)   the company is liable to a fine, and

(b)   if any officer of the company knowingly and wilfully authorised or permitted the contravention, he is liable to imprisonment or a fine, or both.

(4)   The money sum specified in sub-paragraph (1) is subject to increase or reduction by order under section 417A in Part XV.

Disposals and payments

18   (1)   Subject to sub-paragraph (2), the company may only dispose of any of its property if –

(a)   there are reasonable grounds for believing that the disposal will benefit the company, and

(b)   the disposal is approved by the committee established under paragraph 35(1) or, where there is no such committee, by the nominee.

(2)   Sub-paragraph (1) does not apply to a disposal made in the ordinary way of the company's business.

(3)   If the company makes a disposal in contravention of sub-paragraph (1) otherwise than in pursuance of an order of the court –

(a)   the company is liable to a fine, and

(b)   if any officer of the company authorised or permitted the contravention, without reasonable excuse, he is liable to imprisonment or a fine, or both.

19   (1)   Subject to sub-paragraph (2), the company may only make any payment in respect of any debt or other liability of the company in existence before the beginning of the moratorium if –

(a)   there are reasonable grounds for believing that the payment will benefit the company, and

(b)   the payment is approved by the committee established under paragraph 35(1) or, where there is no such committee, by the nominee.

(2) Sub-paragraph (1) does not apply to a payment required by paragraph 20(6).

(3) If the company makes a payment in contravention of sub-paragraph (1) otherwise than in pursuance of an order of the court –

   (a) the company is liable to a fine, and

   (b) if any officer of the company authorised or permitted the contravention, without reasonable excuse, he is liable to imprisonment or a fine, or both.

Disposal of charged property, etc.

20 (1) This paragraph applies where –

   (a) any property of the company is subject to a security, or

   (b) any goods are in the possession of the company under a hire-purchase agreement.

(2) If the holder of the security consents, or the court gives leave, the company may dispose of the property as if it were not subject to the security.

(3) If the owner of the goods consents, or the court gives leave, the company may dispose of the goods as if all rights of the owner under the hire-purchase agreement were vested in the company.

(4) Where property subject to a security which, as created, was a floating charge is disposed of under sub-paragraph (2), the holder of the security has the same priority in respect of any property of the company directly or indirectly representing the property disposed of as he would have had in respect of the property subject to the security.

(5) Sub-paragraph (6) applies to the disposal under sub-paragraph (2) or (as the case may be) sub-paragraph (3) of –

   (a) any property subject to a security other than a security which, as created, was a floating charge, or

   (b) any goods in the possession of the company under a hire-purchase agreement.

(6) It shall be a condition of any consent or leave under sub-paragraph (2) or (as the case may be) sub-paragraph (3) that –

   (a) the net proceeds of the disposal, and

   (b) where those proceeds are less than such amount as may be agreed, or determined by the court, to be the net amount which would be realised on a sale of the property or goods in the open market by a willing vendor, such sums as may be required to make good the deficiency,

shall be applied towards discharging the sums secured by the security or payable under the hire-purchase agreement.

(7) Where a condition imposed in pursuance of sub-paragraph (6) relates to two or more securities, that condition requires –

   (a) the net proceeds of the disposal, and

   (b) where paragraph (b) of sub-paragraph (6) applies, the sums mentioned in that paragraph,

to be applied towards discharging the sums secured by those securities in the order of their priorities.

(8) Where the court gives leave for a disposal under sub-paragraph (2) or (3), the directors shall, within 14 days after leave is given, send an office copy of the order giving leave to the registrar of companies.

(9) If the directors without reasonable excuse fail to comply with sub-paragraph (8), they are liable to a fine.

21 (1) Where property is disposed of under paragraph 20 in its application to Scotland, the company shall grant to the disponee an appropriate document of transfer or conveyance of the property, and

    (a) that document, or

    (b) where any recording, intimation or registration of the document is a legal requirement for completion of title to the property, that recording, intimation or registration,

has the effect of disencumbering the property of, or (as the case may be) freeing the property from, the security.

(2) Where goods in the possession of the company under a hire-purchase agreement are disposed of under paragraph 20 in its application to Scotland, the disposal has the effect of extinguishing, as against the disponee, all rights of the owner of the goods under the agreement.

22 (1) If the company –

    (a) without any consent or leave under paragraph 20, disposes of any of its property which is subject to a security otherwise than in accordance with the terms of the security,

    (b) without any consent or leave under paragraph 20, disposes of any goods in the possession of the company under a hire-purchase agreement otherwise than in accordance with the terms of the agreement, or

    (c) fails to comply with any requirement imposed by paragraph 20 or 21,

it is liable to a fine.

(2) If any officer of the company, without reasonable excuse, authorises or permits any such disposal or failure to comply, he is liable to imprisonment or a fine, or both.

Market contracts, etc.

23 (1) If the company enters into any transaction to which this paragraph applies –

    (a) the company is liable to a fine, and

    (b) if any officer of the company, without reasonable excuse, authorised or permitted the company to enter into the transaction, he is liable to imprisonment or a fine, or both.

(2) A company enters into a transaction to which this paragraph applies if it –

    (a) enters into a market contract, a money market contract or a related contract,

    (b) gives a transfer order,

    (c) grants a market charge, a money market charge or a system-charge, or

    (d) provides any collateral security.

(3) The fact that a company enters into a transaction in contravention of this paragraph does not –

    (a) make the transaction void, or

    (b) make it to any extent unenforceable by or against the company.

(4) Where during the moratorium a company enters into a transaction to which this paragraph applies, nothing done by or in pursuance of the transaction is to be treated as done in contravention of paragraphs 12(1)(g), 14 or 16 to 22.

(5) Paragraph 20 does not apply in relation to any property which is subject to a market charge, a money market charge, a system-charge or a collateral security charge.

(6) In this paragraph, "transfer order", "collateral security" and "collateral security charge" have the same meanings as in the settlement finality regulations.

PART IV   NOMINEES

Monitoring of company's activities

24 (1) During a moratorium, the nominee shall monitor the company's affairs for the purpose of forming an opinion as to whether –

    (a) the proposed voluntary arrangement or, if he has received notice of proposed modifications under paragraph 31(7), the proposed arrangement with those modifications has a reasonable prospect of being approved and implemented, and

    (b) the company is likely to have sufficient funds available to it during the remainder of the moratorium to enable it to continue to carry on its business.

  (2) The directors shall submit to the nominee any information necessary to enable him to comply with sub-paragraph (1) which he requests from them.

  (3) In forming his opinion on the matters mentioned in sub-paragraph (1), the nominee is entitled to rely on the information submitted to him under sub-paragraph (2) unless he has reason to doubt its accuracy.

  (4) The reference in sub-paragraph (1)(b) to the company's business is to that business as the company proposes to carry it on during the remainder of the moratorium.

Withdrawal of consent to act

25 (1) The nominee may only withdraw his consent to act in the circumstances mentioned in this paragraph.

  (2) The nominee must withdraw his consent to act if, at any time during a moratorium –

    (a) he forms the opinion that –

        (i) the proposed voluntary arrangement or, if he has received notice of proposed modifications under paragraph 31(7), the proposed arrangement with those modifications no longer has a reasonable prospect of being approved or implemented, or

        (ii) the company will not have sufficient funds available to it during the remainder of the moratorium to enable it to continue to carry on its business,

    (b) he becomes aware that, on the date of filing, the company was not eligible for a moratorium, or

    (c) the directors fail to comply with their duty under paragraph 24(2).

  (3) The reference in sub-paragraph (2)(a)(ii) to the company's business is to that business as the company proposes to carry it on during the remainder of the moratorium.

  (4) If the nominee withdraws his consent to act, the moratorium comes to an end.

  (5) If the nominee withdraws his consent to act he must, in accordance with the rules, notify the court, the registrar of companies, the company and any creditor of the company of whose claim he is aware of his withdrawal and the reason for it.

  (6) If the nominee without reasonable excuse fails to comply with sub-paragraph (5), he is liable to a fine.

Challenge of nominee's actions, etc.

26 (1) If any creditor, director or member of the company, or any other person affected by a moratorium, is dissatisfied by any act, omission or decision of the nominee during the moratorium, he may apply to the court.

(2) An application under sub-paragraph (1) may be made during the moratorium or after it has ended.

(3) On an application under sub-paragraph (1) the court may –

(a) confirm, reverse or modify any act or decision of the nominee,

(b) give him directions, or

(c) make such other order as it thinks fit.

(4) An order under sub-paragraph (3) may (among other things) bring the moratorium to an end and make such consequential provision as the court thinks fit.

27 (1) Where there are reasonable grounds for believing that –

(a) as a result of any act, omission or decision of the nominee during the moratorium, the company has suffered loss, but

(b) the company does not intend to pursue any claim it may have against the nominee,

any creditor of the company may apply to the court.

(2) An application under sub-paragraph (1) may be made during the moratorium or after it has ended.

(3) On an application under sub-paragraph (1) the court may –

(a) order the company to pursue any claim against the nominee,

(b) authorise any creditor to pursue such a claim in the name of the company, or

(c) make such other order with respect to such a claim as it thinks fit,

unless the court is satisfied that the act, omission or decision of the nominee was in all the circumstances reasonable.

(4) An order under sub-paragraph (3) may (among other things) –

(a) impose conditions on any authority given to pursue a claim,

(b) direct the company to assist in the pursuit of a claim,

(c) make directions with respect to the distribution of anything received as a result of the pursuit of a claim,

(d) bring the moratorium to an end and make such consequential provision as the court thinks fit.

(5) On an application under sub-paragraph (1) the court shall have regard to the interests of the members and creditors of the company generally.

Replacement of nominee by court

28 (1) The court may –

(a) on an application made by the directors in a case where the nominee has failed to comply with any duty imposed on him under this Schedule or has died, or

(b) on an application made by the directors or the nominee in a case where it is impracticable or inappropriate for the nominee to continue to act as such,

direct that the nominee be replaced as such by another person qualified to act as an insolvency practitioner, or authorised to act as nominee, in relation to the voluntary arrangement.

(2) A person may only be appointed as a replacement nominee under this paragraph if he submits to the court a statement indicating his consent to act.

PART V   CONSIDERATION AND IMPLEMENTATION OF VOLUNTARY ARRANGEMENT

Summoning of meetings

29 (1) Where a moratorium is in force, the nominee shall summon meetings of the company and its creditors for such a time, date (within the period for the time being specified in paragraph 8(3)) and place as he thinks fit.
    (2) The persons to be summoned to a creditors' meeting under this paragraph are every creditor of the company of whose claim the nominee is aware.

Conduct of meetings

30 (1) Subject to the provisions of paragraphs 31 to 35, the meetings summoned under paragraph 29 shall be conducted in accordance with the rules.
    (2) A meeting so summoned may resolve that it be adjourned (or further adjourned).
    (3) After the conclusion of either meeting in accordance with the rules, the chairman of the meeting shall report the result of the meeting to the court, and, immediately after reporting to the court, shall give notice of the result of the meeting to such persons as may be prescribed.

Approval of voluntary arrangement

31 (1) The meetings summoned under paragraph 29 shall decide whether to approve the proposed voluntary arrangement (with or without modifications).
    (2) The modifications may include one conferring the functions proposed to be conferred on the nominee on another person qualified to act as an insolvency practitioner, or authorised to act as nominee, in relation to the voluntary arrangement.
    (3) The modifications shall not include one by virtue of which the proposal ceases to be a proposal such as is mentioned in section 1.
    (4) A meeting summoned under paragraph 29 shall not approve any proposal or modification which affects the right of a secured creditor of the company to enforce his security, except with the concurrence of the creditor concerned.
    (5) Subject to sub-paragraph (6), a meeting so summoned shall not approve any proposal or modification under which –
        (a) any preferential debt of the company is to be paid otherwise than in priority to such of its debts as are not preferential debts, or
        (b) a preferential creditor of the company is to be paid an amount in respect of a preferential debt that bears to that debt a smaller proportion than is borne to another preferential debt by the amount that is to be paid in respect of that other debt.
    (6) The meeting may approve such a proposal or modification with the concurrence of the preferential creditor concerned.
    (7) The directors of the company may, before the beginning of the period of seven days which ends with the meetings (or either of them) summoned

under paragraph 29 being held, give notice to the nominee of any modifications of the proposal for which the directors intend to seek the approval of those meetings.

(8) References in this paragraph to preferential debts and preferential creditors are to be read in accordance with section 386 in Part XII of this Act.

Extension of moratorium

32 (1) Subject to sub-paragraph (2), a meeting summoned under paragraph 29 which resolves that it be adjourned (or further adjourned) may resolve that the moratorium be extended (or further extended), with or without conditions.

(2) The moratorium may not be extended (or further extended) to a day later than the end of the period of two months which begins –

(a) where both meetings summoned under paragraph 29 are first held on the same day, with that day,

(b) in any other case, with the day on which the later of those meetings is first held.

(3) At any meeting where it is proposed to extend (or further extend) the moratorium, before a decision is taken with respect to that proposal, the nominee shall inform the meeting –

(a) of what he has done in order to comply with his duty under paragraph 24 and the cost of his actions for the company, and

(b) of what he intends to do to continue to comply with that duty if the moratorium is extended (or further extended) and the expected cost of his actions for the company.

(4) Where, in accordance with sub-paragraph (3)(b), the nominee informs a meeting of the expected cost of his intended actions, the meeting shall resolve whether or not to approve that expected cost.

(5) If a decision not to approve the expected cost of the nominee's intended actions has effect under paragraph 36, the moratorium comes to an end.

(6) A meeting may resolve that a moratorium which has been extended (or further extended) be brought to an end before the end of the period of the extension (or further extension).

(7) The Secretary of State may by order increase or reduce the period for the time being specified in sub-paragraph (2).

33 (1) The conditions which may be imposed when a moratorium is extended (or further extended) include a requirement that the nominee be replaced as such by another person qualified to act as an insolvency practitioner, or authorised to act as nominee, in relation to the voluntary arrangement.

(2) A person may only be appointed as a replacement nominee by virtue of sub-paragraph (1) if he submits to the court a statement indicating his consent to act.

(3) At any meeting where it is proposed to appoint a replacement nominee as a condition of extending (or further extending) the moratorium –

(a) the duty imposed by paragraph 32(3)(b) on the nominee shall instead be imposed on the person proposed as the replacement nominee, and

(b) paragraphs 32(4) and (5) and 36(1)(e) apply as if the references to the nominee were to that person.

34 (1) If a decision to extend, or further extend, the moratorium takes effect under paragraph 36, the nominee shall, in accordance with the rules, notify the registrar of companies and the court.

(2) If the moratorium is extended, or further extended, by virtue of an order under paragraph 36(5), the nominee shall, in accordance with the rules, send an office copy of the order to the registrar of companies.

(3) If the nominee without reasonable excuse fails to comply with this paragraph, he is liable to a fine.

Moratorium committee

35 (1) A meeting summoned under paragraph 29 which resolves that the moratorium be extended (or further extended) may, with the consent of the nominee, resolve that a committee be established to exercise the functions conferred on it by the meeting.

(2) The meeting may not so resolve unless it has approved an estimate of the expenses to be incurred by the committee in the exercise of the proposed functions.

(3) Any expenses, not exceeding the amount of the estimate, incurred by the committee in the exercise of its functions shall be reimbursed by the nominee.

(4) The committee shall cease to exist when the moratorium comes to an end.

Effectiveness of decisions

36 (1) Sub-paragraph (2) applies to references to one of the following decisions having effect, that is, a decision, under paragraph 31, 32 or 35, with respect to –

(a) the approval of a proposed voluntary arrangement,
(b) the extension (or further extension) of a moratorium,
(c) the bringing of a moratorium to an end,
(d) the establishment of a committee, or
(e) the approval of the expected cost of a nominee's intended actions.

(2) The decision has effect if, in accordance with the rules –

(a) it has been taken by both meetings summoned under paragraph 29, or
(b) (subject to any order made under sub-paragraph (5)) it has been taken by the creditors' meeting summoned under that paragraph.

(3) If a decision taken by the creditors' meeting under any of paragraphs 31, 32 or 35 with respect to any of the matters mentioned in sub-paragraph (1) differs from one so taken by the company meeting with respect to that matter, a member of the company may apply to the court.

(4) An application under sub-paragraph (3) shall not be made after the end of the period of 28 days beginning with –

(a) the day on which the decision was taken by the creditors' meeting, or
(b) where the decision of the company meeting was taken on a later day, that day.

(5) On an application under sub-paragraph (3), the court may –

(a) order the decision of the company meeting to have effect instead of the decision of the creditors' meeting, or
(b) make such other order as it thinks fit.

Effect of approval of voluntary arrangement

37 (1) This paragraph applies where a decision approving a voluntary arrangement
        has effect under paragraph 36.

    (2) The approved voluntary arrangement –

        (a) takes effect as if made by the company at the creditors' meeting, and
        (b) binds every person who in accordance with the rules –

            (i)   was entitled to vote at that meeting (whether or not he was
                  present or represented at it), or
            (ii) would have been so entitled if he had had notice of it,

        as if he were a party to the voluntary arrangement.

    (3) If –

        (a) when the arrangement ceases to have effect any amount payable
             under the arrangement to a person bound by virtue of sub-paragraph
             (2)(b)(ii) has not been paid, and
        (b) the arrangement did not come to an end prematurely,

        the company shall at that time become liable to pay to that person the
        amount payable under the arrangement.

    (4) Where a petition for the winding up of the company, other than an excepted
         petition within the meaning of paragraph 12, was presented before the
         beginning of the moratorium, the court shall dismiss the petition.

    (5) The court shall not dismiss a petition under sub-paragraph (4) –

        (a) at any time before the end of the period of 28 days beginning with
             the first day on which each of the reports of the meetings required by
             paragraph 30(3) has been made to the court, or
        (b) at any time when an application under paragraph 38 or an appeal in
             respect of such an application is pending, or at any time in the period
             within which such an appeal may be brought.

Challenge of decisions

38 (1) Subject to the following provisions of this paragraph, any of the persons
        mentioned in sub-paragraph (2) may apply to the court on one or both
        of the following grounds –

        (a) that a voluntary arrangement approved at one or both of the
             meetings summoned under paragraph 29 and which has taken
             effect unfairly prejudices the interests of a creditor, member or
             contributory of the company,
        (b) that there has been some material irregularity at or in relation to
             either of those meetings.

    (2) The persons who may apply under this paragraph are –

        (a) a person entitled, in accordance with the rules, to vote at either of
             the meetings,
        (b) a person who would have been entitled, in accordance with the
             rules, to vote at the creditors' meeting if he had had notice of it, and
        (c) the nominee.

    (3) An application under this paragraph shall not be made –

        (a) after the end of the period of 28 days beginning with the first day on which
             each of the reports required by paragraph 30(3) has been made to the court,
             or
        (b) in the case of a person who was not given notice of the creditors' meeting,
             after the end of the period of 28 days beginning with the day on which he
             became aware that the meeting had taken place,

but (subject to that) an application made by a person within sub-paragraph (2)(b) on the ground that the arrangement prejudices his interests may be made after the arrangement has ceased to have effect, unless it came to an end prematurely.

(4) Where on an application under this paragraph the court is satisfied as to either of the grounds mentioned in sub-paragraph (1), it may do any of the following –

    (a) revoke or suspend –

        (i) any decision approving the voluntary arrangement which has effect under paragraph 36, or

        (ii) in a case falling within sub-paragraph (1)(b), any decision taken by the meeting in question which has effect under that paragraph,

    (b) give a direction to any person –

        (i) for the summoning of further meetings to consider any revised proposal for a voluntary arrangement which the directors may make, or

        (ii) in a case falling within sub-paragraph (1)(b), for the summoning of a further company or (as the case may be) creditors' meeting to reconsider the original proposal.

(5) Where at any time after giving a direction under sub-paragraph (4)(b)(i) the court is satisfied that the directors do not intend to submit a revised proposal, the court shall revoke the direction and revoke or suspend any decision approving the voluntary arrangement which has effect under paragraph 36.

(6) Where the court gives a direction under sub-paragraph (4)(b), it may also give a direction continuing or, as the case may require, renewing, for such period as may be specified in the direction, the effect of the moratorium.

(7) Sub-paragraph (8) applies in a case where the court, on an application under this paragraph –

    (a) gives a direction under sub-paragraph (4)(b), or

    (b) revokes or suspends a decision under sub-paragraph (4)(a) or (5).

(8) In such a case, the court may give such supplemental directions as it thinks fit and, in particular, directions with respect to –

    (a) things done under the voluntary arrangement since it took effect, and

    (b) such things done since that time as could not have been done if a moratorium had been in force in relation to the company when they were done.

(9) Except in pursuance of the preceding provisions of this paragraph, a decision taken at a meeting summoned under paragraph 29 is not invalidated by any irregularity at or in relation to the meeting.

Implementation of voluntary arrangement

39 (1) This paragraph applies where a voluntary arrangement approved by one or both of the meetings summoned under paragraph 29 has taken effect.

    (2) The person who is for the time being carrying out in relation to the voluntary arrangement the functions conferred –

        (a) by virtue of the approval of the arrangement, on the nominee, or

        (b) by virtue of paragraph 31(2), on a person other than the nominee,

    shall be known as the supervisor of the voluntary arrangement.

(3) If any of the company's creditors or any other person is dissatisfied by any act, omission or decision of the supervisor, he may apply to the court.

(4) On an application under sub-paragraph (3) the court may –

   (a) confirm, reverse or modify any act or decision of the supervisor,

   (b) give him directions, or

   (c) make such other order as it thinks fit.

(5) The supervisor –

   (a) may apply to the court for directions in relation to any particular matter arising under the voluntary arrangement, and

   (b) is included among the persons who may apply to the court for the winding up of the company or for an administration order to be made in relation to it.

(6) The court may, whenever –

   (a) it is expedient to appoint a person to carry out the functions of the supervisor, and

   (b) it is inexpedient, difficult or impracticable for an appointment to be made without the assistance of the court,

   make an order appointing a person who is qualified to act as an insolvency practitioner, or authorised to act as supervisor, in relation to the voluntary arrangement, either in substitution for the existing supervisor or to fill a vacancy.

(7) The power conferred by sub-paragraph (6) is exercisable so as to increase the number of persons exercising the functions of supervisor or, where there is more than one person exercising those functions, so as to replace one or more of those persons.

PART VI   MISCELLANEOUS

Challenge of directors' actions

40 (1) This paragraph applies in relation to acts or omissions of the directors of a company during a moratorium.

   (2) A creditor or member of the company may apply to the court for an order under this paragraph on the ground –

   (a) that the company's affairs, business and property are being or have been managed by the directors in a manner which is unfairly prejudicial to the interests of its creditors or members generally, or of some part of its creditors or members (including at least the petitioner), or

   (b) that any actual or proposed act or omission of the directors is or would be so prejudicial.

   (3) An application for an order under this paragraph may be made during or after the moratorium.

   (4) On an application for an order under this paragraph the court may –

   (a) make such order as it thinks fit for giving relief in respect of the matters complained of,

   (b) adjourn the hearing conditionally or unconditionally, or

   (c) make an interim order or any other order that it thinks fit.

   (5) An order under this paragraph may in particular –

   (a) regulate the management by the directors of the company's affairs, business and property during the remainder of the moratorium,

    (b)   require the directors to refrain from doing or continuing an act complained of by the petitioner, or to do an act which the petitioner has complained they have omitted to do,

    (c)   require the summoning of a meeting of creditors or members for the purpose of considering such matters as the court may direct,

    (d)   bring the moratorium to an end and make such consequential provision as the court thinks fit.

(6) In making an order under this paragraph the court shall have regard to the need to safeguard the interests of persons who have dealt with the company in good faith and for value.

(7) In relation to any time when an administration order is in force in relation to the company, or the company is being wound up, in pursuance of a petition presented before the moratorium came into force, no application for an order under this paragraph may be made by a creditor or member of the company; but such an application may be made instead by the administrator or (as the case may be) liquidator.

Offences

41 (1) This paragraph applies where a moratorium has been obtained for a company.

(2) If, within the period of 12 months ending with the day on which the moratorium came into force, a person who was at the time an officer of the company –

    (a)   did any of the things mentioned in paragraphs (a) to (f) of sub-paragraph (4), or

    (b)   was privy to the doing by others of any of the things mentioned in paragraphs (c), (d) and (e) of that sub-paragraph,

he is to be treated as having committed an offence at that time.

(3) If, at any time during the moratorium, a person who is an officer of the company –

    (a)   does any of the things mentioned in paragraphs (a) to (f) of sub-paragraph (4), or

    (b)   is privy to the doing by others of any of the things mentioned in paragraphs (c), (d) and (e) of that sub-paragraph,

he commits an offence.

(4) Those things are –

    (a)   concealing any part of the company's property to the value of £500 or more, or concealing any debt due to or from the company, or

    (b)   fraudulently removing any part of the company's property to the value of £500 or more, or

    (c)   concealing, destroying, mutilating or falsifying any book or paper affecting or relating to the company's property or affairs, or

    (d)   making any false entry in any book or paper affecting or relating to the company's property or affairs, or

    (e)   fraudulently parting with, altering or making any omission in any document affecting or relating to the company's property or affairs, or

    (f)   pawning, pledging or disposing of any property of the company which has been obtained on credit and has not been paid for (unless the pawning, pledging or disposal was in the ordinary way of the company's business).

(5) For the purposes of this paragraph, "officer" includes a shadow director.

(6) It is a defence –

(a)   for a person charged under sub-paragraph (2) or (3) in respect of the things mentioned in paragraph (a) or (f) of sub-paragraph (4) to prove that he had no intent to defraud, and

(b)   for a person charged under sub-paragraph (2) or (3) in respect of the things mentioned in paragraph (c) or (d) of sub-paragraph (4) to prove that he had no intent to conceal the state of affairs of the company or to defeat the law.

(7)   Where a person pawns, pledges or disposes of any property of a company in circumstances which amount to an offence under sub-paragraph (2) or (3), every person who takes in pawn or pledge, or otherwise receives, the property knowing it to be pawned, pledged or disposed of in circumstances which –

(a)   would, if a moratorium were obtained for the company within the period of 12 months beginning with the day on which the pawning, pledging or disposal took place, amount to an offence under sub-paragraph (2), or

(b)   amount to an offence under sub-paragraph (3),

commits an offence.

(8)   A person guilty of an offence under this paragraph is liable to imprisonment or a fine, or both.

(9)   The money sums specified in paragraphs (a) and (b) of sub-paragraph (4) are subject to increase or reduction by order under section 417A in Part XV.

42   (1)   If, for the purpose of obtaining a moratorium, or an extension of a moratorium, for a company, a person who is an officer of the company –

(a)   makes any false representation, or

(b)   fraudulently does, or omits to do, anything,

he commits an offence.

(2)   Sub-paragraph (1) applies even if no moratorium or extension is obtained.

(3)   For the purposes of this paragraph, "officer" includes a shadow director.

(4)   A person guilty of an offence under this paragraph is liable to imprisonment or a fine, or both.

Void provisions in floating charge documents

43   (1)   A provision in an instrument creating a floating charge is void if it provides for –

(a)   obtaining a moratorium, or

(b)   anything done with a view to obtaining a moratorium (including any preliminary decision or investigation),

to be an event causing the floating charge to crystallise or causing restrictions which would not otherwise apply to be imposed on the disposal of property by the company or a ground for the appointment of a receiver.

(2)   In sub-paragraph (1), "receiver" includes a manager and a person who is appointed both receiver and manager.

Functions of the Financial Services Authority

44   (1)   This Schedule has effect in relation to a moratorium for a regulated company with the modifications in sub-paragraphs (2) to (16) below.

(2)   Any notice or other document required by virtue of this Schedule to be sent to a creditor of a regulated company must also be sent to the Authority.

(3) The Authority is entitled to be heard on any application to the court for leave under paragraph 20(2) or 20(3) (disposal of charged property, etc.).

(4) Where paragraph 26(1) (challenge of nominee's actions, etc.) applies, the persons who may apply to the court include the Authority.

(5) If a person other than the Authority applies to the court under that paragraph, the Authority is entitled to be heard on the application.

(6) Where paragraph 27(1) (challenge of nominee's actions, etc.) applies, the persons who may apply to the court include the Authority.

(7) If a person other than the Authority applies to the court under that paragraph, the Authority is entitled to be heard on the application.

(8) The persons to be summoned to a creditors' meeting under paragraph 29 include the Authority.

(9) A person appointed for the purpose by the Authority is entitled to attend and participate in (but not to vote at) –

(a)   any creditors' meeting summoned under that paragraph,

(b)   any meeting of a committee established under paragraph 35 (moratorium committee).

(10) The Authority is entitled to be heard on any application under paragraph 36(3) (effectiveness of decisions).

(11) Where paragraph 38(1) (challenge of decisions) applies, the persons who may apply to the court include the Authority.

(12) If a person other than the Authority applies to the court under that paragraph, the Authority is entitled to be heard on the application.

(13) Where paragraph 39(3) (implementation of voluntary arrangement) applies, the persons who may apply to the court include the Authority.

(14) If a person other than the Authority applies to the court under that paragraph, the Authority is entitled to be heard on the application.

(15) Where paragraph 40(2) (challenge of directors' actions) applies, the persons who may apply to the court include the Authority.

(16) If a person other than the Authority applies to the court under that paragraph, the Authority is entitled to be heard on the application.

(17) This paragraph does not prejudice any right the Authority has (apart from this paragraph) as a creditor of a regulated company.

(18) In this paragraph –

"the Authority" means the Financial Services Authority, and
"regulated company" means a company which –

(a)   is, or has been, an authorised person within the meaning given by section 31 of the Financial Services and Markets Act 2000,

(b)   is, or has been, an appointed representative within the meaning given by section 39 of that Act, or

(c)   is carrying on, or has carried on, a regulated activity, within the meaning given by section 22 of that Act, in contravention of the general prohibition within the meaning given by section 19 of that Act.

Subordinate legislation

45   (1)   Regulations or an order made by the Secretary of State under this Schedule may make different provision for different cases.

(2)   Regulations so made may make such consequential, incidental, supplemental and transitional provision as may appear to the Secretary of State necessary or expedient.

(3)   Any power of the Secretary of State to make regulations under this Schedule may be exercised by amending or repealing any enactment

contained in this Act (including one contained in this Schedule) or contained in the Company Directors Disqualification Act 1986.

(4) Regulations (except regulations under paragraph 5) or an order made by the Secretary of State under this Schedule shall be made by statutory instrument subject to annulment in pursuance of a resolution of either House of Parliament.

(5) Regulations under paragraph 5 of this Schedule are to be made by statutory instrument and shall only be made if a draft containing the regulations has been laid before and approved by resolution of each House of Parliament.'

5   In section 27(3)(a) (protection of interests of creditors and members when administration order in force), 'section 4 in' is omitted.

6   In section 122(1) (grounds on which company may be wound up by the court), after paragraph (f) there is inserted –

'(fa) at the time at which a moratorium for the company under section 1A comes to an end, no voluntary arrangement approved under Part I has effect in relation to the company'.

7   In section 124 (application for winding up of company), after subsection (3) there is inserted –

'(3A) A winding-up petition on the ground set out in section 122(1)(fa) may only be presented by one or more creditors'.

8   (1)   Section 233 (conditions which may be imposed on supply of gas, water, electricity, etc.) is amended as follows.

(2)   In subsection (1) –

(a)   after paragraph (b) there is inserted –

'(ba) a moratorium under section 1A is in force, or',

(b)   in paragraph (c), for the words from 'under Part I' to 'section 3' there is substituted 'approved under Part I', and

(c)   after 'receiver' (in the second place) there is inserted 'the nominee,'.

(3)   In subsection (4) –

(a)   after paragraph (b) there is inserted –

'(ba) the date on which the moratorium came into force', and

(b)   in paragraph (c), for the words following 'arrangement' there is substituted 'took effect'.

9   In section 387 (date which determines existence and amount of preferential debt), after subsection (2) there is inserted –

'(2A) For the purposes of paragraph 31 of Schedule A1 (meetings to consider company voluntary arrangement where a moratorium under section 1A is in force), the relevant date in relation to a company is the date of filing.'

10   After section 417 there is inserted –

'417A Money sums (company moratorium) – (1) The Secretary of State may by order increase or reduce any of the money sums for the time being specified in the following provisions of Schedule A1 to this Act –

paragraph 17(1) (maximum amount of credit which company may obtain without disclosure of moratorium);
paragraph 41(4) (minimum value of company property concealed or fradulently removed, affecting criminal liability of company's officer).

(2)   An order under this section may contain such transitional provisions as may appear to the Secretary of State necessary or expedient.

(3) An order under this section shall be made by statutory instrument subject to annulment in pursuance of a resolution of either House of Parliament.'

11   In section 432(4) (offences by bodies corporate), at the end there is inserted 'and those under paragraphs 16(2), 17(3)(a), 18(3)(a), 19(3)(a), 22(1) and 23(1)(a) of Schedule A1'.

12   In Schedule 10 (punishment of offences), before the entry relating to paragraph 4(3) of Schedule 7 there are inserted the following entries –

'Sch. A1, para. 9(2).	Directors failing to notify nominee of beginning of moratorium.	1. On indictment. 2. Summary.	2 years or a fine, or both. 6 months or the statutory maximum, or both.
Sch. A1, para. 10(3).	Nominee failing to advertise or notify beginning of moratorium.	Summary.	One-fifth of the statutory maximum.
Sch. A1, para. 11(2).	Nominee failing to advertise or notify end of moratorium.	Summary.	One-fifth of the statutory maximum.
Sch. A1, para. 16(2).	Company and officers failing to state in correspondence etc. that moratorium in force.	Summary.	One-fifth of the statutory maximum.
Sch. A1, para. 17(3)(a).	Company obtaining credit without disclosing existence of moratorium.	1. On indictment. 2. Summary.	A fine. The statutory maximum.
Sch. A1, para. 17(3)(b).	Obtaining credit for company without disclosing existence of moratorium.	1. On indictment. 2. Summary.	2 years or a fine, or both. 6 months or the statutory maximum, or both.
Sch. A1, para. 18(3)(a).	Company disposing of property otherwise than in ordinary way of business.	1. On indictment. 2. Summary.	A fine. The statutory maximum.
Sch. A1, para. 18(3)(b).	Authorising or permitting disposal of company property.	1. On indictment. 2. Summary.	2 years or a fine, or both. 6 months or the statutory maximum, or both.
Sch. A1, para. 19(3)(a).	Company making payments in respect of liabilities existing before beginning of moratorium.	1. On indictment. 2. Summary.	A fine. The statutory maximum.
Sch. A1, para. 19(3)(b).	Authorising or permitting such a payment.	1. On indictment. 2. Summary.	2 years or a fine, or both. 6 months or the statutory maximum, or both.
Sch. A1, para. 20(9).	Directors failing to send to registrar office copy of court order permitting disposal of charged property.	Summary.	One-fifth of the statutory maximum.
Sch. A1, para. 22(1).	Company disposing of charged property.	1. On indictment. 2. Summary.	A fine. The statutory maximum.
Sch. A1, para. 22(2).	Authorising or permitting such a disposal.	1. On indictment. 2. Summary.	2 years or a fine, or both. 6 months or the statutory maximum, or both.
Sch. A1, para. 23(1)(a).	Company entering into market contract, etc.	1. On indictment. 2. Summary.	A fine. The statutory maximum.
Sch. A1, para. 23(1)(b).	Authorising or permitting company to do so.	1. On indictment. 2. Summary.	2 years or a fine, or both. 6 months or the statutory maximum, or both.

Sch. A1, para. 25(6).	Nominee failing to give notice of withdrawal of consent to act.	Summary.	One-fifth of the statutory maximum.
Sch. A1, para. 34(3).	Nominee failing to give notice of extension of moratorium.	Summary.	One-fifth of the statutory maximum.
Sch. A1, para. 41(2).	Fraud or privity to fraud in anticipation of moratorium.	1. On indictment. 2. Summary.	7 years or a fine, or both. 6 months or the statutory maximum, or both.
Sch. A1, para. 41(3).	Fraud or privity to fraud during moratorium.	1. On indictment. 2. Summary.	7 years or a fine, or both. 6 months or the statutory maximum, or both.
Sch. A1, para. 41(7).	Knowingly taking in pawn or pledge, or otherwise receiving, company property.	1. On indictment. 2. Summary.	7 years or a fine, or both. 6 months or the statutory maximum, or both.
Sch. A1, para. 42(1).	False representation or fraud for purpose of obtaining or extending moratorium	1. On indictment. 2. Summary.	7 years or a fine, or both. 6 months or the statutory maximum, or both.'

SCHEDULE 2   COMPANY VOLUNTARY ARRANGEMENTS

PART I   AMENDMENTS OF THE INSOLVENCY ACT 1986

1   The Insolvency Act 1986 is amended as follows.

2   In section 1(2) (proposal for a voluntary arrangement), for 'in relation to the company' there is substituted 'or authorised to act as nominee, in relation to the voluntary arrangement'.

3   In section 2 (procedure where nominee is not the liquidator or administrator) –

(a)   in subsection (2)(a), at the beginning there is inserted –

'whether, in his opinion, the proposed voluntary arrangement has a reasonable prospect of being approved and implemented, (aa)'.

(b)   for subsection (4) there is substituted –

'(4)   The court may –

(a)   on an application made by the person intending to make the proposal, in a case where the nominee has failed to submit the report required by this section or has died, or

(b)   on an application made by that person or the nominee, in a case where it is impracticable or inappropriate for the nominee to continue to act as such,

direct that the nominee be replaced as such by another person qualified to act as an insolvency practitioner, or authorised to act as nominee, in relation to the voluntary arrangement.'

4   In section 4(2) (decisions of meetings), for 'in relation to the company' there is substituted 'or authorised to act as nominee, in relation to the voluntary arrangement'.

5   After section 4 there is inserted –

'4A Approval of arrangement.

(1) This section applies to a decision, under section 4, with respect to the approval of a proposed voluntary arrangement.

(2) The decision has effect if, in accordance with the rules –

    (a)   it has been taken by both meetings summoned under section 3, or

    (b)   (subject to any order made under subsection (4)) it has been taken by the creditors' meeting summoned under that section.

(3) If the decision taken by the creditors' meeting differs from that taken by the company meeting, a member of the company may apply to the court.

(4) An application under subsection (3) shall not be made after the end of the period of 28 days beginning with –

    (a)   the day on which the decision was taken by the creditors' meeting, or

    (b)   where the decision of the company meeting was taken on a later day, that day.

(5) Where a member of a regulated company, within the meaning given by paragraph 44 of Schedule A1, applies to the court under subsection (3), the Financial Services Authority is entitled to be heard on the application.

(6) On an application under subsection (3), the court may –

    (a)   order the decision of the company meeting to have effect instead of the decision of the creditors' meeting, or

    (b)   make such other order as it thinks fit.'

6   In section 5 (effect of approval of voluntary arrangement) –

    (a)   for subsection (1) there is substituted –

        '(1) This section applies where a decision approving a voluntary arrangement has effect under section 4A.',

    (b)   in subsections (2) and (3), 'approved' is omitted,

    (c)   in subsection (2), for paragraph (b) there is substituted –

        '(b) binds every person who in accordance with the rules –

            (i)   was entitled to vote at that meeting (whether or not he was present or represented at it), or

            (ii)   would have been so entitled if he had had notice of it,

        as if he were a party to the voluntary arrangement.

        (2A) If –

            (a)   when the arrangement ceases to have effect any amount payable under the arrangement to a person bound by virtue of subsection (2)(b)(ii) has not been paid, and

            (b)   the arrangement did not come to an end prematurely,

        the company shall at that time become liable to pay to that person the amount payable under the arrangement.'

7   (1) Section 6 (challenge of decisions) is amended as follows.

    (2) In subsection (1)(a), for 'approved at the meetings summoned under section 3' there is substituted 'which has effect under section 4A'.

    (3) In subsection (2), after paragraph (a) there is inserted –

        '(aa) a person who would have been entitled, in accordance with the rules, to vote at the creditors' meeting if he had had notice of it'.

    (4) In subsection (3) –

        (a)   after 'be made' there is inserted '(a)',

        (b)   at the end there is inserted 'or

(b)   in the case of a person who was not given notice of the creditors' meeting, after the end of the period of 28 days beginning with the day on which he became aware that the meeting had taken place,

but (subject to that) an application made by a person within subsection (2)(aa) on the ground that the voluntary arrangement prejudices his interests may be made after the arrangement has ceased to have effect, unless it came to an end prematurely.'

(5) In subsection (4)(a) –

(a)   for 'the approvals given by the meetings' there is substituted 'any decision approving the voluntary arrangement which has effect under section 4A',

(b)   for 'approval given by the meeting in question' there is substituted 'decision taken by the meeting in question which has effect under that section'.

(6) In subsection (5), for 'approval given at the previous meetings' there is substituted 'decision approving the voluntary arrangement which has effect under section 4A'.

(7) In subsection (6), for the words from 'since' to the end there is substituted 'under the voluntary arrangement since it took effect'.

(8) In subsection (7), for 'an approval given' there is substituted 'a decision taken'.

8   After that section there is inserted –

'6A False representations, etc.

(1) If, for the purpose of obtaining the approval of the members or creditors of a company to a proposal for a voluntary arrangement, a person who is an officer of the company –

(a)   makes any false representation, or

(b)   fraudulently does, or omits to do, anything,

he commits an offence.

(2) Subsection (1) applies even if the proposal is not approved.

(3) For purposes of this section "officer" includes a shadow director.

(4) A person guilty of an offence under this section is liable to imprisonment or a fine, or both.'

9   In section 7 (implementation of proposal) –

(a)   in subsection (1), for the words following 'voluntary arrangement' there is substituted 'has effect under section 4A',

(b)   in subsection (2), for paragraph (a) there is substituted –

'(a) on the nominee by virtue of the approval given at one or both of the meetings summoned under section 3',

(c)   in subsection (5), for 'in relation to the company' there is substituted 'or authorised to act as supervisor, in relation to the voluntary arrangement'.

10   After that section there is inserted –

'7A Prosecution of delinquent officers of company

(1) This section applies where a moratorium under section 1A has been obtained for a company or the approval of a voluntary arrangement in relation to a company has taken effect under section 4A or paragraph 36 of Schedule A1.

(2) If it appears to the nominee or supervisor that any past or present officer of the company has been guilty of any offence in connection with the moratorium or, as the case may be, voluntary arrangement for which he is criminally liable, the nominee or supervisor shall forthwith –

(a)   report the matter to the appropriate authority, and

(b)   provide the appropriate authority with such information and give the authority such access to and facilities for inspecting and taking copies of documents (being information or documents in the possession or under the control of the nominee or supervisor and relating to the matter in question) as the authority requires.

In this subsection, "the appropriate authority" means –

(i)   in the case of a company registered in England and Wales, the Secretary of State, and

(ii)   in the case of a company registered in Scotland, the Lord Advocate.

(3)   Where a report is made to the Secretary of State under subsection (2), he may, for the purpose of investigating the matter reported to him and such other matters relating to the affairs of the company as appear to him to require investigation, exercise any of the powers which are exercisable by inspectors appointed under section 431 or 432 of the Companies Act to investigate a company's affairs.

(4)   For the purpose of such an investigation any obligation imposed on a person by any provision of the Companies Act to produce documents or give information to, or otherwise to assist, inspectors so appointed is to be regarded as an obligation similarly to assist the Secretary of State in his investigation.

(5)   An answer given by a person to a question put to him in exercise of the powers conferred by subsection (3) may be used in evidence against him.

(6)   However, in criminal proceedings in which that person is charged with an offence to which this subsection applies –

(a)   no evidence relating to the answer may be adduced, and

(b)   no question relating to it may be asked,

by or on behalf of the prosecution, unless evidence relating to it is adduced, or a question relating to it is asked, in the proceedings by or on behalf of that person.

(7)   Subsection (6) applies to any offence other than –

(a)   an offence under section 2 or 5 of the Perjury Act 1911 (false statements made on oath otherwise than in judicial proceedings or made otherwise than on oath), or

(b)   an offence under section 44(1) or (2) of the Criminal Law (Consolidation) (Scotland) Act 1995 (false statements made on oath or otherwise than on oath).

(8)   Where a prosecuting authority institutes criminal proceedings following any report under subsection (2), the nominee or supervisor, and every officer and agent of the company past and present (other than the defendant or defender), shall give the authority all assistance in connection with the prosecution which he is reasonably able to give.

For this purpose –

"agent" includes any banker or solicitor of the company and any person employed by the company as auditor, whether that person is or is not an officer of the company,

"prosecuting authority" means the Director of Public Prosecutions, the Lord Advocate or the Secretary of State.

(9)   The court may, on the application of the prosecuting authority, direct any person referred to in subsection (8) to comply with that subsection if he has failed to do so.

7B Arrangements coming to an end prematurely.

For the purposes of this Part, a voluntary arrangement the approval of which has taken effect under section 4A or paragraph 36 of Schedule A1 comes to an end prematurely if, when it ceases to have effect, it has not been fully implemented in respect of all persons bound by the arrangement by virtue of section 5(2)(b)(i) or, as the case may be, paragraph 37(2)(b)(i) of Schedule A1.'

11 In section 387(2)(b) (date which determines existence and amount of preferential debt), for the words following 'date' there is substituted 'on which the voluntary arrangement takes effect'.

12 In Schedule 10 (punishment of offences), before the entry relating to section 12(2) there is inserted the following entry –

'6A(1).	False representation or fraud for purpose of obtaining members' or creditors' approval of proposed voluntary arrangement.	1. On indictment. 2. Summary.	7 years or a fine, or both. 6 months or the statutory maximum, or both.'

PART II   AMENDMENTS OF THE BUILDING SOCIETIES ACT 1986

13 (1) The Commission may appoint one or more competent persons to investigate and report on any matter reported to the Commission under section 7A(2) of the Insolvency Act 1986; and section 55 of the Building Societies Act 1986 (investigations) applies to such a person and the investigations as it applies to a person appointed under section 55(1) and an investigation under that section.

(2) Section 57(5) to (5B) of that Act (use in evidence of answers given to questions) applies to answers given under section 55(3) as extended by sub-paragraph (1) as it applies to answers given under section 57.

14 (1) Schedule 15A to the Building Societies Act 1986 (application of companies insolvency legislation to building societies) is amended as follows.

(2) In paragraph 1(2)(a), after 'Parts I' there is inserted '(except section 1A)'.

(3) At the end of paragraph 8 there is inserted –

'and subsection (1) of section 2 shall have effect with the omission of the words from "and the directors" to the end.

8A. In subsection (2) of section 4A of the Act (approval of arrangement) as applied to a building society, paragraph (b) and the word "or" immediately preceding that paragraph are omitted.'

(4) After paragraph 9 there is inserted –

'9A. In section 7A of the Act (prosecution of delinquent officers) as applied to a building society –

(a) in subsection (2), for paragraphs (i) and (ii) there is substituted "the Commission",

(b) subsections (3) to (7) are omitted,

(c) in subsection (8), for "Secretary of State" there is substituted "Commission".'

SCHEDULE 3   INDIVIDUAL VOLUNTARY ARRANGEMENTS

1 The Insolvency Act 1986 is amended as follows.

2 In section 252 (interim order of court) –

(a) in subsection (2)(a), after 'with,' there is inserted –

'(aa) no landlord or other person to whom rent is payable may exercise any right of forfeiture by peaceable re-entry in relation to premises let to the debtor in respect of a failure by the debtor to comply with any term or condition of his tenancy of such premises, except with the leave of the court',

(b)   in subsection (2)(b), after 'continued' there is inserted 'and no distress may be levied'.

3   In section 253 (application for interim order) –

(a)   in subsection (1), after 'proposal' there is inserted 'under this Part, that is, a proposal',

(b)   at the end of subsection (2) there is inserted 'and the nominee must be a person who is qualified to act as an insolvency practitioner, or authorised to act as nominee, in relation to the voluntary arrangement',

(c)   in subsection (4), for the words from 'his proposal' to 'arrangement)' there is substituted 'the proposal'.

4   In section 254 (effect of application), in subsection (1) –

(a)   after 'pending' there is inserted –

'(a)   no landlord or other person to whom rent is payable may exercise any right of forfeiture by peaceable re-entry in relation to premises let to the debtor in respect of a failure by the debtor to comply with any term or condition of his tenancy of such premises, except with the leave of the court, and

(b)',

(b)   after 'may' there is inserted –

'forbid the levying of any distress on the debtor's property or its subsequent sale, or both, and'.

5   In section 255 (cases in which interim order can be made), in subsection (1) –

(a)   in paragraph (a), for 'such a proposal as is mentioned in that section' there is substituted 'a proposal under this Part',

(b)   in paragraph (d), the words from 'to his creditors' to 'to the debtor, and' are omitted.

6   In section 256 (nominee's report on debtor's proposal) –

(a)   in subsection (1)(a), at the beginning there is inserted –

'whether, in his opinion, the voluntary arrangement which the debtor is proposing has a reasonable prospect of being approved and implemented,

(aa)'.

(b)   for subsection (3) there is substituted –

'(3)   The court may –

(a)   on an application made by the debtor in a case where the nominee has failed to submit the report required by this section or has died, or

(b)   on an application made by the debtor or the nominee in a case where it is impracticable or inappropriate for the nominee to continue to act as such,

direct that the nominee shall be replaced as such by another person qualified to act as an insolvency practitioner, or authorised to act as nominee, in relation to the voluntary arrangement.

(3A)   The court may, on an application made by the debtor in a case where the nominee has failed to submit the report required by this section, direct that the interim order shall continue, or (if it has ceased to have effect) be renewed, for such further period as the court may specify in the direction.'

7   After section 256 there is inserted –

'Procedure where no interim order made

256A Debtor's proposal and nominee's report

(1) This section applies where a debtor (being an individual) –

    (a) intends to make a proposal under this Part (but an interim order has not been made in relation to the proposal and no application for such an order is pending), and

    (b) if he is an undischarged bankrupt, has given notice of the proposal to the official receiver and, if there is one, the trustee of his estate,

unless a bankruptcy petition presented by the debtor is pending and the court has, under section 273, appointed an insolvency practitioner to inquire into the debtor's affairs and report.

(2) For the purpose of enabling the nominee to prepare a report to the court, the debtor shall submit to the nominee –

    (a) a document setting out the terms of the voluntary arrangement which the debtor is proposing, and

    (b) a statement of his affairs containing –

        (i) such particulars of his creditors and of his debts and other liabilities and of his assets as may be prescribed, and

        (ii) such other information as may be prescribed.

(3) If the nominee is of the opinion that the debtor is an undischarged bankrupt, or is able to petition for his own bankruptcy, the nominee shall, within 14 days (or such longer period as the court may allow) after receiving the document and statement mentioned in subsection (2), submit a report to the court stating –

    (a) whether, in his opinion, the voluntary arrangement which the debtor is proposing has a reasonable prospect of being approved and implemented,

    (b) whether, in his opinion, a meeting of the debtor's creditors should be summoned to consider the debtor's proposal, and

    (c) if in his opinion such a meeting should be summoned, the date on which, and time and place at which, he proposes the meeting should be held.

(4) The court may –

    (a) on an application made by the debtor in a case where the nominee has failed to submit the report required by this section or has died, or

    (b) on an application made by the debtor or the nominee in a case where it is impracticable or inappropriate for the nominee to continue to act as such,

direct that the nominee shall be replaced as such by another person qualified to act as an insolvency practitioner, or authorised to act as nominee, in relation to the voluntary arrangement.

(5) The court may, on an application made by the nominee, extend the period within which the nominee is to submit his report.

Creditors' meeting'

8 In section 257 (summoning of creditors' meeting), in subsection (1) –

    (a) after '256' there is inserted 'or 256A', and

    (b) for '256(3)(a)' there is substituted '256(3) or 256A(4)'.

9 In section 258 (decisions of creditors' meeting), in subsection (3), for 'in relation to the debtor' there is substituted 'or authorised to act as nominee, in relation to the voluntary arrangement' and for 'such as is mentioned in section 253' there is substituted 'under this Part'.

10 In section 260 (effect of approval), for subsection (2)(b) there is substituted –

'(b)   binds every person who in accordance with the rules –

(i)   was entitled to vote at the meeting (whether or not he was present or represented at it), or

(ii)   would have been so entitled if he had had notice of it,

as if he were a party to the arrangement.

(2A) If –

(a)   when the arrangement ceases to have effect any amount payable under the arrangement to a person bound by virtue of subsection (2)(b)(ii) has not been paid, and

(b)   the arrangement did not come to an end prematurely,

the debtor shall at that time become liable to pay to that person the amount payable under the arrangement.'

11   (1)   In section 262 (challenge of meeting's decision), in subsection (2) –

(a)   for paragraph (b) there is substituted –

'(b)   a person who –

(i)   was entitled, in accordance with the rules, to vote at the creditors' meeting, or

(ii)   would have been so entitled if he had had notice of it',

(b)   in paragraph (c), for '256(3)(a)' there is substituted '256(3), 256A(4)'.

(2)   In subsection (3) of that section –

(a)   after 'be made' there is inserted '(a)',

(b)   at the end there is inserted 'or

(b)   in the case of a person who was not given notice of the creditors' meeting, after the end of the period of 28 days beginning with the day on which he became aware that the meeting had taken place,

but (subject to that) an application made by a person within subsection (2)(b)(ii) on the ground that the arrangement prejudices his interests may be made after the arrangement has ceased to have effect, unless it has come to an end prematurely.'

12   After that section there is inserted –

'262A False representations etc.

(1)   If for the purpose of obtaining the approval of his creditors to a proposal for a voluntary arrangement, the debtor –

(a)   makes any false representation, or

(b)   fraudulently does, or omits to do, anything,

he commits an offence.

(2)   Subsection (1) applies even if the proposal is not approved.

(3)   A person guilty of an offence under this section is liable to imprisonment or a fine, or both.

262B Prosecution of delinquent debtors.

(1)   This section applies where a voluntary arrangement approved by a creditors' meeting summoned under section 257 has taken effect.

(2)   If it appears to the nominee or supervisor that the debtor has been guilty of any offence in connection with the arrangement for which he is criminally liable, he shall forthwith –

(a)   report the matter to the Secretary of State, and

(b)   provide the Secretary of State with such information and give the Secretary of State such access to and facilities for inspecting and taking copies of documents (being information or documents in his possession or under his control and relating to the matter in question) as the Secretary of State requires.

(3)   Where a prosecuting authority institutes criminal proceedings following any report under subsection (2), the nominee or, as the case may be, supervisor shall give the authority all assistance in connection with the prosecution which he is reasonably able to give.

For this purpose, "prosecuting authority" means the Director of Public Prosecutions or the Secretary of State.

(4)   The court may, on the application of the prosecuting authority, direct a nominee or supervisor to comply with subsection (3) if he has failed to do so.

262C Arrangements coming to an end prematurely.

For the purposes of this Part, a voluntary arrangement approved by a creditors' meeting summoned under section 257 comes to an end prematurely if, when it ceases to have effect, it has not been fully implemented in respect of all persons bound by the arrangement by virtue of section 260(2)(b)(i).'

13   In section 263 (implementation and supervision of approved voluntary arrangement) –

(a)   in subsection (2), for '256(3)(a)' there is substituted '256(3), 256A(4)', and
(b)   in subsection (5), for 'in relation to the debtor' there is substituted 'or authorised to act as supervisor, in relation to the voluntary arrangement'.

14   In section 347 (distress, etc.) –

(a)   in subsection (1), after '(subject to' there is inserted 'sections 252(2)(b) and 254(1) above and',
(b)   in subsection (8), at the beginning there is inserted 'Subject to sections 252(2)(b) and 254(1) above.'

15   In section 387 (date which determines existence and amount of preferential debt), in subsection (5), for the words following 'undischarged bankrupt' there is substituted –

'(a)   where an interim order has been made under section 252 with respect to his proposal, the date of that order, and
(b)   in any other case, the date on which the voluntary arrangement takes effect.'

16   In Schedule 10 (punishment of offences), after the entry relating to section 235(5) there is inserted the following entry –

'262A(1).	False representation or fraud for purpose of obtaining creditors' approval of proposed voluntary arrangement.	1. On indictment. 2. Summary.	7 years or a fine, or both. 6 months or the statutory maximum, or both.'

SCHEDULE 4   MINOR AND CONSEQUENTIAL AMENDMENTS ABOUT DISQUALIFICATION OF COMPANY DIRECTORS ETC.

PART I   AMENDMENTS OF THE COMPANY DIRECTORS DISQUALIFICATION ACT 1986

1   The Company Directors Disqualification Act 1986 is amended in accordance with this Part.

2   In section 1(3) (disqualification orders), after 'an order' there is inserted 'or to a disqualification undertaking' and after 'those orders' there is inserted 'or, as the case may be, in the order and the undertaking'.

3   In section 2(1) (disqualification on conviction of indictable offence), for the words following 'a company' there is substituted 'with the receivership of a company's property or with his being an administrative receiver of a company'.

4   In section 4 (disqualification for fraud, etc., in winding up), in subsection (1)(b), for 'or receiver or manager of its property' there is substituted 'receiver of the company's property or administrative receiver of the company' and for 'receiver or manager' (in the second place) there is substituted 'receiver or administrative receiver'.

5   (1) In section 6 (disqualification of unfit directors) –

       (a) for subsection (3) there is substituted –

          '(3) In this section and section 7(2), "the court" means –

             (a) where the company in question is being or has been wound up by the court, that court,

             (b) where the company in question is being or has been wound up voluntarily, any court which has or (as the case may be) had jurisdiction to wind it up,

             (c) where neither of the preceding paragraphs applies but an administration order has at any time been made, or an administrative receiver has at any time been appointed, in relation to the company in question, any court which has jurisdiction to wind it up.

         (3A) Sections 117 and 120 of the Insolvency Act 1986 (jurisdiction) shall apply for the purposes of subsection (3) as if the references in the definitions of "registered office" to the presentation of the petition for winding up were references –

             (a) in a case within paragraph (b) of that subsection, to the passing of the resolution for voluntary winding up,

             (b) in a case within paragraph (c) of that subsection, to the making of the administration order or (as the case may be) the appointment of the administrative receiver.

         (3B) Nothing in subsection (3) invalidates any proceedings by reason of their being taken in the wrong court; and proceedings –

             (a) for or in connection with a disqualification order under this section, or

             (b) in connection with a disqualification undertaking accepted under section 7,

            may be retained in the court in which the proceedings were commenced, although it may not be the court in which they ought to have been commenced.

         (3C) In this section and section 7, "director" includes a shadow director'.

6   In section 7 (applications to court under section 6; reporting provisions) –

       (a) in subsection (1)(b), after 'being' there is inserted 'or has been',

       (b) for the sidenote there is substituted 'Disqualification order or undertaking; and reporting provisions'.

7   In section 9 (matters for determining unfitness of directors) –

       (a) in subsection (1), 'or shadow director' is omitted,

       (b) at the end of subsection (2) there is inserted 'and in this section and that Schedule "director" includes a shadow director'.

8   In section 13 (criminal penalties) –

      (a)   after 'disqualification order or' there is inserted 'disqualification undertaking or in contravention',

      (b)   after '12(2)' there is inserted 'or 12A'.

9   In section 14(1) (offences by body corporate), after 'disqualification order' there is inserted 'or disqualification undertaking or in contravention of section 12A'.

10   (1) Section 15 (personal liability for company's debts where person acts while disqualified) is amended as follows.

     (2) In subsection (1) –

      (a)   in paragraph (a), after 'disqualification order or' there is inserted 'disqualification undertaking or in contravention' and after '11' there is inserted 'or 12A',

      (b)   in paragraph (b), after 'disqualification order' there is inserted 'or disqualification undertaking or a disqualification order under Part II of the Companies (Northern Ireland) Order 1989'.

     (3) In subsection (5), after 'disqualification order' there is inserted 'or disqualification undertaking or a disqualification order under Part II of the Companies (Northern Ireland) Order 1989'.

11   (1) In section 16 (application for disqualification order), in subsection (2), for '5' there is substituted '4'.

12   (1) For section 17 (application for leave under an order) there is substituted –

'17 Application for leave under an order or undertaking.

     (1) Where a person is subject to a disqualification order made by a court having jurisdiction to wind up companies, any application for leave for the purposes of section 1(1)(a) shall be made to that court.

     (2) Where –

      (a)   a person is subject to a disqualification order made under section 2 by a court other than a court having jurisdiction to wind up companies, or

      (b)   a person is subject to a disqualification order made under section 5,

     any application for leave for the purposes of section 1(1)(a) shall be made to any court which, when the order was made, had jurisdiction to wind up the company (or, if there is more than one such company, any of the companies) to which the offence (or any of the offences) in question related.

     (3) Where a person is subject to a disqualification undertaking accepted at any time under section 7 or 8, any application for leave for the purposes of section 1A(1)(a) shall be made to any court to which, if the Secretary of State had applied for a disqualification order under the section in question at that time, his application could have been made.

     (4) But where a person is subject to two or more disqualification orders or undertakings (or to one or more disqualification orders and to one or more disqualification undertakings), any application for leave for the purposes of section 1(1)(a) or 1A(1)(a) shall be made to any court to which any such application relating to the latest order to be made, or undertaking to be accepted, could be made.

     (5) On the hearing of an application for leave for the purposes of section 1(1)(a) or 1A(1)(a), the Secretary of State shall appear and call the attention of the court to any matters which seem to him to be relevant, and may himself give evidence or call witnesses.'

13   (1) Section 18 (register of disqualification orders) is amended as follows.

     (2) In subsection (1) –

      (a)   in paragraph (b), after 'order' there is inserted 'or a disqualification undertaking',

      (b)   after paragraph (c) there is inserted 'or

(d)   leave is granted by a court for a person subject to such an undertaking to do anything which otherwise the undertaking prohibits him from doing'.

(3)   After subsection (2) there is inserted –

'(2A) The Secretary of State shall include in the register such particulars as he considers appropriate of disqualification undertakings accepted by him under section 7 or 8 and of cases in which leave has been granted as mentioned in subsection (1)(d).'

(4) In subsection (3) –

(a)   after 'order' there is inserted 'or undertaking',
(b)   at the end there is inserted –

'and, in the case of a disqualification undertaking, any other particulars he has included in the register'.

(5)   After subsection (4) there is inserted –

'(4A) Regulations under this section may extend the preceding provisions of this section, to such extent and with such modifications as may be specified in the regulations, to disqualification orders made under Part II of the Companies (Northern Ireland) Order 1989.'

(6)   For the sidenote there is substituted 'Register of disqualification orders and undertakings'.

14   (1)   Section 21 (interaction with Insolvency Act 1986) is amended as follows.
      (2)   In subsection (2) –

(a)   after 'Sections' there is inserted '1A',
(b)   after '10' there is inserted '13, 14',
(c)   after 'this Act' there is inserted 'and sections 1 and 17 of this Act as they apply for the purposes of those provisions'.

(3)   In subsection (3) –

(a)   after 'sections' there is inserted '1A',
(b)   after '10' there is inserted '13, 14',
(c)   after 'this Act' there is inserted 'and sections 1 and 17 of this Act as they apply for the purposes of those provisions'.

15   (1)   Section 22 (interpretation) is amended as follows.
      (2)   At the end of subsection (3) there is inserted 'and references to acting as an insolvency practitioner are to be read in accordance with section 388 of that Act'.
      (3)   In subsection (4), the words following 'called' are omitted.

PART II   CONSEQUENTIAL AMENDMENTS OF OTHER ENACTMENTS

Insolvency Act 1986 (c. 45)

16   (1)   The Insolvency Act 1986 is amended as follows.
      (2)   In section 390(4)(b) (persons not qualified to act as insolvency practitioners) –

(a)   after 'made' there is inserted 'or a disqualification undertaking accepted',
(b)   after '1986' there is inserted 'or to a disqualification order made under Part II of the Companies (Northern Ireland) Order 1989'.

(3)   In section 426(10) (co-operation between courts) –

(a)   in paragraph (a) –

> > (i)   after 'provision' there is inserted 'extending to England and Wales and',
> > (ii) after 'sections' there is inserted '1A',
> > (iii) for '12, 15' there is substituted '12 to 15',
> > (iv) for 'and extending to England and Wales' there is substituted 'and sections 1 to 17 of that Act as they apply for the purposes of those provisions of that Act',
>
> (b)   in paragraph (b) –
>
> > (i)   after 'sections' there is inserted '1A',
> > (ii) for '12, 15' there is substituted '12 to 15',
> > (iii) after '1986' there is inserted 'and sections 1 to 17 of that Act as they apply for the purposes of those provisions of that Act'.

Law Reform (Miscellaneous Provisions) (Scotland) Act 1990 (c. 40.)

17   In section 8(1)(d) of the Law Reform (Miscellaneous Provisions) (Scotland) Act 1990 (persons disqualified from being concerned in the management and control of a recognised body) –

> (a)   after 'disqualification order' there is inserted 'or disqualification undertaking',
> (b)   after '1986' there is inserted 'or to a disqualification order under Part II of the Companies (Northern Ireland) Order 1989'.

Charities Act 1993 (c. 10)

18   In section 72 of the Charities Act 1993 (persons disqualified for being trustees of a charity) –

> (a)   in subsection (1)(f), after 'disqualification order' there is inserted 'or disqualification undertaking' and after the first mention of '1986' there is inserted 'to a disqualification order under Part II of the Companies (Northern Ireland) Order 1989',
> (b)   for subsection (3)(a) there is substituted –
>
> > '(a)   in the case of a person subject to a disqualification order or disqualification undertaking under the Company Directors Disqualification Act 1986, leave for the purposes of section 1(1)(a) or 1A(1)(a) of that Act has been granted for him to act as director of the charity,
> > (aa) in the case of a person subject to a disqualification order under Part II of the Companies (Northern Ireland) Order 1989, leave has been granted by the High Court in Northern Ireland for him to act as director of the charity',
>
> (c)   in subsection (4)(a) –
>
> > (i)   in sub-paragraph (i), after 'disqualification order' there is inserted 'or disqualification undertaking',
> > (ii) in sub-paragraph (ii), for 'or 12(2)' there is substituted '12(2) or 12A' and after 'order' there is inserted 'Northern Irish disqualification orders'.

Pensions Act 1995 (c. 26)

19   (1)   The Pensions Act 1995 is amended as follows.
(2)   In section 4(1)(e) (suspension orders), after '1986' there is inserted 'or under Part II of the Companies (Northern Ireland) Order 1989'.

(3) In section 29(1)(f) (persons disqualified for being trustees of trust schemes)

(a) after 'disqualification order' there is inserted 'or disqualification undertaking',

(b) after the first mention of '1986' there is inserted 'to a disqualification order under Part II of the Companies (Northern Ireland) Order 1989'.

Police Act 1996 (c. 16)

20 In paragraph 11(1)(c) of Schedule 2, and paragraph 7(1)(c) of Schedule 2A, to the Police Act 1996 (persons disqualified for being members of police authorities) –

(a) after 'disqualification order' there is inserted 'or disqualification undertaking',

(b) after the first mention of '1986' there is inserted 'to a disqualification order under Part II of the Companies (Northern Ireland) Order 1989'.

Housing Act 1996 (c. 52)

21 In paragraph 4(2)(b) of Schedule 1 to the Housing Act 1996 (powers to remove directors, trustees etc. of registered social landlords) –

(a) after 'disqualification order' there is inserted 'or disqualification undertaking',

(b) at the end there is inserted 'or to a disqualification order under Part II of the Companies (Northern Ireland) Order 1989'.

Police Act 1997 (c. 50)

22 (1) The Police Act 1997 is amended as follows.

(2) In section 91 (Commissioners for the purposes of Part III), at the end of subsection (7)(b) there is inserted 'or his disqualification undertaking is accepted under section 7 or 8 of the Company Directors Disqualification Act 1986'.

(3) In Schedule 2 (members of Service Authorities), in paragraph 3(1)(c) –

(a) after 'disqualification order' there is inserted 'or disqualification undertaking',

(b) after '1986 or' there is inserted 'to a disqualification order under'.

SCHEDULE 5   REPEALS

Chapter	Short title	Extent of repeal
1986 c. 45.	The Insolvency Act 1986.	In subsections (2) and (3) of section 5, 'approved'. In section 27(3)(a), 'section 4 in'. In section 218, subsection (2) and, in subsection (6)(b), 'to the prosecuting authority'. In section 255(1)(d), the words from 'to his creditors' to 'to the debtor, and'.
1986 c. 46.	The Company Directors Disqualification Act 1986.	In section 9(1), 'or shadow director'. In section 22(4), the words following 'called'.
1989 c. 40.	The Companies Act 1989.	Section 78.

ENTERPRISE ACT 2002, PART 10

PART 10   INSOLVENCY

Companies etc.

248 Replacement of Part II of Insolvency Act 1986

(1) The following shall be substituted for Part II of the Insolvency Act 1986 (c. 45) (administration orders) –

'PART II   ADMINISTRATION

8 Administration

Schedule B1 to this Act (which makes provision about the administration of companies) shall have effect.'

(2) The Schedule B1 set out in Schedule 16 to this Act shall be inserted after Schedule A1 to the Insolvency Act 1986.

(3) Schedule 17 (minor and consequential amendments relating to administration) shall have effect.

(4) The Secretary of State may by order amend an enactment in consequence of this section.

(5) An order under subsection (4) –

    (a) must be made by statutory instrument, and

    (b) shall be subject to annulment in pursuance of a resolution of either House of Parliament.

249 Special administration regimes

(1) Section 248 shall have no effect in relation to –

    (a) a company holding an appointment under Chapter I of Part II of the Water Industry Act 1991 (c. 56) (water and sewerage undertakers),

    (b) a protected railway company within the meaning of section 59 of the Railways Act 1993 (c. 43) (railway administration order) (including that section as it has effect by virtue of section 19 of the Channel Tunnel Rail Link Act 1996 (c. 61) (administration)),

    (c) a licence company within the meaning of section 26 of the Transport Act 2000 (c. 38) (air traffic services),

    (d) a public-private partnership company within the meaning of section 210 of the Greater London Authority Act 1999 (c. 29) (public-private partnership agreement), or

    (e) a building society within the meaning of section 119 of the Building Societies Act 1986 (c. 53) (interpretation).

(2) A reference in an Act listed in subsection (1) to a provision of Part II of the Insolvency Act 1986 (or to a provision which has effect in relation to a provision of that Part of that Act) shall, in so far as it relates to a company or society listed in subsection (1),

continue to have effect as if it referred to Part II as it had effect immediately before the coming into force of section 248.

(3) But the effect of subsection (2) in respect of a particular class of company or society may be modified by order of –

(a) the Treasury, in the case of building societies, or
(b) the Secretary of State, in any other case.

(4) An order under subsection (3) may make consequential amendment of an enactment.
(5) An order under subsection (3) –

(a) must be made by statutory instrument, and
(b) may not be made unless a draft has been laid before and approved by resolution of each House of Parliament.

(6) An amendment of the Insolvency Act 1986 (c. 45) made by this Act is without prejudice to any power conferred by Part VII of the Companies Act 1989 (c. 40) (financial markets) to modify the law of insolvency.

250 Prohibition of appointment of administrative receiver

(1) The following shall be inserted after Chapter III of Part III of the Insolvency Act 1986 (receivership: receivers' powers) –

'CHAPTER IV   PROHIBITION OF APPOINTMENT OF ADMINISTRATIVE RECEIVER

72A Floating charge holder not to appoint administrative receiver

(1) The holder of a qualifying floating charge in respect of a company's property may not appoint an administrative receiver of the company.
(2) In Scotland, the holder of a qualifying floating charge in respect of a company's property may not appoint or apply to the court for the appointment of a receiver who on appointment would be an administrative receiver of property of the company.
(3) In subsections (1) and (2) –

"holder of a qualifying floating charge in respect of a company's property" has the same meaning as in paragraph 14 of Schedule B1 to this Act, and
"administrative receiver" has the meaning given by section 251.

(4) This section applies –

(a) to a floating charge created on or after a date appointed by the Secretary of State by order made by statutory instrument, and
(b) in spite of any provision of an agreement or instrument which purports to empower a person to appoint an administrative receiver (by whatever name).

(5) An order under subsection (4)(a) may –

(a) make provision which applies generally or only for a specified purpose;
(b) make different provision for different purposes;
(c) make transitional provision.

(6) This section is subject to the exceptions specified in sections 72B to 72G.

72B First exception: capital market

(1) Section 72A does not prevent the appointment of an administrative receiver in pursuance of an agreement which is or forms part of a capital market arrangement if –

(a)   a party incurs or, when the agreement was entered into was expected to incur, a debt of at least £50 million under the arrangement, and

(b)   the arrangement involves the issue of a capital market investment.

(2)   In subsection (1) –

"capital market arrangement" means an arrangement of a kind described in paragraph 1 of Schedule 2A, and

"capital market investment" means an investment of a kind described in paragraph 2 or 3 of that Schedule.

72C Second exception: public-private partnership

(1)   Section 72A does not prevent the appointment of an administrative receiver of a project company of a project which –

(a)   is a public-private partnership project, and

(b)   includes step-in rights.

(2)   In this section "public-private partnership project" means a project –

(a)   the resources for which are provided partly by one or more public bodies and partly by one or more private persons, or

(b)   which is designed wholly or mainly for the purpose of assisting a public body to discharge a function.

(3)   In this section –

"step-in rights" has the meaning given by paragraph 6 of Schedule 2A, and

"project company" has the meaning given by paragraph 7 of that Schedule.

72D Third exception: utilities

(1)   Section 72A does not prevent the appointment of an administrative receiver of a project company of a project which –

(a)   is a utility project, and

(b)   includes step-in rights.

(2)   In this section –

(a)   "utility project" means a project designed wholly or mainly for the purpose of a regulated business,

(b)   "regulated business" means a business of a kind listed in paragraph 10 of Schedule 2A,

(c)   "step-in rights" has the meaning given by paragraph 6 of that Schedule, and

(d)   "project company" has the meaning given by paragraph 7 of that Schedule.

72E Fourth exception: project finance

(1)   Section 72A does not prevent the appointment of an administrative receiver of a project company of a project which –

(a)   is a financed project, and

(b)   includes step-in rights.

(2)   In this section –

(a)   a project is "financed" if under an agreement relating to the project a project company incurs, or when the agreement is entered into is expected to incur, a debt of at least £50 million for the purposes of carrying out the project,

(b)   "project company" has the meaning given by paragraph 7 of Schedule 2A, and

(c)   "step-in rights" has the meaning given by paragraph 6 of that Schedule.

72F Fifth exception: financial market

Section 72A does not prevent the appointment of an administrative receiver of a company by virtue of –

    (a)   a market charge within the meaning of section 173 of the Companies Act 1989 (c. 40),

    (b)   a system-charge within the meaning of the Financial Markets and Insolvency Regulations 1996 (S.I. 1996/1469),

    (c)   a collateral security charge within the meaning of the Financial Markets and Insolvency (Settlement Finality) Regulations 1999 (S.I. 1999/2979).

72G Sixth exception: registered social landlord

Section 72A does not prevent the appointment of an administrative receiver of a company which is registered as a social landlord under Part I of the Housing Act 1996 (c. 52) or under Part 3 of the Housing (Scotland) Act 2001 (asp 10).

72H Sections 72A to 72G: supplementary

(1)   Schedule 2A (which supplements sections 72B to 72G) shall have effect.

(2)   The Secretary of State may by order –

    (a)   insert into this Act provision creating an additional exception to section 72A(1) or (2);

    (b)   provide for a provision of this Act which creates an exception to section 72A(1) or (2) to cease to have effect;

    (c)   amend section 72A in consequence of provision made under paragraph (a) or (b);

    (d)   amend any of sections 72B to 72G;

    (e)   amend Schedule 2A.

(3)   An order under subsection (2) must be made by statutory instrument.

(4)   An order under subsection (2) may make –

    (a)   provision which applies generally or only for a specified purpose;

    (b)   different provision for different purposes;

    (c)   consequential or supplementary provision;

    (d)   transitional provision.

(5)   An order under subsection (2) –

    (a)   in the case of an order under subsection (2)(e), shall be subject to annulment in pursuance of a resolution of either House of Parliament,

    (b)   in the case of an order under subsection (2)(d) varying the sum specified in section 72B(1)(a) or 72E(2)(a) (whether or not the order also makes consequential or transitional provision), shall be subject to annulment in pursuance of a resolution of either House of Parliament, and

    (c)   in the case of any other order under subsection (2)(a) to (d), may not be made unless a draft has been laid before and approved by resolution of each House of Parliament.'

(2)   The Schedule 2A set out in Schedule 18 to this Act shall be inserted after Schedule 2 to the Insolvency Act 1986 (c. 45).

251 Abolition of Crown preference

(1)   The following paragraphs of Schedule 6 to the Insolvency Act 1986 (categories of preferential debts) shall cease to have effect –

   (a)   paragraphs 1 and 2 (debts due to Inland Revenue),

   (b)   paragraphs 3 to 5C (debts due to Customs and Excise), and

   (c)   paragraphs 6 and 7 (social security contributions).

(2) The following paragraphs of Schedule 3 to the Bankruptcy (Scotland) Act 1985 (c. 66) (list of preferred debts) shall cease to have effect –

(a) paragraph 1 (debts due to Inland Revenue),
(b) paragraph 2 (debts due to Customs and Excise), and
(c) paragraph 3 (social security contributions).

(3) In section 386 of the Insolvency Act 1986 (categories of preferential debts) for the parenthetical words after 'Schedule 6 to this Act' there shall be substituted '(contributions to occupational pension schemes; remuneration, &c. of employees; levies on coal and steel production)'.

252 Unsecured creditors

The following shall be inserted after section 176 of the Insolvency Act 1986 (winding up: preferential debt) –

'Property subject to floating charge

176A Share of assets for unsecured creditors

(1) This section applies where a floating charge relates to property of a company –

(a) which has gone into liquidation,
(b) which is in administration,
(c) of which there is a provisional liquidator, or
(d) of which there is a receiver.

(2) The liquidator, administrator or receiver –

(a) shall make a prescribed part of the company's net property available for the satisfaction of unsecured debts, and
(b) shall not distribute that part to the proprietor of a floating charge except in so far as it exceeds the amount required for the satisfaction of unsecured debts.

(3) Subsection (2) shall not apply to a company if –

(a) the company's net property is less than the prescribed minimum, and
(b) the liquidator, administrator or receiver thinks that the cost of making a distribution to unsecured creditors would be disproportionate to the benefits.

(4) Subsection (2) shall also not apply to a company if or in so far as it is disapplied by –

(a) a voluntary arrangement in respect of the company, or
(b) a compromise or arrangement agreed under section 425 of the Companies Act (compromise with creditors and members).

(5) Subsection (2) shall also not apply to a company if –

(a) the liquidator, administrator or receiver applies to the court for an order under this subsection on the ground that the cost of making a distribution to unsecured creditors would be disproportionate to the benefits, and
(b) the court orders that subsection (2) shall not apply.

(6) In subsections (2) and (3) a company's net property is the amount of its property which would, but for this section, be available for satisfaction of claims of holders of debentures secured by, or holders of, any floating charge created by the company.

(7) An order under subsection (2) prescribing part of a company's net property may, in particular, provide for its calculation –

(a) as a percentage of the company's net property, or
(b) as an aggregate of different percentages of different parts of the company's net property.

(8) An order under this section –

    (a)   must be made by statutory instrument, and

    (b)   shall be subject to annulment pursuant to a resolution of either House of Parliament.

(9) In this section –

    "floating charge" means a charge which is a floating charge on its creation and which is created after the first order under subsection (2)(a) comes into force, and

    "prescribed" means prescribed by order by the Secretary of State.

(10) An order under this section may include transitional or incidental provision.'

253 Liquidator's powers

The following shall be inserted in Part I of Schedule 4 to the Insolvency Act 1986 (c. 45) (liquidator's powers in winding up: powers exercisable only with sanction) after paragraph 3 –

    '3A. Power to bring legal proceedings under section 213, 214, 238, 239, 242, 243 or 423.'

254 Application of insolvency law to foreign company

(1)   The Secretary of State may by order provide for a provision of the Insolvency Act 1986 to apply (with or without modification) in relation to a company incorporated outside Great Britain.

(2)   An order under this section –

    (a)   may make provision generally or for a specified purpose only,

    (b)   may make different provision for different purposes, and

    (c)   may make transitional, consequential or incidental provision.

(3)   An order under this section –

    (a)   must be made by statutory instrument, and

    (b)   shall be subject to annulment in pursuance of a resolution of either House of Parliament.

255 Application of law about company arrangement or administration to non-company

(1)   The Treasury may with the concurrence of the Secretary of State by order provide for a company arrangement or administration provision to apply (with or without modification) in relation to –

    (a)   a society registered under the Industrial and Provident Societies Act 1965 (c. 12),

    (b)   a society registered under section 7(1)(b), (c), (d), (e) or (f) of the Friendly Societies Act 1974 (c. 46),

    (c)   a friendly society within the meaning of the Friendly Societies Act 1992 (c. 40), or

    (d)   an unregistered friendly society.

(2)   In subsection (1) 'company arrangement or administration provision' means –

    (a)   a provision of Part I of the Insolvency Act 1986 (company voluntary arrangements),

    (b)   a provision of Part II of that Act (administration), and

    (c)   section 425 of the Companies Act 1985 (c. 6) (compromise or arrangement with creditors).

(3)   An order under this section may not provide for a company arrangement or administration provision to apply in relation to a society which is registered as a social landlord under Part I of the Housing Act 1996 (c. 52) or under Part 3 of the Housing (Scotland) Act 2001 (asp 10).

(4) An order under this section –

    (a) may make provision generally or for a specified purpose only,

    (b) may make different provision for different purposes, and

    (c) may make transitional, consequential or incidental provision,

(5) Provision by virtue of subsection (4)(c) may, in particular –

    (a) apply an enactment (with or without modification);

    (b) amend an enactment.

(6) An order under this section –

    (a) must be made by statutory instrument, and

    (b) shall be subject to annulment in pursuance of a resolution of either House of Parliament.

Individuals

256 Duration of bankruptcy

(1) The following shall be substituted for section 279 of the Insolvency Act 1986 (c. 45) (duration of bankruptcy) –

'279 Duration

(1) A bankrupt is discharged from bankruptcy at the end of the period of one year beginning with the date on which the bankruptcy commences.

(2) If before the end of that period the official receiver files with the court a notice stating that investigation of the conduct and affairs of the bankrupt under section 289 is unnecessary or concluded, the bankrupt is discharged when the notice is filed.

(3) On the application of the official receiver or the trustee of a bankrupt's estate, the court may order that the period specified in subsection (1) shall cease to run until –

    (a) the end of a specified period, or

    (b) the fulfilment of a specified condition.

(4) The court may make an order under subsection (3) only if satisfied that the bankrupt has failed or is failing to comply with an obligation under this Part.

(5) In subsection (3)(b) "condition" includes a condition requiring that the court be satisfied of something.

(6) In the case of an individual who is adjudged bankrupt on a petition under section 264(1)(d) –

    (a) subsections (1) to (5) shall not apply, and

    (b) the bankrupt is discharged from bankruptcy by an order of the court under section 280.

(7) This section is without prejudice to any power of the court to annul a bankruptcy order.'

(2) Schedule 19 (which makes transitional provision in relation to this section) –

    (a) shall have effect, and

    (b) is without prejudice to the generality of section 276.

257 Post-discharge restrictions

(1) The following shall be inserted after section 281 of the Insolvency Act 1986 (c. 45) (bankruptcy: effect of discharge) –

'281A Post-discharge restrictions

Schedule 4A to this Act (bankruptcy restrictions order and bankruptcy restrictions undertaking) shall have effect.'

(2) The Schedule 4A set out in Schedule 20 to this Act shall be inserted after Schedule 4 to the Insolvency Act 1986.

(3) The amendments set out in Schedule 21 (which specify the effect of a bankruptcy restrictions order or undertaking) shall have effect.

258 Investigation by official receiver

The following shall be substituted for section 289 of the Insolvency Act 1986 (official receiver's duty to investigate) –

'289 Investigatory duties of official receiver

(1) The official receiver shall –

    (a) investigate the conduct and affairs of each bankrupt (including his conduct and affairs before the making of the bankruptcy order), and

    (b) make such report (if any) to the court as the official receiver thinks fit.

(2) Subsection (1) shall not apply to a case in which the official receiver thinks an investigation under that subsection unnecessary.

(3) Where a bankrupt makes an application for discharge under section 280 –

    (a) the official receiver shall make a report to the court about such matters as may be prescribed, and

    (b) the court shall consider the report before determining the application.

(4) A report by the official receiver under this section shall in any proceedings be prima facie evidence of the facts stated in it.'

259 Income payments order

(1) Section 310 of the Insolvency Act 1986 (income payments order) shall be amended as follows.

(2) In subsection (1) omit ', on the application of the trustee,'.

(3) After subsection (1) insert –

'(1A) An income payments order may be made only on an application instituted –

    (a) by the trustee, and

    (b) before the discharge of the bankrupt.'

(4) For subsection (6) substitute –

'(6) An income payments order must specify the period during which it is to have effect; and that period –

    (a) may end after the discharge of the bankrupt, but

    (b) may not end after the period of three years beginning with the date on which the order is made.

(6A) An income payments order may (subject to subsection (6)(b)) be varied on the application of the trustee or the bankrupt (whether before or after discharge).'

260 Income payments agreement

The following shall be inserted after section 310 of the Insolvency Act 1986 (c. 45) (income payments order) –

'310A Income payments agreement

(1) In this section "income payments agreement" means a written agreement between a bankrupt and his trustee or between a bankrupt and the official receiver which provides –

    (a) that the bankrupt is to pay to the trustee or the official receiver an amount equal to a specified part or proportion of the bankrupt's income for a specified period, or

(b)   that a third person is to pay to the trustee or the official receiver a specified proportion of money due to the bankrupt by way of income for a specified period.

(2) A provision of an income payments agreement of a kind specified in subsection (1)(a) or (b) may be enforced as if it were a provision of an income payments order.

(3) While an income payments agreement is in force the court may, on the application of the bankrupt, his trustee or the official receiver, discharge or vary an attachment of earnings order that is for the time being in force to secure payments by the bankrupt.

(4) The following provisions of section 310 shall apply to an income payments agreement as they apply to an income payments order –

(a)   subsection (5) (receipts to form part of estate), and
(b)   subsections (7) to (9) (meaning of income).

(5) An income payments agreement must specify the period during which it is to have effect; and that period –

(a)   may end after the discharge of the bankrupt, but
(b)   may not end after the period of three years beginning with the date on which the agreement is made.

(6) An income payments agreement may (subject to subsection (5)(b)) be varied –

(a)   by written agreement between the parties, or
(b)   by the court on an application made by the bankrupt, the trustee or the official receiver.

(7) The court –

(a)   may not vary an income payments agreement so as to include provision of a kind which could not be included in an income payments order, and
(b)   shall grant an application to vary an income payments agreement if and to the extent that the court thinks variation necessary to avoid the effect mentioned in section 310(2).'

261 Bankrupt's home

(1) The following shall be inserted after section 283 of the Insolvency Act 1986 (definition of bankrupt's estate) –

'283A Bankrupt's home ceasing to form part of estate

(1) This section applies where property comprised in the bankrupt's estate consists of an interest in a dwelling-house which at the date of the bankruptcy was the sole or principal residence of –

(a)   the bankrupt,
(b)   the bankrupt's spouse, or
(c)   a former spouse of the bankrupt.

(2) At the end of the period of three years beginning with the date of the bankruptcy the interest mentioned in subsection (1) shall –

(a)   cease to be comprised in the bankrupt's estate, and
(b)   vest in the bankrupt (without conveyance, assignment or transfer).

(3) Subsection (2) shall not apply if during the period mentioned in that subsection –

(a)   the trustee realises the interest mentioned in subsection (1),
(b)   the trustee applies for an order for sale in respect of the dwelling-house,
(c)   the trustee applies for an order for possession of the dwelling-house,
(d)   the trustee applies for an order under section 313 in Chapter IV in respect of that interest, or

(e)   the trustee and the bankrupt agree that the bankrupt shall incur a specified liability to his estate (with or without the addition of interest from the date of the agreement) in consideration of which the interest mentioned in subsection (1) shall cease to form part of the estate.

(4)   Where an application of a kind described in subsection (3)(b) to (d) is made during the period mentioned in subsection (2) and is dismissed, unless the court orders otherwise the interest to which the application relates shall on the dismissal of the application –

(a)   cease to be comprised in the bankrupt's estate, and
(b)   vest in the bankrupt (without conveyance, assignment or transfer).

(5)   If the bankrupt does not inform the trustee or the official receiver of his interest in a property before the end of the period of three months beginning with the date of the bankruptcy, the period of three years mentioned in subsection (2) –

(a)   shall not begin with the date of the bankruptcy, but
(b)   shall begin with the date on which the trustee or official receiver becomes aware of the bankrupt's interest.

(6)   The court may substitute for the period of three years mentioned in subsection (2) a longer period –

(a)   in prescribed circumstances, and
(b)   in such other circumstances as the court thinks appropriate.

(7)   The rules may make provision for this section to have effect with the substitution of a shorter period for the period of three years mentioned in subsection (2) in specified circumstances (which may be described by reference to action to be taken by a trustee in bankruptcy).

(8)   The rules may also, in particular, make provision –

(a)   requiring or enabling the trustee of a bankrupt's estate to give notice that this section applies or does not apply;
(b)   about the effect of a notice under paragraph (a);
(c)   requiring the trustee of a bankrupt's estate to make an application to the Chief Land Registrar.

(9)   Rules under subsection (8)(b) may, in particular –

(a)   disapply this section;
(b)   enable a court to disapply this section;
(c)   make provision in consequence of a disapplication of this section;
(d)   enable a court to make provision in consequence of a disapplication of this section;
(e)   make provision (which may include provision conferring jurisdiction on a court or tribunal) about compensation.'

(2)   Section 313 of the Insolvency Act 1986 (c. 45) (charge on bankrupt's home) shall be amended as follows –

(a)   in subsection (2) for ', up to the value from time to time of the property secured,' substitute ', up to the charged value from time to time,',
(b)   after subsection (2) insert –

'(2A) In subsection (2) the charged value means –

(a)   the amount specified in the charging order as the value of the bankrupt's interest in the property at the date of the order, plus
(b)   interest on that amount from the date of the charging order at the prescribed rate.

(2B) In determining the value of an interest for the purposes of this section the court shall disregard any matter which it is required to disregard by the rules.', and

(c) at the end insert –

'(5) But an order under section 3(5) of that Act may not vary a charged value.'

(3) The following shall be inserted after section 313 of that Act –

'313A Low value home: application for sale, possession or charge

(1) This section applies where –

(a) property comprised in the bankrupt's estate consists of an interest in a dwelling-house which at the date of the bankruptcy was the sole or principal residence of –

    (i) the bankrupt,
    (ii) the bankrupt's spouse, or
    (iii) a former spouse of the bankrupt, and

(b) the trustee applies for an order for the sale of the property, for an order for possession of the property or for an order under section 313 in respect of the property.

(2) The court shall dismiss the application if the value of the interest is below the amount prescribed for the purposes of this subsection.

(3) In determining the value of an interest for the purposes of this section the court shall disregard any matter which it is required to disregard by the order which prescribes the amount for the purposes of subsection (2).'

(4) The following shall be inserted after section 307(2)(a) of the Insolvency Act 1986 (c. 45) (after-acquired property: exclusions) –

'(aa) any property vesting in the bankrupt by virtue of section 283A in Chapter II,'.

(5) In section 384(2) of that Act (prescribed amounts) after 'section 273;' insert –

'section 313A;'.

(6) In section 418(1) of that Act (monetary limits in bankruptcy) after the entry for section 273 insert –

'section 313A (value of property below which application for sale, possession or charge to be dismissed);'.

(7) In subsection (8) –

(a) 'pre-commencement bankrupt' means an individual who is adjudged bankrupt on a petition presented before subsection (1) above comes into force, and

(b) 'the transitional period' is the period of three years beginning with the date on which subsection (1) above comes into force.

(8) If a pre-commencement bankrupt's estate includes an interest in a dwelling-house which at the date of the bankruptcy was the sole or principal residence of him, his spouse or a former spouse of his, at the end of the transitional period that interest shall –

(a) cease to be comprised in the estate, and

(b) vest in the bankrupt (without conveyance, assignment or transfer).

(9) But subsection (8) shall not apply if before or during the transitional period –

(a) any of the events mentioned in section 283A(3) of the Insolvency Act 1986 (c. 45) (inserted by subsection (1) above) occurs in relation to the interest or the dwelling-house, or

(b) the trustee obtains any order of a court, or makes any agreement with the bankrupt, in respect of the interest or the dwelling-house.

(10) Subsections 283A(4) to (9) of that Act shall have effect, with any necessary modifications, in relation to the provision made by subsections (7) to (9) above; in
particular –

    (a)   a reference to the period mentioned in section 283A(2) shall be construed
as a reference to the transitional period,

    (b)   in the application of section 283A(5) a reference to the date of the bank-
ruptcy shall be construed as a reference to the date on which subsection (1)
above comes into force, and

    (c)   a reference to the rules is a reference to rules made under section 412 of the
Insolvency Act 1986 (for which purpose this section shall be treated as
forming part of Parts VIII to XI of that Act).

262 Powers of trustee in bankruptcy

The following shall be inserted in Part I of Schedule 5 to the Insolvency Act 1986 (powers
of trustee in bankruptcy: powers exercisable only with sanction) after paragraph 2 –

    '2A. Power to bring legal proceedings under section 339, 340 or 423.'

263 Repeal of certain bankruptcy offences

The following sections of the Insolvency Act 1986 shall cease to have effect –

    (a)   section 361 (offence of failure to keep proper accounting records), and
    (b)   section 362 (offence of gambling and speculation).

264 Individual voluntary arrangement

(1)   Schedule 22 (which makes provision about individual voluntary arrangements) shall
have effect.

(2)   The Secretary of State may by order amend the Insolvency Act 1986 so as to extend
the provisions of sections 263B to 263G (which are inserted by Schedule 22 and provide a fast-track procedure for making an individual voluntary arrangement) to some
or all cases other than those specified in section 263A as inserted by Schedule 22.

(3)   An order under subsection (2) –

    (a)   must be made by statutory instrument, and
    (b)   may not be made unless a draft has been laid before and approved by each House
of Parliament.

(4)   An order under subsection (2) may make –

    (a)   consequential provision (which may include provision amending the Insolvency
Act 1986 or another enactment);
    (b)   transitional provision.

265 Disqualification from office: justice of the peace

Section 65 of the Justices of the Peace Act 1997 (c. 25) (disqualification of bankrupt from
appointment as justice of the peace) shall cease to have effect.

266 Disqualification from office: Parliament

(1)   The following shall be inserted before section 427 of the Insolvency Act 1986 (c. 45)
(the title to which becomes 'Disqualification from Parliament (Scotland and Northern
Ireland)') –

    '426A Disqualification from Parliament (England and Wales)

    (1)   A person in respect of whom a bankruptcy restrictions order has effect shall be
disqualified –

        (a)   from membership of the House of Commons,
        (b)   from sitting or voting in the House of Lords, and

      (c) from sitting or voting in a committee of the House of Lords or a joint committee of both Houses.

(2) If a member of the House of Commons becomes disqualified under this section, his seat shall be vacated.

(3) If a person who is disqualified under this section is returned as a member of the House of Commons, his return shall be void.

(4) No writ of summons shall be issued to a member of the House of Lords who is disqualified under this section.

(5) If a court makes a bankruptcy restrictions order or interim order in respect of a member of the House of Commons or the House of Lords the court shall notify the Speaker of that House.

(6) If the Secretary of State accepts a bankruptcy restrictions undertaking made by a member of the House of Commons or the House of Lords, the Secretary of State shall notify the Speaker of that House.

426B Devolution

(1) If a court makes a bankruptcy restrictions order or interim order in respect of a member of the Scottish Parliament, the Northern Ireland Assembly or the National Assembly for Wales, the court shall notify the presiding officer of that body.

(2) If the Secretary of State accepts a bankruptcy restrictions undertaking made by a member of the Scottish Parliament, the Northern Ireland Assembly or the National Assembly for Wales, the Secretary of State shall notify the presiding officer of that body.

426C Irrelevance of privilege

(1) An enactment about insolvency applies in relation to a member of the House of Commons or the House of Lords irrespective of any Parliamentary privilege.

(2) In this section "enactment" includes a provision made by or under –

      (a) an Act of the Scottish Parliament, or

      (b) Northern Ireland legislation.'

(2) In section 427 of the Insolvency Act 1986 the following shall cease to have effect –

      (a) in subsection (1), the words 'England and Wales or', and

      (b) subsection (7).

(3) The Secretary of State may by order –

      (a) provide for section 426A or 426B of that Act (as inserted by subsection (1) above) to have effect in relation to orders made or undertakings accepted in Scotland or Northern Ireland under a system which appears to the Secretary of State to be equivalent to the system operating under Schedule 4A to that Act (as inserted by section 257 of this Act);

      (b) make consequential amendment of section 426A or 426B of that Act (as inserted by subsection (1) above);

      (c) make other consequential amendment of an enactment.

(4) An order under this section may make transitional, consequential or incidental provision.

(5) An order under this section –

      (a) must be made by statutory instrument, and

      (b) may not be made unless a draft has been laid before and approved by resolution of each House of Parliament.

267 Disqualification from office: local government

(1) The following shall be substituted for section 80(1)(b) of the Local Government Act 1972 (c. 70) (disqualification for membership of local authority: bankrupt) –

'(b) is the subject of a bankruptcy restrictions order or interim order;'.

(2) Section 81(1) and (2) of that Act (which amplify the provision substituted by sub-section (1) above) shall cease to have effect.

268 Disqualification from office: general

(1) The Secretary of State may make an order under this section in relation to a disquali-fication provision.

(2) A 'disqualification provision' is a provision which disqualifies (whether permanently or temporarily and whether absolutely or conditionally) a bankrupt or a class of bankrupts from –

(a) being elected or appointed to an office or position,

(b) holding an office or position, or

(c) becoming or remaining a member of a body or group.

(3) In subsection (2) the reference to a provision which disqualifies a person condition-ally includes a reference to a provision which enables him to be dismissed.

(4) An order under subsection (1) may repeal or revoke the disqualification provision.

(5) An order under subsection (1) may amend, or modify the effect of, the disqualification provision –

(a) so as to reduce the class of bankrupts to whom the disqualification provision applies;

(b) so as to extend the disqualification provision to some or all individuals who are subject to a bankruptcy restrictions regime;

(c) so that the disqualification provision applies only to some or all individuals who are subject to a bankruptcy restrictions regime;

(d) so as to make the application of the disqualification provision wholly or partly subject to the discretion of a specified person, body or group.

(6) An order by virtue of subsection (5)(d) may provide for a discretion to be subject to –

(a) the approval of a specified person or body;

(b) appeal to a specified person or body.

(7) An order by virtue of subsection (5)(d) made with the concurrence of the Lord Chancellor may provide for a discretion to be subject to appeal to a specified court or tribunal.

(8) The Secretary of State may specify himself for the purposes of subsection (5)(d) or (6)(a) or (b).

(9) In this section 'bankrupt' means an individual –

(a) who has been adjudged bankrupt by a court in England and Wales or in Northern Ireland,

(b) whose estate has been sequestrated by a court in Scotland, or

(c) who has made an agreement with creditors of his for a composition of debts, for a scheme of arrangement of affairs, for the grant of a trust deed or for some other kind of settlement or arrangement.

(10) In this section 'bankruptcy restrictions regime' means an order or undertaking –

(a) under Schedule 4A to the Insolvency Act 1986 (c. 45) (bankruptcy restrictions orders), or

(b) under any system operating in Scotland or Northern Ireland which appears to the Secretary of State to be equivalent to the system operating under that Schedule.

(11) In this section –

'body' includes Parliament and any other legislative body, and
'provision' means –

    (a)   a provision made by an Act of Parliament passed before or in the same Session as this Act, and

    (b)   a provision made, before or in the same Session as this Act, under an Act of Parliament.

(12) An order under this section –

    (a)   may make provision generally or for a specified purpose only,

    (b)   may make different provision for different purposes, and

    (c)   may make transitional, consequential or incidental provision.

(13) An order under this section –

    (a)   must be made by statutory instrument, and

    (b)   may not be made unless a draft has been laid before and approved by resolution of each House of Parliament.

(14) A reference in this section to the Secretary of State shall be treated as a reference to the National Assembly for Wales in so far as it relates to a disqualification provision which –

    (a)   is made by the National Assembly for Wales, or

    (b)   relates to a function of the National Assembly.

(15) Provision made by virtue of subsection (7) is subject to any order of the Lord Chancellor under section 56(1) of the Access to Justice Act 1999 (c. 22) (appeals: jurisdiction).

269 Minor and consequential amendments

Schedule 23 (minor and consequential amendments relating to individual insolvency) shall have effect.

Money

270 Fees

(1) The following shall be inserted after section 415 of the Insolvency Act 1986 (c. 45) (fees orders: individual insolvency) –

'415A Fees orders (general)

    (1)   The Secretary of State –

        (a)   may by order require a body to pay a fee in connection with the grant or maintenance of recognition of the body under section 391, and

        (b)   may refuse recognition, or revoke an order of recognition under section 391(1) by a further order, where a fee is not paid.

    (2)   The Secretary of State –

        (a)   may by order require a person to pay a fee in connection with the grant or maintenance of authorisation of the person under section 393, and

        (b)   may disregard an application or withdraw an authorisation where a fee is not paid.

    (3)   The Secretary of State may by order require the payment of fees in respect of –

        (a)   the operation of the Insolvency Services Account;

        (b)   payments into and out of that Account.

(4) The following provisions of section 414 apply to fees under this section as they apply to fees under that section –

    (a) subsection (3) (manner of payment),
    (b) subsection (5) (additional provision),
    (c) subsection (6) (statutory instrument),
    (d) subsection (7) (payment into Consolidated Fund), and
    (e) subsection (9) (saving for rules of court).'

(2) An order made by virtue of subsection (1) may relate to the maintenance of recognition or authorisation granted before this section comes into force.

(3) At the end of section 392 of the Insolvency Act 1986 (c. 45) (authorisation of insolvency practitioner) there shall be added –

    '(9) Subsection (3)(c) shall not have effect in respect of an application made to the Secretary of State (but this subsection is without prejudice to section 415A).'

(4) In section 440(2)(c) of that Act (provisions not extending to Scotland) after '415,' there shall be inserted '415A(3),'.

271 Insolvency Services Account: interest

(1) The following shall be inserted after paragraph 16 of Schedule 8 to the Insolvency Act 1986 (company insolvency rules: money) –

'**16A.** Provision enabling the Secretary of State to set the rate of interest paid on sums which have been paid into the Insolvency Services Account.'

(2) The following shall be inserted after paragraph 21 of Schedule 9 to the Insolvency Act 1986 (individual insolvency rules: money) –

'**21A.** Provision enabling the Secretary of State to set the rate of interest paid on sums which have been paid into the Insolvency Services Account.'

272 Insolvency Services Accounts

(1) Section 405 of the Insolvency Act 1986 (operation of Investment Account) shall cease to have effect.

(2) The following shall be substituted for section 408 of that Act (recourse to Consolidated Fund) –

'408 Adjustment of balances

(1) The Treasury may direct the payment out of the Consolidated Fund of sums into –

    (a)   the Insolvency Services Account;
    (b)   the Investment Account.

(2) The Treasury shall certify to the House of Commons the reason for any payment under subsection (1).

(3) The Secretary of State may pay sums out of the Insolvency Services Account into the Consolidated Fund.

(4) The National Debt Commissioners may pay sums out of the Investment Account into the Consolidated Fund.'

Appendix 3

ENTERPRISE ACT 2002, SCHEDULES 16–23

SCHEDULE 16   SCHEDULE B1 TO INSOLVENCY
                   ACT 1986   Section 248

SCHEDULE B1   ADMINISTRATION
                  ARRANGEMENT OF SCHEDULE

Nature of administration	Paragraphs 1 to 9
Appointment of administrator by court	Paragraphs 10 to 13
Appointment of administrator by holder of floating charge	Paragraphs 14 to 21
Appointment of administrator by company or directors	Paragraphs 22 to 34
Administration application: special cases	Paragraphs 35 to 39
Effect of administration	Paragraphs 40 to 45
Process of administration	Paragraphs 46 to 58
Functions of administrator	Paragraphs 59 to 75
Ending administration	Paragraphs 76 to 86
Replacing administrator	Paragraphs 87 to 99
General	Paragraphs 100 to 116

NATURE OF ADMINISTRATION

Administration

1   (1)   For the purposes of this Act 'administrator' of a company means a person appointed under this Schedule to manage the company's affairs, business and property.

      (2)   For the purposes of this Act –

          (a)   a company is 'in administration' while the appointment of an administrator of the company has effect,

          (b)   a company 'enters administration' when the appointment of an administrator takes effect,

          (c)   a company ceases to be in administration when the appointment of an administrator of the company ceases to have effect in accordance with this Schedule, and

          (d)   a company does not cease to be in administration merely because an administrator vacates office (by reason of resignation, death or otherwise) or is removed from office.

2   A person may be appointed as administrator of a company –

          (a)   by administration order of the court under paragraph 10,

          (b)   by the holder of a floating charge under paragraph 14, or

          (c)   by the company or its directors under paragraph 22.

Purpose of administration

3   (1)   The administrator of a company must perform his functions with the objective of –

   (a)   rescuing the company as a going concern, or

   (b)   achieving a better result for the company's creditors as a whole than would be likely if the company were wound up (without first being in administration), or

   (c)   realising property in order to make a distribution to one or more secured or preferential creditors.

   (2)   Subject to sub-paragraph (4), the administrator of a company must perform his functions in the interests of the company's creditors as a whole.

   (3)   The administrator must perform his functions with the objective specified in sub-paragraph (1)(a) unless he thinks either –

   (a)   that it is not reasonably practicable to achieve that objective, or

   (b)   that the objective specified in sub-paragraph (1)(b) would achieve a better result for the company's creditors as a whole.

   (4)   The administrator may perform his functions with the objective specified in sub-paragraph (1)(c) only if –

   (a)   he thinks that it is not reasonably practicable to achieve either of the objectives specified in sub-paragraph (1)(a) and (b), and

   (b)   he does not unnecessarily harm the interests of the creditors of the company as a whole.

4   The administrator of a company must perform his functions as quickly and efficiently as is reasonably practicable.

Status of administrator

5   An administrator is an officer of the court (whether or not he is appointed by the court).

General restrictions

6   A person may be appointed as administrator of a company only if he is qualified to act as an insolvency practitioner in relation to the company.

7   A person may not be appointed as administrator of a company which is in administration (subject to the provisions of paragraphs 90 to 97 and 100 to 103 about replacement and additional administrators).

8   (1)   A person may not be appointed as administrator of a company which is in liquidation by virtue of –

   (a)   a resolution for voluntary winding up, or

   (b)   a winding-up order.

   (2)   Sub-paragraph (1)(a) is subject to paragraph 38.

   (3)   Sub-paragraph (1)(b) is subject to paragraphs 37 and 38.

9   (1)   A person may not be appointed as administrator of a company which –

   (a)   has a liability in respect of a deposit which it accepted in accordance with the Banking Act 1979 (c. 37) or 1987 (c. 22), but

   (b)   is not an authorised deposit taker.

   (2)   A person may not be appointed as administrator of a company which effects or carries out contracts of insurance.

(3) But sub-paragraph (2) does not apply to a company which –

(a)   is exempt from the general prohibition in relation to effecting or carrying out contracts of insurance, or

(b)   is an authorised deposit taker effecting or carrying out contracts of insurance in the course of a banking business.

(4) In this paragraph –

'authorised deposit taker' means a person with permission under Part IV of the Financial Services and Markets Act 2000 (c. 8) to accept deposits, and

'the general prohibition' has the meaning given by section 19 of that Act.

(5) This paragraph shall be construed in accordance with –

(a)   section 22 of the Financial Services and Markets Act 2000 (classes of regulated activity and categories of investment),

(b)   any relevant order under that section, and

(c)   Schedule 2 to that Act (regulated activities).

APPOINTMENT OF ADMINISTRATOR BY COURT

Administration order

10   An administration order is an order appointing a person as the administrator of a company.

Conditions for making order

11   The court may make an administration order in relation to a company only if satisfied –

(a)   that the company is or is likely to become unable to pay its debts, and

(b)   that the administration order is reasonably likely to achieve the purpose of administration.

Administration application

12   (1) An application to the court for an administration order in respect of a company (an 'administration application') may be made only by –

(a)   the company,

(b)   the directors of the company,

(c)   one or more creditors of the company,

(d)   the justices' chief executive for a magistrates' court in the exercise of the power conferred by section 87A of the Magistrates' Courts Act 1980 (c. 43) (fine imposed on company), or

(e)   a combination of persons listed in paragraphs (a) to (d).

(2) As soon as is reasonably practicable after the making of an administration application the applicant shall notify –

(a)   any person who has appointed an administrative receiver of the company,

(b)   any person who is or may be entitled to appoint an administrative receiver of the company,

(c)   any person who is or may be entitled to appoint an administrator of the company under paragraph 14, and

(d)   such other persons as may be prescribed.

(3) An administration application may not be withdrawn without the permission of the court.

(4) In sub-paragraph (1) 'creditor' includes a contingent creditor and a prospective creditor.

Powers of court

13 (1) On hearing an administration application the court may –

(a) make the administration order sought;
(b) dismiss the application;
(c) adjourn the hearing conditionally or unconditionally;
(d) make an interim order;
(e) treat the application as a winding-up petition and make any order which the court could make under section 125;
(f) make any other order which the court thinks appropriate.

(2) An appointment of an administrator by administration order takes effect –

(a) at a time appointed by the order, or
(b) where no time is appointed by the order, when the order is made.

(3) An interim order under sub-paragraph (1)(d) may, in particular –

(a) restrict the exercise of a power of the directors or the company;
(b) make provision conferring a discretion on the court or on a person qualified to act as an insolvency practitioner in relation to the company.

(4) This paragraph is subject to paragraph 39.

APPOINTMENT OF ADMINISTRATOR BY HOLDER OF FLOATING CHARGE

Power to appoint

14 (1) The holder of a qualifying floating charge in respect of a company's property may appoint an administrator of the company.

(2) For the purposes of sub-paragraph (1) a floating charge qualifies if created by an instrument which –

(a) states that this paragraph applies to the floating charge,
(b) purports to empower the holder of the floating charge to appoint an administrator of the company,
(c) purports to empower the holder of the floating charge to make an appointment which would be the appointment of an administrative receiver within the meaning given by section 29(2), or
(d) purports to empower the holder of a floating charge in Scotland to appoint a receiver who on appointment would be an administrative receiver.

(3) For the purposes of sub-paragraph (1) a person is the holder of a qualifying floating charge in respect of a company's property if he holds one or more debentures of the company secured –

(a) by a qualifying floating charge which relates to the whole or substantially the whole of the company's property,
(b) by a number of qualifying floating charges which together relate to the whole or substantially the whole of the company's property, or
(c) by charges and other forms of security which together relate to the whole or substantially the whole of the company's property and at least one of which is a qualifying floating charge.

Restrictions on power to appoint

15 (1) A person may not appoint an administrator under paragraph 14 unless –

    (a) he has given at least two business days' written notice to the holder of any prior floating charge which satisfies paragraph 14(2), or

    (b) the holder of any prior floating charge which satisfies paragraph 14(2) has consented in writing to the making of the appointment.

  (2) One floating charge is prior to another for the purposes of this paragraph if –

    (a) it was created first, or

    (b) it is to be treated as having priority in accordance with an agreement to which the holder of each floating charge was party.

  (3) Sub-paragraph (2) shall have effect in relation to Scotland as if the following were substituted for paragraph (a) –

    '(a) it has priority of ranking in accordance with section 464(4)(b) of the Companies Act 1985 (c. 6),'.

16 An administrator may not be appointed under paragraph 14 while a floating charge on which the appointment relies is not enforceable.

17 An administrator of a company may not be appointed under paragraph 14 if –

    (a) a provisional liquidator of the company has been appointed under section 135, or

    (b) an administrative receiver of the company is in office.

Notice of appointment

18 (1) A person who appoints an administrator of a company under paragraph 14 shall file with the court –

    (a) a notice of appointment, and

    (b) such other documents as may be prescribed.

  (2) The notice of appointment must include a statutory declaration by or on behalf of the person who makes the appointment –

    (a) that the person is the holder of a qualifying floating charge in respect of the company's property,

    (b) that each floating charge relied on in making the appointment is (or was) enforceable on the date of the appointment, and

    (c) that the appointment is in accordance with this Schedule.

  (3) The notice of appointment must identify the administrator and must be accompanied by a statement by the administrator –

    (a) that he consents to the appointment,

    (b) that in his opinion the purpose of administration is reasonably likely to be achieved, and

    (c) giving such other information and opinions as may be prescribed.

  (4) For the purpose of a statement under sub-paragraph (3) an administrator may rely on information supplied by directors of the company (unless he has reason to doubt its accuracy).

  (5) The notice of appointment and any document accompanying it must be in the prescribed form.

  (6) A statutory declaration under sub-paragraph (2) must be made during the prescribed period.

  (7) A person commits an offence if in a statutory declaration under sub-paragraph (2) he makes a statement –

    (a) which is false, and

    (b) which he does not reasonably believe to be true.

Commencement of appointment

19   The appointment of an administrator under paragraph 14 takes effect when the requirements of paragraph 18 are satisfied.

20   A person who appoints an administrator under paragraph 14 –

    (a)   shall notify the administrator and such other persons as may be prescribed as soon as is reasonably practicable after the requirements of paragraph 18 are satisfied, and

    (b)   commits an offence if he fails without reasonable excuse to comply with paragraph (a).

Invalid appointment: indemnity

21   (1)   This paragraph applies where –

    (a)   a person purports to appoint an administrator under paragraph 14, and

    (b)   the appointment is discovered to be invalid.

(2)   The court may order the person who purported to make the appointment to indemnify the person appointed against liability which arises solely by reason of the appointment's invalidity.

APPOINTMENT OF ADMINISTRATOR BY COMPANY OR DIRECTORS

Power to appoint

22   (1)   A company may appoint an administrator.

(2)   The directors of a company may appoint an administrator.

Restrictions on power to appoint

23   (1)   This paragraph applies where an administrator of a company is appointed –

    (a)   under paragraph 22, or

    (b)   on an administration application made by the company or its directors.

(2)   An administrator of the company may not be appointed under paragraph 22 during the period of 12 months beginning with the date on which the appointment referred to in sub-paragraph (1) ceases to have effect.

24   (1)   If a moratorium for a company under Schedule A1 ends on a date when no voluntary arrangement is in force in respect of the company, this paragraph applies for the period of 12 months beginning with that date.

(2)   This paragraph also applies for the period of 12 months beginning with the date on which a voluntary arrangement in respect of a company ends if –

    (a)   the arrangement was made during a moratorium for the company under Schedule A1, and

    (b)   the arrangement ends prematurely (within the meaning of section 7B).

(3)   While this paragraph applies, an administrator of the company may not be appointed under paragraph 22.

25   An administrator of a company may not be appointed under paragraph 22 if –

    (a)   a petition for the winding up of the company has been presented and is not yet disposed of,

    (b)   an administration application has been made and is not yet disposed of, or

    (c)   an administrative receiver of the company is in office.

Notice of intention to appoint

26 (1) A person who proposes to make an appointment under paragraph 22 shall give at least five business days' written notice to –

    (a) any person who is or may be entitled to appoint an administrative receiver of the company, and

    (b) any person who is or may be entitled to appoint an administrator of the company under paragraph 14.

  (2) A person who proposes to make an appointment under paragraph 22 shall also give such notice as may be prescribed to such other persons as may be prescribed.

  (3) A notice under this paragraph must –

    (a) identify the proposed administrator, and

    (b) be in the prescribed form.

27 (1) A person who gives notice of intention to appoint under paragraph 26 shall file with the court as soon as is reasonably practicable a copy of –

    (a) the notice, and

    (b) any document accompanying it.

  (2) The copy filed under sub-paragraph (1) must be accompanied by a statutory declaration made by or on behalf of the person who proposes to make the appointment –

    (a) that the company is or is likely to become unable to pay its debts,

    (b) that the company is not in liquidation, and

    (c) that, so far as the person making the statement is able to ascertain, the appointment is not prevented by paragraphs 23 to 25, and

    (d) to such additional effect, and giving such information, as may be prescribed.

  (3) A statutory declaration under sub-paragraph (2) must –

    (a) be in the prescribed form, and

    (b) be made during the prescribed period.

  (4) A person commits an offence if in a statutory declaration under sub-paragraph (2) he makes a statement –

    (a) which is false, and

    (b) which he does not reasonably believe to be true.

28 (1) An appointment may not be made under paragraph 22 unless the person who makes the appointment has complied with any requirement of paragraphs 26 and 27 and –

    (a) the period of notice specified in paragraph 26(1) has expired, or

    (b) each person to whom notice has been given under paragraph 26(1) has consented in writing to the making of the appointment.

  (2) An appointment may not be made under paragraph 22 after the period of ten business days beginning with the date on which the notice of intention to appoint is filed under paragraph 27(1).

Notice of appointment

29 (1) A person who appoints an administrator of a company under paragraph 22 shall file with the court –

    (a) a notice of appointment, and

    (b) such other documents as may be prescribed.

(2)   The notice of appointment must include a statutory declaration by or on behalf of the person who makes the appointment –

(a)   that the person is entitled to make an appointment under paragraph 22,

(b)   that the appointment is in accordance with this Schedule, and

(c)   that, so far as the person making the statement is able to ascertain, the statements made and information given in the statutory declaration filed with the notice of intention to appoint remain accurate.

(3)   The notice of appointment must identify the administrator and must be accompanied by a statement by the administrator –

(a)   that he consents to the appointment,

(b)   that in his opinion the purpose of administration is reasonably likely to be achieved, and

(c)   giving such other information and opinions as may be prescribed.

(4)   For the purpose of a statement under sub-paragraph (3) an administrator may rely on information supplied by directors of the company (unless he has reason to doubt its accuracy).

(5)   The notice of appointment and any document accompanying it must be in the prescribed form.

(6)   A statutory declaration under sub-paragraph (2) must be made during the prescribed period.

(7)   A person commits an offence if in a statutory declaration under sub-paragraph (2) he makes a statement –

(a)   which is false, and

(b)   which he does not reasonably believe to be true.

30   In a case in which no person is entitled to notice of intention to appoint under paragraph 26(1) (and paragraph 28 therefore does not apply) –

(a)   the statutory declaration accompanying the notice of appointment must include the statements and information required under paragraph 27(2), and

(b)   paragraph 29(2)(c) shall not apply.

Commencement of appointment

31   The appointment of an administrator under paragraph 22 takes effect when the requirements of paragraph 29 are satisfied.

32   A person who appoints an administrator under paragraph 22 –

(a)   shall notify the administrator and such other persons as may be prescribed as soon as is reasonably practicable after the requirements of paragraph 29 are satisfied, and

(b)   commits an offence if he fails without reasonable excuse to comply with paragraph (a).

33   If before the requirements of paragraph 29 are satisfied the company enters administration by virtue of an administration order or an appointment under paragraph 14 –

(a)   the appointment under paragraph 22 shall not take effect, and

(b)   paragraph 32 shall not apply.

Invalid appointment: indemnity

34   (1)   This paragraph applies where –

(a)   a person purports to appoint an administrator under paragraph 22, and

(b)   the appointment is discovered to be invalid.

(2) The court may order the person who purported to make the appointment to indemnify the person appointed against liability which arises solely by reason of the appointment's invalidity.

ADMINISTRATION APPLICATION – SPECIAL CASES

Application by holder of floating charge

35 (1) This paragraph applies where an administration application in respect of a company –

   (a) is made by the holder of a qualifying floating charge in respect of the company's property, and

   (b) includes a statement that the application is made in reliance on this paragraph.

   (2) The court may make an administration order –

   (a) whether or not satisfied that the company is or is likely to become unable to pay its debts, but

   (b) only if satisfied that the applicant could appoint an administrator under paragraph 14.

Intervention by holder of floating charge

36 (1) This paragraph applies where –

   (a) an administration application in respect of a company is made by a person who is not the holder of a qualifying floating charge in respect of the company's property, and

   (b) the holder of a qualifying floating charge in respect of the company's property applies to the court to have a specified person appointed as administrator (and not the person specified by the administration applicant).

   (2) The court shall grant an application under sub-paragraph (1)(b) unless the court thinks it right to refuse the application because of the particular circumstances of the case.

Application where company in liquidation

37 (1) This paragraph applies where the holder of a qualifying floating charge in respect of a company's property could appoint an administrator under paragraph 14 but for paragraph 8(1)(b).

   (2) The holder of the qualifying floating charge may make an administration application.

   (3) If the court makes an administration order on hearing an application made by virtue of sub-paragraph (2) –

   (a) the court shall discharge the winding-up order,

   (b) the court shall make provision for such matters as may be prescribed,

   (c) the court may make other consequential provision,

   (d) the court shall specify which of the powers under this Schedule are to be exercisable by the administrator, and

   (e) this Schedule shall have effect with such modifications as the court may specify.

38 (1) The liquidator of a company may make an administration application.

(2) If the court makes an administration order on hearing an application made by virtue of sub-paragraph (1) –

    (a)   the court shall discharge any winding-up order in respect of the company,

    (b)   the court shall make provision for such matters as may be prescribed,

    (c)   the court may make other consequential provision,

    (d)   the court shall specify which of the powers under this Schedule are to be exercisable by the administrator, and

    (e)   this Schedule shall have effect with such modifications as the court may specify.

Effect of administrative receivership

39 (1) Where there is an administrative receiver of a company the court must dismiss an administration application in respect of the company unless –

    (a)   the person by or on behalf of whom the receiver was appointed consents to the making of the administration order,

    (b)   the court thinks that the security by virtue of which the receiver was appointed would be liable to be released or discharged under sections 238 to 240 (transaction at undervalue and preference) if an administration order were made,

    (c)   the court thinks that the security by virtue of which the receiver was appointed would be avoided under section 245 (avoidance of floating charge) if an administration order were made, or

    (d)   the court thinks that the security by virtue of which the receiver was appointed would be challengeable under section 242 (gratuitous alienations) or 243 (unfair preferences) or under any rule of law in Scotland.

(2) Sub-paragraph (1) applies whether the administrative receiver is appointed before or after the making of the administration application.

EFFECT OF ADMINISTRATION

Dismissal of pending winding-up petition

40 (1) A petition for the winding up of a company –

    (a)   shall be dismissed on the making of an administration order in respect of the company, and

    (b)   shall be suspended while the company is in administration following an appointment under paragraph 14.

(2) Sub-paragraph (1)(b) does not apply to a petition presented under –

    (a)   section 124A (public interest), or

    (b)   section 367 of the Financial Services and Markets Act 2000 (c. 8) (petition by Financial Services Authority).

(3) Where an administrator becomes aware that a petition was presented under a provision referred to in sub-paragraph (2) before his appointment, he shall apply to the court for directions under paragraph 63.

Dismissal of administrative or other receiver

41 (1) When an administration order takes effect in respect of a company any administrative receiver of the company shall vacate office.

(2) Where a company is in administration, any receiver of part of the company's property shall vacate office if the administrator requires him to.

(3) Where an administrative receiver or receiver vacates office under sub-paragraph (1) or (2) –

   (a) his remuneration shall be charged on and paid out of any property of the company which was in his custody or under his control immediately before he vacated office, and

   (b) he need not take any further steps under section 40 or 59.

(4) In the application of sub-paragraph (3)(a) –

   (a) 'remuneration' includes expenses properly incurred and any indemnity to which the administrative receiver or receiver is entitled out of the assets of the company,

   (b) the charge imposed takes priority over security held by the person by whom or on whose behalf the administrative receiver or receiver was appointed, and

   (c) the provision for payment is subject to paragraph 43.

Moratorium on insolvency proceedings

42 (1) This paragraph applies to a company in administration.

   (2) No resolution may be passed for the winding up of the company.

   (3) No order may be made for the winding up of the company.

   (4) Sub-paragraph (3) does not apply to an order made on a petition presented under –

   (a) section 124A (public interest), or

   (b) section 367 of the Financial Services and Markets Act 2000 (c. 8) (petition by Financial Services Authority).

   (5) If a petition presented under a provision referred to in sub-paragraph (4) comes to the attention of the administrator, he shall apply to the court for directions under paragraph 63.

Moratorium on other legal process

43 (1) This paragraph applies to a company in administration.

   (2) No step may be taken to enforce security over the company's property except –

   (a) with the consent of the administrator, or

   (b) with the permission of the court.

   (3) No step may be taken to repossess goods in the company's possession under a hire-purchase agreement except –

   (a) with the consent of the administrator, or

   (b) with the permission of the court.

   (4) A landlord may not exercise a right of forfeiture by peaceable re-entry in relation to premises let to the company except –

   (a) with the consent of the administrator, or

   (b) with the permission of the court.

   (5) In Scotland, a landlord may not exercise a right of irritancy in relation to premises let to the company except –

   (a) with the consent of the administrator, or

   (b) with the permission of the court.

(6) No legal process (including legal proceedings, execution, distress and diligence) may be instituted or continued against the company or property of the company except –

    (a)   with the consent of the administrator, or

    (b)   with the permission of the court.

(7) Where the court gives permission for a transaction under this paragraph it may impose a condition on or a requirement in connection with the transaction.

(8) In this paragraph 'landlord' includes a person to whom rent is payable.

Interim moratorium

44 (1) This paragraph applies where an administration application in respect of a company has been made and –

    (a)   the application has not yet been granted or dismissed, or

    (b)   the application has been granted but the administration order has not yet taken effect.

(2) This paragraph also applies from the time when a copy of notice of intention to appoint an administrator under paragraph 14 is filed with the court until –

    (a)   the appointment of the administrator takes effect, or

    (b)   the period of five business days beginning with the date of filing expires without an administrator having been appointed.

(3) Sub-paragraph (2) has effect in relation to a notice of intention to appoint only if it is in the prescribed form.

(4) This paragraph also applies from the time when a copy of notice of intention to appoint an administrator is filed with the court under paragraph 27(1) until –

    (a)   the appointment of the administrator takes effect, or

    (b)   the period specified in paragraph 28(2) expires without an administrator having been appointed.

(5) The provisions of paragraphs 42 and 43 shall apply (ignoring any reference to the consent of the administrator).

(6) If there is an administrative receiver of the company when the administration application is made, the provisions of paragraphs 42 and 43 shall not begin to apply by virtue of this paragraph until the person by or on behalf of whom the receiver was appointed consents to the making of the administration order.

(7) This paragraph does not prevent or require the permission of the court for –

    (a)   the presentation of a petition for the winding up of the company under a provision mentioned in paragraph 42(4),

    (b)   the appointment of an administrator under paragraph 14,

    (c)   the appointment of an administrative receiver of the company, or

    (d)   the carrying out by an administrative receiver (whenever appointed) of his functions.

Publicity

45 (1) While a company is in administration every business document issued by or on behalf of the company or the administrator must state –

    (a)   the name of the administrator, and

    (b)   that the affairs, business and property of the company are being managed by him.

(2) Any of the following commits an offence if without reasonable excuse he authorises or permits a contravention of sub-paragraph (1) –

    (a) the administrator,

    (b) an officer of the company, and

    (c) the company.

(3) In sub-paragraph (1) 'business document' means –

    (a) an invoice,

    (b) an order for goods or services, and

    (c) a business letter.

PROCESS OF ADMINISTRATION

Announcement of administrator's appointment

46 (1) This paragraph applies where a person becomes the administrator of a company.

    (2) As soon as is reasonably practicable the administrator shall –

      (a) send a notice of his appointment to the company, and

      (b) publish a notice of his appointment in the prescribed manner.

    (3) As soon as is reasonably practicable the administrator shall –

      (a) obtain a list of the company's creditors, and

      (b) send a notice of his appointment to each creditor of whose claim and address he is aware.

    (4) The administrator shall send a notice of his appointment to the registrar of companies before the end of the period of 7 days beginning with the date specified in sub-paragraph (6).

    (5) The administrator shall send a notice of his appointment to such persons as may be prescribed before the end of the prescribed period beginning with the date specified in sub-paragraph (6).

    (6) The date for the purpose of sub-paragraphs (4) and (5) is –

      (a) in the case of an administrator appointed by administration order, the date of the order,

      (b) in the case of an administrator appointed under paragraph 14, the date on which he receives notice under paragraph 20, and

      (c) in the case of an administrator appointed under paragraph 22, the date on which he receives notice under paragraph 32.

    (7) The court may direct that sub-paragraph (3)(b) or (5) –

      (a) shall not apply, or

      (b) shall apply with the substitution of a different period.

    (8) A notice under this paragraph must –

      (a) contain the prescribed information, and

      (b) be in the prescribed form.

    (9) An administrator commits an offence if he fails without reasonable excuse to comply with a requirement of this paragraph.

Statement of company's affairs

47 (1) As soon as is reasonably practicable after appointment the administrator of a company shall by notice in the prescribed form require one or more relevant persons to provide the administrator with a statement of the affairs of the company.

(2) The statement must –

    (a) be verified by a statement of truth in accordance with Civil Procedure Rules,

    (b) be in the prescribed form,

    (c) give particulars of the company's property, debts and liabilities,

    (d) give the names and addresses of the company's creditors,

    (e) specify the security held by each creditor,

    (f) give the date on which each security was granted, and

    (g) contain such other information as may be prescribed.

(3) In sub-paragraph (1) 'relevant person' means –

    (a) a person who is or has been an officer of the company,

    (b) a person who took part in the formation of the company during the period of one year ending with the date on which the company enters administration,

    (c) a person employed by the company during that period, and

    (d) a person who is or has been during that period an officer or employee of a company which is or has been during that year an officer of the company.

(4) For the purpose of sub-paragraph (3) a reference to employment is a reference to employment through a contract of employment or a contract for services.

(5) In Scotland, a statement of affairs under sub-paragraph (1) must be a statutory declaration made in accordance with the Statutory Declarations Act 1835 (c. 62) (and sub-paragraph (2)(a) shall not apply).

48 (1) A person required to submit a statement of affairs must do so before the end of the period of 11 days beginning with the day on which he receives notice of the requirement.

(2) The administrator may –

    (a) revoke a requirement under paragraph 47(1), or

    (b) extend the period specified in sub-paragraph (1) (whether before or after expiry).

(3) If the administrator refuses a request to act under sub-paragraph (2) –

    (a) the person whose request is refused may apply to the court, and

    (b) the court may take action of a kind specified in sub-paragraph (2).

(4) A person commits an offence if he fails without reasonable excuse to comply with a requirement under paragraph 47(1).

Administrator's proposals

49 (1) The administrator of a company shall make a statement setting out proposals for achieving the purpose of administration.

(2) A statement under sub-paragraph (1) must, in particular –

    (a) deal with such matters as may be prescribed, and

    (b) where applicable, explain why the administrator thinks that the objective mentioned in paragraph 3(1)(a) or (b) cannot be achieved.

(3) Proposals under this paragraph may include –

    (a) a proposal for a voluntary arrangement under Part I of this Act (although this paragraph is without prejudice to section 4(3));

    (b) a proposal for a compromise or arrangement to be sanctioned under section 425 of the Companies Act (compromise with creditors or members).

(4) The administrator shall send a copy of the statement of his proposals –

    (a) to the registrar of companies,

(b)   to every creditor of the company of whose claim and address he is aware, and

(c)   to every member of the company of whose address he is aware.

(5)   The administrator shall comply with sub-paragraph (4) –

   (a)   as soon as is reasonably practicable after the company enters administration, and

   (b)   in any event, before the end of the period of eight weeks beginning with the day on which the company enters administration.

(6)   The administrator shall be taken to comply with sub-paragraph (4)(c) if he publishes in the prescribed manner a notice undertaking to provide a copy of the statement of proposals free of charge to any member of the company who applies in writing to a specified address.

(7)   An administrator commits an offence if he fails without reasonable excuse to comply with sub-paragraph (5).

(8)   A period specified in this paragraph may be varied in accordance with paragraph 107.

Creditors' meeting

50   (1)   In this Schedule 'creditors' meeting' means a meeting of creditors of a company summoned by the administrator –

   (a)   in the prescribed manner, and

   (b)   giving the prescribed period of notice to every creditor of the company of whose claim and address he is aware.

(2)   A period prescribed under sub-paragraph (1)(b) may be varied in accordance with paragraph 107.

(3)   A creditors' meeting shall be conducted in accordance with the rules.

Requirement for initial creditors' meeting

51   (1)   Each copy of an administrator's statement of proposals sent to a creditor under paragraph 49(4)(b) must be accompanied by an invitation to a creditors' meeting (an 'initial creditors' meeting').

(2)   The date set for an initial creditors' meeting must be –

   (a)   as soon as is reasonably practicable after the company enters administration, and

   (b)   in any event, within the period of ten weeks beginning with the date on which the company enters administration.

(3)   An administrator shall present a copy of his statement of proposals to an initial creditors' meeting.

(4)   A period specified in this paragraph may be varied in accordance with paragraph 107.

(5)   An administrator commits an offence if he fails without reasonable excuse to comply with a requirement of this paragraph.

52   (1)   Paragraph 51(1) shall not apply where the statement of proposals states that the administrator thinks –

   (a)   that the company has sufficient property to enable each creditor of the company to be paid in full,

   (b)   that the company has insufficient property to enable a distribution to be made to unsecured creditors other than by virtue of section 176A(2)(a), or

(c)   that neither of the objectives specified in paragraph 3(1)(a) and (b) can be achieved.

(2)   But the administrator shall summon an initial creditors' meeting if it is requested –

(a)   by creditors of the company whose debts amount to at least 10% of the total debts of the company,

(b)   in the prescribed manner, and

(c)   in the prescribed period.

(3)   A meeting requested under sub-paragraph (2) must be summoned for a date in the prescribed period.

(4)   The period prescribed under sub-paragraph (3) may be varied in accordance with paragraph 107.

Business and result of initial creditors' meeting

53   (1)   An initial creditors' meeting to which an administrator's proposals are presented shall consider them and may –

(a)   approve them without modification, or

(b)   approve them with modification to which the administrator consents.

(2)   After the conclusion of an initial creditors' meeting the administrator shall as soon as is reasonably practicable report any decision taken to –

(a)   the court,

(b)   the registrar of companies, and

(c)   such other persons as may be prescribed.

(3)   An administrator commits an offence if he fails without reasonable excuse to comply with sub-paragraph (2).

Revision of administrator's proposals

54   (1)   This paragraph applies where –

(a)   an administrator's proposals have been approved (with or without modification) at an initial creditors' meeting,

(b)   the administrator proposes a revision to the proposals, and

(c)   the administrator thinks that the proposed revision is substantial.

(2)   The administrator shall –

(a)   summon a creditors' meeting,

(b)   send a statement in the prescribed form of the proposed revision with the notice of the meeting sent to each creditor,

(c)   send a copy of the statement, within the prescribed period, to each member of the company of whose address he is aware, and

(d)   present a copy of the statement to the meeting.

(3)   The administrator shall be taken to have complied with sub-paragraph (2)(c) if he publishes a notice undertaking to provide a copy of the statement free of charge to any member of the company who applies in writing to a specified address.

(4)   A notice under sub-paragraph (3) must be published –

(a)   in the prescribed manner, and

(b)   within the prescribed period.

(5)   A creditors' meeting to which a proposed revision is presented shall consider it and may –

(a) approve it without modification, or

(b) approve it with modification to which the administrator consents.

(6) After the conclusion of a creditors' meeting the administrator shall as soon as is reasonably practicable report any decision taken to –

(a) the court,

(b) the registrar of companies, and

(c) such other persons as may be prescribed.

(7) An administrator commits an offence if he fails without reasonable excuse to comply with sub-paragraph (6).

Failure to obtain approval of administrator's proposals

55 (1) This paragraph applies where an administrator reports to the court that –

(a) an initial creditors' meeting has failed to approve the administrator's proposals presented to it, or

(b) a creditors' meeting has failed to approve a revision of the administrator's proposals presented to it.

(2) The court may –

(a) provide that the appointment of an administrator shall cease to have effect from a specified time;

(b) adjourn the hearing conditionally or unconditionally;

(c) make an interim order;

(d) make an order on a petition for winding up suspended by virtue of paragraph 40(1)(b);

(e) make any other order (including an order making consequential provision) that the court thinks appropriate.

Further creditors' meetings

56 (1) The administrator of a company shall summon a creditors' meeting if –

(a) it is requested in the prescribed manner by creditors of the company whose debts amount to at least 10% of the total debts of the company, or

(b) he is directed by the court to summon a creditors' meeting.

(2) An administrator commits an offence if he fails without reasonable excuse to summon a creditors' meeting as required by this paragraph.

Creditors' committee

57 (1) A creditors' meeting may establish a creditors' committee.

(2) A creditors' committee shall carry out functions conferred on it by or under this Act.

(3) A creditors' committee may require the administrator –

(a) to attend on the committee at any reasonable time of which he is given at least seven days' notice, and

(b) to provide the committee with information about the exercise of his functions.

Correspondence instead of creditors' meeting

58   (1)   Anything which is required or permitted by or under this Schedule to be done at a creditors' meeting may be done by correspondence between the administrator and creditors –

(a)   in accordance with the rules, and
(b)   subject to any prescribed condition.

(2)   A reference in this Schedule to anything done at a creditors' meeting includes a reference to anything done in the course of correspondence in reliance on sub-paragraph (1).

(3)   A requirement to hold a creditors' meeting is satisfied by conducting correspondence in accordance with this paragraph.

FUNCTIONS OF ADMINISTRATOR

General powers

59   (1)   The administrator of a company may do anything necessary or expedient for the management of the affairs, business and property of the company.

(2)   A provision of this Schedule which expressly permits the administrator to do a specified thing is without prejudice to the generality of sub-paragraph (1).

(3)   A person who deals with the administrator of a company in good faith and for value need not inquire whether the administrator is acting within his powers.

60   The administrator of a company has the powers specified in Schedule 1 to this Act.

61   The administrator of a company –

(a)   may remove a director of the company, and
(b)   may appoint a director of the company (whether or not to fill a vacancy).

62   The administrator of a company may call a meeting of members or creditors of the company.

63   The administrator of a company may apply to the court for directions in connection with his functions.

64   (1)   A company in administration or an officer of a company in administration may not exercise a management power without the consent of the administrator.

(2)   For the purpose of sub-paragraph (1) –

(a)   'management power' means a power which could be exercised so as to interfere with the exercise of the administrator's powers,
(b)   it is immaterial whether the power is conferred by an enactment or an instrument, and
(c)   consent may be general or specific.

Distribution

65   (1)   The administrator of a company may make a distribution to a creditor of the company.

(2)   Section 175 shall apply in relation to a distribution under this paragraph as it applies in relation to a winding up.

(3)   A payment may not be made by way of distribution under this paragraph to a creditor of the company who is neither secured nor preferential unless the court gives permission.

66   The administrator of a company may make a payment otherwise than in accordance with paragraph 65 or paragraph 13 of Schedule 1 if he thinks it likely to assist achievement of the purpose of administration.

General duties

67   The administrator of a company shall on his appointment take custody or control of all the property to which he thinks the company is entitled.

68   (1)   Subject to sub-paragraph (2), the administrator of a company shall manage its affairs, business and property in accordance with –

(a)   any proposals approved under paragraph 53,

(b)   any revision of those proposals which is made by him and which he does not consider substantial, and

(c)   any revision of those proposals approved under paragraph 54.

(2)   If the court gives directions to the administrator of a company in connection with any aspect of his management of the company's affairs, business or property, the administrator shall comply with the directions.

(3)   The court may give directions under sub-paragraph (2) only if –

(a)   no proposals have been approved under paragraph 53,

(b)   the directions are consistent with any proposals or revision approved under paragraph 53 or 54,

(c)   the court thinks the directions are required in order to reflect a change in circumstances since the approval of proposals or a revision under paragraph 53 or 54, or

(d)   the court thinks the directions are desirable because of a misunderstanding about proposals or a revision approved under paragraph 53 or 54.

Administrator as agent of company

69   In exercising his functions under this Schedule the administrator of a company acts as its agent.

Charged property: floating charge

70   (1)   The administrator of a company may dispose of or take action relating to property which is subject to a floating charge as if it were not subject to the charge.

(2)   Where property is disposed of in reliance on sub-paragraph (1) the holder of the floating charge shall have the same priority in respect of acquired property as he had in respect of the property disposed of.

(3)   In sub-paragraph (2) 'acquired property' means property of the company which directly or indirectly represents the property disposed of.

Charged property: non-floating charge

71   (1)   The court may by order enable the administrator of a company to dispose of property which is subject to a security (other than a floating charge) as if it were not subject to the security.

(2)   An order under sub-paragraph (1) may be made only –

(a)   on the application of the administrator, and

(b)   where the court thinks that disposal of the property would be likely to promote the purpose of administration in respect of the company.

(3)   An order under this paragraph is subject to the condition that there be applied towards discharging the sums secured by the security –

(a)   the net proceeds of disposal of the property, and

(b)   any additional money required to be added to the net proceeds so as to produce the amount determined by the court as the net amount which would
be realised on a sale of the property at market value.

(4)   If an order under this paragraph relates to more than one security, application of
money under sub-paragraph (3) shall be in the order of the priorities of the
securities.

(5)   An administrator who makes a successful application for an order under this
paragraph shall send a copy of the order to the registrar of companies before the
end of the period of 14 days starting with the date of the order.

(6)   An administrator commits an offence if he fails to comply with sub-paragraph
(5) without reasonable excuse.

Hire-purchase property

72   (1)   The court may by order enable the administrator of a company to dispose of
goods which are in the possession of the company under a hire-purchase agreement as if all the rights of the owner under the agreement were vested in the
company.

(2)   An order under sub-paragraph (1) may be made only –

(a)   on the application of the administrator, and

(b)   where the court thinks that disposal of the goods would be likely to promote the purpose of administration in respect of the company.

(3)   An order under this paragraph is subject to the condition that there be applied
towards discharging the sums payable under the hire-purchase agreement –

(a)   the net proceeds of disposal of the goods, and

(b)   any additional money required to be added to the net proceeds so as to produce the amount determined by the court as the net amount which would
be realised on a sale of the goods at market value.

(4)   An administrator who makes a successful application for an order under this
paragraph shall send a copy of the order to the registrar of companies before the
end of the period of 14 days starting with the date of the order.

(5)   An administrator commits an offence if he fails without reasonable excuse to
comply with sub-paragraph (4).

Protection for secured or preferential creditor

73   (1)   An administrator's statement of proposals under paragraph 49 may not include
any action which –

(a)   affects the right of a secured creditor of the company to enforce his security,

(b)   would result in a preferential debt of the company being paid otherwise
than in priority to its non-preferential debts, or

(c)   would result in one preferential creditor of the company being paid a
smaller proportion of his debt than another.

(2)   Sub-paragraph (1) does not apply to –

(a)   action to which the relevant creditor consents,

(b)   a proposal for a voluntary arrangement under Part I of this Act (although
this sub-paragraph is without prejudice to section 4(3)), or

(c)   a proposal for a compromise or arrangement to be sanctioned under section
425 of the Companies Act (compromise with creditors or members).

(3)   The reference to a statement of proposals in sub-paragraph (1) includes a reference to a statement as revised or modified.

Challenge to administrator's conduct of company

74   (1)   A creditor or member of a company in administration may apply to the court claiming that –

   (a)   the administrator is acting or has acted so as unfairly to harm the interests of the applicant (whether alone or in common with some or all other members or creditors), or

   (b)   the administrator proposes to act in a way which would unfairly harm the interests of the applicant (whether alone or in common with some or all other members or creditors).

   (2)   A creditor or member of a company in administration may apply to the court claiming that the administrator is not performing his functions as quickly or as efficiently as is reasonably practicable.

   (3)   The court may –

   (a)   grant relief;

   (b)   dismiss the application;

   (c)   adjourn the hearing conditionally or unconditionally;

   (d)   make an interim order;

   (e)   make any other order it thinks appropriate.

   (4)   In particular, an order under this paragraph may –

   (a)   regulate the administrator's exercise of his functions;

   (b)   require the administrator to do or not do a specified thing;

   (c)   require a creditors' meeting to be held for a specified purpose;

   (d)   provide for the appointment of an administrator to cease to have effect;

   (e)   make consequential provision.

   (5)   An order may be made on a claim under sub-paragraph (1) whether or not the action complained of –

   (a)   is within the administrator's powers under this Schedule;

   (b)   was taken in reliance on an order under paragraph 71 or 72.

   (6)   An order may not be made under this paragraph if it would impede or prevent the implementation of –

   (a)   a voluntary arrangement approved under Part I,

   (b)   a compromise or arrangement sanctioned under section 425 of the Companies Act (compromise with creditors and members), or

   (c)   proposals or a revision approved under paragraph 53 or 54 more than 28 days before the day on which the application for the order under this paragraph is made.

Misfeasance

75   (1)   The court may examine the conduct of a person who –

   (a)   is or purports to be the administrator of a company, or

   (b)   has been or has purported to be the administrator of a company.

   (2)   An examination under this paragraph may be held only on the application of –

   (a)   the official receiver,

   (b)   the administrator of the company,

   (c)   the liquidator of the company,

   (d)   a creditor of the company, or

   (e)   a contributory of the company.

   (3)   An application under sub-paragraph (2) must allege that the administrator –

   (a)   has misapplied or retained money or other property of the company,

    (b)   has become accountable for money or other property of the company,

    (c)   has breached a fiduciary or other duty in relation to the company, or

    (d)   has been guilty of misfeasance.

(4)   On an examination under this paragraph into a person's conduct the court may order him –

    (a)   to repay, restore or account for money or property;

    (b)   to pay interest;

    (c)   to contribute a sum to the company's property by way of compensation for breach of duty or misfeasance.

(5)   In sub-paragraph (3) 'administrator' includes a person who purports or has purported to be a company's administrator.

(6)   An application under sub-paragraph (2) may be made in respect of an administrator who has been discharged under paragraph 98 only with the permission of the court.

ENDING ADMINISTRATION

Automatic end of administration

76   (1)   The appointment of an administrator shall cease to have effect at the end of the period of one year beginning with the date on which it takes effect.

    (2)   But –

       (a)   on the application of an administrator the court may by order extend his term of office for a specified period, and

       (b)   an administrator's term of office may be extended for a specified period not exceeding six months by consent.

77   (1)   An order of the court under paragraph 76 –

       (a)   may be made in respect of an administrator whose term of office has already been extended by order or by consent, but

       (b)   may not be made after the expiry of the administrator's term of office.

    (2)   Where an order is made under paragraph 76 the administrator shall as soon as is reasonably practicable notify the registrar of companies.

    (3)   An administrator who fails without reasonable excuse to comply with sub-paragraph (2) commits an offence.

78   (1)   In paragraph 76(2)(b) 'consent' means consent of –

       (a)   each secured creditor of the company, and

       (b)   if the company has unsecured debts, creditors whose debts amount to more than 50% of the company's unsecured debts, disregarding debts of any creditor who does not respond to an invitation to give or withhold consent.

    (2)   But where the administrator has made a statement under paragraph 52(1)(b) 'consent' means –

       (a)   consent of each secured creditor of the company, or

       (b)   if the administrator thinks that a distribution may be made to preferential creditors, consent of –

          (i)   each secured creditor of the company, and

         (ii)   preferential creditors whose debts amount to more than 50% of the preferential debts of the company, disregarding debts of any creditor who does not respond to an invitation to give or withhold consent.

(3) Consent for the purposes of paragraph 76(2)(b) may be –

(a) written, or

(b) signified at a creditors' meeting.

(4) An administrator's term of office –

(a) may be extended by consent only once,

(b) may not be extended by consent after extension by order of the court, and

(c) may not be extended by consent after expiry.

(5) Where an administrator's term of office is extended by consent he shall as soon as is reasonably practicable –

(a) file notice of the extension with the court, and

(b) notify the registrar of companies.

(6) An administrator who fails without reasonable excuse to comply with sub-paragraph (5) commits an offence.

Court ending administration on application of administrator

79 (1) On the application of the administrator of a company the court may provide for the appointment of an administrator of the company to cease to have effect from a specified time.

(2) The administrator of a company shall make an application under this paragraph if –

(a) he thinks the purpose of administration cannot be achieved in relation to the company,

(b) he thinks the company should not have entered administration, or

(c) a creditors' meeting requires him to make an application under this paragraph.

(3) The administrator of a company shall make an application under this paragraph if –

(a) the administration is pursuant to an administration order, and

(b) the administrator thinks that the purpose of administration has been sufficiently achieved in relation to the company.

(4) On an application under this paragraph the court may –

(a) adjourn the hearing conditionally or unconditionally;

(b) dismiss the application;

(c) make an interim order;

(d) make any order it thinks appropriate (whether in addition to, in conse-quence of or instead of the order applied for).

Termination of administration where objective achieved

80 (1) This paragraph applies where an administrator of a company is appointed under paragraph 14 or 22.

(2) If the administrator thinks that the purpose of administration has been suf-ficiently achieved in relation to the company he may file a notice in the prescribed form –

(a) with the court, and

(b) with the registrar of companies.

(3) The administrator's appointment shall cease to have effect when the require-ments of sub-paragraph (2) are satisfied.

(4) Where the administrator files a notice he shall within the prescribed period send a copy to every creditor of the company of whose claim and address he is aware.

(5) The rules may provide that the administrator is taken to have complied with sub-paragraph (4) if before the end of the prescribed period he publishes in the prescribed manner a notice undertaking to provide a copy of the notice under sub-paragraph (2) to any creditor of the company who applies in writing to a specified address.

(6) An administrator who fails without reasonable excuse to comply with sub-paragraph (4) commits an offence.

Court ending administration on application of creditor

81 (1) On the application of a creditor of a company the court may provide for the appointment of an administrator of the company to cease to have effect at a specified time.

(2) An application under this paragraph must allege an improper motive –

(a) in the case of an administrator appointed by administration order, on the part of the applicant for the order, or

(b) in any other case, on the part of the person who appointed the administrator.

(3) On an application under this paragraph the court may –

(a) adjourn the hearing conditionally or unconditionally;

(b) dismiss the application;

(c) make an interim order;

(d) make any order it thinks appropriate (whether in addition to, in consequence of or instead of the order applied for).

Public interest winding-up

82 (1) This paragraph applies where a winding-up order is made for the winding up of a company in administration on a petition presented under –

(a) section 124A (public interest), or

(b) section 367 of the Financial Services and Markets Act 2000 (c. 8) (petition by Financial Services Authority).

(2) This paragraph also applies where a provisional liquidator of a company in administration is appointed following the presentation of a petition under any of the provisions listed in sub-paragraph (1).

(3) The court shall order –

(a) that the appointment of the administrator shall cease to have effect, or

(b) that the appointment of the administrator shall continue to have effect.

(4) If the court makes an order under sub-paragraph (3)(b) it may also –

(a) specify which of the powers under this Schedule are to be exercisable by the administrator, and

(b) order that this Schedule shall have effect in relation to the administrator with specified modifications.

Moving from administration to creditors' voluntary liquidation

83 (1) This paragraph applies in England and Wales where the administrator of a company thinks –

(a) that the total amount which each secured creditor of the company is likely to receive has been paid to him or set aside for him, and

(b)   that a distribution will be made to unsecured creditors of the company (if there are any).

(2)   This paragraph applies in Scotland where the administrator of a company thinks –

(a)   that each secured creditor of the company will receive payment in respect of his debt, and

(b)   that a distribution will be made to unsecured creditors (if there are any).

(3)   The administrator may send to the registrar of companies a notice that this paragraph applies.

(4)   On receipt of a notice under sub-paragraph (3) the registrar shall register it.

(5)   If an administrator sends a notice under sub-paragraph (3) he shall as soon as is reasonably practicable –

(a)   file a copy of the notice with the court, and

(b)   send a copy of the notice to each creditor of whose claim and address he is aware.

(6)   On the registration of a notice under sub-paragraph (3) –

(a)   the appointment of an administrator in respect of the company shall cease to have effect, and

(b)   the company shall be wound up as if a resolution for voluntary winding up under section 84 were passed on the day on which the notice is registered.

(7)   The liquidator for the purposes of the winding up shall be –

(a)   a person nominated by the creditors of the company in the prescribed manner and within the prescribed period, or

(b)   if no person is nominated under paragraph (a), the administrator.

(8)   In the application of Part IV to a winding up by virtue of this paragraph –

(a)   section 85 shall not apply,

(b)   section 86 shall apply as if the reference to the time of the passing of the resolution for voluntary winding up were a reference to the beginning of the date of registration of the notice under sub-paragraph (3),

(c)   section 89 does not apply,

(d)   sections 98, 99 and 100 shall not apply,

(e)   section 129 shall apply as if the reference to the time of the passing of the resolution for voluntary winding up were a reference to the beginning of the date of registration of the notice under sub-paragraph (3), and

(f)   any creditors' committee which is in existence immediately before the company ceases to be in administration shall continue in existence after that time as if appointed as a liquidation committee under section 101.

Moving from administration to dissolution

84   (1)   If the administrator of a company thinks that the company has no property which might permit a distribution to its creditors, he shall send a notice to that effect to the registrar of companies.

(2)   The court may on the application of the administrator of a company disapply sub-paragraph (1) in respect of the company.

(3)   On receipt of a notice under sub-paragraph (1) the registrar shall register it.

(4)   On the registration of a notice in respect of a company under sub-paragraph (1) the appointment of an administrator of the company shall cease to have effect.

(5)   If an administrator sends a notice under sub-paragraph (1) he shall as soon as is reasonably practicable –

(a)   file a copy of the notice with the court, and

(b)   send a copy of the notice to each creditor of whose claim and address he is aware.

(6) At the end of the period of three months beginning with the date of registration of a notice in respect of a company under sub-paragraph (1) the company is deemed to be dissolved.

(7) On an application in respect of a company by the administrator or another interested person the court may –

    (a) extend the period specified in sub-paragraph (6),

    (b) suspend that period, or

    (c) disapply sub-paragraph (6).

(8) Where an order is made under sub-paragraph (7) in respect of a company the administrator shall as soon as is reasonably practicable notify the registrar of companies.

(9) An administrator commits an offence if he fails without reasonable excuse to comply with sub-paragraph (5).

Discharge of administration order where administration ends

85 (1) This paragraph applies where –

    (a) the court makes an order under this Schedule providing for the appointment of an administrator of a company to cease to have effect, and

    (b) the administrator was appointed by administration order.

(2) The court shall discharge the administration order.

Notice to Companies Registrar where administration ends

86 (1) This paragraph applies where the court makes an order under this Schedule providing for the appointment of an administrator to cease to have effect.

(2) The administrator shall send a copy of the order to the registrar of companies within the period of 14 days beginning with the date of the order.

(3) An administrator who fails without reasonable excuse to comply with sub-paragraph (2) commits an offence.

REPLACING ADMINISTRATOR

Resignation of administrator

87 (1) An administrator may resign only in prescribed circumstances.

(2) Where an administrator may resign he may do so only –

    (a) in the case of an administrator appointed by administration order, by notice in writing to the court,

    (b) in the case of an administrator appointed under paragraph 14, by notice in writing to the person who appointed him,

    (c) in the case of an administrator appointed under paragraph 22(1), by notice in writing to the company, or

    (d) in the case of an administrator appointed under paragraph 22(2), by notice in writing to the directors of the company.

Removal of administrator from office

88 The court may by order remove an administrator from office.

Administrator ceasing to be qualified

89 (1) The administrator of a company shall vacate office if he ceases to be qualified to act as an insolvency practitioner in relation to the company.

  (2) Where an administrator vacates office by virtue of sub-paragraph (1) he shall give notice in writing –

  (a) in the case of an administrator appointed by administration order, to the court,

  (b) in the case of an administrator appointed under paragraph 14, to the person who appointed him,

  (c) in the case of an administrator appointed under paragraph 22(1), to the company, or

  (d) in the case of an administrator appointed under paragraph 22(2), to the directors of the company.

  (3) An administrator who fails without reasonable excuse to comply with sub-paragraph (2) commits an offence.

Supplying vacancy in office of administrator

90 Paragraphs 91 to 95 apply where an administrator –

  (a) dies,

  (b) resigns,

  (c) is removed from office under paragraph 88, or

  (d) vacates office under paragraph 89.

91 (1) Where the administrator was appointed by administration order, the court may replace the administrator on an application under this sub-paragraph made by –

  (a) a creditors' committee of the company,

  (b) the company,

  (c) the directors of the company,

  (d) one or more creditors of the company, or

  (e) where more than one person was appointed to act jointly or concurrently as the administrator, any of those persons who remains in office.

  (2) But an application may be made in reliance on sub-paragraph (1)(b) to (d) only where –

  (a) there is no creditors' committee of the company,

  (b) the court is satisfied that the creditors' committee or a remaining administrator is not taking reasonable steps to make a replacement, or

  (c) the court is satisfied that for another reason it is right for the application to be made.

92 Where the administrator was appointed under paragraph 14 the holder of the floating charge by virtue of which the appointment was made may replace the administrator.

93 (1) Where the administrator was appointed under paragraph 22(1) by the company it may replace the administrator.

  (2) A replacement under this paragraph may be made only –

  (a) with the consent of each person who is the holder of a qualifying floating charge in respect of the company's property, or

  (b) where consent is withheld, with the permission of the court.

94 (1) Where the administrator was appointed under paragraph 22(2) the directors of the company may replace the administrator.

(2) A replacement under this paragraph may be made only –

    (a) with the consent of each person who is the holder of a qualifying floating charge in respect of the company's property, or

    (b) where consent is withheld, with the permission of the court.

95 The court may replace an administrator on the application of a person listed in paragraph 91(1) if the court –

    (a) is satisfied that a person who is entitled to replace the administrator under any of paragraphs 92 to 94 is not taking reasonable steps to make a replacement, or

    (b) that for another reason it is right for the court to make the replacement.

Substitution of administrator: competing floating charge-holder

96 (1) This paragraph applies where an administrator of a company is appointed under paragraph 14 by the holder of a qualifying floating charge in respect of the company's property.

    (2) The holder of a prior qualifying floating charge in respect of the company's property may apply to the court for the administrator to be replaced by an administrator nominated by the holder of the prior floating charge.

    (3) One floating charge is prior to another for the purposes of this paragraph if –

        (a) it was created first, or

        (b) it is to be treated as having priority in accordance with an agreement to which the holder of each floating charge was party.

    (4) Sub-paragraph (3) shall have effect in relation to Scotland as if the following were substituted for paragraph (a) –

        '(a) it has priority of ranking in accordance with section 464(4)(b) of the Companies Act 1985 (c. 6),'.

Substitution of administrator appointed by company or directors: creditors' meeting

97 (1) This paragraph applies where –

    (a) an administrator of a company is appointed by a company or directors under paragraph 22, and

    (b) there is no holder of a qualifying floating charge in respect of the company's property.

    (2) A creditors' meeting may replace the administrator.

    (3) A creditors' meeting may act under sub-paragraph (2) only if the new administrator's written consent to act is presented to the meeting before the replacement is made.

Vacation of office: discharge from liability

98 (1) Where a person ceases to be the administrator of a company (whether because he vacates office by reason of resignation, death or otherwise, because he is removed from office or because his appointment ceases to have effect) he is discharged from liability in respect of any action of his as administrator.

    (2) The discharge provided by sub-paragraph (1) takes effect –

    (a) in the case of an administrator who dies, on the filing with the court of notice of his death,

    (b) in the case of an administrator appointed under paragraph 14 or 22, at a time appointed by resolution of the creditors' committee or, if there is no committee, by resolution of the creditors, or

    (c) in any case, at a time specified by the court.

(3) For the purpose of the application of sub-paragraph (2)(b) in a case where the administrator has made a statement under paragraph 52(1)(b), a resolution shall be taken as passed if (and only if) passed with the approval of –

    (a) each secured creditor of the company, or

    (b) if the administrator has made a distribution to preferential creditors or thinks that a distribution may be made to preferential creditors –

        (i) each secured creditor of the company, and

        (ii) preferential creditors whose debts amount to more than 50% of the preferential debts of the company, disregarding debts of any creditor who does not respond to an invitation to give or withhold approval.

(4) Discharge –

    (a) applies to liability accrued before the discharge takes effect, and

    (b) does not prevent the exercise of the court's powers under paragraph 75.

Vacation of office: charges and liabilities

99 (1) This paragraph applies where a person ceases to be the administrator of a company (whether because he vacates office by reason of resignation, death or otherwise, because he is removed from office or because his appointment ceases to have effect).

  (2) In this paragraph –

      'the former administrator' means the person referred to in sub-paragraph (1), and

      'cessation' means the time when he ceases to be the company's administrator.

  (3) The former administrator's remuneration and expenses shall be –

    (a) charged on and payable out of property of which he had custody or control immediately before cessation, and

    (b) payable in priority to any security to which paragraph 70 applies.

  (4) A sum payable in respect of a debt or liability arising out of a contract entered into by the former administrator or a predecessor before cessation shall be –

    (a) charged on and payable out of property of which the former administrator had custody or control immediately before cessation, and

    (b) payable in priority to any charge arising under sub-paragraph (3).

  (5) Sub-paragraph (4) shall apply to a liability arising under a contract of employment which was adopted by the former administrator or a predecessor before cessation; and for that purpose –

    (a) action taken within the period of 14 days after an administrator's appointment shall not be taken to amount or contribute to the adoption of a contract,

    (b) no account shall be taken of a liability which arises, or in so far as it arises, by reference to anything which is done or which occurs before the adoption of the contract of employment, and

    (c) no account shall be taken of a liability to make a payment other than wages or salary.

  (6) In sub-paragraph (5)(c) 'wages or salary' includes –

    (a) a sum payable in respect of a period of holiday (for which purpose the sum shall be treated as relating to the period by reference to which the entitlement to holiday accrued),

    (b)   a sum payable in respect of a period of absence through illness or other good cause,

    (c)   a sum payable in lieu of holiday,

    (d)   in respect of a period, a sum which would be treated as earnings for that period for the purposes of an enactment about social security, and

    (e)   a contribution to an occupational pension scheme.

GENERAL

Joint and concurrent administrators

100 (1) In this Schedule –

    (a)   a reference to the appointment of an administrator of a company includes a reference to the appointment of a number of persons to act jointly or concurrently as the administrator of a company, and

    (b)   a reference to the appointment of a person as administrator of a company includes a reference to the appointment of a person as one of a number of persons to act jointly or concurrently as the administrator of a company.

  (2) The appointment of a number of persons to act as administrator of a company must specify –

    (a)   which functions (if any) are to be exercised by the persons appointed acting jointly, and

    (b)   which functions (if any) are to be exercised by any or all of the persons appointed.

101 (1) This paragraph applies where two or more persons are appointed to act jointly as the administrator of a company.

  (2) A reference to the administrator of the company is a reference to those persons acting jointly.

  (3) But a reference to the administrator of a company in paragraphs 87 to 99 of this Schedule is a reference to any or all of the persons appointed to act jointly.

  (4) Where an offence of omission is committed by the administrator, each of the persons appointed to act jointly –

    (a)   commits the offence, and

    (b)   may be proceeded against and punished individually.

  (5) The reference in paragraph 45(1)(a) to the name of the administrator is a reference to the name of each of the persons appointed to act jointly.

  (6) Where persons are appointed to act jointly in respect of only some of the functions of the administrator of a company, this paragraph applies only in relation to those functions.

102 (1) This paragraph applies where two or more persons are appointed to act concurrently as the administrator of a company.

  (2) A reference to the administrator of a company in this Schedule is a reference to any of the persons appointed (or any combination of them).

103 (1) Where a company is in administration, a person may be appointed to act as administrator jointly or concurrently with the person or persons acting as the administrator of the company.

  (2) Where a company entered administration by administration order, an appointment under sub-paragraph (1) must be made by the court on the application of –

    (a)   a person or group listed in paragraph 12(1)(a) to (e), or

    (b)   the person or persons acting as the administrator of the company.

(3) Where a company entered administration by virtue of an appointment under paragraph 14, an appointment under sub-paragraph (1) must be made by –

   (a) the holder of the floating charge by virtue of which the appointment was made, or

   (b) the court on the application of the person or persons acting as the administrator of the company.

(4) Where a company entered administration by virtue of an appointment under paragraph 22(1), an appointment under sub-paragraph (1) above must be made either by the court on the application of the person or persons acting as the administrator of the company or –

   (a) by the company, and

   (b) with the consent of each person who is the holder of a qualifying floating charge in respect of the company's property or, where consent is withheld, with the permission of the court.

(5) Where a company entered administration by virtue of an appointment under paragraph 22(2), an appointment under sub-paragraph (1) must be made either by the court on the application of the person or persons acting as the administrator of the company or –

   (a) by the directors of the company, and

   (b) with the consent of each person who is the holder of a qualifying floating charge in respect of the company's property or, where consent is withheld, with the permission of the court.

(6) An appointment under sub-paragraph (1) may be made only with the consent of the person or persons acting as the administrator of the company.

Presumption of validity

104 An act of the administrator of a company is valid in spite of a defect in his appointment or qualification.

Majority decision of directors

105 A reference in this Schedule to something done by the directors of a company includes a reference to the same thing done by a majority of the directors of a company.

Penalties

106 (1) A person who is guilty of an offence under this Schedule is liable to a fine (in accordance with section 430 and Schedule 10).

   (2) A person who is guilty of an offence under any of the following paragraphs of this Schedule is liable to a daily default fine (in accordance with section 430 and Schedule 10) –

   (a) paragraph 20,
   (b) paragraph 32,
   (c) paragraph 46,
   (d) paragraph 48,
   (e) paragraph 49,
   (f) paragraph 51,
   (g) paragraph 53,
   (h) paragraph 54,

(i)   paragraph 56,
(j)   paragraph 71,
(k)   paragraph 72,
(l)   paragraph 77,
(m) paragraph 78,
(n)   paragraph 80,
(o)   paragraph 84,
(p)   paragraph 86, and
(q)   paragraph 89.

Extension of time limit

107 (1) Where a provision of this Schedule provides that a period may be varied in accordance with this paragraph, the period may be varied in respect of a company –

(a)   by the court, and
(b)   on the application of the administrator.

(2) A time period may be extended in respect of a company under this paragraph –

(a)   more than once, and
(b)   after expiry.

108 (1) A period specified in paragraph 49(5), 50(1)(b) or 51(2) may be varied in respect of a company by the administrator with consent.

(2) In sub-paragraph (1) 'consent' means consent of –

(a)   each secured creditor of the company, and
(b)   if the company has unsecured debts, creditors whose debts amount to more than 50% of the company's unsecured debts, disregarding debts of any creditor who does not respond to an invitation to give or withhold consent.

(3) But where the administrator has made a statement under paragraph 52(1)(b) 'consent' means –

(a)   consent of each secured creditor of the company, or
(b)   if the administrator thinks that a distribution may be made to preferential creditors, consent of –

(i)   each secured creditor of the company, and
(ii) preferential creditors whose debts amount to more than 50% of the total preferential debts of the company, disregarding debts of any creditor who does not respond to an invitation to give or withhold consent.

(4) Consent for the purposes of sub-paragraph (1) may be –

(a)   written, or
(b)   signified at a creditors' meeting.

(5) The power to extend under sub-paragraph (1) –

(a)   may be exercised in respect of a period only once,
(b)   may not be used to extend a period by more than 28 days,
(c)   may not be used to extend a period which has been extended by the court, and
(d)   may not be used to extend a period after expiry.

109 Where a period is extended under paragraph 107 or 108, a reference to the period shall be taken as a reference to the period as extended.

Amendment of provision about time

110 (1) The Secretary of State may by order amend a provision of this Schedule which –

      (a) requires anything to be done within a specified period of time,

      (b) prevents anything from being done after a specified time, or

      (c) requires a specified minimum period of notice to be given.

  (2) An order under this paragraph –

      (a) must be made by statutory instrument, and

      (b) shall be subject to annulment in pursuance of a resolution of either House of Parliament.

Interpretation

111 (1) In this Schedule –

      'administrative receiver' has the meaning given by section 251,

      'administrator' has the meaning given by paragraph 1 and, where the context requires, includes a reference to a former administrator,

      'company' includes a company which may enter administration by virtue of Article 3 of the EC Regulation,

      'correspondence' includes correspondence by telephonic or other electronic means,

      'creditors' meeting' has the meaning given by paragraph 50,

      'enters administration' has the meaning given by paragraph 1,

      'floating charge' means a charge which is a floating charge on its creation,

      'in administration' has the meaning given by paragraph 1,

      'hire-purchase agreement' includes a conditional sale agreement, a chattel leasing agreement and a retention of title agreement,

      'holder of a qualifying floating charge' in respect of a company's property has the meaning given by paragraph 14,

      'market value' means the amount which would be realised on a sale of property in the open market by a willing vendor,

      'the purpose of administration' means an objective specified in paragraph 3, and

      'unable to pay its debts' has the meaning given by section 123.

  (2) A reference in this Schedule to a thing in writing includes a reference to a thing in electronic form.

  (3) In this Schedule a reference to action includes a reference to inaction.

Scotland

112 In the application of this Schedule to Scotland –

      (a) a reference to filing with the court is a reference to lodging in court, and

      (b) a reference to a charge is a reference to a right in security.

113 Where property in Scotland is disposed of under paragraph 70 or 71, the administrator shall grant to the disponee an appropriate document of transfer or conveyance of the property, and –

      (a) that document, or

      (b) recording, intimation or registration of that document (where recording, intimation or registration of the document is a legal requirement for completion of title to the property),

has the effect of disencumbering the property of or, as the case may be, freeing the property from, the security.

114 In Scotland, where goods in the possession of a company under a hire-purchase agreement are disposed of under paragraph 72, the disposal has the effect of extinguishing as against the disponee all rights of the owner of the goods under the agreement.

115 (1)   In Scotland, the administrator of a company may make, in or towards the satisfaction of the debt secured by the floating charge, a payment to the holder of a floating charge which has attached to the property subject to the charge.

(2)   In Scotland, where the administrator thinks that the company has insufficient property to enable a distribution to be made to unsecured creditors other than by virtue of section 176A(2)(a), he may file a notice to that effect with the registrar of companies.

(3)   On delivery of the notice to the registrar of companies, any floating charge granted by the company shall, unless it has already so attached, attach to the property which is subject to the charge and that attachment shall have effect as if each floating charge is a fixed security over the property to which it has attached.

116 In Scotland, the administrator in making any payment in accordance with paragraph 115 shall make such payment subject to the rights of any of the following categories of persons (which rights shall, except to the extent provided in any instrument, have the following order of priority) –

(a)   the holder of any fixed security which is over property subject to the floating charge and which ranks prior to, or pari passu with, the floating charge,

(b)   creditors in respect of all liabilities and expenses incurred by or on behalf of the administrator,

(c)   the administrator in respect of his liabilities, expenses and remuneration and any indemnity to which he is entitled out of the property of the company,

(d)   the preferential creditors entitled to payment in accordance with paragraph 65,

(e)   the holder of the floating charge in accordance with the priority of that charge in relation to any other floating charge which has attached, and

(f)   the holder of a fixed security, other than one referred to in paragraph (a), which is over property subject to the floating charge.

SCHEDULE 17   ADMINISTRATION: MINOR AND CONSEQUENTIAL AMENDMENTS   Section 248

General

1   In any instrument made before section 248(1) to (3) of this Act comes into force –

(a)   a reference to the making of an administration order shall be treated as including a reference to the appointment of an administrator under paragraph 14 or 22 of Schedule B1 to the Insolvency Act 1986 (c. 45) (inserted by section 248(2) of this Act), and

(b)   a reference to making an application for an administration order by petition shall be treated as including a reference to making an administration application under that Schedule, appointing an administrator under paragraph 14 or 22 of that Schedule or giving notice under paragraph 15 or 26 of that Schedule.

Magistrates' Courts Act 1980 (c. 43)

2   In section 87A(1) of the Magistrates' Court Act 1980 (fine imposed on company) for 'section 9 or 124 of the Insolvency Act 1986' substitute 'section 124 of, or paragraph 12 of Schedule B1 to, the Insolvency Act 1986'.

Companies Act 1985 (c. 6)

3   The Companies Act 1985 shall be amended as follows.

4   In section 225 (alteration of accounting reference date) –

   (a)   in subsection (4) for 'an administration order is in force' substitute 'the company is in administration', and

   (b)   in subsection (6) for 'An accounting reference period may not in any case, unless an administration order is in force' substitute 'A company's accounting reference period may not in any case, unless the company is in administration'.

5   In section 425(1) (power of company to compromise) for 'an administration order being in force in relation to a company' substitute 'in administration'.

6   In section 427A(3) (mergers and divisions of public companies) for 'an administration order being in force in relation to the company' substitute 'where the company is in administration'.

7   In section 652B(3) (duty when applying to strike off defunct company) for paragraph (c) substitute –

   '(c)   the company is in administration under Part II of that Act;

   (ca)   an application to the court for an administration order in respect of the company has been made and not finally dealt with or withdrawn;

   (cb)   a copy of notice of intention to appoint an administrator of the company under paragraph 14 of Schedule B1 to that Act has been filed with the court and neither of the events mentioned in paragraph 44(2)(a) and (b) of that Schedule has occurred;

   (cc)   a copy of notice of intention to appoint an administrator of the company under paragraph 22 of that Schedule has been filed with the court and neither of the events mentioned in paragraph 44(4)(a) and (b) of that Schedule has occurred;'.

8   In section 652C(4) (director's duty following application to strike off defunct company) for paragraph (d) substitute –

   '(d)   an application to the court for an administration order in respect of the company is made under paragraph 12 of Schedule B1 to that Act;

   (da)   an administrator is appointed in respect of the company under paragraph 14 or 22 of that Schedule;

   (db)   a copy of notice of intention to appoint an administrator of the company under paragraph 14 or 22 of that Schedule is filed with the court;'.

Insolvency Act 1986 (c. 45)

9   The Insolvency Act 1986 shall be amended as follows.

10   In section 1 (proposal for company voluntary arrangement) –

   (a)   in subsection (1) for '(other than one for which an administration order is in force, or which is being wound up)' substitute '(other than one which is in administration or being wound up)', and

   (b)   in subsection (3) for paragraph (a) substitute –

   '(a)   where the company is in administration, by the administrator,'.

11   In section 5(3) (approval of company voluntary arrangement) –

    (a)   for 'an administration order is in force' substitute 'is in administration', and

    (b)   for 'discharge the administration order' substitute 'provide for the appointment of the administrator to cease to have effect'.

12   In section 6(2)(c) (challenge of decision in relation to company voluntary arrangement) for 'an administration order is in force' substitute 'is in administration'.

13   In section 51 (power to appoint receiver: Scotland) after subsection (2) insert –

    '(2A) Subsections (1) and (2) are subject to section 72A.'

14   At the end of section 100 (creditors' voluntary winding up of company: appointment of liquidator) add –

    '(4)   The court shall grant an application under subsection (3) made by the holder of a qualifying floating charge in respect of the company's property (within the meaning of paragraph 14 of Schedule B1) unless the court thinks it right to refuse the application because of the particular circumstances of the case.'

15   At the end of section 127 (winding-up: avoidance of property disposition) (which becomes subsection (1)) add –

    '(2)   This section has no effect in respect of anything done by an administrator of a company while a winding-up petition is suspended under paragraph 40 of Schedule B1.'

16   After section 129(1) (commencement of winding up) insert –

    '(1A) Where the court makes a winding-up order by virtue of paragraph 13(1)(e) of Schedule B1, the winding up is deemed to commence on the making of the order.'

17   In section 140 (appointment by court of liquidator following administration or voluntary arrangement) for subsection (1) substitute –

    '(1)   Where a winding-up order is made immediately upon the appointment of an administrator ceasing to have effect, the court may appoint as liquidator of the company the person whose appointment as administrator has ceased to have effect.'

18   In section 212 (misfeasance of officers) –

    (a)   in subsection (1)(b) omit ', administrator',

    (b)   in subsection (2) omit (in each place) 'or administrator', and

    (c)   in subsection (4) –

        (i)   omit 'or administrator', and

        (ii)   for 'that person' substitute 'he'.

19   Section 230(1) (administrator to be qualified insolvency practitioner) shall cease to have effect.

20   In section 231(1) and (2) (appointment to office of two or more persons) omit the word 'administrator,'.

21   In section 232 (validity of office-holder's act) omit the word 'administrator,'.

22   In section 233 (utility supplies) –

    (a)   for subsection (1)(a) substitute –

    '(a)   the company enters administration,', and

    (b)   for subsection (4)(a) substitute –

    '(a)   the date on which the company entered administration'.

23   For section 234(1)(a) (getting in the company's property) substitute –

    '(a)   the company enters administration,'.

24   For section 235(4)(a) (co-operation with office-holder) substitute –

'(a)   the date on which the company entered administration,'.

25   For section 238(1)(a) (transactions at an undervalue: England and Wales) substitute –

'(a) the company enters administration,'.

26   (1)   Section 240 (relevant time for sections 238 and 239) shall be amended as follows.
     (2)   For subsection (1)(c) substitute –

'(c)   in either case, at a time between the making of an administration application in respect of the company and the making of an administration order
on that application, and
(d)   in either case, at a time between the filing with the court of a copy of notice
of intention to appoint an administrator under paragraph 14 or 22 of
Schedule B1 and the making of an appointment under that paragraph.'

     (3)   The word 'and' after subsection (1)(b) shall cease to have effect.
     (4)   For subsection (3)(a), (aa) and (b) substitute –

'(a)   in a case where section 238 or 239 applies by reason of an administrator of
a company being appointed by administration order, the date on which the
administration application is made,
(b)   in a case where section 238 or 239 applies by reason of an administrator of
a company being appointed under paragraph 14 or 22 of Schedule B1 following filing with the court of a copy of a notice of intention to appoint
under that paragraph, the date on which the copy of the notice is filed,
(c)   in a case where section 238 or 239 applies by reason of an administrator of
a company being appointed otherwise than as mentioned in paragraph (a)
or (b), the date on which the appointment takes effect,
(d)   in a case where section 238 or 239 applies by reason of a company going
into liquidation either following conversion of administration into winding
up by virtue of Article 37 of the EC Regulation or at the time when the
appointment of an administrator ceases to have effect, the date on which
the company entered administration (or, if relevant, the date on which the
application for the administration order was made or a copy of the notice
of intention to appoint was filed), and
(e)   in a case where section 238 or 239 applies by reason of a company going
into liquidation at any other time, the date of the commencement of the
winding up.'

27   (1)   Section 241 (order under section 238 or 239) shall be amended as follows.
     (2)   For subsection (3A) substitute –

'(3A) Where section 238 or 239 applies by reason of a company's entering administration, a person has notice of the relevant proceedings if he has notice
that –

(a)   an administration application has been made,
(b)   an administration order has been made,
(c)   a copy of a notice of intention to appoint an administrator under
paragraph 14 or 22 of Schedule B1 has been filed, or
(d)   notice of the appointment of an administrator has been filed under
paragraph 18 or 29 of that Schedule.'

     (3)   For subsection (3B) substitute –

'(3B) Where section 238 or 239 applies by reason of a company's going into
liquidation at the time when the appointment of an administrator of the
company ceases to have effect, a person has notice of the relevant proceedings if he has notice that –

(a)   an administration application has been made,
(b)   an administration order has been made,

      (c)   a copy of a notice of intention to appoint an administrator under paragraph 14 or 22 of Schedule B1 has been filed,

      (d)   notice of the appointment of an administrator has been filed under paragraph 18 or 29 of that Schedule, or

      (e)   the company has gone into liquidation.'

28 (1) Section 242 (gratuitous alienations: Scotland) shall be amended as follows.

    (2) In subsection (1)(b) for 'an administration order is in force in relation to a company' substitute 'a company enters administration'.

    (3) In subsection (3)(a)(ii) for 'the administration order is made' substitute 'the company enters administration'.

29 (1) Section 243 (unfair preferences: Scotland) shall be amended as follows.

    (2) In subsection (1) for 'the making of an administration order in relation to the company' substitute 'the company enters administration'.

    (3) In subsection (4)(b) for 'in the case of an administration order' substitute 'where the company has entered administration'.

30 In section 244(2) (extortionate credit transaction) for 'the day on which the administration order was made or (as the case may be) the company went into liquidation' substitute 'the day on which the company entered administration or went into liquidation'.

31 (1) Section 245 (avoidance of floating charge) shall be amended as follows.

    (2) The word 'or' after subsection (3)(b) shall cease to have effect.

    (3) For subsection (3)(c) substitute –

      '(c)   in either case, at a time between the making of an administration application in respect of the company and the making of an administration order on that application, or

      (d)   in either case, at a time between the filing with the court of a copy of notice of intention to appoint an administrator under paragraph 14 or 22 of Schedule B1 and the making of an appointment under that paragraph.'

    (4) For subsection (5)(a) and (b) substitute –

      '(a)   in a case where this section applies by reason of an administrator of a company being appointed by administration order, the date on which the administration application is made,

      (b)   in a case where this section applies by reason of an administrator of a company being appointed under paragraph 14 or 22 of Schedule B1 following filing with the court of a copy of notice of intention to appoint under that paragraph, the date on which the copy of the notice is filed,

      (c)   in a case where this section applies by reason of an administrator of a company being appointed otherwise than as mentioned in paragraph (a) or (b), the date on which the appointment takes effect, and

      (d)   in a case where this section applies by reason of a company going into liquidation, the date of the commencement of the winding up.'

32 For section 246(1)(a) (unenforceability of lien on records) substitute –

      '(a)   the company enters administration,'.

33 (1) Section 247 (meaning of 'insolvency' and 'go into liquidation') shall be amended as follows.

    (2) In subsection (1) for 'the making of an administration order or the appointment of an administrative receiver' substitute 'or the appointment of an administrator or administrative receiver'.

    (3) For subsection (3) substitute –

      '(3)   The reference to a resolution for voluntary winding up in subsection (2) includes a reference to a resolution which is deemed to occur by virtue of –

          (a)   paragraph 83(6)(b) of Schedule B1, or

    (b)   an order made following conversion of administration or a voluntary arrangement into winding up by virtue of Article 37 of the EC Regulation.'

34 (1) Section 387 (preferential debts: 'the relevant date') shall be amended as follows.

    (2) In subsection (2) for paragraphs (a) and (b) substitute –

      '(a)   if the company is in administration, the date on which it entered administration, and

      (b)   if the company is not in administration, the date on which the voluntary arrangement takes effect.'

    (3) In subsection (3) –

      (a)   in paragraphs (a), (aa) and (ab) for 'the date of the making of the administration order' substitute 'the date on which the company entered administration',

      (b)   after paragraph (b) insert –

        '(ba) if the case does not fall within paragraph (a), (aa), (ab) or (b) and the company is being wound up following administration pursuant to paragraph 83 of Schedule B1, the relevant date is the date on which the company entered administration;', and

      (c)   in paragraph (c) for 'paragraph (a), (aa), (ab) or (b)' substitute 'paragraph (a), (aa), (ab), (b) or (ba)'.

    (4) After subsection (3) insert –

      '(3A) In relation to a company which is in administration (and to which no other provision of this section applies) the relevant date is the date on which the company enters administration.'

35 In section 422 (power to apply first Group of Parts to banks, &c.) for subsection (1) substitute –

      '(1) The Secretary of State may by order made with the concurrence of the Treasury and after consultation with the Financial Services Authority provide that specified provisions in the first Group of Parts shall apply with specified modifications in relation to any person who –

      (a)   has a liability in respect of a deposit which he accepted in accordance with the Banking Act 1979 (c. 37) or 1987 (c. 22), but

      (b)   does not have permission under Part IV of the Financial Services and Markets Act 2000 (c. 8) (regulated activities) to accept deposits.

    (1A) Subsection (1)(b) shall be construed in accordance with –

      (a)   section 22 of the Financial Services and Markets Act 2000 (classes of regulated activity and categories of investment),

      (b)   any relevant order under that section, and

      (c)   Schedule 2 to that Act (regulated activities).'

36 In section 424(1)(a) (application for order in relation to transaction defrauding creditor) for 'in relation to which an administration order is in force' substitute 'is in administration'.

37 (1) Schedule A1 (moratorium where directors propose voluntary arrangement) shall be amended as follows.

    (2) In paragraph 4(1) (exclusion from eligibility for moratorium) –

      (a)   for paragraph (a) substitute –

        '(a)   the company is in administration,', and

      (b)   after paragraph (f) (and before the word 'or') insert –

        '(fa) an administrator appointed under paragraph 22 of Schedule B1 has held office in the period of 12 months ending with the date of filing,'.

(3) In paragraph 12(1) (effect of moratorium on creditor) for paragraph (d) substitute –

'(d) no administration application may be made in respect of the company,

(da) no administrator of the company may be appointed under paragraph 14 or 22 of Schedule B1,'.

(4) In paragraph 40 (challenge of directors' actions during moratorium) for sub-paragraph (7) substitute –

'(7) Sub-paragraph (8) applies where –

(a) the appointment of an administrator has effect in relation to the company and the appointment took effect before the moratorium came into force, or

(b) the company is being wound up in pursuance of a petition presented before the moratorium came into force.

(8) No application for an order under this paragraph may be made by a creditor or member of the company; but such an application may be made instead by the administrator or (as the case may be) the liquidator.'

38 (1) Schedule 8 (scope of insolvency rules) shall be amended as follows.

(2) At the end of paragraph 2 (which becomes sub-paragraph (1)) add –

'(2) Rules made by virtue of this paragraph about the consequence of failure to comply with practice or procedure may, in particular, include provision about the termination of administration.'

(3) In paragraph 10 (provision as to committees) for 'section 26, 49, 68, 101, 141 or 142 of this Act' substitute 'section 49, 68, 101, 141 or 142 of, or paragraph 57 of Schedule B1 to, this Act'.

(4) After paragraph 14 insert –

'14A. Provision about the application of section 176A of this Act which may include, in particular –

(a) provision enabling a receiver to institute winding up proceedings;

(b) provision requiring a receiver to institute winding up proceedings.'

(5) After paragraph 14A (inserted by sub-paragraph (4) above) insert –

'*Administration*

14B. Provision which –

(a) applies in relation to administration, with or without modifications, a provision of Parts IV to VII of this Act, or

(b) serves a purpose in relation to administration similar to a purpose that may be served by the rules in relation to winding up by virtue of a provision of this Schedule.'

(6) In paragraph 29 (general provision) for 'section 22, 47, 66, 131, 143(2) or 235 of this Act' substitute 'section 47, 66, 131, 143(2) or 235 of, or paragraph 47 of Schedule B1 to, this Act'.

39 (1) Schedule 10 (punishment of offences) shall be amended as follows.

(2) After the entries for Schedule A1 insert –

'Sch. B1, para. 18(7).	Making false statement in statutory declaration where administrator appointed by holder of floating charge.	1. On indictment. 2. Summary.	2 years, or a fine or both. 6 months, or the statutory maximum or both.	
Sch. B1, para. 20.	Holder of floating charge failing to notify administrator or others of commencement of appointment.	1. On indictment. 2. Summary.	2 years, or a fine or both. 6 months, or the statutory maximum or both.	One-tenth of the statutory maximum.

Sch. B1, para. 27(4).	Making false statement in statutory declaration where appointment of administrator proposed by company or directors.	1. On indictment. 2. Summary.	2 years, or a fine or both. 6 months, or the statutory maximum or both.	
Sch. B1, para. 29(7).	Making false statement in statutory declaration where administrator appointed by company or directors.	1. On indictment. 2. Summary.	2 years, or a fine or both. 6 months, or the statutory maximum or both.	
Sch. B1, para. 32.	Company or directors failing to notify administrator or others of commencement of appointment.	1. On indictment. 2. Summary.	2 years, or a fine or both. 6 months, or the statutory maximum or both.	One-tenth of the statutory maximum.
Sch. B1, para. 45(2).	Administrator, company or officer failing to state in business document that administrator appointed.	Summary.	One-fifth of the statutory maximum.	
Sch. B1, para. 46(9).	Administrator failing to give notice of his appointment.	Summary.	One-fifth of the statutory maximum.	One-fiftieth of the statutory maximum.
Sch. B1, para. 48(4).	Failing to comply with provisions about statement of affairs where administrator appointed.	1. On indictment. 2. Summary.	A fine. The statutory maximum.	One-tenth of the statutory maximum.
Sch. B1, para. 49(7).	Administrator failing to send out statement of his proposals.	Summary.	One-fifth of the statutory maximum.	One-fiftieth of the statutory maximum.
Sch. B1, para. 51(5).	Administrator failing to arrange initial creditors' meeting.	Summary.	One-fifth of the statutory maximum.	One-fiftieth of the statutory maximum.
Sch. B1, para. 53(3).	Administrator failing to report decision taken at initial creditors' meeting.	Summary.	One-fifth of the statutory maximum.	One-fiftieth of the statutory maximum.
Sch. B1, para. 54(7).	Administrator failing to report decision taken at creditors' meeting summoned to consider revised proposal.	Summary	One-fifth of the statutory maximum.	One-fiftieth of the statutory maximum.
Sch. B1, para. 56(2).	Administrator failing to summon creditors' meeting.	Summary.	One-fifth of the statutory maximum.	One-fiftieth of the statutory maximum.
Sch. B1, para. 71(6).	Administrator failing to file court order enabling disposal of charged property.	Summary.	One-fifth of the statutory maximum.	One-fiftieth of the statutory maximum.
Sch. B1, para. 72(5).	Administrator failing to file court order enabling disposal of hire-purchase property.	Summary.	One-fifth of the statutory maximum.	One-fiftieth of the statutory maximum.
Sch. B1, para. 77(3).	Administrator failing to notify Registrar of Companies of automatic end of administration.	Summary.	One-fifth of the statutory maximum.	One-fiftieth of the statutory maximum.
Sch. B1, para. 78(6).	Administrator failing to give notice of extension by consent of term of office.	Summary.	One-fifth of the statutory maximum.	One-fiftieth of the statutory maximum.

Sch. B1, para. 80(6).	Administrator failing to give notice of termination of administration where objective achieved.	Summary.	One-fifth of the statutory maximum.	One-fiftieth of the statutory maximum.
Sch. B1, para. 84(9).	Administrator failing to comply with provisions where company moves to dissolution.	Summary.	One-fifth of the statutory maximum.	One-fiftieth of the statutory maximum.
Sch. B1, para. 86(3).	Administrator failing to notify Registrar of Companies where court terminates administration.	Summary.	One-fifth of the statutory maximum.	One-fiftieth of the statutory maximum.
Sch. B1, para. 89(3).	Administrator failing to give notice on ceasing to be qualified.	Summary.	One-fifth of the statutory maximum.	One-fiftieth of the statutory maximum.'

(3) Omit the entries for the following provisions –

    (a) section 12(2),

    (b) section 15(8),

    (c) section 18(5),

    (d) section 21(3),

    (e) section 22(6),

    (f) section 23(3),

    (g) section 24(7), and

    (h) section 27(6).

Company Directors Disqualification Act 1986 (c. 46)

40 The Company Directors Disqualification Act 1986 shall be amended as follows.

41 In section 6 (duty of court to disqualify unfit director of insolvent company) –

    (a) for subsection (2)(b) substitute –

      '(b) the company enters administration,',

    (b) for subsection (3)(c) substitute –

      '(c) where neither paragraph (a) nor (b) applies but an administrator or administrative receiver has at any time been appointed in respect of the company in question, any court which has jurisdiction to wind it up.', and

    (c) for subsection (3A)(b) substitute –

      '(b) in a case within paragraph (c) of that subsection, to the appointment of the administrator or (as the case may be) administrative receiver.'

42 In section 7(3) (duty of office-holder to report to Secretary of State) for paragraph (c) substitute –

      '(c) in the case of a company which is in administration, the administrator,'.

Companies Act 1989 (c. 40)

43 The Companies Act 1989 shall be amended as follows.

44 In section 158 (modification of insolvency law) –

    (a) in subsection (3) for paragraph (b) substitute –

      '(b) the application for an administration order or the presentation of a winding-up petition or the passing of a resolution for voluntary winding up,', and

(b)   after subsection (3) insert –

'(3A) In subsection (3)(h) the reference to an application for an administration order shall be taken to include a reference to –

(a)   in a case where an administrator is appointed under paragraph 14 or 22 of Schedule B1 to the Insolvency Act 1986 (appointment by floating charge holder, company or directors) following filing with the court of a copy of a notice of intention to appoint under that paragraph, the filing of the copy of the notice, and

(b)   in a case where an administrator is appointed under either of those paragraphs without a copy of a notice of intention to appoint having been filed with the court, the appointment of the administrator.'

45   In section 161(4) (disapplication of enactments to default proceedings) for 'sections 10(1)(c), 11(3), 126, 128, 130, 185 or 285 of the Insolvency Act 1986' substitute 'section 126, 128, 130, 185 or 285 of, or paragraph 42 or 43 (including paragraph 43(6) as applied by paragraph 44) of Schedule B1 to, the Insolvency Act 1986'.

46   After section 167(1) (application by exchange or clearing house about taking default proceedings) insert –

'(1A) In subsection (1) a reference to an administration order shall be taken to include a reference to the appointment of an administrator under –

(a)   paragraph 14 of Schedule B1 to the Insolvency Act 1986 (c.45) (appointment by holder of qualifying floating charge), or

(b)   paragraph 22 of that Schedule (appointment by company or directors).'

47   (1)   Section 175 (financial markets: administration) shall be amended as follows.

(2)   For subsection (1) substitute –

'(1)   The following provisions of Schedule B1 to the Insolvency Act 1986 (administration) do not apply in relation to a market charge –

(a)   paragraph 43(2) and (3) (restriction on enforcement of security or repossession of goods) (including that provision as applied by paragraph 44 (interim moratorium)), and

(b)   paragraphs 70, 71 and 72 (power of administrator to deal with charged or hire-purchase property).

(1A)   Paragraph 41(2) of that Schedule (receiver to vacate office at request of administrator) does not apply to a receiver appointed under a market charge.'

(3)   In subsection (2) for 'an administration order has been made or a petition for an administration order has been presented' substitute 'the occurrence of an event to which subsection (2A) applies'.

(4)   After subsection (2) insert –

'(2A) This subsection applies to –

(a)   making an administration application under paragraph 12 of Schedule B1 to the Insolvency Act 1986,

(b)   appointing an administrator under paragraph 14 or 22 of that Schedule (appointment by floating charge holder, company or directors),

(c)   filing with the court a copy of notice of intention to appoint an administrator under either of those paragraphs.'

Coal Industry Act 1994 (c. 21)

48   (1)   Section 36 of the Coal Industry Act 1994 (insolvency of licensed operator) shall be amended as follows.

(2)   After subsection (2) insert –

'(2A) Where the administrator of a company which is or has been a licensed operator files a notice with the registrar of companies under paragraph 84(1) of Schedule B1 to the Insolvency Act 1986 (c. 45) (administration: moving to dissolution), he shall at the same time send a copy to the Authority.'

(3)   In subsection (3) –

(a)   after 'liquidator' insert 'or administrator', and
(b)   after 'subsection (2)' insert 'or (2A)'.

Employment Rights Act 1996 (c. 18)

49   (1)   The Employment Rights Act 1996 shall be amended as follows.

(2)   In section 166(7) (application by employee for payment by Secretary of State) –

(a)   in paragraph (a) omit 'or an administration order', and
(b)   after paragraph (a) insert –

'(aa) if the company is in administration for the purposes of the Insolvency Act 1986,'.

(3)   In section 183(3)(a) (insolvency of employer) –

(a)   in paragraph (a) omit 'or an administration order', and
(b)   after paragraph (a) insert –

'(aa) if the company is in administration for the purposes of the Insolvency Act 1986,'.

(4)   Omit section 189(4) (transfer to Secretary of State of rights and remedies: priority of preferential debts).

Housing Act 1996 (c. 52)

50   The Housing Act 1996 shall be amended as follows.

51   At the end of section 40 (initial notice to be given to Housing Corporation or Housing for Wales) add –

'(7)   Subsections (8) and (9) apply in relation to the reference in subsection (3) to applying for an administration order.

(8)   In a case where an administrator is appointed under paragraph 14 or 22 of Schedule B1 to the Insolvency Act 1986 (appointment by floating charge holder, company or directors) –

(a)   the reference includes a reference to appointing an administrator under that paragraph, and
(b)   in respect of an appointment under either of those paragraphs the reference to the applicant shall be taken as a reference to the person making the appointment.

(9)   In a case where a copy of a notice of intention to appoint an administrator under either of those paragraphs is filed with the court –

(a)   the reference shall be taken to include a reference to the filing of the copy of the notice, and
(b)   in respect of the filing of a copy of a notice of intention to appoint

under either of those paragraphs the reference to the applicant shall be taken as a reference to the person giving the notice.'

52   At the end of section 41 (further notice to be given to Housing Corporation or Housing for Wales) add –

'(6) In subsection (3) –

(a)   the reference to the making of an administration order includes a reference to appointing an administrator under paragraph 14 or 22 of Schedule B1 to the Insolvency Act 1986 (administration), and

(b)   in respect of an appointment under either of those paragraphs the reference to the applicant shall be taken as a reference to the person making the appointment.'

Financial Services and Markets Act 2000 (c. 8)

53   The Financial Services and Markets Act 2000 shall be amended as follows.

54   (1)   Section 215 (provision of Financial Services Compensation Scheme in relation to insolvency) shall be amended as follows.

(2)   In subsection (3) for 'presents a petition under section 9 of the 1986 Act or Article 22 of the 1989 Order' substitute 'makes an administration application under Schedule B1 to the 1986 Act or presents a petition under Article 22 of the 1989 Order'.

(3)   After subsection (3) insert –

'(3A)   In subsection (3) the reference to making an administration application includes a reference to –

(a)   appointing an administrator under paragraph 14 or 22 of Schedule B1 to the 1986 Act, or

(b)   filing with the court a copy of notice of intention to appoint an administrator under either of those paragraphs.'

55   For section 359 (administration order) substitute –

'**359 Administration order**

(1)   The Authority may make an administration application under Schedule B1 to the 1986 Act (or present a petition under Article 22 of the 1989 Order) in relation to a company or insolvent partnership which –

(a)   is or has been an authorised person,

(b)   is or has been an appointed representative, or

(c)   is carrying on or has carried on a regulated activity in contravention of the general prohibition.

(2)   Subsection (3) applies in relation to an administration application made (or a petition presented) by the Authority by virtue of this section.

(3)   Any of the following shall be treated for the purpose of paragraph 11(a) of Schedule B1 to the 1986 Act (or Article 21(1)(a) of the 1989 Order) as unable to pay its debts –

(a)   a company or partnership in default on an obligation to pay a sum due and payable under an agreement, and

(b)   an authorised deposit taker in default on an obligation to pay a sum due and payable in respect of a relevant deposit.

(4)   In this section –

"agreement" means an agreement the making or performance of which constitutes or is part of a regulated activity carried on by the company or partnership, "authorised deposit taker" means a person with a Part IV permission to accept deposits (but not a person who has a Part IV permission to accept deposits only for the purpose of carrying on another regulated activity in accordance with that permission),

"company" means a company –

    (a)   in respect of which an administrator may be appointed under Schedule B1 to the 1986 Act, or

    (b)   to which Article 21 of the 1989 Order applies, and

"relevant deposit" shall, ignoring any restriction on the meaning of deposit arising from the identity of the person making the deposit, be construed in accordance with –

    (a)   section 22,

    (b)   any relevant order under that section, and

    (c)   Schedule 2.

(5)   The definition of "authorised deposit taker" in subsection (4) shall be construed in accordance with –

    (a)   section 22,

    (b)   any relevant order under that section, and

    (c)   Schedule 2.'

56   For section 361 (administrator to report to Authority) substitute –

'361 Administrator's duty to report to Authority

(1)   This section applies where a company or partnership is –

    (a)   in administration within the meaning of Schedule B1 to the 1986 Act, or

    (b)   the subject of an administration order under Part III of the 1989 Order.

(2)   If the administrator thinks that the company or partnership is carrying on or has carried on a regulated activity in contravention of the general prohibition, he must report to the Authority without delay.

(3)   Subsection (2) does not apply where the administration arises out of an administration order made on an application made or petition presented by the Authority.'

57   In section 362 (Financial Services Authority's right to participate in proceedings) –

    (a)   in subsection (1) for 'presents a petition to the court under section 9 of the 1986 Act (or Article 22 of the 1989 Order)' substitute 'makes an administration application under Schedule B1 to the 1986 Act (or presents a petition under Article 22 of the 1989 Order)',

    (b)   after subsection (1) insert –

'(1A) This section also applies in relation to –

    (a)   the appointment under paragraph 14 or 22 of Schedule B1 to the 1986 Act of an administrator of a company of a kind described in subsection (1)(a) to (c), or

    (b)   the filing with the court of a copy of notice of intention to appoint an administrator under either of those paragraphs.',

    (c)   in subsection (2)(a) for 'petition' substitute 'administration application or the petition',

    (d)   for subsection (4) substitute –

'(4)   The Authority may apply to the court under paragraph 74 of Schedule B1 to the 1986 Act (or Article 39 of the 1989 Order).

(4A) In respect of an application under subsection (4) –

    (a)   paragraph 74(1)(a) and (b) shall have effect as if for the words "harm the interests of the applicant (whether alone or in common with some or all other members or creditors)" there were substituted the words "harm the interests of some or all members or creditors", and

    (b)   Article 39 of the 1989 Order shall have effect with the omission of the words "(including at least himself')".", and

(e)   in subsection (5)(b) for 'section 26 of the 1986 Act' substitute 'paragraph 57 of Schedule B1 to the 1986 Act'.

58   After section 362 insert –

'362A Administrator appointed by company or directors

(1)   This section applies in relation to a company of a kind described in section 362(1)(a) to (c).

(2)   An administrator of the company may not be appointed under paragraph 22 of Schedule B1 to the 1986 Act without the consent of the Authority.

(3)   Consent under subsection (2) –

    (a)   must be in writing, and

    (b)   must be filed with the court along with the notice of intention to appoint under paragraph 27 of that Schedule.

(4)   In a case where no notice of intention to appoint is required –

    (a)   subsection (3)(b) shall not apply, but

    (b)   consent under subsection (2) must accompany the notice of appointment filed under paragraph 29 of that Schedule.'

59   In section 427A(3) (mergers and divisions of public companies) for 'an administration order being in force in relation to the company' substitute 'where the company is in administration'.

SCHEDULE 18   SCHEDULE 2A TO INSOLVENCY ACT 1986

Section 250

SCHEDULE 2A   EXCEPTIONS TO PROHIBITION ON APPOINTMENT OF ADMINISTRATIVE RECEIVER: SUPPLEMENTARY PROVISIONS

Capital market arrangement

1   (1)   For the purposes of section 72B an arrangement is a capital market arrangement if –

    (a)   it involves a grant of security to a person holding it as trustee for a person who holds a capital market investment issued by a party to the arrangement, or

    (b)   at least one party guarantees the performance of obligations of another party, or

    (c)   at least one party provides security in respect of the performance of obligations of another party, or

    (d)   the arrangement involves an investment of a kind described in articles 83 to 85 of the Financial Services and Markets Act 2000 (Regulated Activities) Order 2001 (S.I. 2001/544) (options, futures and contracts for differences).

(2)   For the purposes of sub-paragraph (1) –

    (a)   a reference to holding as trustee includes a reference to holding as nominee or agent,

(b) a reference to holding for a person who holds a capital market investment includes a reference to holding for a number of persons at least one of whom holds a capital market investment, and

(c) a person holds a capital market investment if he has a legal or beneficial interest in it.

(3) In section 72B(1) and this paragraph 'party' to an arrangement includes a party to an agreement which –

(a) forms part of the arrangement,

(b) provides for the raising of finance as part of the arrangement, or

(c) is necessary for the purposes of implementing the arrangement.

Capital market investment

2 (1) For the purposes of section 72B an investment is a capital market investment if it –

(a) is within article 77 of the Financial Services and Markets Act 2000 (Regulated Activities) Order 2001 (S.I. 2001/544) (debt instruments), and

(b) is rated, listed or traded or designed to be rated, listed or traded.

(2) In sub-paragraph (1) –

'rated' means rated for the purposes of investment by an internationally recognised rating agency,

'listed' means admitted to the official list within the meaning given by section 103(1) of the Financial Services and Markets Act 2000 (c. 8) (interpretation), and

'traded' means admitted to trading on a market established under the rules of a recognised investment exchange or on a foreign market.

(3) In sub-paragraph (2) –

'recognised investment exchange' has the meaning given by section 285 of the Financial Services and Markets Act 2000 (recognised investment exchange), and

'foreign market' has the same meaning as 'relevant market' in article 67(2) of the Financial Services and Markets Act 2000 (Financial Promotion) Order 2001 (S.I. 2001/1335) (foreign markets).

3 (1) An investment is also a capital market investment for the purposes of section 72B if it consists of a bond or commercial paper issued to one or more of the following –

(a) an investment professional within the meaning of article 19(5) of the Financial Services and Markets Act 2000 (Financial Promotion) Order 2001,

(b) a person who is, when the agreement mentioned in section 72B(1) is entered into, a certified high net worth individual in relation to a communication within the meaning of article 48(2) of that order,

(c) a person to whom article 49(2) of that order applies (high net worth company, &c.),

(d) a person who is, when the agreement mentioned in section 72B(1) is entered into, a certified sophisticated investor in relation to a communication within the meaning of article 50(1) of that order, and

(e) a person in a State other than the United Kingdom who under the law of that State is not prohibited from investing in bonds or commercial paper.

(2) In sub-paragraph (1) –

'bond' shall be construed in accordance with article 77 of the Financial

Services and Markets Act 2000 (Regulated Activities) Order 2001 (S.I. 2001/544), and

'commercial paper' has the meaning given by article 9(3) of that order.

(3) For the purposes of sub-paragraph (1) –

    (a)   in applying article 19(5) of the Financial Promotion Order for the purposes of sub-paragraph (1)(a) –

        (i)   in article 19(5)(b), ignore the words after 'exempt person',

        (ii)   in article 19(5)(c)(i), for the words from 'the controlled activity' to the end substitute 'a controlled activity', and

        (iii)   in article 19(5)(e) ignore the words from 'where the communication' to the end, and

    (b)   in applying article 49(2) of that order for the purposes of sub-paragraph (1)(c), ignore article 49(2)(e).

'Agreement'

4   For the purposes of sections 72B and 72E and this Schedule 'agreement' includes an agreement or undertaking effected by –

    (a)   contract,

    (b)   deed, or

    (c)   any other instrument intended to have effect in accordance with the law of England and Wales, Scotland or another jurisdiction.

Debt

5   The debt of at least £50 million referred to in section 72B(1)(a) or 72E(2)(a) –

    (a)   may be incurred at any time during the life of the capital market arrangement or financed project, and

    (b)   may be expressed wholly or partly in foreign currency (in which case the sterling equivalent shall be calculated as at the time when the arrangement is entered into or the project begins).

Step-in rights

6   (1) For the purposes of sections 72C to 72E a project has 'step-in rights' if a person who provides finance in connection with the project has a conditional entitlement under an agreement to –

    (a)   assume sole or principal responsibility under an agreement for carrying out all or part of the project, or

    (b)   make arrangements for carrying out all or part of the project.

    (2) In sub-paragraph (1) a reference to the provision of finance includes a reference to the provision of an indemnity.

Project company

7   (1) For the purposes of sections 72C to 72E a company is a 'project company' of a project if –

    (a)   it holds property for the purpose of the project,

    (b)   it has sole or principal responsibility under an agreement for carrying out all or part of the project,

    (c)   it is one of a number of companies which together carry out the project,

    (d)   it has the purpose of supplying finance to enable the project to be carried out, or

    (e)   it is the holding company of a company within any of paragraphs (a) to (d).

(2)   But a company is not a 'project company' of a project if –

    (a)   it performs a function within sub-paragraph (1)(a) to (d) or is within sub-paragraph (1)(e), but

    (b)   it also performs a function which is not –

       (i)   within sub-paragraph (1)(a) to (d),

       (ii)   related to a function within sub-paragraph (1)(a) to (d), or

       (iii)   related to the project.

(3)   For the purposes of this paragraph a company carries out all or part of a project whether or not it acts wholly or partly through agents.

'Resources'

8   In section 72C 'resources' includes –

    (a)   funds (including payment for the provision of services or facilities),

    (b)   assets,

    (c)   professional skill,

    (d)   the grant of a concession or franchise, and

    (e)   any other commercial resource.

'Public body'

9 (1)   In section 72C 'public body' means –

    (a)   a body which exercises public functions,

    (b)   a body specified for the purposes of this paragraph by the Secretary of State, and

    (c)   a body within a class specified for the purposes of this paragraph by the Secretary of State.

(2)   A specification under sub-paragraph (1) may be –

    (a)   general, or

    (b)   for the purpose of the application of section 72C to a specified case.

Regulated business

10 (1)   For the purposes of section 72D a business is regulated if it is carried on –

    (a)   in reliance on a licence granted to a person under section 7 of the Telecommunications Act 1984 (c. 12) (telecommunications service),

    (b)   in reliance on a licence under section 7 or 7A of the Gas Act 1986 (c. 44) (transport and supply of gas),

    (c)   in reliance on a licence granted by virtue of section 41C of that Act (power to prescribe additional licensable activity),

    (d)   in reliance on a licence under section 6 of the Electricity Act 1989 (c. 29) (supply of electricity),

    (e)   by a water undertaker,

    (f)   by a sewerage undertaker,

    (g)   by a universal service provider within the meaning given by section 4(3) and (4) of the Postal Services Act 2000 (c. 26),

    (h)   by the Post Office company within the meaning given by section 62 of that Act (transfer of property),

(i)   by a relevant subsidiary of the Post Office Company within the meaning given by section 63 of that Act (government holding),

(j)   in reliance on a licence under section 8 of the Railways Act 1993 (c. 43) (railway services),

(k)   in reliance on a licence exemption under section 7 of that Act (subject to sub-paragraph (2) below),

(l)   by the operator of a system of transport which is deemed to be a railway for a purpose of Part I of that Act by virtue of section 81(2) of that Act (tramways, &c.), or

(m)   by the operator of a vehicle carried on flanged wheels along a system within paragraph (l).

(2)   Sub-paragraph (1)(k) does not apply to the operator of a railway asset on a railway unless on some part of the railway there is a permitted line speed exceeding 40 kilometres per hour.

'Person'

11   A reference to a person in this Schedule includes a reference to a partnership or another unincorporated group of persons.

SCHEDULE 19   DURATION OF BANKRUPTCY: TRANSITIONAL PROVISIONS   Section 256

Introduction

1   This Schedule applies to an individual who immediately before commencement –

(a)   has been adjudged bankrupt, and

(b)   has not been discharged from the bankruptcy.

2   In this Schedule –

'commencement' means the date appointed under section 279 for the commencement of section 256, and

'pre-commencement bankrupt' means an individual to whom this Schedule applies.

Neither old law nor new law to apply

3   Section 279 of the Insolvency Act 1986 (c. 45) (bankruptcy: discharge) shall not apply to a pre-commencement bankrupt (whether in its pre-commencement or its post-commencement form).

General rule for discharge from pre-commencement bankruptcy

4   (1)   A pre-commencement bankrupt is discharged from bankruptcy at whichever is the earlier of –

(a)   the end of the period of one year beginning with commencement, and

(b)   the end of the relevant period applicable to the bankrupt under section 279(1)(b) of the Insolvency Act 1986 (duration of bankruptcy) as it had effect immediately before commencement.

(2)   An order made under section 279(3) of that Act before commencement –

(a)   shall continue to have effect in respect of the pre-commencement bankrupt after commencement, and

(b)   may be varied or revoked after commencement by an order under section 279(3) as substituted by section 256 of this Act.

(3)   Section 279(3) to (5) of that Act as substituted by section 256 of this Act shall have effect after commencement in relation to the period mentioned in sub-paragraph (1)(a) or (b) above.

Second-time bankruptcy

5   (1)   This paragraph applies to a pre-commencement bankrupt who was an undischarged bankrupt at some time during the period of 15 years ending with the day before the date on which the pre-commencement bankruptcy commenced.

(2)   The pre-commencement bankrupt shall not be discharged from bankruptcy in accordance with paragraph 4 above.

(3)   An order made before commencement under section 280(2)(b) or (c) of the Insolvency Act 1986 (c. 45) (discharge by order of the court) shall continue to have effect after commencement (including any provision made by the court by virtue of section 280(3)).

(4)   A pre-commencement bankrupt to whom this paragraph applies (and in respect of whom no order is in force under section 280(2)(b) or (c) on commencement) is discharged –

(a)   at the end of the period of five years beginning with commencement, or

(b)   at such earlier time as the court may order on an application under section 280 of the Insolvency Act 1986 (discharge by order) heard after commencement.

(5)   Section 279(3) to (5) of the Insolvency Act 1986 as substituted by section 256 of this Act shall have effect after commencement in relation to the period mentioned in sub-paragraph (4)(a) above.

(6)   A bankruptcy annulled under section 282 shall be ignored for the purpose of sub-paragraph (1).

Criminal bankruptcy

6   A pre-commencement bankrupt who was adjudged bankrupt on a petition under section 264(1)(d) of the Insolvency Act 1986 (criminal bankruptcy) –

(a)   shall not be discharged from bankruptcy in accordance with paragraph 4 above, but

(b)   may be discharged from bankruptcy by an order of the court under section 280 of that Act.

Income payments order

7   (1)   This paragraph applies where –

(a)   a pre-commencement bankrupt is discharged by virtue of paragraph 4(1)(a), and

(b)   an income payments order is in force in respect of him immediately before his discharge.

(2)   If the income payments order specifies a date after which it is not to have effect, it shall continue in force until that date (and then lapse).

(3)   But the court may on the application of the pre-commencement bankrupt –

(a)   vary the income payments order;

(b) provide for the income payments order to cease to have effect before the date referred to in sub-paragraph (2).

Bankruptcy restrictions order or undertaking

8   A provision of this Schedule which provides for an individual to be discharged from bankruptcy is subject to –

(a) any bankruptcy restrictions order (or interim order) which may be made in relation to that individual, and

(b) any bankruptcy restrictions undertaking entered into by that individual.

SCHEDULE 20   SCHEDULE 4A TO INSOLVENCY ACT 1986

Section 257

SCHEDULE 4A   BANKRUPTCY RESTRICTIONS ORDER AND UNDERTAKING

Bankruptcy restrictions order

1   (1) A bankruptcy restrictions order may be made by the court.

(2) An order may be made only on the application of –

(a) the Secretary of State, or

(b) the official receiver acting on a direction of the Secretary of State.

Grounds for making order

2   (1) The court shall grant an application for a bankruptcy restrictions order if it thinks it appropriate having regard to the conduct of the bankrupt (whether before or after the making of the bankruptcy order).

(2) The court shall, in particular, take into account any of the following kinds of behaviour on the part of the bankrupt –

(a) failing to keep records which account for a loss of property by the bankrupt, or by a business carried on by him, where the loss occurred in the period beginning 2 years before petition and ending with the date of the application;

(b) failing to produce records of that kind on demand by the official receiver or the trustee;

(c) entering into a transaction at an undervalue;

(d) giving a preference;

(e) making an excessive pension contribution;

(f) a failure to supply goods or services which were wholly or partly paid for which gave rise to a claim provable in the bankruptcy;

(g) trading at a time before commencement of the bankruptcy when the bankrupt knew or ought to have known that he was himself to be unable to pay his debts;

(h) incurring, before commencement of the bankruptcy, a debt which the bankrupt had no reasonable expectation of being able to pay;

(i) failing to account satisfactorily to the court, the official receiver or the trustee for a loss of property or for an insufficiency of property to meet bankruptcy debts;

(j)   carrying on any gambling, rash and hazardous speculation or unreasonable extravagance which may have materially contributed to or increased the extent of the bankruptcy or which took place between presentation of the petition and commencement of the bankruptcy;

(k)   neglect of business affairs of a kind which may have materially contributed to or increased the extent of the bankruptcy;

(l)   fraud or fraudulent breach of trust;

(m)   failing to cooperate with the official receiver or the trustee.

(3)   The court shall also, in particular, consider whether the bankrupt was an undischarged bankrupt at some time during the period of six years ending with the date of the bankruptcy to which the application relates.

(4)   For the purpose of sub-paragraph (2) –

'before petition' shall be construed in accordance with section 351(c),

'excessive pension contribution' shall be construed in accordance with section 342A,

'preference' shall be construed in accordance with section 340, and

'undervalue' shall be construed in accordance with section 339.

Timing of application for order

3   (1)   An application for a bankruptcy restrictions order in respect of a bankrupt must be made –

(a)   before the end of the period of one year beginning with the date on which the bankruptcy commences, or

(b)   with the permission of the court.

(2)   The period specified in sub-paragraph (1)(a) shall cease to run in respect of a bankrupt while the period set for his discharge is suspended under section 279(3).

Duration of order

4   (1)   A bankruptcy restrictions order –

(a)   shall come into force when it is made, and

(b)   shall cease to have effect at the end of a date specified in the order.

(2)   The date specified in a bankruptcy restrictions order under sub-paragraph (1)(b) must not be –

(a)   before the end of the period of two years beginning with the date on which the order is made, or

(b)   after the end of the period of 15 years beginning with that date.

Interim bankruptcy restrictions order

5   (1)   This paragraph applies at any time between –

(a)   the institution of an application for a bankruptcy restrictions order, and

(b)   the determination of the application.

(2)   The court may make an interim bankruptcy restrictions order if the court thinks that –

(a)   there are prima facie grounds to suggest that the application for the bankruptcy restrictions order will be successful, and

(b)   it is in the public interest to make an interim order.

(3)   An interim order may be made only on the application of –

    (a)   the Secretary of State, or

    (b)   the official receiver acting on a direction of the Secretary of State.

(4)   An interim order –

    (a)   shall have the same effect as a bankruptcy restrictions order, and

    (b)   shall come into force when it is made.

(5)   An interim order shall cease to have effect –

    (a)   on the determination of the application for the bankruptcy restrictions order,

    (b)   on the acceptance of a bankruptcy restrictions undertaking made by the bankrupt, or

    (c)   if the court discharges the interim order on the application of the person who applied for it or of the bankrupt.

6   (1)   This paragraph applies to a case in which both an interim bankruptcy restrictions order and a bankruptcy restrictions order are made.

  (2)   Paragraph 4(2) shall have effect in relation to the bankruptcy restrictions order as if a reference to the date of that order were a reference to the date of the interim order.

Bankruptcy restrictions undertaking

7   (1)   A bankrupt may offer a bankruptcy restrictions undertaking to the Secretary of State.

  (2)   In determining whether to accept a bankruptcy restrictions undertaking the Secretary of State shall have regard to the matters specified in paragraph 2(2) and (3).

8   A reference in an enactment to a person in respect of whom a bankruptcy restrictions order has effect (or who is 'the subject of' a bankruptcy restrictions order) includes a reference to a person in respect of whom a bankruptcy restrictions undertaking has effect.

9   (1)   A bankruptcy restrictions undertaking –

    (a)   shall come into force on being accepted by the Secretary of State, and

    (b)   shall cease to have effect at the end of a date specified in the undertaking.

  (2)   The date specified under sub-paragraph (1)(b) must not be –

    (a)   before the end of the period of two years beginning with the date on which the undertaking is accepted, or

    (b)   after the end of the period of 15 years beginning with that date.

  (3)   On an application by the bankrupt the court may –

    (a)   annul a bankruptcy restrictions undertaking;

    (b)   provide for a bankruptcy restrictions undertaking to cease to have effect before the date specified under sub-paragraph (1)(b).

Effect of annulment of bankruptcy order

10   Where a bankruptcy order is annulled under section 282(1)(a) or (2) –

    (a)   any bankruptcy restrictions order, interim order or undertaking which is in force in respect of the bankrupt shall be annulled,

    (b)   no new bankruptcy restrictions order or interim order may be made in respect of the bankrupt, and

    (c)   no new bankruptcy restrictions undertaking by the bankrupt may be accepted.

11   Where a bankruptcy order is annulled under section 261, 263D or 282(1)(b) –

    (a)   the annulment shall not affect any bankruptcy restrictions order, interim order or undertaking in respect of the bankrupt,

    (b)   the court may make a bankruptcy restrictions order in relation to the bankrupt on an application instituted before the annulment,

    (c)   the Secretary of State may accept a bankruptcy restrictions undertaking offered before the annulment, and

    (d)   an application for a bankruptcy restrictions order or interim order in respect of the bankrupt may not be instituted after the annulment.

Registration

12   The Secretary of State shall maintain a register of –

    (a)   bankruptcy restrictions orders,

    (b)   interim bankruptcy restrictions orders, and

    (c)   bankruptcy restrictions undertakings.

SCHEDULE 21   EFFECT OF BANKRUPTCY RESTRICTIONS ORDER AND UNDERTAKING   Section 257

Disqualification for acting as receiver or manager

1   The following shall be substituted for section 31 of the Insolvency Act 1986 (c. 45) (receiver and manager: disqualification) –

'31 Disqualification of bankrupt

(1)   A person commits an offence if he acts as receiver or manager of the property of a company on behalf of debenture holders while –

    (a)   he is an undischarged bankrupt, or

    (b)   a bankruptcy restrictions order is in force in respect of him.

(2)   A person guilty of an offence under subsection (1) shall be liable to imprisonment, a fine or both.

(3)   This section does not apply to a receiver or manager acting under an appointment made by the court.'

Bankruptcy offences after discharge

2   After section 350(3) of the Insolvency Act 1986 (c. 45) (bankruptcy offences: general: no liability after discharge) there shall be inserted –

    '(3A) Subsection (3) is without prejudice to any provision of this Chapter which applies to a person in respect of whom a bankruptcy restrictions order is in force.'

3   At the end of section 360 of that Act (obtaining credit and doing business) there shall be inserted –

    '(5)   This section applies to the bankrupt after discharge while a bankruptcy restrictions order is in force in respect of him.

    (6)   For the purposes of subsection (1)(a) as it applies by virtue of subsection (5), the relevant information about the status of the person in question is the information that a bankruptcy restrictions order is in force in respect of him.'

Disqualification for acting as insolvency practitioner

4   At the end of section 390 of that Act (disqualification for insolvency practitioner) there shall be added –

'(5)   A person is not qualified to act as an insolvency practitioner while a bankruptcy restrictions order is in force in respect of him.'

Prohibition against involvement in company

5   The following shall be substituted for section 11(1) of the Company Directors Disqualification Act 1986 (c. 46) (bankrupt) –

'(1)   It is an offence for a person to act as director of a company or directly or indirectly to take part in or be concerned in the promotion, formation or management of a company, without the leave of the court, at a time when –

(a)   he is an undischarged bankrupt, or

(b)   a bankruptcy restrictions order is in force in respect of him.'

SCHEDULE 22   INDIVIDUAL VOLUNTARY ARRANGEMENT

Section 264

Annulment of bankruptcy on making of voluntary arrangement

1   The following shall be substituted for section 261 of the Insolvency Act 1986 (effect of voluntary arrangement: undischarged bankrupt) –

'261 Additional effect on undischarged bankrupt

(1)   This section applies where –

(a)   the creditors' meeting summoned under section 257 approves the proposed voluntary arrangement (with or without modifications), and

(b)   the debtor is an undischarged bankrupt.

(2)   Where this section applies the court shall annul the bankruptcy order on an application made –

(a)   by the bankrupt, or

(b)   where the bankrupt has not made an application within the prescribed period, by the official receiver.

(3)   An application under subsection (2) may not be made –

(a)   during the period specified in section 262(3)(a) during which the decision of the creditors' meeting can be challenged by application under section 262,

(b)   while an application under that section is pending, or

(c)   while an appeal in respect of an application under that section is pending or may be brought.

(4)   Where this section applies the court may give such directions about the conduct of the bankruptcy and the administration of the bankrupt's estate as it thinks appropriate for facilitating the implementation of the approved voluntary arrangement.'

Fast-track for making voluntary arrangement

2   The following shall be inserted after section 263 of that Act (implementation of voluntary arrangement) –

'Fast-track voluntary arrangement

263A Availability

Section 263B applies where an individual debtor intends to make a proposal to his creditors for a voluntary arrangement and –

(a)   the debtor is an undischarged bankrupt,

(b)   the official receiver is specified in the proposal as the nominee in relation to the voluntary arrangement, and

(c)   no interim order is applied for under section 253.

263B Decision

(1)   The debtor may submit to the official receiver –

(a)   a document setting out the terms of the voluntary arrangement which the debtor is proposing, and

(b)   a statement of his affairs containing such particulars as may be prescribed of his creditors, debts, other liabilities and assets and such other information as may be prescribed.

(2)   If the official receiver thinks that the voluntary arrangement proposed has a reasonable prospect of being approved and implemented, he may make arrangements for inviting creditors to decide whether to approve it.

(3)   For the purposes of subsection (2) a person is a 'creditor' only if –

(a)   he is a creditor of the debtor in respect of a bankruptcy debt, and

(b)   the official receiver is aware of his claim and his address.

(4)   Arrangements made under subsection (2) –

(a)   must include the provision to each creditor of a copy of the proposed voluntary arrangement,

(b)   must include the provision to each creditor of information about the criteria by reference to which the official receiver will determine whether the creditors approve or reject the proposed voluntary arrangement, and

(c)   may not include an opportunity for modifications to the proposed voluntary arrangement to be suggested or made.

(5)   Where a debtor submits documents to the official receiver under subsection (1) no application under section 253 for an interim order may be made in respect of the debtor until the official receiver has –

(a)   made arrangements as described in subsection (2), or

(b)   informed the debtor that he does not intend to make arrangements (whether because he does not think the voluntary arrangement has a reasonable prospect of being approved and implemented or because he declines to act).

263C Result

As soon as is reasonably practicable after the implementation of arrangements under section 263B(2) the official receiver shall report to the court whether the proposed voluntary arrangement has been approved or rejected.

263D Approval of voluntary arrangement

(1)   This section applies where the official receiver reports to the court under section 263C that a proposed voluntary arrangement has been approved.

(2) The voluntary arrangement –

    (a) takes effect,

    (b) binds the debtor, and

    (c) binds every person who was entitled to participate in the arrangements made under section 263B(2).

(3) The court shall annul the bankruptcy order in respect of the debtor on an application made by the official receiver.

(4) An application under subsection (3) may not be made –

    (a) during the period specified in section 263F(3) during which the voluntary arrangement can be challenged by application under section 263F(2),

    (b) while an application under that section is pending, or

    (c) while an appeal in respect of an application under that section is pending or may be brought.

(5) The court may give such directions about the conduct of the bankruptcy and the administration of the bankrupt's estate as it thinks appropriate for facilitating the implementation of the approved voluntary arrangement.

(6) The Deeds of Arrangement Act 1914 (c. 47) does not apply to the voluntary arrangement.

(7) A reference in this Act or another enactment to a voluntary arrangement approved under this Part includes a reference to a voluntary arrangement which has effect by virtue of this section.

263E Implementation

Section 263 shall apply to a voluntary arrangement which has effect by virtue of section 263D(2) as it applies to a voluntary arrangement approved by a creditors' meeting.

263F Revocation

(1) The court may make an order revoking a voluntary arrangement which has effect by virtue of section 263D(2) on the ground –

    (a) that it unfairly prejudices the interests of a creditor of the debtor, or

    (b) that a material irregularity occurred in relation to the arrangements made under section 263B(2).

(2) An order under subsection (1) may be made only on the application of –

    (a) the debtor,

    (b) a person who was entitled to participate in the arrangements made under section 263B(2),

    (c) the trustee of the bankrupt's estate, or

    (d) the official receiver.

(3) An application under subsection (2) may not be made after the end of the period of 28 days beginning with the date on which the official receiver makes his report to the court under section 263C.

(4) But a creditor who was not made aware of the arrangements under section 263B(2) at the time when they were made may make an application under subsection (2) during the period of 28 days beginning with the date on which he becomes aware of the voluntary arrangement.

263G Offences

(1) Section 262A shall have effect in relation to obtaining approval to a proposal for a voluntary arrangement under section 263D.

(2) Section 262B shall have effect in relation to a voluntary arrangement which has effect by virtue of section 263D(2) (for which purposes the words "by a creditors' meeting summoned under section 257" shall be disregarded).'

Role of official receiver

3   The following shall be inserted after section 389A of that Act (authorisation of nominees and supervisors) –

'389B Official receiver as nominee or supervisor

(1)   The official receiver is authorised to act as nominee or supervisor in relation to a voluntary arrangement approved under Part VIII provided that the debtor is an undischarged bankrupt when the arrangement is proposed.

(2)   The Secretary of State may by order repeal the proviso in subsection (1).

(3)   An order under subsection (2) –

(a)   must be made by statutory instrument, and

(b)   shall be subject to annulment in pursuance of a resolution of either House of Parliament.'

SCHEDULE 23   INDIVIDUAL INSOLVENCY: MINOR AND CONSEQUENTIAL AMENDMENTS   Section 269

1   The Insolvency Act 1986 (c. 45) shall be amended as follows.

2   Section 275 (bankruptcy: summary administration) shall cease to have effect.

3   In section 280(1) (bankruptcy: discharge by order of court) –

(a)   for 'section 279(1)(a)' substitute 'section 279(6)', and

(b)   for 'commencement of the bankruptcy' substitute 'date on which the bankruptcy commences'.

4   In section 282 (annulment of bankruptcy) –

(a)   in subsection (4) (effect of annulment) after 'section 261' insert 'or 263D', and

(b)   omit subsection (5) (previous bankruptcy: disregard of annulled bankruptcy).

5   For section 291(4) (co-operation with official receiver) substitute –

'(4)   The bankrupt shall give the official receiver such inventory of his estate and such other information, and shall attend on the official receiver at such times, as the official receiver may reasonably require –

(a)   for a purpose of this Chapter, or

(b)   in connection with the making of a bankruptcy restrictions order.'

6   In section 292(1)(a) (trustee in bankruptcy: power to appoint) omit the words 'except at a time when a certificate for the summary administration of the bankrupt's estate is in force,'.

7   In section 293(1) (trustee in bankruptcy: meeting to appoint) omit the words 'and no certificate for the summary administration of the bankrupt's estate has been issued,'.

8   In section 294(1) (power of creditors to requisition meeting) omit the words –

'and

(b)   a certificate for the summary administration of the estate is not for the time being in force,'.

9   In section 297 (trustee: special cases) –

(a)   omit subsections (2) and (3), and

(b)   in subsection (4) omit the words 'but no certificate for the summary administration of the estate is issued'.

10   Omit section 298(3) (removal of trustee: summary administration).

11   In section 300 (trustee: vacancy) –

    (a)   omit subsection (5), and

    (b)   in subsections (6) and (7) omit the words 'or (5)'.

12   In section 354(3) (concealment of property) after 'the official receiver' insert ', the trustee'.

13   At the end of section 355 (concealment and falsification of records) add –

    '(4)   In their application to a trading record subsections (2)(d) and (3)(b) shall have effect as if the reference to 12 months were a reference to two years.

    (5)   In subsection (4) "trading record" means a book, document or record which shows or explains the transactions or financial position of a person's business, including –

        (a)   a periodic record of cash paid and received,

        (b)   a statement of periodic stock-taking, and

        (c)   except in the case of goods sold by way of retail trade, a record of goods sold and purchased which identifies the buyer and seller or enables them to be identified.'

14   In the following provisions of section 399 (appointment of official receiver) for 'or winding up' substitute ', winding up or individual voluntary arrangement' –

    (a)   subsection (1) (twice), and

    (b)   subsection (4).

15   In section 429(2)(b) (disability imposed on revoking administration order under County Courts Act 1984) for 'not exceeding 2 years' there shall be substituted 'not exceeding one year'.

16   (1)   Schedule 9 (scope of insolvency rules) shall be amended as follows.

    (2)   After paragraph 8 (registration of voluntary arrangements) insert –

        'Official receiver acting on voluntary arrangement

        8A.   Provision about the official receiver acting as nominee or supervisor in relation to a voluntary arrangement under Part VIII of this Act, including –

           (a)   provision requiring the official receiver to act in specified circumstances;

           (b)   provision about remuneration;

           (c)   provision prescribing terms or conditions to be treated as forming part of a voluntary arrangement in relation to which the official receiver acts as nominee or supervisor;

           (d)   provision enabling those terms or conditions to be varied or excluded, in specified circumstances or subject to specified conditions, by express provision in an arrangement.'

    (3)   After paragraph 29 (records) insert –

        'Bankruptcy restrictions orders and undertakings

        29A.   Provision about bankruptcy restrictions orders, interim orders and undertakings, including –

           (a)   provision about evidence;

           (b)   provision enabling the amalgamation of the register mentioned in paragraph 12 of Schedule 4A with another register;

           (c)   provision enabling inspection of that register by the public.'

17   In Schedule 10 (punishment of offences) –

    (a)   in the entry for section 31 omit 'Undischarged', and

    (b)   omit the entries for sections 361 and 362.

BIBLIOGRAPHY

The following works have been of assistance to the authors and hence may be of interest to the reader:

BOOKS

Bailey, E., Groves, H. & Smith, C. (1992) *Corporate Insolvency Law and Practice* (2nd Ed), Butterworths Law.

Berry, C., Bailey, E. & Schaw Miller, S. (2001) *Personal Insolvency Law and Practice*, Butterworths Law.

Bruce, M. (2002) *Rights and Duties of Directors*, Butterworths Law.

Campbell, D. (1992) *International Corporate Insolvency Law*, Butterworths Law.

Fletcher, I. (1990) *The Law of Insolvency* (3rd Ed), Sweet & Maxwell.

Fletcher, I., Higham, J. & Trower, W. (1994) *The Law and Practice of Corporate Administrations*, Butterworths Law.

Frieze, S. (1992) *Handbook of Bankruptcy & Personal Insolvency*, Sweet & Maxwell.

Gerty, C. & Davies, S. (2000) *Insolvency Practice on the Human Rights Act 1988 – Special Bulletin*, Jordans.

Goode, R. (1997) *Principles of Corporate Insolvency Law* (2nd Ed), Sweet & Maxwell.

Goode, R. (1998) *Commercial Law* (2nd Ed), Butterworths Law.

Grier, I. & Floyd, R. (1988) *Company Administration Orders and Voluntary Arrangements*, Sweet & Maxwell.

Harris, D., O'Boyle, M. & Warbrick, C. (2000) *Law of the European Convention of Human Rights*, Butterworths Law.

INSOL International (2001) *Directors in the Twilight Zone*, International Federation of Insolvency Practitioners.

Kerr, R. & Hunter, M. (1992) *Kerr on the Law and Practice as to Receivers and Administrators* (17th Ed), Sweet & Maxwell.

Lightman, G. & Moss, G. (2000) *The Law of Receivers and Administrators of Companies* (3rd Ed), Sweet & Maxwell.

Lingard, J. (1989) *Corporate Rescues and Insolvency* (2nd Ed), Butterworths Law.

Loose, P. (1997) *Loose on Liquidators* (4th Ed), Jordans.

McCormack, G. (1996) *Proprietary Claims and Insolvency*, Sweet & Maxwell.

McMullen, J. (1998) *Business Transfers and Employee Rights*, Butterworths Law.

Palmers Corporate Insolvency, Sweet & Maxwell (Looseleaf).

Picarda, H. (2000) *The Law Relating to Receivers, Managers and Administrators* (3rd Ed), Butterworths Law.

Pollard, D. (2000) *Corporate Insolvency: Employment and Pensions Rights*, Butterworths Law.

Rajak, H., Horricks, P. & Bannister, J. (1994) *European Corporate Insolvency Law*, Chancery Wiley Law Publications.

Rajani, S. (1994) *Tolley's Corporate Insolvency* (2nd Ed), Tolley Publishing.

Sealy, L. & Milman, D. (2002) *Annotated Guide to the Insolvency Legislation*, Sweet & Maxwell.

Simor, J. & Emmerson, B. (2002) *Human Rights Practice*, Sweet & Maxwell.

Smart, P. (1998) *Cross Border Insolvency* (2nd Ed), Butterworths Law.

Starmer, K. (1999) *European Human Rights Law – The Human Rights Act 1998: The European Convention of Human Rights*, The Legal Action Group.

Tomasic, R. & Little, P. (1997) *Insolvency Law and Practice in Asia*, Sweet & Maxwell Asia.

Totty, P. & Moss, G. *Insolvency*, Sweet & Maxwell (Looseleaf).

Various, *Insolvency Law*, Tolleys Publishing (Looseleaf).

Wallington, P. (2000) *Butterworths Employment Law Handbook* (9th Ed), Butterworths Law.

ARTICLES

Anderson, H., 'Insolvent Insolvencies', *Tolleys IL&P*, Vol.17, No.3, 2001.

Andrews, M., 'Working Party Review Promotes Rescue Culture', *International Law Office – Legal Newsletter*, 14 December 1999.

Andrews, M., 'Taking things one step at a time', *The Lawyer*, 20 November 2002.

Archer, D., 'A Bankrupt's Pension: Whose Is It?', *Solicitors Journal*, Vol. 144, No.22.

Archer, G., 'Insolvency Act 2000', *Solicitors Journal*, Vol. 145, No.5.

Baistar, S., 'Insolvency Proceedings in Europe', *Legal Gazette*, 2 May 2002.

Baister, S., 'Voluntary Arrangements: The Failures', *Gazette*, 18 July 2002.

Beger, A., 'Coslett – Section 395 and set off in the House of Lords', *Insolvency Intelligence 2002*. Vol 15, Parts 2 & 3.

Bennet, D., 'Bankruptcy and Insolvency Law Reform', *Business Law*, Issue 53, September 2001.

Birch, R., 'Human rights, Directors and Legal Aid: Part 1', *New Law Journal*, Vol.151, No.6970.

Braithwaite (QC), B., 'The Woolf Reforms', *The Lawyer*, 25 February 2002.

Briggs, J., 'A Wife's Equity of Exoneration: The Doctrine Re-Visited', *Insolvency Intelligence 2001*, Vol.14(5).

Briggs, J., 'Forfeiture on Bankruptcy Clauses in personal pension schemes', *Insolvency Intelligence 2000*, Vol.13.

Brougham, C. & Briggs, J., 'Current Issues in Insolvency: Bankruptcy Reform Proposals', *Insolvency Intelligence 2002*, Vol 15, No.3.

Cain, B., 'Insolvency: Effect Upon Employees', *Tolley's Employment Law – Iine Newsletter*, October 2001.

Cappa, C. & McHugh, L., 'Wither, the Floating Charge', *Insolvency Lawyer*, [1999] 162.

Capper, D., 'Fixed Charges over Book Debts: Back to Basics, but how far back?', (2002) *LMCLQ* 246.

Corr, P., 'Wrongful trading: a deterrent of making profit', *Finance and Credit Law*, July/August 2001, No.7.

Coulson, F., 'The End of Banking as we know it', *Legal Week*, 28 July 2001.

Davey, M., 'Insolvency in the Family Home', *Insolvency Lawyer*, [2000], No.12.

De Kerloy, K., 'Replacing a Resigning Office Holder in Insolvency Administrations', *Tolley's IL&P*, Vol.15, No.2, 1999.

Deacock, A. & Martin, A., 'The Rights of a Trustee in Bankruptcy to the Bankrupt's Pension: Pension Industry v. Insolvency Practitioners', *Tolley's IL&P*, Vol.16, No.4.

Dennis, V., 'Bankruptcy Reform: A Start in the Wrong Direction', *Tolley's IL&P*, Vol.16, No.5.

Dennis, V., 'Enterprise Bill: Administration the Key to Corporate Rescue', *New Law Journal*, Vol.152, No.7055.

Dennis, V., 'The Future of Corporate Rescue', *Financier World Wide*, July/August 2002.

Elliott, L., 'Ensuring Change', *The Lawyer*, 25 March 2002.

Elwes, S., 'Charges: fixed or floating', *Tolley's IL&P*, Vol.17, No.6.

Elwes, S., 'Transactions defrauding creditors', *Tolley's IL&P*, Vol.17, No.1.

Fennessy, M., 'Reversal of Fortune for Creditors after Administration', *Tolley's IL&P*, Vol.17, No.1.

Fidler, P., 'Wrongful trading after continental insurance', *Tolley's IL&P*, Vol.17, No.6.

Floyd, R., 'Pleased as Punch! A Delegate's Impression of the 10th Annual Congress of the Association Business Recovery Professionals 2000', *Insolvency Law & Practice*, Vol.16, No.4.

Foster, S. & Perkin, C., 'Bankrupt's Correspondence and Article 8 of the European Convention of Human Rights', *New Law Journal*, 8 September 2000.

Friedman, P., 'Transactions defrauding creditors', *New Law Journal*, 7 September 2001.

Frieze, S., 'Bankruptcy & Pensions', *Insolvency Intelligence 1999*, Vol.13, No.5.

Frieze, S., 'Exit from Administration', *Insolvency Intelligence 2001*, Vol.14, No.6.

Frisby, S., 'Making a silk purse out of a pig's ear: Medford v. Blake', [2000] MLR 413.

Gearty, C., 'Insolvency . . . and Human Rights', *Insolvency Lawyer*, 2000, Pt1.

Gearty, C., 'Insolvency . . . and Human Rights', *Insolvency Lawyer*, 2000, Pt2.

Greenstreet, I., 'Pensions & Bankruptcy: Recent Development', *Tolley's IL&P*, Vol.16, No.2.

Greenstreet, I., 'Pensions & Bankruptcy: Recent Developments', *Tolley's IL&P*, Vol.17, No.2.

Griffiths, N., 'Human Rights Issues and Insolvency', *International Law Office – Legal Newsletter*, 18 August 2000.

Griffiths, N., 'Impact on Decision on Security over Book Debts', *International Law Office – Legal Newsletter*, 27 July 2001.

Griffiths, N., 'Revised Enterprise Bill Brings Reforms One Step Closer', *International Law Office – Legal Newsletter*, 26 July 2002.

Hardy, S., 'Some TUPE Implications for Insolvency Lawyers', *Insolvency Lawyer*, 2001, Issue 4.

Hawkins, R., 'A clarion call for clarity', *Estate Gazette*, 6 January 2001.

Hemsworth, M., 'Directors' Powers during Administrative Receivership: The Power to take Legal Proceedings', *Insolvency Law*, 1999, Issue 3.

Henderson, A., 'Defining the Limits of Silence (2)', *Solicitor's Journal*, 31 May 2001.

Hickman, N., 'Bankruptcy: the Pensions Saga', *Gazette*, Vol.99, No.14.

Hicks, A., 'Directors' Disqualification: The National Audit Office Follows Up', *Insolvency Law & Practice*, Vol.15, No.4.

Hodgson, R., 'Set for Reform', *International Law Office – Legal Newsletter*, 3 April 2002.

Ife, L., 'Liability of Receivers and Banks in selling a mortgage in property', *Insolvency Intelligence 2001*, Vol.61, No.??.

Lloyd-Dawson, K., 'A Quick End', *The Lawyer*, 25 March 2002.

MacDonald, I. & Moujalli, D., 'A Very English Concept: The Receiver appointed out of Court', *Insolvency Intelligence 2001*, Vol.14, No.10.

Marshall, J., 'Insolvency Act 2000: A Taste of Things to Come?', *PLC*, June 2001.

McCartney, P., 'Insolvency Procedures and Landlord's Rights of Peaceable Re-Entry', *Insolvency Intelligence 2000*, Vol.13, No.10.

McIntosh, M., 'Insolvency Act 2000: Landlord's Rights of Peaceful Re-Entry', *Tolleys IL&P*, Vol.17, No.2.

Miller, G., 'Application by Trustee in Bankruptcy for the Sale of the Family Home', *Tolley's IL&P*, Vol.15, No.6.

Miller, G., 'Income Payments Order', *Tolley's IL&P*, Vol.18, No.2.

Milman, D., 'Under the Liquidation Expense Principle', *Insolvency Lawyer*, No.126.

Milman, D., 'Enterprise Bill', *Insolvency Law*, 2002, Issue 4.

Morton, J., 'The Impact of the Rules on Limitation in the Context of Section 238 to 241 Insolvency Act 1986', *Corporate Briefing*, June 2002.

Moss, G., 'Conditional Resolutions and Exit from Administration Orders', *Insolvency Intelligence 2000*, Vol.13, No.4.

Murphy, J., 'Mond v. Hyde: Negligence Immunity for the Official Receiver?', *Insolvency Lawyer* [1999], Issue 5.

O'Flynn, K., 'Insolvency: Australia Overview, *International Law Office – Legal Newsletter*, November 2001.

O'Neil, B., 'Insolvency: Ireland Overview', *International Law Office – Legal Newsletter*, February 2002.

Obank, R., 'Cross Border Harmonisation of Insolvency Proceedings and the Quest for Comity', *Butterworths JIBFL*, February 2002.

Obank, R., 'Cross Border Harmonisation of Insolvency Proceedings and the Quest for Comity Part 2', *Butterworths JIBFL*, March 2002.

Obank, R., 'Cross Border Harmonisation of Insolvency Proceedings and the Quest for Comity Part 3', *Butterworths JIBFL*, April 2002.

Oditah, F., 'Fixed Charges over Book Debts after Brumark', *Insolvency Intelligence 2001*, Vol.14, No.7.

Peel, M., 'Case opens door for creditors to seize pensions', *Financial Times*, 11 July 2001.

Phillips, M., 'To the Rescue?', *Recovery*, June 2002.

Pike, N., 'The Human Rights Act 1998 and Its Impact on Insolvency Practitioners', *Insolvency Lawyer*, 1 February 2001.

Plainer, A., 'Administrator: When to go to Court', *Finance and Credit Law*, November/December 2002.

Plainer, A. & Parker, C., 'Challenging an Administrator re: C E King (In Administration)', *Insolvency Bulletin 5*, July/August 1999.

Pond, K., 'New Rules and New Roles for the Individual Voluntary Arrangements', *Tolley's IL&P*, Vol.18, No.1.

Pond, K., 'A Decade of Change for Individual Voluntary Arrangements', *Tolley's IL&P*, Vol.14, No.6.

Pope, T. & Woollard, M., 'Balance of Power in the Expenses Regime', *Insolvency Intelligence 2001*, Vol.14, No.2.

Prime, V, *Tolley's Company Insolvency Monthly Newsletter*, December 2001.

Pugh, C., 'Section 426 of the Insolvency Act Recent Developments', *ILMP*, Vol.16, No.1.

Pullen, S., 'Classification of certain causes in building contractors registrable floating charges', *Finance and Credit Law*, February 2002.

R3, *Technical Bulletin*, Issue No.52, July 2002.

R3, *Technical Bulletin*, Issue No.54, December 2002.

R3 – SPI, 'Statement of Insolvency Practice: A Receiver's responsibility to preferential creditors', *Insolvency Bulletin 9*, 14 June 1999.

Rajani, S., 'Director Disqualification Undertaking & Blackspur Case', *Tolley's IL&P*, Vol.18, No.1.

Readett, H., 'Cross-Border Insolvencies', *New Law Journal*, 2002, 152 (7040).

Redhead, S., 'Directors Disqualification: Defending DTI Actions', *Solicitors Journal*, 24 September 1999.

Rook, D., 'Property Law and the Human Rights Act 1998: A Review of the First Years', *Conveyancer*, July/August 2002.

Rutstein, M., 'In the spirit of Enterprise', *Accountancy*, September 2001.

Sargeant, M., 'New Transfer Regulations', *Industrial Law Journal*, Vol.31, No.2.

Schiller, C., 'Insolvency Germany Overview', *International Law Office – Legal Newsletter*, July 2002.

Schiller, C., 'The Insolvency Plan: Success Story or Stumbling Block', *International Law Office – Legal Newsletter*, 10 May 2002.

Sergeant, M., 'New Transfer Regulations', *Industrial Law Journal*, 31 March 2002.

Shafran, H., 'New Value Plans under the Bankruptcy Code', *International Law Office – Legal Newsletter*, 21 June 2002.

Shafran, H., 'Foreign Representatives in Chapter 11 Cases', *International Law Office – Legal Newsletter*, 6 July 2001.

Shafran, H., 'Insolvency USA Overview', *International Law Office – Legal Newsletter*, April 2001.

Shah, R., 'Integrating Insolvency', *Legal Week*, 9 July 2002.

Shanro, S. & Derrick, C., 'Falling Apart: Rescue Mechanisms and Insolvency', *www.Practical Law.com*, A21397.

Short, P., 'Administration: Peaceable Re-Entry by a Landlord Revisited', *Insolvency Lawyer*, Vol.1999, No.6.

Simmons, M., 'Wrongful Trading', *Insolvency Lawyer*, Vol.1999, No.6.

Simmons, M., 'Human Rights and Insolvency: An Update', *Tolley's IL&P*, Vol.17, No.6.

Simmons, M. & Smith, T., 'The Human Rights Act 1998: The Practical Impact on Insolvency', *Tolley's IL&P*, Vol.16, No.5.

Smith, A. & Neill, M., 'The Insolvency Act 2000', *Insolvency Law & Practice*, Vol.17, No.3.

Spon-Smith, R., 'Pension Lump Sums and Bankruptcy', *Family Law*, July 2000.

Steinberg, A., 'Insolvency USA Overview', *International Law Office – Legal Newsletter*, December 2002.

Steiner, M., 'Receivers v. the Liquidators v. Preferential Creditors v. Unsecured Creditors: Practitioners Beware', *Tolley's IL&P*, Vol.17, No.1.

Stewart, R., 'Reconciling International Insolvency Law', *Legal Gazette*, 31 January 2002.

Trower, W., 'Human Rights: Article 6 Reality and Myth', *Insolvency Law 48*, 2001.

Trower, W., 'Bringing Human Rights Home to the Insolvency Practitioner: Part I', *Insolvency Intelligence 2000*, Vol.13, No.6.

Trower, W., 'Bringing Human Rights Home to the Insolvency Practitioner: Part II', *Insolvency Intelligence 2000*, Vol.30, No.7.

Verrill, J., 'Brumark Investments and Fixed Charges on Book Debts', *Finance and Credit Law*, Vol.3, No.2.

Wadham, J., 'Half Measures', *Solicitor's Journal*, 15 November 2001.

Walker, A., 'Claims by a Trustee in Bankruptcy in Relation to Land Situated Abroad', *Insolvency Lawyer*, Vol.2000, No.5.

Walters, A., 'Directors' Disqualification after the Insolvency Act 2000: The New Regime', *Insolvency Lawyer*, Vol.2001, No.3.

Weintroub, I., 'Unfit Directors: The Amended Position', *Legal Gazette*, 3 May 2001.

West, I., 'Exiting Administrations: Who Bears the Cost', *Tolley's IL&P*, Vol.15, No.2.

Whiteson, J., 'Enterprise Bill: Insolvency Proposals', *Tolley's Company Law and Insolvency Newsletter*, May 2002.

Whiteson, J., 'Enterprise Bill: Insolvency Proposals Part 2', *Tolley's Company Law and Insolvency*, Vol.1, No.12.

Willcok, J., 'The Twilight Zone', *Legal Week*, 13 September 2001.

Willcok, J., 'How the Banks won the battle for the Enterprise Bill', *Recovery*, June 2002.

Wise, L., 'Directors Running for Cover', *Solicitors Journal*, Vol.142, No.36.

Wise, L., 'No More Bacon', *Tolley's IL&P*, Vol.15, No.3.

Wise, L., 'Safeguards Leave Door Open for Directors', *Gazette*, 21 November 2002.

Wyatt, W., 'On the Road to Recovery', *Pensions World*, October 2002.

Yeowart, G., 'Administrative Receivership: Abolition or Reform?', *Butterworths JIBFL*, Vol.17, No.1.

Yeowart, G., 'Enterprise Bill: Impact on Financing Transactions', *Butterworths JIBFL*, Vol.17, No.5.

Other resources

DTI, 'Transfer of Undertakings (Protection of Employment) Regulations 1981 (1981): Government Proposals for Reform: Detailed Background Paper' (URN 01/1158).

DTI, 'Transfer of Undertakings (Protection of Employment) Regulations 1981 (1981): Government Proposals for Reform: Public Consultation Document' (URN 01/1133).

DTI Press Release, 'Company winding up and bankruptcy petition statistics', 2 August 2002 (available to view at **www.nds.coi.gov.uk**).

DTI Press Release, 'Insolvencies in the third quarter 2002', 1 November 2002 (available to view at **www.nds.coi.gov.uk**).

Home Office, 'Rights Brought Home: The Human Rights Bill Command Paper', October 1997, Cm 3782

LNN Times, 'Company/Commercial: Disqualification – Shadow, De Factor and Nominee Directors', Issue 372, 19/10/01 (notes to video).

R3 Association of Business Recovery of Professions, 9th Annual Survey of Business Recovery in the UK, (unpublished – available to view at **wwwr3.org.uk**).

R3 Corporate Insolvency in the UK: A Decade of Change, June 2002.

INDEX

administration
  compulsory 1.4.13
  Cork Committee 1.2.5, 1.2.6, 1.2.10,
    1.2.11
  creation of 1.2.5
  disabilities on revocation of
    administration order against an
    individual 9.4.11
  dissolution following 7.10.30–7.10.31
  effect
    interim moratorium 7.6.18–7.6.20
    moratorium 7.6.10–7.6.17
    publicity requirements
      7.6.21–7.6.22
    receivership 7.6.5–7.6.9
    winding-up petition 7.6.1–7.6.4
  ending 7.10
  funding of process 10.1.12
  generally 1.2.5, 1.2.6, 1.2.10, 1.2.11,
    10.1.12–10.1.13
  initial creditors' meeting
    7.7.19–7.7.28
  landlords' rights of action, and
    3.7.1–3.7.4
  moratorium 7.6.10–7.6.17
    interim 7.6.18–7.6.20
  one-year limitation period
    7.10.1–7.10.3
    extension 7.10.4–7.10.9
  process
    administrator's proposals
      7.7.7–7.7.15
    initial creditors' meeting
      7.7.19–7.7.28
    notice of appointment 7.7.1–7.7.3
    sale of business prior to creditors'
      approval of proposals to
      7.7.16–7.7.18
    statement of affairs 7.7.4–7.7.6
  publicity requirements 7.6.21–6.22

purposes
  better result than winding up
    7.2.11–7.2.13
  generally 7.2.1–7.2.5
  realisation of property for
    purposes of secured or
    preferential creditors
    7.2.14–7.2.18
  rescuing company as going concern
    7.2.6–7.2.10
  receivership, effect on 7.6.5–7.6.9
  restrictions on use 7.2.21
  sale of business prior to creditors'
    approval of proposals 7.7.16–7.7.18
  US Chapter 11 proceedings compared
    2.2.14–2.2.15, 10.1.12
  winding-up petition, effect on
    7.6.1–7.6.4
administrative receiver
  definition 5.1.6
administrative receivership
  abolition of 1.4.15, 5.2.1, 5.2.3–5.2.7,
    10.1.3
  administration order, effect of
    7.6.5–7.6.9
  banks, and 1.2.11, 1.4.12,
    5.1.9–5.1.12
  capital market arrangements
    5.3.8–5.3.10
  costs 5.1.11
  criticism 1.4.3
  debentures entered into before
    Enterprise Act 2002 5.2.1–5.2.7
  decline in use 1.2.11
  Enterprise Act 2002 reforms
    exemptions to new procedures
      5.3.7–5.3.22
    generally 5.3.1–5.3.6, 7.1.1, 7.1.3
    power to amend or vary exceptions
      5.3.22–5.3.24

administrative receivership *cont.*
  reasons for reform 1.4.1–1.4.4,
    5.1.8–5.1.20
  review process 1.4.5–1.4.8
  financial market operations 5.3.19
  foreign incorporated companies
    5.3.27
  friendly societies 5.3.28
  generally 1.2.10
  industrial societies 5.3.28
  misuse 1.4.2
  project finance 5.3.16–5.3.18
  public private partnership
    5.3.11–5.3.14
  receivership distinguished 5.1.6–5.1.7
  registered social landlords
    5.3.20–5.3.21
  special administration regimes
    5.3.25–5.3.26
  utilities 5.3.15
  widespread use 1.2.9, 1.4.1, 1.4.2
administrator
  agent of company, as 7.8.3
  appointment
    cessation
      administrator, by
        7.10.10–7.10.15
      consequences 7.10.20–7.10.29
      creditor's application, by
        7.10.16–7.10.18
      public interest winding-up
        petition 7.10.19
    company or directors, by
      initiating the procedure
        7.5.1–7.5.3
      notice of appointment
        7.5.10–7.5.15
      notice of intention to appoint
        7.5.6–7.5.9
      restrictions on appointment
        7.5.4–7.5.5
    court, by
      application before court
        7.3.20–7.3.23
      floating charge holder, and
        7.3.11–7.3.20
      notice provisions 7.3.10
      persons applying 7.3.7–7.3.9
      pre-conditions 7.3.1–7.3.6
    floating chargeholder, by
      generally 7.2.15, 7.3.11–7.3.12,
        7.4.1–7.4.3, 7.10.13
      notice of appointment
        7.4.11–7.4.14
      pre-conditions 7.4.4–7.4.5

      restrictions on appointment
        7.4.6–7.4.10
    winding-up petitions 7.6.2–7.6.4
    notice of 7.7.1–7.7.3
  challenge regarding conduct
    court's powers 7.9.4–7.9.11
    pre-conditions 7.9.1–7.9.3
  charged property, dealing with
    7.8.11–7.8.14
  contracts of employment
    7.11.10–7.11.13
  court directions to 7.8.6
  distribution of funds 7.8.5, 7.10.23,
    7.10.24
  duties 1.4.3, 7.8.8–7.8.10
  expenses claim 7.11.11
  functions 7.8
  hire purchase agreement, property
    subject to 7.8.15–8.17
  offences 7.10.12
  powers 7.8.1–7.8.7
    charged property 7.8.11–7.8.14
    hire purchase, property subject to
      7.8.15–8.17
    payment of secured, preferential
      and unsecured creditors 7.8.5,
      7.10.23
  proposals for administration
    7.7.7–7.7.15
    sale of business prior to approval
      7.7.16–7.7.18
  removal
    charges and liabilities
      7.11.8–7.11.13
    circumstances for 7.11.1
    effect of vacation of office 7.11.7
    replacement 7.11.2–7.11.6
  remuneration 7.11.11
  statement of affairs 7.7.4–7.7.6
  status of 7.2.19–7.2.20
after acquired property 1.5.17, 9.2.12
'after the event' insurance 6.2.10
Alexander, Douglas 2.1.3, 6.3.5, 7.2.9
annulment of bankruptcy order 8.1.10,
  9.3.3–9.3.5
Asia
  bankruptcy 2.5.11–2.5.12
  corporate rescue 2.5.7–2.5.10
  generally 2.5.1–2.5.6
asset based lending 1.4.3
Association of Business Recovery
  Professionals (R3) 1.3.6
Australia
  bankruptcy 2.4.6
    discharge 2.4.6

corporate rescue 2.4.1, 2.4.2–2.4.4
creditors' committee 2.4.2
deed of arrangements 2.4.2
moratorium 2.4.2
receivership 5.1.4
scheme of arrangement procedure
    2.4.4
secured creditors 2.4.2
super-priority financing 2.4.2
voluntary administration 2.4.2–2.4.3

Bank of England 4.6.4
bankruptcy
    after acquired property 1.5.17, 9.2.12
    annulment of order 8.1.10,
        9.3.3–9.3.5
    Asia 2.5.11–2.5.12
    Australia 2.4.6
    bankruptcy offences after discharge
        9.4.9
    bankrupt's business, restrictions on
        9.4.10
    Canada 2.4.7
    certificate of misfortune 1.5.5
    commencing on or after 29 May 2000
        approved pensions, exclusion of
            4.2.22–4.2.23
        exclusion order application, factors
            taken into account by court 4.2.26
        generally 4.2.21
        seizure of bankrupt's pension
            benefits 4.2.27–4.2.29
        time limits 4.2.25
        unapproved pension arrangements,
            exclusion of 4.2.24
    concealment and falsification of
        records 9.1.6–9.1.9
    consumer bankruptcy
        United Kingdom 2.2.20
        United States 1.5.6, 1.5.13, 2.2.19
    culpable and non-culpable 1.5.5,
        1.5.8, 1.5.19–1.5.20, 8.2.3, 8.3.1,
        10.2.3
    debtor education programmes 2.4.8
    development of law 1.5.1–1.5.10
    disabilities on revocation of
        administration order against an
        individual 9.4.11
    discharge
        Australia 2.4.6
        automatic 1.5.8, 1.5.15
        bankruptcy offences after 9.4.9
        bankruptcy restrictions order, effect
            on 8.2.11
        criminal bankruptcy 8.1.11

general bankruptcy offences after
    9.4.9
generally 1.5.4, 1.5.7, 8.2.2
Germany 2.3.9–2.3.10
Ireland 2.3.11
Italy 2.3.12
Official Receiver, by 8.1.5, 9.1.3,
    9.1.4
reduction in period of
    1.5.15–1.5.18
suspension of bankruptcy period
    8.1.9–8.1.11
disclosure of fact of 9.4.13
discrimination on grounds of 1.5.15,
    10.2.10
disqualification from office
    generally 9.4.5
    Justices of the Peace 9.4.2
    local government 9.4.4
    parliament 9.4.3
duration of order 8.1.1–8.1.4
    former regime 8.1.4
    new regime 8.1.5–8.1.8
    suspension of bankruptcy period
        8.1.9–8.1.11
Enterprise Act 2002
    criminal pre-commencement
        bankruptcy 8.2.5
    generally 1.5.14–1.5.21,
        10.2.11–10.2.13
    'repeat' pre-commencement
        bankrupt 8.2.6–8.2.10
    transitional provisions 8.2
family home see family home
Germany 2.3.9–2.3.10
insolvency practitioner,
    disqualification from acting as 9.4.8
interest on sums held in insolvency
    services account 3.8.4
involvement in company 9.4.10
Ireland 2.3.11
Italy 2.3.12
Justices of the Peace 9.4.2
law merchant 1.5.1
manager, bankrupt acting as 9.4.7
offences
    after discharge 9.4.9
    repeal of 9.4.12
pension benefits, and 1.5.17,
    4.2.1–4.2.33
receiver, bankrupt acting as 9.4.7
rise in 1.5.11
since 1986 1.5.11–1.5.13
stigma 1.5.4–1.5.5, 1.5.12, 2.1.2
United States see United States

bankruptcy period
Australia 2.4.6
Canada 2.4.7
duration of order 8.1.1–8.1.4
former regime 8.1.4
new regime 8.1.5–8.1.8
Germany 2.3.9–2.3.10
Ireland 2.3.11
Italy 2.3.12
suspension of 8.1.9–8.1.11
bankruptcy restriction order (BRO)
annulment, effect of 8.5.1–8.5.4
disqualification from office
local government 9.4.4
parliament 9.4.3
duration 8.3.4, 8.6.5
effect of discharge on 8.2.11
excessive pension contributions
4.2.31
fast-track IVAs, and 9.3.19–9.3.21
generally 1.5.19, 1.5.21, 8.1.11, 8.3.1,
10.2.6
grounds for making 8.3.2–8.3.4
interim 8.3.5–8.3.7, 8.6.1
limitation period 8.3.3
new regime 8.6.1–8.6.7
register 8.6.1
bankruptcy restriction undertaking (BRU)
annulment, effect of 8.5.1–8.5.4
disqualification from office
local government 9.4.4
parliament 9.4.3
generally 8.1.11, 8.4.1
nature 8.4.2
new regime 8.6.1–8.6.7
register 8.6.1
banks
administrative receivership, and
1.2.11, 1.4.12, 5.1.9–5.1.12
appointment of receiver 1.2.4
corporate rescue, and 1.2.4, 1.2.11
self-regulation 1.4.3
book debts
fixed charges over 1.4.13,
10.1.6–10.110
business rescue see corporate rescue

Canada
bankruptcy 2.4.7
receivership 5.1.4
capital market arrangements 5.3.8–5.3.10
certificate of misfortune 1.5.5
China
corporate rescue 2.5.9
insolvency regime 2.5.4

cohabitees
rights of 4.3.14, 4.3.20
Commonwealth jurisdictions
corporate rescue 2.4.1–2.4.5
receivership 5.1.4
company
creation 1.2.1
definition 1.2.1
joint stock company 1.2.1
legal personality 1.2.1
limited liability 1.2.1
prohibition against bankrupt's
involvement in 9.4.10
winding up 1.2.1
company directors see directors
company voluntary arrangements
administration order, effect of 3.2.1
aim of procedure 1.2.7
approval 1.4.13, 3.3.4
effect of 3.2.48–3.2.49
binding 'unknown' creditors
3.2.48–3.2.49, 3.3.6–3.3.7
challenges to decisions 3.2.50–3.2.51
creation of 1.2.5
false representations 3.2.57, 3.3.8
general reforms 3.3
generally 1.2.5, 1.2.7, 6.1.8
implementation 3.2.52–3.2.54
Insolvency Act 1986 3.2.1
Insolvency Act 2000 3.2.2–3.3.14
moratorium 1.4.13, 3.2.3,
3.2.4–3.2.13
court orders during 3.2.18–3.2.20,
3.2.40–3.2.41
credit, obtaining 3.2.27
disposal of property during
3.2.28–3.2.29
documentation 3.2.13
effect of 3.2.24–3.2.34
eligibility criteria 3.2.5–3.2.9
ending 3.2.21, 3.2.23
extension 3.2.15–3.2.17
meetings to consider CVA proposals
3.2.43–3.2.47
moratorium committee 3.2.34
moratorium period 3.2.14–3.2.21
nominee's role 3.2.11–3.2.12,
3.2.35–3.2.42
notification procedures
3.2.22–3.2.23
offences 3.2.55–3.2.57
public utility companies 3.2.31
replacement of nominee 3.2.17
security, grant of 3.2.30
special purpose vehicles 3.2.9

uncrystallised floating charge, effect
    on 3.2.26
winding-up petition, staying of
    3.2.25
nominee
    acting as insolvency practitioner
        3.5.1–3.5.2
    challenging actions of
        3.2.28–3.2.29
    costs for actions 3.2.16
    duty 3.2.1, 3.3.2
    information to 3.2.37
    moratorium, role in 3.2.11–3.2.12,
        3.2.35–3.2.42
    replacement 3.2.17, 3.2.42, 3.3.3
    statement to directors
        3.2.11–3.2.12
    supervisor of voluntary
        arrangement, as 3.2.52–3.2.53,
        3.5.1–3.5.2
    withdrawing consent to act 3.2.21,
        3.2.36
    offences 3.2.55–3.2.57
    premature ending 3.3.12
    prosecution of company officers
        3.2.57, 3.3.8–3.3.11
    small companies 3.2
    supervisor of 3.2.52–3.2.54
compulsion
    powers of 3.8.2
compulsory administration 1.4.13
conditional fee arrangements 6.2.10
consumer bankruptcy
    United Kingdom 2.2.20
    United States 1.5.6, 1.5.13, 2.2.19
Cork Committee
    administration 1.2.5, 1.2.6, 1.2.10,
        1.2.11
    corporate rescue 1.2.4–1.2.10,
        1.3.1–1.3.2, 1.4.5, 1.5.7, 1.5.8
    Crown preference 6.1.5–6.1.7
    insolvency practitioners 1.3.1–1.3.2
    officeholders proceedings 6.2.2, 6.2.3
    receivership 1.2.4, 1.2.10
    ring-fenced sum 6.3.1
corporate insolvency law
    development 1.2.1
    reform
        Cork Committee 1.2.4–1.2.10,
            1.3.1–1.3.2, 1.4.5, 1.5.7, 1.5.8,
            6.1.5–6.1.7
        Enterprise Act 2002 1.4.9–1.4.15
        Joint Review Group 1.4.6–1.4.8
        necessity for 1.4.1–1.4.4
        review process 1.4.5–1.4.8

corporate reconstruction
    international see international
        corporate reconstruction
corporate rescue
    Asia 2.5.7–2.5.10
    Australia 2.4.1, 2.4.2–2.4.4
    banks, and 1.2.11
    China 2.5.9
    Commonwealth jurisdictions
        2.4.1–2.4.5
    company voluntary arrangements
        1.2.5, 1.2.9, 1.2.7
    Cork Committee 1.2.4–1.2.10,
        1.3.1–1.3.2, 1.4.5, 1.5.7, 1.5.8
    development 1.2.4–1.2.11
    France 2.3.7
    Germany 2.3.2–2.3.6, 7.1.3
    Ireland 2.3.8
    Malaysia 2.5.7
    New Zealand 2.4.1, 2.4.5
    receivership 1.2.4, 1.2.10
    Singapore 2.5.7, 2.5.8
    Taiwan 2.5.9
    Thailand 2.5.10
    United States see United States
credit 1.1.1, 1.5.6
cross-border insolvency
    Asia 2.5.1
    EC Regulation on Insolvency
        Proceedings 4.5.7–4.5.19, 4.5.36
        collective insolvency proceedings
            4.5.10
        main proceedings 4.5.12,
            4.5.13–4.5.14, 4.5.16, 4.5.19
        secondary proceedings 4.5.12,
            4.5.15
        territorial proceedings 4.5.12,
            4.5.15–4.5.18
    generally 4.5.1–4.5.2
    Insolvency Act 1986 4.5.3–4.5.6
    Insolvency Act 2000 3.8.5
    recognition
        common law 4.5.2
        effect 4.5.34
        pre-action relief 4.5.35
        procedure 4.5.32
        statutory obligation 4.5.3–4.5.6
        UNCITRAL Model Law
            4.5.26–4.5.35
    UNCITRAL Model Law 2.5.2, 3.8.5,
        4.5.20–4.5.35
Crown preference
    abolition of 1.4.15, 6.1.2,
        6.1.10–6.1.13
    Cork Committee 6.1.5–6.1.7

Crown preference *cont.*
   Enterprise Act 2002 1.4.15, 6.1.2,
      6.1.10–6.1.14
   preferential debts 6.1.1–6.1.4
   reasons for retention 6.1.5–6.1.7
   reform process 1.4.8, 6.1.5–6.1.9
   unsecured creditors, benefit to 6.2.1,
      6.3.1

debentures 1.2.4, 5.2.1–5.2.7
debtor education programmes 2.4.8
Dickens, Charles 1.5.3
directors
   bankrupts as 9.4.10
   disqualification proceedings
      3.6.1–3.6.8
disabilities on revocation of
   administration order against an
   individual 9.4.11
discounting 1.4.3
discrimination
   bankrupts, against 1.5.15, 10.2.10
disqualification from office
   generally 9.4.5
   Justices of the Peace 9.4.2
   local government 9.4.4
   parliament 9.4.3

economic recession
   effects of 1.2.9, 1.4.1, 1.4.2, 1.4.4,
      4.3.21–4.3.23
employment law reform *see* transfer of
   undertakings
Enterprise Act 2002
   administration *see* administration
   administrative receivership
      capital market 5.3.8–5.3.10
      exemptions to new procedures
         5.3.7–5.3.22
      financial markets 5.3.19
      foreign incorporated companies
         5.3.27
      friendly societies 5.3.28
      generally 5.3.1–5.3.6
      industrial societies 5.3.28
      power to amend or vary exceptions
         5.3.22–5.3.24
      project finance 5.3.16–5.3.18
      public private partnership
         5.3.11–5.3.14
      reasons for reform 1.4.1–1.4.4,
         5.1.8–5.1.20
      registered social landlords
         5.3.20–5.3.21
      review process 1.4.5–1.4.8

   special administration regimes
      5.3.25–5.3.26
   utilities 5.3.15
bankruptcy
   criminal pre-commencement
      bankruptcy 8.2.5
   generally 1.5.14–1.5.21,
      10.2.11–10.2.13
   'repeat' pre-commencement
      bankrupt 8.2.6–8.2.10
   restrictions 9.4
   transitional provisions 8.2
Crown preference, abolition of 1.4.15,
   6.1.2, 6.1.10–6.1.14
culpable and non-culpable bankrupt
   1.5.19–1.5.20, 8.2.3, 8.3.1, 10.2.3
family home
   limitation period 4.3.26, 4.3.28
   low value exception 4.3.27–4.3.29
   necessity for reform 4.3.21–4.3.23
   sunset provision 1.5.16,
      4.3.24–4.3.26, 4.3.29, 10.2.9
   generally 1.4.9–1.4.15, 7.1.1–7.1.4
   implementation 10.3.1–10.3.4
   insolvency 1.3.8
   personal insolvency 1.5.15–1.5.18
   secured creditors, role of
      10.1.3–10.1.11
   transitional provisions 8.2

factoring 1.4.3
family home
   assessing value of interest in
      beneficial interest 4.3.6–4.3.7
      registered interest 4.3.4
      third party interests 4.3.5, 4.3.8
   cohabitees, rights of 4.3.14, 4.3.20
   economic recession, effects of
      4.3.21–4.3.23
   Enterprise Act 2002
      limitation period 4.3.26, 4.3.28
      low value exception 4.3.27–4.3.29
      necessity for reform 4.3.21–4.3.23
      sunset provision 1.5.16,
         4.3.24–4.3.26, 4.3.29, 10.2.9
   Family Law Act 1996 4.3.11–4.3.15
   family versus creditors' rights
      4.3.1–4.3.3
   generally 1.5.9, 4.1.14, 4.1.31
   homestead exemption 2.2.18, 4.3.30
   Human Rights Act 1998 4.1.14,
      4.1.31, 4.3.19–4.3.20
   orders, application for 4.3.10,
      4.3.12–4.3.14
   registration of interest 4.3.4, 4.3.11

third party interests 4.3.5, 4.3.8,
    4.3.12
Trustees of Land and Appointment of
    Trustees Act 1996 4.3.16–4.3.18
financial markets
    administrative receivership, and 5.3.19
floating charge
    moratorium, effect of 3.2.26
    proceeds of book debts, over
        10.1.6–10.110
    ring-fenced sum 6.3.1–6.3.9, 10.1.11
floating chargeholder
    appointment of administrator
        company or directors, by
            7.5.6–7.5.9, 7.5.15
        court appointment 7.3.11–7.3.19
        generally 1.2.6, 5.2.2, 7.2.15,
            7.3.11–7.3.12, 7.4.1–7.4.3,
            7.10.13
        notice of appointment
            7.4.11–7.4.14
        pre-conditions 7.4.4–7.4.5
        restrictions on appointment
            7.4.6–7.4.10
        winding-up petitions 7.6.2–7.6.4
    generally 1.2.4, 1.4.3
France
    corporate rescue 2.3.7

Germany
    bankruptcy 2.3.9–2.3.10
    corporate rescue 2.3.2–2.3.6, 7.1.3
global trends 2.1.1–2.1.5

hire purchase agreements 7.8.15–8.17
Hong Kong
    insolvency regime 2.5.5
Human Rights Act 1998
    assets not forming part of bankrupt's
        estate 4.1.30–4.1.31
    concurrent civil and criminal
        proceedings 4.1.20
    defending claim 4.1.12–4.1.15
    delay in completing insolvency
        process 4.1.19
    family home, and 4.1.14, 4.1.31,
        4.3.19–4.3.20
    generally 4.1.1–4.1.8
    insolvency fees, reasonableness of
        4.1.27
    insolvency profession, effect on 4.1.3,
        4.1.16–4.1.17
    justifiable interference 4.1.13, 4.1.23
    legislation incompatible with 4.1.9
    limitation period 4.1.2, 4.1.11

mail redirection orders 4.1.29
Official Receiver, immunity of 4.1.28
principal obligations 4.1.9–4.1.10
public authority 4.1.9, 4.1.10
requirements for commencing claim
    4.1.11
retrospective effect 4.1.2
silence, right to 4.1.22–4.1.26
utmost fairness, duty of 4.1.21

imprisonment for debt 1.5.3, 1.5.4
income payments agreement
    background to reforms 9.2.1–9.2.3
    new procedure 9.2.6–9.2.8
income payments order
    after acquired property 9.2.12
    background to reforms 9.2.1–9.2.3
    new procedure 9.2.4–9.2.5
    pension benefits 9.2.14
    statutory protection for bankrupt
        9.2.9–9.2.11
    transitional provisions 9.2.13
India
    insolvency regime 2.5.5
individual voluntary arrangements
    annulment of bankruptcy order
        9.3.3–9.3.5
    approval, effect of 3.4.10
    background to reforms 9.3.1
    binding of creditors 3.4.10–3.4.11
    creditors' meeting 3.4.8–3.4.9
    effect of 9.3.3–9.3.5
    false representations 3.4.12
    fast-track 9.3.2
        alternatives to 9.3.17–9.3.18
        BROS, and 9.3.19–9.3.21
        procedure 9.3.6–9.3.12
        revocation 9.3.13–9.3.16
    general amendments to procedure
        3.4.8–3.4.14
    generally 1.5.11
    Insolvency Act 2000 3.4.2–3.4.14
    nationalisation 9.3.1
    no interim order, where 3.4.2–3.4.7
    offences 3.4.12–3.4.13
    Official Receiver, role of 9.3.1–9.3.27
    premature ending 3.4.14
    United States 9.3.1
Indonesia
    insolvency regime 2.5.4
Insolvency Act 2000
    company director disqualification
        proceedings 3.6.1–3.6.8
    company voluntary arrangements
        3.2.2–3.3.14

Insolvency Act 2000 *cont.*
　cross-border insolvency 3.8.5
　generally 3.1.1–3.1.3
　implementation 3.9.1
　individual voluntary arrangements
　　3.4.2–3.4.14
　interest on sums held in insolvency
　　services account 3.8.4
　investigation and prosecution of
　　malpractice 3.8.1
　landlords' rights of action 3.7.4
　powers of compulsion 3.8.2
　trustee of deceased insolvent's estate,
　　powers of 3.8.3
insolvency practitioners
　bankrupt disqualified from acting as
　　9.4.8
　changing perception of 1.3.1–1.3.8
　Cork Committee 1.3.1–1.3.2
　generally 2.2.4
　Human Rights Act 1998
　　examples of application of
　　　4.1.18–4.1.31
　　general effect of 4.1.3, 4.1.16–4.1.17
　inspection 1.3.5
　nominees as 3.5.1–3.5.2
　personal liability 4.1.3
　professional standards 1.3.5
　qualification 1.3.4
　recognised professional bodies 1.3.3,
　　1.3.6
　unethical conduct 1.3.5
　unqualified persons 1.3.2–1.3.3
insolvency services account
　interest on sums in 3.8.4
international corporate reconstruction
　Financial Services and Markets Act
　　2000 4.6.20–4.6.23
　future of informal work out models
　　4.6.12–4.6.14
　generally 4.6.1–4.6.3, 10.1.14
　global principles for multi-creditor
　　work out 4.6.9–4.6.11
　London Approach 2.5.2, 4.6.4–4.6.8,
　　4.6.9
　schemes of arrangement 4.6.15–4.6.19
Ireland
　bankruptcy 2.3.11
　corporate rescue 2.3.8
Italy
　bankruptcy 2.3.12

Japan
　insolvency regime 2.5.4
Joint Insolvency Monitoring Unit 1.3.5

joint stock companies 1.2.1
Justice of the Peace
　bankrupt as 9.4.2

landlords
　administration, effect of 7.6.16–7.6.17
　registered social landlords
　　5.3.20–5.3.21
　rights of action 3.7.1–3.7.4
law merchant 1.5.1
lessors
　administration, effect of 7.6.16–7.6.17
liberalisation
　effects of 10.2.1–10.2.7
limited liability 1.2.1
liquidation 1.2.3, 1.2.5, 4.1.19,
　7.10.25–7.10.29
　expenses of 6.2.2–6.2.10
　ring-fenced sum 6.3.1–6.3.9, 10.1.11
local government
　disqualification from office 9.4.4
London Approach 2.5.2, 4.6.4–4.6.8, 4.6.9

mail redirection orders 4.1.29
Malaysia
　corporate rescue 2.5.7
　insolvency regime 2.5.5
malpractice
　investigation and prosecution 3.8.1
manager
　bankrupt acting as 9.4.7
Mandleson, Peter 1.5.12, 2.1.2
matrimonial home *see* family home
misfortune, certificate of 1.5.5

New Zealand
　corporate rescue 2.4.1, 2.4.5
　receivership 5.1.4

Official Receiver
　discharge of bankrupt 8.1.5, 9.1.3
　　obligation to report on 9.1.4
　immunity 4.1.28
　individual voluntary arrangements
　　9.3.1–9.3.27
　investigatory duties
　　concealment and falsification of
　　　records by bankrupt 9.1.6–9.1.9
　　duty to investigate 9.1.1–9.1.3

'pari passu' principle 6.1.3
parliament
　disqualification from office 9.4.3
pension benefits
　approved pensions 4.2.22–4.2.23

asset for creditors, as 1.5.17,
4.2.1–4.2.33
bankruptcies commencing on or after
29 May 2000 4.2.21–4.2.29
bankruptcies declared before
Insolvency Act 1986 4.2.3–4.2.7
bankruptcies declared during
'intervening period' 4.2.8–4.2.20
bankruptcy restriction orders 4.2.31
exclusion order applications 4.2.26
forfeiture 4.2.31
income payments order 9.2.14
occupational pension schemes
4.2.14–4.2.17
personal pension schemes
4.2.11–4.2.13
property rights 4.2.8
seizure of 4.2.27–4.2.29, 9.2.14
state retirement pension and SERPs
4.2.18
time limits 4.2.25
unapproved pension arrangements
4.2.24
preferential debts
Cork Committee 6.1.5–6.1.7
meaning 6.1.1–6.1.4
see also Crown preference
project finance 5.3.16–5.3.18
public private partnerships 5.3.11–5.3.14

receiver
administrative receiver distinguished
5.1.6
appointed by bank 1.2.4
definition 5.1.5
duties 5.1.15–5.1.19
generally 1.2.4
manager distinguished 5.1.5
restriction on bankrupt acting as
9.4.7
receivership
administration, effect of 7.6.5–7.6.9
administrative receivership
distinguished 5.1.6–5.1.7
Commonwealth jurisdictions 5.1.4
Cork Committee 1.2.4, 1.2.10
historical perspective 5.1.1–5.1.4
recession see economic recession
redirection of mail 4.1.29
Review Committee on Insolvency Law
(Cork Committee) 1.2.4–1.2.10,
1.3.1–1.3.2, 1.4.5, 1.5.7, 1.5.8,
6.1.5–6.1.7
ring-fenced sum 6.3.1–6.3.9, 10.1.11
risk 1.1.2

secured creditors
Australia 2.4.2
powers of 2.4.3
role 10.1.3–10.1.11
United States 2.2.8, 2.2.11
silence, right to
insolvency investigations, and
4.1.22–4.1.26
Singapore
corporate rescue 2.5.7, 2.5.8
insolvency regime 2.5.5
South Korea
insolvency regime 2.5.4
super-priority financing 1.4.13, 10.1.12
Australia 2.4.2
United States 2.2.9

Taiwan
corporate rescue 2.5.9
insolvency regime 2.5.4
Thailand
corporate rescue 2.5.10
transfer of undertakings
changes to terms and conditions
4.4.14
dismissals 4.4.9–4.4.10
employee liability information
4.4.15–4.4.19
existing position 4.4.4–4.4.10
pre-existing debts 4.4.13
transfer of employees on existing
terms and conditions 4.4.5–4.4.8
TUPE
effect of 4.4.1–4.4.10
reform 4.4.11–4.4.19
trustee in bankruptcy
concealment and falsification of
records by bankrupt 9.1.6–9.1.9
family home, sale of 4.1.14, 4.1.31,
4.3.4–4.3.31
mail redirection orders 4.1.29
matrimonial home 1.5.16, 1.5.17
pension benefits, seizure of
4.2.27–4.2.29, 9.2.14
powers of 1.5.17, 9.1.5
restrictions on 1.5.17
trustee of insolvent's estate
powers of 3.8.3

United States
Chapter 7 bankruptcy 1.5.13,
2.2.17–2.2.18
homestead exemption 2.2.18
Chapter 11 corporate reconstruction
model 1.4.4, 2.2.1, 2.2.2–2.2.16

United States *cont.*
    creditors committee 2.2.7
    debtor in possession 2.2.4
    debtor in possession financing 2.2.9
    involuntary application 2.2.6
    management of company 2.2.4
    moratorium 2.2.3, 2.2.7, 2.2.11
    no prior insolvency requirement
        2.2.5
    ongoing contracts 2.2.10
    plan of reorganisation 2.2.3, 2.2.7,
        2.2.12, 2.2.13
    product liability claims 2.2.5
    secured creditors 2.2.8, 2.2.11
    super-priority financing 2.2.9
    treatment of creditors 2.2.12–2.2.13
    UK administration procedure
        compared 2.2.14–2.2.15, 10.1.12
    voluntary application 2.2.6

Chapter 13 compositions 1.5.13
    consumer bankruptcy 1.5.6, 1.5.13,
        2.2.19
    generally 1.5.6, 1.5.13, 1.5.15, 1.5.21,
        2.1.1–2.1.3, 2.2.1–2.2.20
    individual voluntary arrangements
        9.3.1
    law 1.5.12
    number of filings 1.5.13
utilities
    administrative receivership 5.3.15
    company voluntary arrangements
        3.2.31

winding-up petition
    administration, effect of 7.6.1–7.6.4
    CVA moratorium, effect of 3.2.25
    public interest 7.10.19
    staying of 3.2.25